Difference and Repetition

Gilles Deleuze

Difference and Repetition

Translated by
Paul Patton

COLUMBIA UNIVERSITY PRESS

Columbia University Press
New York

The publishers wish to express their appreciation of assistance given by the government of France through the French Ministry of Culture in the preparation of this translation.

Library of Congress Cataloging-in-Publication Data

Deleuze, Gilles.
[Différence et répétition. English]
Difference and repetition/Gilles Deleuze : translated by Paul Patton.
p. cm.
Includes bibliographical references and index.
ISBN 0-231-08158-8
1. Difference (Philosophy) 2. Repetition (Philosophy)
3. Philosophy, French—20th century. I. Title.
B2430.D453D4513 1993 93 & 41815
111—dc20 CIP

Printed in Great Britain on acid-free paper.

c 10 9 8 7 6 5 4 3 2 1

Contents

Translator's Preface

Difference and Repetition was first published in 1968. It was Deleuze's principal thesis for the Doctorat D'Etat. *Expressionism in Philosophy: Spinoza*, published in the same year, was his accompanying secondary thesis. *The Logic of Sense* (Athlone, 1990) appeared the following year. This interrelated body of writing marks the border between two phases of Deleuze's career: one side facing the earlier texts of an unorthodox historian of philosophy, the other facing his subsequent work, alone and with Guattari. If the study of Spinoza is the more strictly scholarly undertaking, then *Difference and Repetition* is the first book in which Deleuze begins to write on his own behalf. As such, it occupies a pivotal place in his *œuvre*.

Difference and Repetition is a work of prodigious conceptual invention in which Deleuze draws upon his earlier readings of Plato, Hume, Bergson, Nietzsche and Kant, as well as elements of contemporary science and art, to weave together a physics and a metaphysics of difference. If this amounts to a critique of the philosophy of representation which has dominated European thought since Plato, then it does so in the same manner that *Anti-Oedipus* (Athlone, 1984) amounts to a critique of psychoanalysis – namely, by proposing a retrospective analysis on the basis of an alternative. The different kinds of multiplicity found in Bergson, the ontology of eternal return understood as the being of that which differs and a transcendental empiricism of the faculties are among the elements of Deleuze's earlier studies which are here woven into a systematic philosophy of difference. 'Representation' is replaced by the expression or actualization of Ideas, where this is understood in terms of the complex notion of 'different/ciation'. The system is 'grounded' only in the repetition of difference, or the repetition of Ideal problems, which precisely amounts to a non-ground or groundlessness.

As befits the exposition of a novel metaphysical system, there is occasional recourse to neologisms. These include some terms which are Deleuze's own inventions, and which I have attempted to render into appropriate English equivalents, such as 'a-presentation' (p.24) or the recurrent notion of 'the disparate' [*le dispars*]. A more significant case arises from the need to make a terminological distinction in English where no equivalent exists for the corresponding French terms. Thus, Deleuze makes significant use of the distinction in French between *différencier*, to make or become different, and *différentier*, which is restricted to the mathematical operation. Because of the extent and significance of his use of this distinction (which becomes apparent in Chapter IV), I have had to follow his terminology and introduce 'differenciate' as a term of art in English.

On the whole, however, *Difference and Repetition* achieves its effects by means of 'no typographical cleverness, no lexical agility, no blending or creation of words, no syntactical boldness...'.[1] The problems which it poses for the translator are of another order. These include, first, problems raised by the diversity of philosophical languages deployed in the course of this book. For the most part, I have followed the terminology employed in the standard English translations of the primary texts in question: for example, following the authorized translations of Bergson in using 'extensity' for *étendue* (see Chapter V). In some cases, however, where standard French terminology differs from the English in ways which relate to important aspects of Deleuze's project, I have followed the French. For example, Deleuze uses the term 'Ideas', in standard Platonic or Kantian senses, but then develops his own concept of Ideas which owes as much to Leibniz and contemporary structuralism as it does to Kant or Plato. In order to maintain the continuity in Deleuze's use of this term, I have used the term 'Ideas' with reference to Plato in some contexts where standard English translations would use 'Forms'.

Secondly, in the pursuit of his own distinctive style of philosophizing – which combines an extreme sobriety in the use of language with an extraordinary vitality in the use of concepts – Deleuze often draws upon existing words to create a terminology for concepts of his own making. In some cases, this involves the use of technical terms taken from the sciences or particular philosophies. For example, the term 'multiplicity', which is now well established in the translations of Deleuze's work, is derived from the French mathematical term [*multiplicité*] used to refer to those Reimannian objects which English mathematicians would call 'manifolds'. In other cases, Deleuze employs apparently ordinary words to designate important concepts of his own making. This is true of *point remarquable*, which I have rendered as 'distinctive point'. This term has been variously translated as 'prominent', 'exceptional' or 'remarkable' point. In fact, there is nothing remarkable about these points: they are the points or pre-individual singularities which distinguish one Idea, problem or multiplicity from another. Initially introduced alongside the mathematical concept of 'singular point', which is employed to designate those points which characterize or define a given function, 'distinctive point' takes on a life of its own as a non-mathematical term of art in Deleuze's work. It is not to be confused with the 'distinctive traits' referred to by structural linguistics. Nor should it be confused with the 'shining points' to which Bergson refers in his discussion of memory, although in this book and in *Bergsonism* Deleuze does establish a connection between these two terms.

A further difficulty arises in cases where a single word in French has multiple English equivalents. A frequently occurring word of this type is *moi*, which may be rendered either as 'ego' or as 'self'. Here, the attempt to follow standard English terminology has led me to use 'self' in all contexts except those where it is explicitly a question of psychoanalysis, in which case I have used 'ego'. In this case, readers should be aware that I have maintained continuity with the existing English terminology for particular philosophies, at the cost of introducing a discontinuity into Deleuze's text which is not present in the original.

Another case of this type is the word *fond*, which may be either 'ground' or 'bottom'. This term occurs widely in conjunction and opposition with a series of cognate French words, *fondé, fondement, fondation*, as well as the important term *sans-fond* and Deleuze's own *effondement*. I have retained Deleuze's distinction between 'foundation' [*fondation*] and 'ground' [*fondement*]. However, while the French *fonder* often occurs in contexts in which the appropriate English term would be the verb 'to found', I have mostly preferred 'ground' in order to maintain the connection with Deleuze's important usage of *le fond* and *fondement*. Both these terms are connected with the philosophical concept which is regularly rendered as 'ground' in English translations of German philosophy, while his notion of the 'groundless' [*sans-fond*] is explicitly linked to the German *Ungrund* (p.229). For this reason, I have also used 'ungrounding' for *effondement*. This family of terms is further complicated by the occasional play upon *fond* (bottom or depths) and *profond* (deep, profound). However, since Deleuze contrasts a concept of depth [*profondeur*] with that of ground [*fond*] in Chapter V, I have used 'ground' for *le fond* throughout.

Additional translator's notes on particular points, along with references to texts cited, have been included in the Notes. These are indicated by an asterisk*.

Many colleagues have read sections, offered assistance or answered my queries in the course of preparing this translation. In particular, I would like to thank Genevieve Lloyd, Paul Crittenden, Kim Lycos and Paul Thom for their scholarly assistance; the dean, Richard Campbell, and the Faculty of Arts at The Australian National University for awarding me a Faculty Research Fund Grant; Rex Butler for his considerable efforts as research assistant and reader; Hugh Tomlinson, who suggested that I undertake this task; Constantin V. Boundas, who sent me his draft translation of the entire text, thereby providing me with an invaluable means of checking the accuracy of my own; Martin Joughin, Timothy S. Murphy and Amitavo Islam for their comments; and Brian Massumi for his scrupulous and helpful Reader's review. I am grateful to Peter Cook for his help with proof-reading and printing the final text, and with compiling the Index. Throughout the course of this project, I have been fortunate to enjoy the support, encouragement and scholarly assistance of Moira Gatens.

Preface to the English Edition

There is a great difference between writing history of philosophy and writing philosophy. In the one case, we study the arrows or the tools of a great thinker, the trophies and the prey, the continents discovered. In the other case, we trim our own arrows, or gather those which seem to us the finest in order to try to send them in other directions, even if the distance covered is not astronomical but relatively small. We try to speak in our own name only to learn that a proper name designates no more than the outcome of a body of work – in other words, the concepts discovered, on condition that we were able to express these and imbue them with life using all the possibilities of language.

After I had studied Hume, Spinoza, Nietzsche and Proust, all of whom fired me with enthusiasm, *Difference and Repetition* was the first book in which I tried to 'do philosophy'. All that I have done since is connected to this book, including what I wrote with Guattari (obviously, I speak from my own point of view). It is very difficult to say why one becomes attached to a particular problem: why was it difference and repetition which preoccupied me rather than something else, and why the two together rather than separately? These were not exactly new problems, since the history of philosophy, and especially contemporary philosophy, dealt with them constantly. But perhaps the majority of philosophers had subordinated difference to identity or to the Same, to the Similar, to the Opposed or to the Analogous: they had introduced difference into the identity of the concept, they had put difference in the concept itself, thereby reaching a conceptual difference, but not a concept of difference.

We tend to subordinate difference to identity in order to think it (from the point of view of the concept or the subject: for example, specific difference presupposes an identical concept in the form of a genus). We also have a tendency to subordinate it to resemblance (from the point of view of perception), to opposition (from the point of view of predicates), and to analogy (from the point of view of judgement). In other words, we do not think difference in itself. With Aristotle, Philosophy was able to provide itself with an organic representation of difference, with Leibniz and Hegel an orgiastic representation: it has not, for all that, reached difference in itself.

The situation was perhaps no better with regard to repetition: in another manner, this too is thought in terms of the identical, the similar, the equal or the opposed. In this case, we treat it as a difference without concept: two things repeat one another when they are different even while they have exactly the same concept. Henceforth, everything which causes repetition to vary seems to us to cover or hide it at the same time. Here again, we do not reach a concept of repetition. By contrast, might we not form such a concept once we realize that variation is not added to repetition in order to hide it, but is rather its condition or constitutive element, the interiority of repetition *par excellence*? Disguise no less than displacement forms part of repetition, and of difference: a common transport or diaphora. At the limit, might there not be a single power of difference or of repetition, but one which operates only in the multiple and determines multiplicities?

Every philosophy must achieve its own manner of speaking about the arts and sciences, as though it established alliances with them. It is very difficult, since philosophy obviously cannot claim the least superiority, but also creates and expounds its own concepts only in relation to what it can grasp of scientific functions and artistic constructions. A philosophical concept can never be confused with a scientific function or an artistic construction, but finds itself in affinity with these in this or that domain of science or style of art. The scientific or artistic content of a philosophy may be very elementary, since it is not obliged to advance art or science, but it can advance itself only by forming properly philosophical concepts from a given function or construction, however elementary. Philosophy cannot be undertaken independently of science or art. It is in this sense that we tried to constitute a philosophical concept from the mathematical function of differen*t*iation and the biological function of differen*c*iation, in asking whether there was not a statable relation between these two concepts which could not appear at the level of their respective objects. Art, science and philosophy seemed to us to be caught up in mobile relations in which each is obliged to respond to the other, but by its own means.

Finally, in this book it seemed to me that the powers of difference and repetition could be reached only by putting into question the traditional image of thought. By this I mean not only that we think according to a given method, but also that there is a more or less implicit, tacit or presupposed image of thought which determines our goals when we try to think. For example, we suppose that thought possesses a good nature, and the thinker a good will (naturally to 'want' the true); we take as a model the process of recognition – in other words, a common sense or employment of all the faculties on a supposed same object; we designate error, nothing but error, as the enemy to be fought; and we suppose that the true concerns solutions – in other words, propositions capable of serving as answers. This is the classic image of thought, and as long as the critique has not been carried to the heart of that image it is difficult to conceive of thought as encompassing those problems which point beyond the propositional mode; or as involving encounters which escape all recognition; or as confronting its true enemies, which are quite different from thought; or as attaining that which tears thought from its natural torpor and notorious bad will, and forces us to think. A new image of thought – or rather, a liberation of thought from those images which imprison it: this is what I had already sought to discover in Proust. Here, however, in *Difference and Repetition*, this search is autonomous and it becomes the condition for the discovery of these two concepts. It is therefore the third chapter which now seems to me the most necessary and the most concrete, and which serves to introduce subsequent books up to and including the research undertaken with Guattari where we invoked a vegetal model of thought: the rhizome in opposition to the tree, a rhizome-thought instead of an arborescent thought.

Preface

The weaknesses of a book are often the counterparts of empty intentions that one did not know how to implement. In this sense, a declaration of intent is evidence of real modesty in relation to the ideal book. It is often said that prefaces should be read only at the end. Conversely, conclusions should be read at the outset. This is true of the present book, the conclusion of which could make reading the rest unnecessary.

The subject dealt with here is manifestly in the air. The signs may be noted: Heidegger's more and more pronounced orientation towards a philosophy of ontological Difference; the structuralist project, based upon a distribution of differential characters within a space of coexistence; the contemporary novelist's art which revolves around difference and repetition, not only in its most abstract reflections but also in its effective techniques; the discovery in a variety of fields of a power peculiar to repetition, a power which also inhabits the unconscious, language and art. All these signs may be attributed to a generalized anti-Hegelianism: difference and repetition have taken the place of the identical and the negative, of identity and contradiction. For difference implies the negative, and allows itself to lead to contradiction, only to the extent that its subordination to the identical is maintained. The primacy of identity, however conceived, defines the world of representation. But modern thought is born of the failure of representation, of the loss of identities, and of the discovery of all the forces that act under the representation of the identical. The modern world is one of simulacra. Man did not survive God, nor did the identity of the subject survive that of substance. All identities are only simulated, produced as an optical 'effect' by the more profound game of difference and repetition. We propose to think difference in itself independently of the forms of representation which reduce it to the Same, and the relation of different to different independently of those forms which make them pass through the negative.

Modern life is such that, confronted with the most mechanical, the most stereotypical repetitions, inside and outside ourselves, we endlessly extract from them little differences, variations and modifications. Conversely, secret, disguised and hidden repetitions, animated by the perpetual displacement of a difference, restore bare, mechanical and stereotypical repetitions, within and without us. In simulacra, repetition already plays upon repetitions, and difference already plays upon differences. Repetitions repeat themselves, while the differenciator differenciates itself. The task of life is to make all these repetitions coexist in a space in which difference is distributed. Two lines of research lie at the origin of this book: one concerns a concept of difference without negation, precisely because unless it is subordinated to the identical, difference would not extend or 'would not have to extend' as far as opposition and contradiction; the other concerns a concept of repetition in which physical, mechanical or bare repetitions (repetition of the Same) would find their *raison d'être* in the more profound structures of a hidden repetition in which a 'differential' is disguised and displaced. These two lines of research spontaneously came together, because on every occasion *these concepts of a pure difference and a complex repetition* seemed to connect and coalesce. The perpetual divergence and decentring of difference corresponded closely to a displacement and a disguising within repetition.

There are certainly many dangers in invoking pure differences which have become independent of the negative and liberated from the identical. The greatest danger is that of lapsing into the representations of a beautiful soul: there are only reconcilable and federative differences, far removed from bloody struggles. The beautiful soul says: we are different, but not opposed... . The *notion of a problem*, which we see linked to that of difference, also seems to nurture the sentiments of the beautiful soul: only problems and questions matter... . Nevertheless, we believe that when these problems attain their proper degree of *positivity*, and when difference becomes the object of a corresponding *affirmation*, they release a power of aggression and selection which destroys the beautiful soul by depriving it of its very identity and breaking its good will. The problematic and the differential determine struggles or destructions in relation to which those of the negative are only appearances, and the wishes of the beautiful soul are so many mystifications trapped in appearances. The simulacrum is not just a copy, but that which overturns all copies by *also* overturning the models: every thought becomes an aggression.

A book of philosophy should be in part a very particular species of detective novel, in part a kind of science fiction. By detective novel we mean that concepts, with their zones of presence, should intervene to resolve local situations. They themselves change along with the problems. They have spheres of influence where, as we shall see, they operate in relation to 'dramas' and by means of a certain 'cruelty'. They must have a coherence among themselves, but that coherence must not come from themselves. They must receive their coherence from elsewhere.

This is the secret of empiricism. Empiricism is by no means a reaction against concepts, nor a simple appeal to lived experience. On the contrary, it undertakes the most insane creation of concepts ever seen or heard. Empiricism is a mysticism and a mathematicism of concepts, but precisely one which treats the concept as object of an encounter, as a here-and-now, or rather as an *Erewhon* from which emerge inexhaustibly ever new, differently distributed 'heres' and 'nows'. Only an empiricist could say: concepts are indeed things, but things in their free and wild state, beyond 'anthropological predicates'. I make, remake and unmake my concepts along a moving horizon, from an always decentred centre, from an always displaced periphery which repeats and differenciates them. The task of modern philosophy is to overcome the alternatives temporal/non-temporal, historical/eternal and particular/universal. Following Nietzsche we discover, as more profound than time and eternity, the untimely: philosophy is neither a philosophy of history, nor a philosophy of the eternal, but untimely, always and only untimely – that is to say, 'acting counter to our time and thereby acting on our time and, let us hope, for the benefit of a time to come'.[1] Following Samuel Butler, we discover *Erewhon*, signifying at once the originary 'nowhere' and the displaced, disguised, modified and always re-created 'here-and-now'. Neither empirical particularities nor abstract universals: a Cogito for a dissolved self. We believe in a world in which individuations are impersonal, and singularities are pre-individual: the splendour of the pronoun 'one' – whence the science-fiction aspect, which necessarily derives from this *Erewhon*. What this book should therefore have made apparent is the advent of a coherence which is no more our own, that of mankind, than that of God or the world. In this sense, it should have been an apocalyptic book (the third time in the series of times).

Science fiction in yet another sense, one in which the weaknesses become manifest. How else can one write but of those things which one doesn't know, or knows badly? It is precisely there that we imagine having something to say. We write only at the frontiers of our knowledge, at the border which separates our knowledge from our ignorance and transforms the one into the other. Only in this manner are we resolved to write. To satisfy ignorance is to put off writing until tomorrow – or rather, to make it impossible. Perhaps writing has a relation to silence altogether more threatening than that which it is supposed to entertain with death. We are therefore well aware, unfortunately, that we have spoken about science in a manner which was not scientific.

The time is coming when it will hardly be possible to write a book of philosophy as it has been done for so long: 'Ah! the old style...'. The search for new means of philosophical expression was begun by Nietzsche and must be pursued today in relation to the renewal of certain other arts, such as the theatre or the cinema. In this context, we can now raise the question of the utilization of the history of philosophy. It seems to us that the history of philosophy should play a role roughly analogous to that of *collage* in painting. The history of philosophy is the reproduction of philosophy itself. In the history of philosophy, a commentary should act as a veritable double and bear the maximal modification appropriate to a double. (One imagines a *philosophically* bearded Hegel, a *philosophically* clean-shaven Marx, in the same way as a moustached Mona Lisa.) It should be possible to recount a real book of past philosophy as if it were an imaginary and feigned book. Borges, we know, excelled in recounting imaginary books. But he goes further when he considers a real book, such as *Don Quixote*, as though it were an imaginary book, itself reproduced by an imaginary author, Pierre Menard, who in turn he considers to be real. In this case, the most exact, the most strict repetition has as its correlate the maximum of difference ('The text of Cervantes and that of Menard are verbally identical, but the second is almost infinitely richer...'[2]). Commentaries in the history of philosophy should represent a kind of slow motion, a congelation or immobilisation of the text: *not only* of the text to which they relate, *but also* of the text in which they are inserted – so much so that they have a double existence and a corresponding ideal: the pure repetition of the former text and the present text *in one another*. It is in order to approach this double existence that we have sometimes had to integrate historical notes into the present text.

Introduction: Repetition and Difference

Repetition is not generality. Repetition and generality must be distinguished in several ways. Every formula which implies their confusion is regrettable: for example, when we say that two things are as alike as two drops of water; or when we identify 'there is only a science of the general' with 'there is only a science of that which is repeated'. Repetition and resemblance are different in kind – extremely so.

Generality presents two major orders: the qualitative order of resemblances and the quantitative order of equivalences. Cycles and equalities are their respective symbols. But in any case, generality expresses a point of view according to which one term may be exchanged or substituted for another. The exchange or substitution of particulars defines our conduct in relation to generality. That is why the empiricists are not wrong to present general ideas as particular ideas in themselves, so long as they add the belief that each of these can be replaced by any other particular idea which resembles it in relation to a given word. By contrast, we can see that repetition is a necessary and justified conduct only in relation to that which cannot be replaced. Repetition as a conduct and as a point of view concerns non-exchangeable and non-substitutable singularities. Reflections, echoes, doubles and souls do not belong to the domain of resemblance or equivalence; and it is no more possible to exchange one's soul than it is to substitute real twins for one another. If exchange is the criterion of generality, theft and gift are those of repetition. There is, therefore, an economic difference between the two.

To repeat is to behave in a certain manner, but in relation to something unique or singular which has no equal or equivalent. And perhaps this repetition at the level of external conduct echoes, for its own part, a more secret vibration which animates it, a more profound, internal repetition within the singular. This is the apparent paradox of festivals: they repeat an 'unrepeatable'. They do not add a second and a third time to the first, but carry the first time to the 'nth' power. With respect to this power, repetition interiorizes and thereby reverses itself: as Péguy says, it is not Federation Day which commemorates or represents the fall of the Bastille, but the fall of the Bastille which celebrates and repeats in advance all the Federation Days; or Monet's first water lily which repeats all the others.[1] Generality, as generality of the particular, thus stands opposed to repetition as universality of the singular. The repetition of a work of art is like a singularity without concept, and it is not by chance that a poem must be learned by heart. The head is the organ of exchange, but the heart is the amorous organ of repetition. (It is true that repetition also concerns the head, but precisely because it is its terror or paradox.) Pius Servien rightly distinguished two languages: the language of science, dominated by the symbol of equality, in which each term may be replaced by others; and lyrical language, in which every term is irreplaceable and can only be repeated.[2] Repetition can always be 'represented' as extreme resemblance or perfect equivalence, but the fact that one can pass by degrees from one thing to another does not prevent their being different in kind.

On the other hand, generality belongs to the order of laws. However, law determines only the resemblance of the subjects ruled by it, along with their equivalence to terms which it designates. Far from grounding repetition, law shows, rather, how repetition would remain impossible for pure subjects of law – particulars. It condemns them to change. As an empty form of difference, an invariable form of variation, a law compels its subjects to illustrate it only at the cost of their own change. No doubt there are as many constants as variables among the terms designated by laws, and as many permanences and perseverations as there are fluxes and variations in nature. However, a perseveration is still not a repetition. The constants of one law are in turn variables of a more general law, just as the hardest rocks become soft and fluid matter on the geological scale of millions of years. So at each level, it is in relation to large, permanent natural objects that the subject of a law experiences its own powerlessness to repeat and discovers that this powerlessness is already contained in the object, reflected in the permanent object wherein it sees itself condemned. Law unites the change of the water and the permanence of the river. Elie Faure said of Watteau: 'He imbued with the utmost transitoriness those things which our gaze encounters as the most enduring, namely space and forests.' This is the eighteenth-century method. Wolmar, in *La Nouvelle Héloïse*, made a system of it: the impossibility of repetition, and change as a general condition to which all particular creatures are subject by the law of Nature, were understood in relation to fixed terms (themselves, no doubt, variables in relation to other permanences and in function of other, more general laws). This is the meaning of the grove, the grotto and the 'sacred' object. Saint-Preux learns that he cannot repeat, not only because of his own change and that of Julie, but also because of the great natural permanences, which assume a symbolic value and exclude him no less from true repetition. If repetition is possible, it is due to miracle rather than to law. It is against the law: against the similar form and the equivalent content of law. If repetition can be found, even in nature, it is in the name of a power which affirms itself against the law, which works underneath laws, perhaps superior to laws. If repetition exists, it expresses at once a singularity opposed to the general, a universality opposed to the particular, a distinctive opposed to the ordinary, an instantaneity opposed to variation and an eternity opposed to permanence. In every respect, repetition is a transgression. It puts law into question, it denounces its nominal or general character in favour of a more profound and more artistic reality.

From the point of view of scientific experiment, it seems difficult to deny a relationship between repetition and law. However, we must ask under what conditions experimentation ensures repetition. Natural phenomena are produced in a free state, where any inference is possible among the vast cycles of resemblance: in this sense, everything reacts on everything else, and everything resembles everything else (resemblance of the diverse with itself). However, experimentation constitutes relatively closed environments in which phenomena are defined in terms of a small number of chosen factors (a minimum of two – for example, Space and Time for the movement of bodies in a vacuum). Consequently, there is no reason to question the application of mathematics to physics: physics is already mathematical, since the closed environments or chosen factors also constitute systems of geometrical co-ordinates. In these conditions, phenomena necessarily appear as *equal* to a certain quantitative relation between the chosen factors. Experimentation is thus a matter of substituting one order of generality for another: an order of equality for an order of resemblance. Resemblances are unpacked in order to discover an equality which allows the identification of a phenomenon under the particular conditions of the experiment. Repetition appears here only in the passage from one order of generality to another, emerging with the help of – or on the occasion of – this passage. It is as if repetition momentarily appeared between or underneath the two generalities. Here too, however, there is a risk of mistaking a difference in kind for a difference of degree. For generality only represents and presupposes a hypothetical repetition: 'given the same circumstances, then...'. This formula says that in similar situations one will always be able to select and retain the same factors, which represent the being-equal of the phenomena. This, however, does not account for what gives rise to repetition, nor for what is categorical or important for repetition in principle (what is important in principle is 'n' times as the power of a single time, without the need to pass through a second or a third time). In its essence, repetition refers to a singular power which differs in kind from generality, even when, in order to appear, it takes advantage of the artificial passage from one order of generality to another.

Expecting repetition from the law of nature is the 'Stoic' error. The wise must be converted into the virtuous; the dream of finding a law which would make repetition possible passes over to the moral sphere. There is always a task to recommence, a fidelity to be revived within a daily life indistinguishable from the reaffirmation of Duty. Büchner makes Danton say:

> 'It is so wearisome. First you put on your shirt, then your trousers; you drag yourself into bed at night and in the morning drag yourself out again; and always you put one foot in front of the other. There is little hope that it will ever change. Millions have always done it like that and millions more will do so after us. Moreover, since we're made up of two halves which both do the same thing, everything's done twice. It's all very boring and very, very sad.'[3]

However, what good is moral law if it does not sanctify reiteration, above all if it does not make reiteration possible and give us a legislative power from which we are excluded by the law of nature? Moralists sometimes present the categories of Good and Evil in the following manner: every time we try to repeat according to nature or as natural beings (repetition of a pleasure, of a past, of a passion) we throw ourselves into a demonic and already damned exercise which can end only in despair or boredom. The Good, by contrast, holds out the possibility of repetition, of successful repetition and of the spirituality of repetition, because it depends not upon a law of nature but on a law of duty, of which, as moral beings, we cannot be subjects without also being legislators. What is Kant's 'highest test' if not a criterion which should decide what *can* in principle be reproduced – in other words, what can be repeated without contradiction in the form of moral law? The man of duty invented a 'test' of repetition; he decided what in principle could be repeated. He thought he had thereby defeated both the demonic and the wearisome. Moreover, as an echo of Danton's concerns or a response to them, is there not a moralism in that repetition apparatus described with such precision by Kant's biographers, right down to the astonishing garters that he made for himself, and the regularity of his daily promenades (in the sense that neglecting one's toilet and missing exercise are among those conducts whose maxim cannot, without contradiction, be regarded as a universal law, nor, therefore, be the object of rightful repetition)?

Conscience, however, suffers from the following ambiguity: it can be conceived only by supposing the moral law to be external, superior and indifferent to the natural law; but the application of the moral law can be conceived only by restoring to conscience itself the image and the model of the law of nature. As a result, the moral law, far from giving us true repetition, still leaves us in generality. This time, the generality is not that of nature but that of habit as a second nature. It is useless to point to the existence of immoral or bad habits: it is the form of habit – or, as Bergson used to say, the habit of acquiring habits (the whole of obligation) – which is essentially moral or has the form of the good. Furthermore, in this whole or generality of habit we again find the two major orders: that of resemblance, in the variable conformity of the elements of action with a given model in so far as the habit has not been acquired; and that of equivalence, with the equality of the elements of action in different situations once the habit has been acquired. As a result, habit never gives rise to true repetition: sometimes the action changes and is perfected while the intention remains constant; sometimes the action remains the same in different contexts and with different intentions. There again, if repetition is possible, it would appear only between or beneath the two generalities of perfection and integration, testifying to the presence of a quite different power, at the risk of overturning these two generalities.

If repetition is possible, it is as much opposed to moral law as it is to natural law. There are two known ways to overturn moral law. One is by ascending towards the principles: challenging the law as secondary, derived, borrowed or 'general'; denouncing it as involving a second-hand principle which diverts an original force or usurps an original power. The other way, by contrast, is to overturn the law by descending towards the consequences, to which one submits with a too-perfect attention to detail. By adopting the law, a falsely submissive soul manages to evade it and to taste pleasures it was supposed to forbid. We can see this in demonstration by absurdity and working to rule, but also in some forms of masochistic behaviour which mock by submission. The first way of overturning the law is ironic, where irony appears as an art of principles, of ascent towards the principles and of overturning principles. The second is humour, which is an art of consequences and descents, of suspensions and falls. Must we understand that repetition appears in both this suspense and this ascent, as though existence recommenced and 'reiterated' itself once it is no longer constrained by laws? Repetition belongs to humour and irony; it is by nature transgression or exception, always revealing a singularity opposed to the particulars subsumed under laws, a universal opposed to the generalities which give rise to laws.

There is a force common to Kierkegaard and Nietzsche. (Péguy would have to be added in order to form the triptych of priest, Antichrist and Catholic. Each of the three, in his own way, makes repetition not only a power peculiar to language and thought, a superior pathos and pathology, but also the fundamental category of a philosophy of the future. To each corresponds a Testament as well as a Theatre, a conception of the theatre, and a hero of repetition as a principal character in this theatre: Job–Abraham, Dionysus–Zarathustra, Joan of Arc–Clio). What separates them is considerable, evident and well-known. But nothing can hide this prodigious encounter in relation to a philosophy of repetition: *they oppose repetition to all forms of generality*. Nor do they take the word 'repetition' in a metaphorical sense: on the contrary, they have a way of taking it literally and of introducing it into their style. We can – or rather, must – first of all list the principal propositions which indicate the points on which they coincide:

1. Make something new of repetition itself: connect it with a test, with a selection or selective test; make it the supreme object of the will and of freedom. Kierkegaard specifies that it is not a matter of drawing something new from repetition, of extracting something new from it. Only contemplation or the mind which contemplates from without 'extracts'. It is rather a matter of acting, of making repetition as such a novelty; that is, a freedom and a task of freedom. In the case of Nietzsche: liberate the will from everything which binds it by making repetition the very object of willing. No doubt it is repetition which already binds; but if we die of repetition we are also saved and healed by it – healed, above all, by the other repetition. The whole mystical game of loss and salvation is therefore contained in repetition, along with the whole theatrical game of life and death and the whole positive game of illness and health (cf. Zarathustra ill and Zarathustra convalescent by virtue of one and the same power which is that of repetition in the eternal return).

2. In consequence, oppose repetition to the laws of nature. Kierkegaard declares that he does not speak at all of repetition in nature, of cycles and seasons, exchanges and equalities. Furthermore, if repetition concerns the most interior element of the will, this is because everything *changes* around the will, in accordance with the law of nature. According to the law of nature, repetition is impossible. For this reason, Kierkegaard condemns as aesthetic repetition every attempt to obtain repetition from the laws of nature by identifying with the legislative principle, whether in the Epicurean or the Stoic manner. It will be said that the situation is not so clear with Nietzsche. Nietzsche's declarations are nevertheless explicit. If he discovers repetition in the *Physis* itself, this is because he discovers in the *Physis* something superior to the reign of laws: a will willing itself through all change, a power opposed to law, an interior of the earth opposed to the laws of its surface. Nietzsche opposes 'his' hypothesis to the cyclical hypothesis. He conceives of repetition in the eternal return as Being, but he opposes this being to every legal form, to the being-similar as much as to the being-equal. How could the thinker who goes furthest in criticising the notion of law reintroduce eternal return as a law of nature? How could such a connoisseur of the Greeks be justified in regarding his own thought as prodigious and new, if he were content to formulate that natural platitude, that generality regarding nature well known to the Ancients? On two occasions, Zarathustra corrects erroneous interpretations of the eternal return: with anger, directed at his demon ('Spirit of Gravity ... do not treat this too lightly'); with kindness, directed at his animals ('O buffoons and barrel-organs ... you have already made a refrain out of it'). The refrain is the eternal return as cycle or circulation, as being-similar and being-equal – in short, as natural animal certitude and as sensible law of nature.

3. Oppose repetition to moral law, to the point where it becomes the suspension of ethics, a thought beyond good and evil. Repetition appears

as the logos of the solitary and the singular, the logos of the 'private thinker'. Both Kierkegaard and Nietzsche develop the opposition between the private thinker, the thinker-comet and bearer of repetition, and the public professor and doctor of law, whose second-hand discourse proceeds by mediation and finds its moralising source in the generality of concepts (cf. Kierkegaard against Hegel, Nietzsche against Kant and Hegel; and from this point of view, Péguy against the Sorbonne). Job is infinite contestation and Abraham infinite resignation, but these are one and the same thing. Job challenges the law in an ironic manner, refusing all second-hand explanations and dismissing the general in order to reach the most singular as principle or as universal. Abraham submits humorously to the law, but finds in that submission precisely the singularity of his only son whom the law commanded him to sacrifice. As Kierkegaard understands it, repetition is the transcendent correlate shared by the psychical intentions of contestation and resignation. (We rediscover the two aspects in Péguy's doubling of Joan of Arc and Gervaise.) In Nietzsche's striking atheism, hatred of the law and *amor fati* (love of fate), aggression and acquiescence are the two faces of Zarathustra, gathered from the Bible and turned back against it. Further, in a certain sense one can see Zarathustra's moral test of repetition as competing with Kant. The eternal return says: whatever you will, will it in such a manner that you also will its eternal return. There is a 'formalism' here which overturns Kant on his own ground, a test which goes further since, instead of relating repetition to a supposed moral law, it seems to make repetition itself the only form of a law beyond morality. In reality, however, things are even more complicated. The form of repetition in the eternal return is the brutal form of the immediate, that of the universal and the singular reunited, which dethrones every general law, dissolves the mediations and annihilates the particulars subjected to the law. Just as irony and black humour are combined in Zarathustra, so there is a within-the-law and a beyond-the-law united in the eternal return.

4. Oppose repetition not only to the generalities of habit but also to the particularities of memory. For it is perhaps habit which manages to 'draw' something new from a repetition contemplated from without. With habit, we act only on the condition that there is a little Self within us which contemplates: it is this which extracts the new – in other words, the general – from the pseudo-repetition of particular cases. Memory, then, perhaps recovers the particulars dissolved in generality. These psychological movements are of little consequence: for both Nietzsche and Kierkegaard they fade away in the face of repetition proposed as the double condemnation of habit and memory. In this way, repetition is the thought of the future: it is opposed to both the ancient category of reminiscence and the modern category of *habitus*. It is in repetition and by repetition that Forgetting becomes a positive power while the unconscious becomes a

positive and superior unconscious (for example, forgetting as a force is an integral part of the lived experience of eternal return). Everything is summed up in power. When Kierkegaard speaks of repetition as the second power of consciousness, 'second' means not a second time but the infinite which belongs to a single time, the eternity which belongs to an instant, the unconscious which belongs to consciousness, the 'nth' power. And when Nietzsche presents the eternal return as the immediate expression of the will to power, will to power does not at all mean 'to want power' but, on the contrary: whatever you will, carry it to the 'nth' power – in other words, separate out the superior form by virtue of the selective operation of thought in the eternal return, by virtue of the singularity of repetition in the eternal return itself. Here, in the superior form of everything that is, we find the immediate identity of the eternal return and the Overman.[4]

We are not suggesting any resemblance whatsoever between Nietzsche's Dionysus and Kierkegaard's God. On the contrary, we believe that the difference is insurmountable. But this is all the more reason to ask why their coincidence concerning this fundamental objective, the theme of repetition, even though they understand this objective differently? Kierkegaard and Nietzsche are among those who bring to philosophy new means of expression. In relation to them we speak readily of an overcoming of philosophy. Furthermore, in all their work, *movement* is at issue. Their objection to Hegel is that he does not go beyond false movement – in other words, the abstract logical movement of 'mediation'. They want to put metaphysics in motion, in action. They want to make it act, and make it carry out immediate acts. It is not enough, therefore, for them to propose a new representation of movement; representation is already mediation. Rather, it is a question of producing within the work a movement capable of affecting the mind outside of all representation; it is a question of making movement itself a work, without interposition; of substituting direct signs for mediate representations; of inventing vibrations, rotations, whirlings, gravitations, dances or leaps which directly touch the mind. This is the idea of a man of the theatre, the idea of a director before his time. In this sense, something completely new begins with Kierkegaard and Nietzsche. They no longer reflect on the theatre in the Hegelian manner. Neither do they set up a philosophical theatre. They invent an incredible equivalent of theatre within philosophy, thereby founding simultaneously this theatre of the future and a new philosophy. It will be said that, at least from the point of view of theatre, there was no production: neither the profession of priest and Copenhagen around 1840, nor the break with Wagner and Bayreuth, was a favourable condition. One thing, however, is certain: when Kierkegaard speaks of ancient theatre and modern drama, the environment has already changed; we are no longer in the element of reflection. We find here a thinker who lives the problem of masks, who experiences the inner emptiness of masks and seeks to fill it, to complete it, albeit with the 'absolutely different' – that is, by putting into it all the difference between the finite and the infinite, thereby creating the idea of a theatre of humour and of faith. When Kierkegaard explains that the knight of faith so resembles a bourgeois in his Sunday best as to be capable of being mistaken for one, this philosophical instruction must be taken as the remark of a director showing how the knight of faith should be *played*. And when he comments on Job or Abraham, when he imagines the variations of *Agnes and the Triton*, he rewrites the tale in a manner which is clearly that of a scenario. Mozart's music resonates even in Abraham and Job; it is a matter of 'leaping' to the tune of this music. 'I look only at movements' is the language of a director who poses the highest theatrical problem, the problem of a movement which would directly touch the soul, which would be that of the soul.[5]

Even more so with Nietzsche. *The Birth of Tragedy* is not a reflection on ancient theatre so much as the practical foundation of a theatre of the future, the opening up of a path along which Nietzsche still thinks it possible to push Wagner. The break with Wagner is not a matter of theory, nor of music; it concerns the respective roles of text, history, noise, music, light, song, dance and décor in this theatre of which Nietzsche dreams. Zarathustra incorporates the two attempts at dramatizing Empedocles. Moreover, if Bizet is better than Wagner, it is from the point of view of theatre and for Zarathustra's dances. Nietzsche's reproach to Wagner is that he inverted and distorted 'movement', giving us a nautical theatre in which we must paddle and swim rather than one in which we can walk and dance. *Zarathustra* is conceived entirely within philosophy, but also entirely for the stage. Everything in it is scored and visualised, put in motion and made to walk or dance. How can it be read without searching for the exact sound of the cries of the higher man, how can the prologue be read without staging the episode of the tightrope walker which opens the whole story? At certain moments, it is a comic opera about terrible things; and it is not by chance that Nietzsche speaks of the comic character of the Overman. Remember the song of Ariadne from the mouth of the old Sorcerer: here, two masks are superimposed – that of a young woman, almost of a *Korē*, which has just been laid over the mask of a repugnant old man. The actor must play the role of an old man playing the role of the *Korē*. Here too, for Nietzsche, it is a matter of filling the inner emptiness of the mask within a theatrical space: by multiplying the superimposed masks and inscribing the omnipresence of Dionysus in that superimposition, by inserting both the infinity of real movement and the form of the absolute difference given in the repetition of eternal return. When Nietzsche says that the Overman resembles Borgia rather than Parsifal, or when he suggests that the Overman belongs at once to both the Jesuit Order and the Prussian officer corps, we can understand these texts only by taking them for what they are: the remarks of a director indicating how the Overman should be 'played'.

Theatre is real movement, and it extracts real movement from all the arts it employs. This is what we are told: this movement, the essence and the interiority of movement, is *not opposition*, *not mediation*, but repetition. Hegel is denounced as the one who proposes an abstract movement of concepts instead of a movement of the *Physis* and the *Psyche*. Hegel substitutes the abstract relation of the particular to the concept in general for the true relation of the singular and the universal in the Idea. He thus remains in the reflected element of 'representation', within simple generality. He represents concepts instead of dramatizing Ideas: he creates a false theatre, a false drama, a false movement. We must see how Hegel betrays and distorts the immediate in order to ground his dialectic in that incomprehension, and to introduce mediation in a movement which is no more than that of his own thought and its generalities. When we say, on the contrary, that movement is repetition and that this is our true theatre, we are not speaking of the effort of the actor who 'repeats' because he has not yet learned the part. We have in mind the theatrical space, the emptiness of that space, and the manner in which it is filled and determined by the signs and masks through which the actor plays a role which plays other roles; we think of how repetition is woven from one distinctive point to another, including the differences within itself. (When Marx also criticizes the abstract false movement or mediation of the Hegelians, he finds himself drawn to an idea, which he indicates rather than develops, an essentially 'theatrical' idea: to the extent that history is theatre, then repetition, along with the tragic and the comic within repetition, forms a condition of movement under which the 'actors' or the 'heroes' produce something effectively new in history.) The theatre of repetition is opposed to the theatre of representation, just as movement is opposed to the concept and to representation which refers it back to the concept. In the theatre of repetition, we experience pure forces, dynamic lines in space which act without intermediary upon the spirit, and link it directly with nature and history, with a language which speaks before words, with gestures which develop before organised bodies, with masks before faces, with spectres and phantoms before characters – the whole apparatus of repetition as a 'terrible power'.

It then becomes easy to speak of the differences between Kierkegaard and Nietzsche. Even this question, however, must no longer be posed at the speculative level of the ultimate nature of the God of Abraham or the Dionysus of Zarathustra. It is rather a matter of knowing what it means to 'produce movement', to repeat or to obtain repetition. Is it a matter of leaping, as Kierkegaard believes? Or is it rather a matter of dancing, as Nietzsche thinks? He does not like the confusion of dancing and leaping (only Zarathustra's ape, his demon, his dwarf, his buffoon, leaps).[6]

Kierkegaard offers us a theatre of faith; he opposes spiritual movement, the movement of faith, to logical movement. He can thus invite us to go beyond all aesthetic repetition, beyond irony and even humour, all the while painfully aware that he offers us only the aesthetic, ironic and humoristic image of such a going-beyond. With Nietzsche, it is a theatre of unbelief, of movement as *Physis*, already a theatre of cruelty. Here, humour and irony are indispensable and fundamental operations of nature. And what would eternal return be, if we forgot that it is a vertiginous movement endowed with a force: not one which causes the return of the Same in general, but one which selects, one which expels as well as creates, destroys as well as produces? Nietzsche's leading idea is to ground the repetition in eternal return on both the death of God and the dissolution of the self. However, it is a quite different alliance in the theatre of faith: Kierkegaard dreams of an alliance between a God and a self rediscovered. All sorts of differences follow: is the movement in the sphere of the mind, or in the entrails of the earth which knows neither God nor self? Where will it be better protected against generalities, against mediations? Is repetition supernatural, to the extent that it is over and above the laws of nature? Or is it rather the most natural will of Nature in itself and willing itself as *Physis*, because Nature is by itself superior to its own kingdoms and its own laws? Has Kierkegaard not mixed all kinds of things together in his condemnation of 'aesthetic' repetition: a pseudo-repetition attributable to general laws of nature and a true repetition in nature itself; a pathological repetition of the passions and a repetition in art and the work of art? We cannot now resolve any of these problems; it has been enough for us to find theatrical confirmation of an irreducible difference between generality and repetition.

Repetition and generality are opposed from the point of view of conduct and from the point of view of law. It remains to specify a third opposition from the point of view of concepts or representation. Let us pose a question *quid juris*: a concept may be in principle the concept of a particular existing thing, thus having an infinite comprehension. Infinite comprehension is the correlate of an extension = 1. It is very important that this infinity of comprehension be supposed actual, not virtual or simply indefinite. It is on this condition that predicates in the form of moments of concepts are preserved, and have an effect on the subject to which they are attributed. Infinite comprehension thus makes possible remembering and recognition, memory and self-consciousness (even when these two faculties are not themselves infinite). The relation of a concept to its object under this double aspect, in the form that it assumes in this memory and this self-consciousness, is called representation. From this may be drawn the principles of a vulgarized Leibnizianism. According to a principle of difference, every determination is conceptual in the last instance, or actually belongs to the comprehension of a concept. According to a principle of sufficient reason, there is always one concept per particular thing. According to the reciprocal principle of the identity of indiscernibles, there is one and only one thing per concept. Together, these principles expound a theory of difference as conceptual difference, or develop the account of representation as mediation.

However, a concept can always be blocked at the level of each of its determinations or each of the predicates that it includes. In so far as it serves as a determination, a predicate must remain fixed in the concept while becoming something else in the thing (animal becomes something other in man and in horse; humanity something other in Peter and in Paul). This is why the comprehension of the concept is infinite; having become other in the thing, the predicate is like the object of another predicate in the concept. But this is also why each determination remains general or defines a resemblance, to the extent that it remains fixed in the concept and applicable by right to an infinity of things. Here, the concept is thus constituted in such a fashion that, in its real use, its comprehension extends to infinity, but in its logical use, this comprehension is always liable to an artificial blockage. Every logical limitation of the comprehension of a concept endows it with an extension greater than 1, in principle infinite, and thus of a generality such that no existing individual *can* correspond to it *hic et nunc* (rule of the inverse relation of comprehension and extension). Thus, the principle of difference understood as difference in the concept does not oppose but, on the contrary, allows the greatest space possible for the apprehension of resemblances. Even from the point of view of conundrums, the question 'What difference is there?' may always be transformed into: 'What resemblance is there?' But above all, in classification, the determination of species implies and supposes a continual evaluation of resemblances. Undoubtedly, resemblance is not a partial identity, but that is only because the predicate in the concept is not, by virtue of its becoming other in the thing, a part of that thing.

We wish to indicate the difference between this type of artificial blockage and a quite different type which must be called a natural blockage of the concept. One refers to logic pure and simple, but the other refers to a transcendental logic or a dialectic of existence. Let us suppose that a concept, taken at a particular moment when its comprehension is finite, is forcibly assigned a place in space and time – that is, an existence corresponding normally to the extension = 1. We would say, then, that a genus or species passes into existence *hic et nunc* without any augmentation of comprehension. There is a rift between that extension = 1 imposed upon the concept and the extension = ∞ that its weak comprehension demands in principle. The result will be a 'discrete extension' – that is, a pullulation of individuals absolutely identical in respect of their concept, and participating in the same singularity in existence (the paradox of doubles or twins).[7] This phenomenon of discrete extension implies a natural blockage of the concept, different in kind from a logical blockage: it forms a true repetition in existence rather than an order of resemblance in thought. There is a significant difference between generality, which always designates a logical power of concepts, and repetition, which testifies to their powerlessness or their real limits. Repetition is the pure fact of a concept with finite comprehension being forced to pass as such into existence: can we find examples of such a passage? Epicurean atoms would be one: individuals localised in space, they nevertheless have a meagre comprehension, which is made up for in discrete extension, to the point where there exists an infinity of atoms of the same shape and size. The existence of Epicurean atoms may be doubted. On the other hand, the existence of words, which are in a sense linguistic atoms, cannot be doubted. Words possess a comprehension which is necessarily finite, since they are by nature the objects of a merely nominal definition. We have here a reason why the comprehension of the concept *cannot* extend to infinity: we define a word by only a finite number of words. Nevertheless, speech and writing, from which words are inseparable, give them an existence *hic et nunc*; a genus thereby passes into existence as such; and here again extension is made up for in dispersion, in discreteness, under the sign of a repetition which forms the real power of language in speech and writing.

The question is: are there other natural blockages besides those of discrete extension and finite comprehension? Let us assume a concept with indefinite comprehension (virtually infinite). However far one pursues that comprehension, one can always think that it subsumes perfectly identical objects. By contrast with the actual infinite, where the concept is sufficient by right to distinguish its object from *every* other object, in this case the concept can pursue its comprehension indefinitely, always subsuming a plurality of objects which is itself indefinite. Here again, the concept is the Same – indefinitely the same – for objects which are distinct. We must therefore recognise the existence of non-conceptual differences between these objects. It is Kant who best indicates the correlation between objects endowed with only an indefinite specification, and purely spatio–temporal or oppositional, non-conceptual determinations (the paradox of symmetrical objects).[8] However, these determinations are precisely only the figures of repetition: space and time are themselves repetitive milieux; and real opposition is not a maximum of difference but a minimum of repetition – a repetition reduced to two, echoing and returning on itself; a repetition which has found the means to *define* itself. Repetition thus appears as difference without a concept, repetition which escapes indefinitely continued conceptual difference. It expresses a power peculiar to the existent, a stubbornness of the existent in intuition, which resists every specification by concepts no matter how far this is taken. However far you go in the concept, Kant says, you can always repeat – that is, make several objects correspond to it, or at least two: one for the left and one for the right, one for the more and one for the less, one for the positive and one for the negative.

Such a situation may be better understood if we consider that concepts with indefinite comprehension are concepts of Nature. As such, they are always in something else: they are not in Nature but in the mind which contemplates it or observes it, and represents it to itself. That is why it is said that Nature is alienated mind or alienated concept, opposed to itself. Corresponding to such concepts are those objects which themselves lack memory – that is, which neither possess nor collect in themselves their own moments. The question is asked why Nature repeats: because it is *partes extra partes, mens momentanea*. Novelty then passes to the mind which represents itself: because the mind has a memory or acquires habits, it is capable of forming concepts in general and of drawing something new, of subtracting something new from the repetition that it contemplates.

Concepts with finite comprehension are nominal concepts; concepts with indefinite comprehension but without memory are concepts of Nature. Yet these two cases still do not exhaust the examples of natural blockage. Take an individual notion or a particular representation with infinite comprehension, endowed with memory but lacking self-consciousness. The comprehensive representation is indeed in-itself, the memory is there, embracing all the particularity of an act, a scene, an event or a being. What is missing, however, for a determinate natural reason, is the for-itself of consciousness or recognition. What is missing in the memory is remembrance – or rather, the working through of memory. Consciousness establishes between the I and the representation a relation much more profound than that which appears in the expression 'I have a representation': it relates the representation to the I as if to a free faculty which does not allow itself to be confined within any one of its products, but for which each product is already thought and recognised as past, the occasion of a determinant change in inner meaning. When the consciousness of knowledge or the working through of memory is missing, the knowledge in itself is only the repetition of its object: it is *played*, that is to say repeated, enacted instead of being known. Repetition here appears as the unconscious of the free concept, of knowledge or of memory, the unconscious of representation. It fell to Freud to assign the natural reason for such a blockage: repression or resistance, which makes repetition itself a veritable 'constraint', a 'compulsion'. Here, then, is a third case of blockage, one which concerns, this time, the concepts of freedom. Here too, from the standpoint of a certain Freudianism, we can discover the principle of an inverse relation between repetition and consciousness, repetition and remembering, repetition and recognition (the paradox of the 'burials' or buried objects): the less one remembers, the less one is conscious of remembering one's past, the more one repeats it – remember and work through the memory in order not to repeat it.[9] Self-consciousness in recognition appears as the faculty of the future or the function of the future, the function of the new. Is it not true that the only dead who return are those whom one has buried too quickly and too deeply, without paying them the necessary respects, and that remorse testifies less to an excess of memory than to a powerlessness or to a failure in the working through of a memory?

There is a tragic and a comic repetition. Indeed, repetition always appears twice, once in the tragic destiny and once in the comic aspect. In the theatre, the hero repeats precisely because he is separated from an essential, infinite knowledge. This knowledge is in him, it is immersed in him and acts in him, but acts like something hidden, like a blocked representation. The difference between the comic and the tragic pertains to two elements: first, the nature of the repressed knowledge – in the one case immediate natural knowledge, a simple given of common sense, in the other terrible esoteric knowledge; second, as a result, the manner in which the character is excluded from this knowledge, the manner in which 'he does not know that he knows'. In general the practical problem consists in this: this unknown knowledge must be represented as bathing the whole scene, impregnating all the elements of the play and comprising in itself all the powers of mind and nature, but at the same time the hero cannot represent it to *himself* – on the contrary, he must enact it, play it and repeat it until the acute moment that Aristotle called 'recognition'. At this point, repetition and representation confront one another and merge, without, however, confusing their two levels, the one reflecting itself in and being sustained by the other, the knowledge as it is represented on stage and as repeated by the actor then being recognised as the same.

The discrete, the alienated and the repressed are the three cases of natural blockage, corresponding respectively to nominal concepts, concepts of nature and concepts of freedom. In all these cases, however, conceptual identity or Sameness of representation is invoked to account for repetition: repetition is attributed to elements which are really distinct but nevertheless share strictly the same concept. Repetition thus appears as a difference, but a difference absolutely without concept; in this sense, an indifferent difference. The words 'really', 'strictly', 'absolutely' are supposed to refer to the phenomenon of natural blockage, in opposition to logical blockage which only determines a generality. However, an important drawback compromises this whole endeavour. As long as we invoke absolute conceptual identity for distinct objects, we suggest a purely negative explanation, an explanation by default. The fact that this default should be grounded in the nature of concepts or representations themselves changes nothing. In the first case, repetition occurs because nominal concepts naturally possess a finite comprehension. In the second case, repetition occurs because concepts of nature are naturally devoid of memory, alienated and outside themselves. In the third case, because the concept of freedom remains unconscious while memories and representations remain repressed. In all these cases, *that which* repeats does so only by dint of not 'comprehending', not remembering, not knowing or not being conscious. Throughout, the inadequacy of concepts and of their representative concomitants (memory and self-consciousness, remembrance and recognition) is supposed to account for repetition. Such is therefore the default of every argument grounded in the form of identity in the concept: these arguments give us only a nominal definition and a negative explanation of repetition. No doubt the formal identity which corresponds to simple logical blockage may be opposed to real identity (*the Same*) as this appears in natural blockage. But natural blockage itself requires a positive supra-conceptual force capable of explaining it, and of thereby explaining repetition.

Let us return to the example of psychoanalysis: we repeat because we repress ... Freud was never satisfied with such a negative schema, in which repetition is explained by amnesia. It is true that, from the beginning, repression was considered a positive power. However, he borrowed this positivity from the pleasure principle or from the reality principle: it was merely a derived positivity, one of opposition. The turning point of Freudianism appears in *Beyond the Pleasure Principle*: the death instinct is discovered, not in connection with the destructive tendencies, not in connection with aggressivity, but as a result of a direct consideration of repetition phenomena. Strangely, the death instinct serves as a positive, originary principle for repetition; this is its domain and its meaning. It plays the role of a transcendental principle, whereas the pleasure principle is only psychological. For this reason, it is above all silent (not given in experience), whereas the pleasure principle is noisy. The first question, then, is: How is it that the theme of death, which appears to draw together the most negative elements of psychological life, can be in itself the most positive element, transcendentally positive, to the point of affirming repetition? How can it be related to a primordial *instinct*? But a second question immediately arises: Under what form is repetition affirmed and prescribed by the death instinct? Ultimately, it is a question of the relation between repetition and disguises. Do the disguises found in the work of dreams or symptoms – condensation, displacement, dramatisation – rediscover while attenuating a bare, brute repetition (repetition of the Same)? From the first theory of repression, Freud indicated another path: Dora elaborates her own role, and repeats her love for the father, only through other roles filled by others, which she herself adopts in relation to those others (K., Frau K., the governess ...). The disguises and the variations, the masks or costumes, do not come 'over and above': they are, on the contrary, the internal genetic elements of repetition itself, its integral and constituent parts. This path would have been able to lead the analysis of the unconscious towards a veritable theatre. However, if it did not do so, this was because Freud was unable to prevent himself maintaining the model of a brute repetition, at least as a tendency. We see this when he attributes fixation to the Id: disguise is then understood from the perspective of a simple opposition of forces; disguised repetition is only the fruit of a secondary compromise between the opposed forces of the Ego and the Id. Even beyond the pleasure principle, the form of a bare repetition persists, since Freud interprets the death instinct as a tendency to return to the state of inanimate matter, one which upholds the model of a wholly physical or material repetition.

Death has nothing to do with a material model. On the contrary, the death instinct may be understood in relation to masks and costumes. Repetition is truly that which disguises itself in constituting itself, that which constitutes itself only by disguising itself. It is not underneath the masks, but is formed from one mask to another, as though from one distinctive point to another, from one privileged instant to another, with and within the variations. The masks do not hide anything except other masks. There is no first term which is repeated, and even our childhood love for the mother repeats other adult loves with regard to other women, rather like the way in which the hero of *In Search of Lost Time* replays with his mother Swann's passion for Odette. There is therefore nothing repeated which may be isolated or abstracted from the repetition in which it was formed, but in which it is also hidden. There is no bare repetition which may be abstracted or inferred from the disguise itself. The same thing is both disguising and disguised. A decisive moment in psychoanalysis occurred when Freud gave up, in certain respects, the hypothesis of real childhood events, which would have played the part of ultimate disguised terms, in order to substitute the power of fantasy which is immersed in the death instinct, where everything is already masked and disguised. In short, repetition is in its essence symbolic; symbols or simulacra are the letter of repetition itself. Difference is included in repetition by way of disguise and by the order of the symbol. This is why the variations do not come from without, do not express a secondary compromise between a repressing instance and a repressed instance, and must not be understood on the basis of the still negative forms of opposition, reversal or overturning. The variations express, rather, the differential mechanisms which belong to the essence and origin of that which is repeated. We should even overturn the relations between 'covered' and 'uncovered' within repetition. Take an uncovered or bare repetition (repetition of the Same) such as an obsessional ceremony or a schizophrenic stereotype: the mechanical element in the repetition, the element of action apparently repeated, serves as a cover for a more profound repetition, which is played in another dimension, a secret verticality in which the roles and masks are furnished by the death instinct. Theatre of terror, Binswanger said of schizophrenia. There, the 'never seen' is not the contrary of the 'already seen': both signify the same thing, and are lived each in the other. Nerval's *Sylvie* already introduced us into this theatre, and the *Gradiva*, so close to a Nervalian inspiration, shows us the hero who lives at once both repetition as such and the repeated which is always disguised in the repetition. In the analysis of obsession, the appearance of the theme of death coincides with the moment at which the obsessed has command of all the characters of his drama and brings them together in a repetition of which the 'ceremony' is only the external envelope. The mask, the costume, the covered is everywhere the truth of the uncovered. The mask is the true subject of repetition. Because repetition differs in kind from representation, the repeated cannot be represented: rather, it must always be signified, masked by what signifies it, itself masking what it signifies.

I do not repeat because I repress. I repress because I repeat, I forget because I repeat. I repress, because I can live certain things or certain experiences only in the mode of repetition. I am determined to repress whatever would prevent me from living them thus: in particular, the representation which mediates the lived by relating it to the form of a similar or identical object. Eros and Thanatos are distinguished in that Eros must be repeated, can be lived only through repetition, whereas Thanatos (as transcendental principle) is that which gives repetition to Eros, that which submits Eros to repetition. Only such a point of view is capable of advancing us in the obscure problems of the origin of repression, its nature, its causes and the exact terms on which it bears. For when Freud shows – beyond repression 'properly speaking', which bears upon *representations* – the necessity of supposing a primary repression which concerns first and foremost pure *presentations*, or the manner in which the drives are necessarily lived, we believe that he comes closest to a positive internal principle of repetition. This later appears to him determinable in the form of the death instinct, and it is this which, far from being explained by it, must explain the blockage of representation in repression properly speaking. This is why the law of an inverse relation between repetition and remembering is in every respect hardly satisfactory, in so far as it makes repetition depend upon repression.

Freud noted from the beginning that in order to stop repeating it was not enough to remember in the abstract (without affect), nor to form a concept in general, nor even to represent the repressed event in all its particularity: it was necessary to seek out the memory there where it was, to install oneself directly in the past in order to accomplish a living connection between the knowledge and the resistance, the representation and the blockage. We are not, therefore, healed by simple anamnesis, any more than we are made ill by amnesia. Here as elsewhere, becoming conscious counts for little. The more theatrical and dramatic operation by which healing takes place – or does not take place – has a name: transference. Now transference is still repetition: above all it is repetition.[10] If repetition makes us ill, it also heals us; if it enchains and destroys us, it also frees us, testifying in both cases to its 'demonic' power. All cure is a voyage to the bottom of repetition. There is indeed something analogous to scientific experimentation in transference, since the patient is supposed to repeat the whole of his disturbance in privileged, artificial conditions, taking the person of the analyst as 'object'. In transference, however, repetition does not so much serve to identify events, persons and passions as to *authenticate* the roles and select the masks. Transference is not an experiment but a principle which grounds the entire analytic experience. The roles themselves are by nature erotic, but the verification of these roles appeals to the highest principle and the most profound judge, the death instinct. In effect, reflection on transference was a determinant motive behind the discovery of a 'beyond'. In this sense, repetition constitutes by itself the selective game of our illness *and* our health, of our loss *and* our salvation. How can this game be related to the death instinct? No doubt in a sense close to that in which Miller, in his wonderful book on Rimbaud, says: 'I realized that I was free, that the death I had gone through had liberated me.'[11] It seems that the idea of a death instinct must be understood in terms of three paradoxical and complementary requirements: to give repetition an original, positive principle, but also an autonomous disguising power; and finally, to give it an immanent meaning in which terror is closely mingled with the movement of selection and freedom.

Our problem concerns the essence of repetition. It is a question of knowing why repetition cannot be explained by the form of identity in concepts or representations; in what sense it demands a superior 'positive' principle. This enquiry must embrace all the concepts of nature and freedom. Consider, on the border between these two cases, the repetition of a decorative motif: a figure is reproduced, while the concept remains absolutely identical ... . However, this is not how artists proceed in reality. They do not juxtapose instances of the figure, but rather each time combine an element of one instance with *another* element of a following instance. They introduce a disequilibrium into the dynamic process of construction, an instability, dissymmetry or gap of some kind which disappears only in the overall effect. Commenting on such a case, Lévi-Strauss writes: 'These elements interlock with each other through dislocation, and it is only at the end that the pattern achieves a stability which both confirms and belies the dynamic process according to which it has been carried out.'[12] These remarks stand for the notion of causality in general. For it is not the elements of symmetry present which matter for artistic or natural causality, but those which are missing and are not in the cause; what matters is the possibility of the cause having less symmetry than the effect. Moreover, causality would remain eternally conjectural, a simple logical category, if that possibility were not at some moment or other effectively fulfilled. For this reason, the logical relation of causality is inseparable from a physical process of signalling, without which it would not be translated into action. By 'signal' we mean a system with orders of disparate size, endowed with elements of dissymmetry; by 'sign' we mean what happens within such a system, what flashes across the intervals when a communication takes place between disparates. The sign is indeed an effect, but an effect with two aspects: in one of these it expresses, *qua* sign, the productive dissymmetry; in the other it tends to cancel it. The sign is not entirely of the order of the symbol; nevertheless, it makes way for it by implying an internal difference (while leaving the conditions of its reproduction still external).

The negative expression 'lack of symmetry' should not mislead us: it indicates the origin and positivity of the causal process. It is positivity itself. For us, as the example of the decorative motif suggests, it is essential to break down the notion of causality in order to distinguish two types of repetition: one which concerns only the overall, abstract effect, and the other which concerns the acting cause. One is a static repetition, the other is dynamic. One results from the work, but the other is like the 'evolution' of a bodily movement. One refers back to a single concept, which leaves only an external difference between the ordinary instances of a figure; the other is the repetition of an internal difference which it incorporates in each of its moments, and carries from one distinctive point to another. One could try to assimilate these two repetitions by saying that the difference between the first and the second is only a matter of a change in the content of the concept, or of the figure being articulated differently, but this would be to fail to recognise the respective order of each repetition. For in the dynamic order there is no representative concept, nor any figure represented in a pre-existing space. There is an Idea, and a pure dynamism which creates a corresponding space.

Studies on rhythm or symmetry confirm this duality. A distinction is drawn between arithmetic symmetry, which refers back to a scale of whole or fractional coefficients, and geometric symmetry, based upon proportions or irrational ratios; a static symmetry which is cubic or hexagonal, and a dynamic symmetry which is pentagonal and appears in a spiral line or in a geometrically progressing pulsation – in short, in a living and mortal 'evolution'. Now, the second of these is at the heart of the first; it is the vital, positive, active procedure. In a network of double squares, we discover radiating lines which have the centre of a pentagon or a pentagram as their asymmetrical pole. The network is like a fabric stretched upon a framework, 'but the outline, the principal rhythm of that framework, is almost always a theme independent of the network': such elements of dissymmetry serve as both genetic principle and principle of reflection for symmetrical figures.[13] The static repetition in the network of double squares thus refers back to a dynamic repetition, formed by a pentagon and 'the decreasing series of pentagrams which may be naturally inscribed therein'. Similarly, the study of rhythm allows us immediately to distinguish two kinds of repetition. Cadence-repetition is a regular division of time, an isochronic recurrence of identical elements. However, a period exists only in so far as it is determined by a tonic accent, commanded by intensities. Yet we would be mistaken about the function of accents if we said that they were reproduced at equal intervals. On the contrary, tonic and intensive values act by creating inequalities or incommensurabilities between metrically equivalent periods or spaces. They create distinctive points, privileged instants which always indicate a poly-rhythm. Here again, the unequal is the most positive element. Cadence is only the envelope of a rhythm, and of a relation between rhythms. The reprise of points of inequality, of inflections or of rhythmic events, is more profound than the reproduction of ordinary homogeneous elements. As a result, we should distinguish cadence-repetition and rhythm-repetition in every case, the first being only the outward appearance or the abstract effect of the second. A bare, material repetition (repetition of the Same) appears only in the sense that another repetition is disguised within it, constituting it and constituting itself in disguising itself. Even in nature, isochronic rotations are only the outward appearance of a more profound movement, the revolving cycles are only abstractions: placed together, they reveal evolutionary cycles or spirals whose principle is a variable curve, and the trajectory of which has two dissymmetrical aspects, as though it had a right and a left. It is always in this gap, which should not be confused with the negative, that creatures weave their repetition and receive at the same time the gift of living and dying.

Finally, to return to nominal concepts: is it the identity of the nominal concept which explains the repetition of a word? Take the example of rhyme: it is indeed verbal repetition, but repetition which includes the difference between two words and inscribes that difference at the heart of a poetic Idea, in a space which it determines. Nor does its meaning lie in marking equal intervals, but rather, as we see in a notion of strong rhyme, in putting tonal values in the service of tonic rhythm, and contributing to the independence of tonic rhythms from arithmetic rhythms. As for the repetition of a single word, we must understand this as a 'generalised rhyme', not rhyme as a restricted repetition. This generalisation can proceed in two ways: either a word taken in two senses ensures a resemblance or a paradoxical identity between the two senses; or a word taken in one sense exercises an attractive force on its neighbours, communicating an extraordinary gravity to them until one of the neighbouring words takes up the baton and becomes in turn a centre of repetition. Raymond Roussel and Charles Péguy were the great repeaters of literature, able to lift the pathological power of language to a higher artistic level. Roussel takes ambiguous words or homonyms and fills the entire distance between their meanings with a story presented twice and with objects themselves doubled. He thereby overcomes homonymity on its own ground and inscribes the maximum difference within repetition, where this is the space opened up in the heart of a word. This space is still presented by Roussel as one of masks and death, in which is developed both a repetition which enchains and a repetition which saves – which saves above all from the one which enchains. Roussel creates an after-language where, once everything has been said, everything is repeated and recommenced.[14] Péguy's technique is very different: it substitutes repetition not for homonymity but for synonymity; it concerns what linguists call the function of contiguity rather than that of similarity; it forms a before-language, an auroral language in which the step-by-step creation of an internal space within words proceeds by tiny differences. This time, everything leads to the problem of aging and premature deaths, but in relation to this problem also to the extraordinary chance to affirm a repetition which saves against that which enchains. Both Péguy and Roussel take language to one of its limits: in the case of Roussel, that of similarity and selection, the 'distinctive feature' between *b*illard and *p*illard; in the case of Péguy, that of contiguity or combination, the famous *tapestry points*. Both substitute a vertical repetition of distinctive points, which takes us inside the words, for the horizontal repetition of ordinary words repeated. Both substitute a positive repetition, one which flows from the excess of a linguistic and stylistic Idea, for a repetition by default which results from the inadequacy of nominal concepts or verbal representations. How does death inspire language, given that it is always present when repetition is affirmed?

The reproduction of the Same is not a motor of bodily movements. We know that even the simplest imitation involves a difference between inside and outside. Moreover, imitation plays only a secondary and regulatory role in the acquisition of a behaviour: it permits the correction of movements being made, but not their instigation. Learning takes place not in the relation between a representation and an action (reproduction of the Same) but in the relation between a sign and a response (encounter with the Other). Signs involve heterogeneity in at least three ways: first, in the object which bears or emits them, and is necessarily on a different level, as though there were two orders of size or disparate realities between which the sign flashes; secondly, in themselves, since a sign envelops another 'object' within the limits of the object which bears it, and incarnates a natural or spiritual power (an Idea); finally, in the response they elicit, since the movement of the response does not 'resemble' that of the sign. The movement of the swimmer does not resemble that of the wave, in particular, the movements of the swimming instructor which we reproduce on the sand bear no relation to the movements of the wave, which we learn to deal with only by grasping the former in practice as signs. That is why it is so difficult to say how someone learns: there is an innate or acquired practical familiarity with signs, which means that there is something amorous – but also something fatal – about all education. We learn nothing from those who say: 'Do as I do'. Our only teachers are those who tell us to 'do with me', and are able to emit signs to be developed in heterogeneity rather than propose gestures for us to reproduce. In other words, there is no ideo-motivity, only sensory-motivity. When a body combines some of its own distinctive points with those of a wave, it espouses the principle of a repetition which is no longer that of the Same, but involves the Other – involves difference, from one wave and one gesture to another, and carries that difference through the repetitive space thereby constituted. To learn is indeed to constitute this space of an encounter with signs, in which the distinctive points renew themselves in each other, and repetition takes shape while disguising itself. Apprenticeship always gives rise to images of death, on the edges of the space it creates and with the help of the heterogeneity it engenders. Signs are deadly when they are lost in the distance, but also when they strike us with full force. Oedipus receives a sign once from too far away, once from too close, and between the two a terrible repetition of the crime is woven. Zarathustra receives his 'sign' either from too near or from too far, and only at the end does he foresee the correct distance which will turn that which in eternal return makes him ill into a liberatory and redemptive repetition. Signs are the true elements of theatre. They testify to the spiritual and natural powers which act beneath the words, gestures, characters and objects represented. They signify repetition as real movement, in opposition to representation which is a false movement of the abstract.

We are right to speak of repetition when we find ourselves confronted by identical elements with exactly the same concept. However, we must distinguish between these discrete elements, these repeated objects, and a secret subject, the real subject of repetition, which repeats itself through them. Repetition must be understood in the pronominal; we must find the Self of repetition, the singularity within that which repeats. For there is no repetition without a repeater, nothing repeated without a repetitious soul. As a result, rather than the repeated and the repeater, the object and the subject, we must distinguish two forms of repetition. In every case repetition is difference without a concept. But in one case, the difference is taken to be only external to the concept; it is a difference between objects represented by the same concept, falling into the indifference of space and time. In the other case, the difference is internal to the Idea; it unfolds as pure movement, creative of a dynamic space and time which correspond to the Idea. The first repetition is repetition of the Same, explained by the identity of the concept or representation; the second includes difference, and includes itself in the alterity of the Idea, in the heterogeneity of an 'a-presentation'. One is negative, occurring by default in the concept; the other affirmative, occurring by excess in the Idea. One is conjectural, the other categorical. One is static, the other dynamic. One is repetition in the effect, the other in the cause. One is extensive, the other intensive. One is ordinary, the other distinctive and singular. One is horizontal, the other vertical. One is developed and explicated, the other enveloped and in need of interpretation. One is revolving, the other evolving. One involves equality, commensurability and symmetry; the other is grounded in inequality, incommensurability and dissymmetry. One is material, the other spiritual, even in nature and in the earth. One is inanimate, the other carries the secret of our deaths and our lives, of our enchainments and our liberations, the demonic and the divine. One is a 'bare' repetition, the other a covered repetition, which forms itself in covering itself, in masking and disguising itself. One concerns accuracy, the other has authenticity as its criterion.

The two repetitions are not independent. One is the singular subject, the interiority and the heart of the other, the depths of the other. The other is only the external envelope, the abstract effect. The repetition of dissymmetry is hidden within symmetrical ensembles or effects; a repetition of distinctive points underneath that of ordinary points; and everywhere the Other in the repetition of the Same. This is the secret, the most profound repetition: it alone provides the principle of the other one, the reason for the blockage of concepts. In this domain, as in *Sartor Resartus*, it is the masked, the disguised or the costumed which turns out to be the truth of the uncovered. Necessarily, since this repetition is not hidden by something else but forms itself by disguising itself; it does not pre-exist its own disguises and, in forming itself, constitutes the bare repetition within which it becomes enveloped. Important consequences follow from this. When we are confronted by a repetition which proceeds masked, or comprises displacements, quickenings, slowdowns, variants or differences which are ultimately capable of leading us far away from the point of departure, we tend to see a mixed state in which repetition is not pure but only approximative: the very word repetition seems to be employed symbolically, by analogy or metaphor. It is true that we have strictly defined repetition as difference without concept. However, we would be wrong to reduce it to a difference which falls back into exteriority, because the concept embodies the form of the Same, without seeing that it can be internal to the Idea and possess in itself all the resources of signs, symbols and alterity which go beyond the concept as such. The examples invoked above concern the most diverse kinds of case, from nominal concepts to concepts of nature and freedom, and we could be charged with having mixed up all kinds of physical and psychical repetitions, even with having run together stereotypical repetitions and latent, symbolic repetitions in the psychical domain. However, we wished to show the coexistence of these instances in every repetitive structure, to show how repetition displays identical elements which necessarily refer back to a latent subject which repeats itself through these elements, forming an 'other' repetition at the heart of the first. We therefore suggest that this other repetition is in no way approximative or metaphorical. It is, on the contrary, the spirit of every repetition. It is the very letter of every repetition, its watermark or constitutive cipher. It forms the essence of that in which every repetition consists: difference without a concept, non-mediated difference. It is both the literal and spiritual primary sense of repetition. The material sense results from this other, as if secreted by it like a shell.

We began by distinguishing generality and repetition. Then we distinguished two forms of repetition. These two distinctions are linked: the consequences of the first are unfolded only in the second. For if we were content to treat repetition abstractly and as devoid of any interior, we would remain incapable of understanding why and how a concept could be naturally blocked, allowing a repetition which has nothing to do with generality to appear. Conversely, when we discover the literal interior of repetition, we have the means not only to understand the outer repetition as a cover, but also to recapture the order of generality (and, following Kierkegaard's wish, to carry out the reconciliation of the singular with the general). For to the extent that the internal repetition projects itself through a bare repetition which covers it, the differences that it includes appear to be so many factors which oppose repetition, which attenuate it and vary it according to 'general' laws. Beneath the general operation of laws, however, there always remains the play of singularities. Cyclical generalities in nature are the masks of a singularity which appears through their interferences; and beneath the generalities of habit in moral life we rediscover singular processes of learning. The domain of laws must be understood, but always on the basis of a Nature and a Spirit superior to their own laws, which weave their repetitions in the depths of the earth and of the heart, where laws do not yet exist. The interior of repetition is always affected by an order of difference: it is only to the extent that something is linked to a repetition of an order other than its own that the repetition appears external and bare, and the thing itself subject to the categories of generality. It is the inadequation between difference and repetition which gives rise to the order of generality. Gabriel Tarde suggested in this sense that resemblance itself was only displaced repetition: real repetition is that which corresponds directly to a difference of the same degree as itself. Better than anyone, Tarde was able to elaborate a new dialectic by discovering in mind and nature the secret effort to establish an ever more perfect correspondence between difference and repetition.[15]

So long as we take difference to be conceptual difference, intrinsically conceptual, and repetition to be an extrinsic difference between objects represented by the same concept, it appears that the problem of their relation may be resolved by the facts. Are there repetitions – yes or no? Or is every difference indeed intrinsic and conceptual in the last instance? Hegel ridiculed Leibniz for having invited the court ladies to undertake experimental metaphysics while walking in the gardens, to see whether two leaves of a tree could not have the same concept. Replace the court ladies by forensic scientists: no two grains of dust are absolutely identical, no two hands have the same distinctive points, no two typewriters have the same strike, no two revolvers score their bullets in the same manner ... . Why, however, do we feel that the problem is not properly defined so long as we look for the criterion of a *principium individuationis* in the facts? It is because a difference can be internal, yet not conceptual (as the paradox of symmetrical objects shows). A dynamic space must be defined from the point of view of an observer tied to that space, not from an external position. There are internal differences which dramatise an Idea before representing an object. Difference here is internal to an Idea, even though it be external to the concept which represents an object. That is why the opposition between Kant and Leibniz seems much less strong to the extent that one takes account of the dynamic factors present in the two doctrines. If, in the forms of intuition, Kant recognised extrinsic differences not reducible to the order of concepts, these are no less 'internal' even though they cannot be regarded as 'intrinsic' by the understanding, and can be represented only in their external relation to space as a whole.[16] In other words, following certain neo-Kantian interpretations, there is a step-by-step, internal, dynamic construction of space which must precede the 'representation' of the whole as a form of exteriority. The element of this internal genesis seems to us to consist of intensive quantity rather than schema, and to be related to Ideas rather than to concepts of the understanding. If the spatial order of extrinsic differences and the conceptual order of intrinsic differences are finally in harmony, as the schema shows they are, this is ultimately due to this intensive differential element, this synthesis of continuity at a given moment which, in the form of a *continua repetitio*, first gives rise internally to the space corresponding to Ideas. With Leibniz, the affinity between extrinsic differences and intrinsic conceptual differences already appealed to the internal process of a *continua repetitio*, grounded upon an intensive differential element which ensures the synthesis of continuity at a point in order to engender space from within.

There are repetitions which are not only extrinsic differences, just as there are internal differences which are neither intrinsic nor conceptual. We are thus in a better position to identify the source of the preceding ambiguities. When we define repetition as difference without concept, we are drawn to conclude that only extrinsic difference is involved in repetition; we consider, therefore, that any internal 'novelty' is sufficient to remove us from repetition proper and can be reconciled only with an approximative repetition, so-called by analogy. Nothing of the sort is true. For we do not yet know what is the essence of repetition, what is positively denoted by the expression 'difference without concept', or the nature of the interiority it may imply. Conversely, when we define difference as conceptual difference, we believe we have done enough to specify the concept of difference as such. Nevertheless, here again we have no idea of difference, no concept of difference as such. Perhaps the mistake of the philosophy of difference, from Aristotle to Hegel via Leibniz, lay in confusing the concept of difference with a merely conceptual difference, in remaining content to inscribe difference in the concept in general. In reality, so long as we inscribe difference in the concept in general we have no singular Idea of difference, we remain only with a difference already mediated by representation. We therefore find ourselves confronted by two questions: what is the concept of difference – one which is not reducible to simple conceptual difference but demands its own Idea, its own singularity at the level of Ideas? On the other hand, what is the essence of repetition – one which is not reducible to difference without concept, and cannot be confused with the apparent character of objects represented by the same concept, but bears witness to singularity as a power of Ideas? The meeting between these two notions, difference and repetition, can no longer be assumed: it must come about as a result of interferences and intersections between these two lines: one concerning the essence of repetition, the other the idea of difference.

Chapter I
Difference in Itself

Indifference has two aspects: the undifferenciated abyss, the black nothingness, the indeterminate animal in which everything is dissolved – but also the white nothingness, the once more calm surface upon which float unconnected determinations like scattered members: a head without a neck, an arm without a shoulder, eyes without brows. The indeterminate is completely indifferent, but such floating determinations are no less indifferent to each other. Is difference intermediate between these two extremes? Or is it not rather the only extreme, the only moment of presence and precision? Difference is the state in which one can speak of determination *as such*. The difference 'between' two things is only empirical, and the corresponding determinations are only extrinsic. However, instead of something distinguished from something else, imagine something which distinguishes itself – and yet that from which it distinguishes itself does not distinguish itself from it. Lightning, for example, distinguishes itself from the black sky but must also trail it behind, as though it were distinguishing itself from that which does not distinguish itself from it. It is as if the ground rose to the surface, without ceasing to be ground. There is cruelty, even monstrosity, on both sides of this struggle against an elusive adversary, in which the distinguished opposes something which cannot distinguish itself from it but continues to espouse that which divorces it. Difference is this state in which determination takes the form of unilateral distinction. We must therefore say that difference is made, or makes itself, as in the expression 'make the difference'. This difference or determination *as such* is also cruelty. The Platonists used to say that the not-One distinguished itself from the One, but not the converse, since the One does not flee that which flees it; and at the other pole, form distinguishes itself from matter or from the ground, but not the converse, since distinction itself is a form. In truth, all the forms are dissolved when they are reflected in this rising ground. It has ceased to be the pure indeterminate which remains below, but the forms also cease to be the coexisting or complementary determinations. The rising ground is no longer below, it acquires autonomous existence; the form reflected in this ground is no longer a form but an abstract line acting directly upon the soul. When the ground rises to the surface, the human face decomposes in this mirror in which both determinations and the indeterminate combine in a single determination which 'makes' the difference. It is a poor recipe for producing monsters to accumulate heteroclite determinations or to overdetermine the animal. It is better to raise up the ground and dissolve the form. Goya worked with aquatint and etching, the grisaille of the one and the severity of the other. Odilon Redon used *chiaroscuro* and the abstract line. The abstract line acquires all its force from giving up the model – that is to say, the plastic symbol of the form – and participates in the ground all the more violently in that it distinguishes itself from it without the ground distinguishing itself from the line.[1] At this point, in such a mirror, faces are distorted. Nor is it certain that it is only the sleep of reason which gives rise to monsters: it is also the vigil, the insomnia of thought, since thought is that moment in which determination makes itself one, by virtue of maintaining a unilateral and precise relation to the indeterminate. Thought 'makes' difference, but difference is monstrous. We should not be surprised that difference should appear accursed, that it should be error, sin or the figure of evil for which there must be expiation. There is no sin other than raising the ground and dissolving the form. Recall Artaud's idea: cruelty is nothing but determination *as such*, that precise point at which the determined maintains its essential relation with the undetermined, that rigorous abstract line fed by *chiaroscuro*.

To rescue difference from its maledictory state seems, therefore, to be the project of the philosophy of difference. Cannot difference become a harmonious organism and relate determination to other determinations within a form – that is to say, within the coherent medium of an organic representation? There are four principal aspects to 'reason' in so far as it is the medium of representation: identity, in the form of the *undetermined* concept; analogy, in the relation between ultimate *determinable* concepts; opposition, in the relation between *determinations* within concepts; resemblance, in the *determined* object of the concept itself. These forms are like the four heads or the four shackles of mediation. Difference is 'mediated' to the extent that it is subjected to the fourfold root of identity, opposition, analogy and resemblance. On the basis of a first impression (difference is evil), it is proposed to 'save' difference by representing it, and to represent it by relating it to the requirements of the concept in general. It is therefore a question of determining a propitious moment – the Greek propitious moment – at which difference is, as it were, reconciled with the concept. Difference must leave its cave and cease to be a monster; or at least only that which escapes at the propitious moment must persist as a monster, that which constitutes only a bad encounter, a bad occasion. At this point the expression 'make the difference' changes its meaning. It now refers to a selective test which must determine which differences may be inscribed within the concept in general, and how. Such a test, such a selection, seems to be effectively realised by the Large and the Small. For the Large and the Small are not naturally said of the One, but first and foremost of difference. The question arises, therefore, how far the difference can and must extend – how large? how small? – in order to remain within the limits of the concept, neither becoming lost within nor escaping beyond it. It is obviously difficult to know whether the problem is well posed in this way: is difference really an evil in itself? Must the question have been posed in these moral terms? Must difference have been 'mediated' in order to render it both livable and thinkable? Must the selection have consisted in that particular test? Must the test have been conceived in that manner and with that aim? But we can answer these questions only once we have more precisely determined the supposed nature of the propitious moment.

Aristotle says: there is a difference which is at once the greatest and the most perfect, *megistē* and *teleios*. Difference in general is distinguished from diversity or otherness. For two terms differ when they are other, not in themselves, but in something else; thus when they also agree in something else: in genus when they are differences in species, in species for differences in number, or even 'in being, according to the analogy' for differences in genus. Under these conditions, what is the greatest difference? The greatest difference is always an opposition, but of all the forms of opposition, which is the most perfect, the most complete, that which 'agrees' best? Related terms belong to one another; contradiction already belongs to a subject, but only in order to make its subsistence impossible and to qualify the change by which it begins or ceases to be; privation again expresses a determinate incapacity on behalf of an existing subject. Contrariety alone expresses the capacity of a subject to bear opposites while remaining substantially the same (in matter or in genus). Under what conditions, however, does contrariety impart its perfection to difference? So long as we consider the concrete being with respect to its matter, the contrarieties which affect it are corporeal modifications which give us only the empirical, accidental concept of a still extrinsic difference [*extra quidditatem*]. Accidents may be separable from the subject, as 'white' and 'black' are from 'man'; or inseparable, as 'male' and 'female' are from 'animal': accordingly, the difference will be called either *communis* or *propria*, but in so far as it pertains to matter, it will always be accidental. Thus, only a contrariety in the essence or in the form gives us the concept of a difference that is itself essential [*differentia essentialis aut propriissima*]. Contraries in this case are modifications which affect a subject with respect to its genus. Genera are in effect divided by differences in essence which take the form of contraries, such as 'with feet' and 'with wings'. In short, contrariety in the genus is the perfect and maximal difference, and contrariety in the genus is specific difference. Above and below that, difference tends to become simple otherness and almost to escape the identity of the concept: generic difference is too large, being established between uncombinable objects which do not enter into relations of contrariety; while individual difference is too small, being between indivisible objects which have no contrariety either.[2]

It seems indeed, on the other hand, that specific difference meets all the requirements of a harmonious concept and an organic representation. It is pure because it is formal, intrinsic because it applies to the essence. It is qualitative, and to the extent that the genus designates the essence, difference is even a very special quality 'according to the essence', a quality of the essence itself. It is synthetic, since the determination of species is composition, and the difference is actually added to the genus in which it was hitherto only virtually included. It is mediated, it is itself mediation, the middle term in person. It is productive, since genera are not divided into differences but divided by differences which give rise to corresponding species. That is why it is always a cause, the formal cause: the shortest distance is the specific difference of the straight line, compression the specific difference of the colour black, dissociation that of the colour white. That is also why it is a predicate of such a peculiar type, since it is attributed to the species but at the same time attributes the genus to it and constitutes the species to which it is attributed. Such a synthetic and constitutive predicate, attributive more than attributed, a veritable rule of production, has one final property: that of carrying with itself that which it attributes. In effect, the quality of the essence is sufficiently special to make the genus something other, and not simply of another quality.[3] It is thus in the nature of genera to remain the same in themselves while becoming other in the differences which divide them. Difference carries with itself the genus and all the intermediary differences. The determination of species links difference with difference across the successive levels of division, like a transport of difference, a *diaphora* (difference) of *diaphora*, until a final difference, that of the *infima species* (lowest species), condenses in the chosen direction the entirety of the essence and its continued quality, gathers them under an intuitive concept and grounds them along with the term to be defined, thereby becoming itself something unique and indivisible [*atomon*, *adiaphoron*, *eidos*]. In this manner, therefore, the determination of species ensures coherence and continuity in the comprehension of the concept.

Return to the expression 'the greatest difference'. It is now evident that specific difference is the greatest only in an entirely relative sense. Absolutely speaking, contradiction is greater than contrariety – and above all, generic difference is greater than specific. Already, the manner in which Aristotle distinguishes between difference and diversity or otherness points the way: only in relation to the supposed identity of a concept is specific difference called the greatest. Furthermore, it is in relation to the form of identity in the generic concept that difference goes as far as opposition, that it is pushed as far as contrariety. Specific difference, therefore, in no way represents a universal concept (that is to say, an Idea) encompassing all the singularities and turnings of difference, but rather refers to a particular moment in which difference is merely reconciled with the concept in general. Thus Aristotle's *diaphora* of the *diaphora* is only a false transport: it never shows difference changing its nature, we never discover in it a differenciator of difference which would relate, in their respective immediacy, the most universal and the most singular. Specific difference refers only to an entirely relative maximum, a point of accommodation for the Greek eye – in particular for the Greek eye which sees the mean, and has lost the sense of Dionysian transports and metamorphoses. Here we find the principle which lies behind a confusion disastrous for the entire philosophy of difference: assigning a distinctive concept of difference is confused with the inscription of difference within concepts in general – the determination of the concept of difference is confused with the inscription of difference in the identity of an undetermined concept. This is the sleight of hand involved in the propitious moment (and perhaps everything else follows: the subordination of difference to opposition, to analogy, and to resemblance, all the aspects of mediation). Difference then can be no more than a predicate in the comprehension of a concept. Aristotle constantly reminds us of this predicative character of specific difference, but he is forced to lend it strange powers such as that of attributing as much as that of being attributed, or of altering the genus as much as of modifying its quality. All of the ways in which specific difference seems to satisfy the requirements of a distinctive concept (purity, interiority, productivity, transportivity ...) are thus shown to be illusory, even contradictory, on the basis of this fundamental confusion.

Specific difference is thus small in relation to a larger difference which concerns the genera themselves. Even in biological classification, it becomes quite small in relation to the large genera; no doubt not a material difference, but nevertheless a simple difference 'in' the material, one which works through the more and the less. The fact is that specific difference is maximal and perfect, but only on condition of the identity of an undetermined concept (genus). It is insignificant, by contrast, in comparison with the difference between genera as ultimate determinable concepts (categories), for these latter are not subject to the condition that they share an identical concept or a common genus. Remember the reason why Being itself is not a genus: it is, Aristotle says, because differences *are* (the genus must therefore be able to attribute itself to its differences in themselves: as if animal was said at one time of the human species, but at another of the difference 'rational' in constituting another species ...).[4] It is therefore an argument borrowed from the nature of specific difference which allows him to conclude that generic differences are of *another* nature. It is as though there were two 'Logoi', differing in nature but intermingled with one another: the logos of Species, the logos of what we think and say, which rests upon the condition of the identity or univocity of concepts in general taken as genera; and the logos of Genera, the logos of what is thought and said through us, which is free of that condition and operates both in the equivocity of Being and in the diversity of the most general concepts. When we speak the univocal, is it not still the equivocal which speaks within us? Must we not recognise here a kind of fracture introduced into thought, one which will not cease to widen in another atmosphere (non-Aristotelian)? But above all, is this not already a new chance for the philosophy of difference? Will it not lead towards an absolute concept, once liberated from the condition which made difference an entirely relative maximum?

Nothing of the kind, however, occurs with Aristotle. The fact is that generic or categorial difference remains a difference in the Aristotelian sense and does not collapse into simple diversity or otherness. An identical or common concept thus still subsists, albeit in a very particular manner. This concept of Being is not collective, like a genus in relation to its species, but only distributive and hierarchical: it has no content in itself, only a content in proportion to the formally different terms of which it is predicated. These terms (categories) need not have an equal relation to being: it is enough that each has an *internal* relation to being. The two characteristics of the concept of being – having no more than a distributive common sense and having a hierarchical primary sense – show clearly that being does not have, in relation to the categories, the role of a genus in relation to univocal species. They also show that the equivocity of being is quite particular: it is a matter of analogy.[5] Now, if we ask what is the instance capable of proportioning the concept to the terms or to the subjects of which it is affirmed, it is clear that it is judgement. For judgement has precisely two essential functions, and only two: distribution, which it ensures by the *partition* of concepts; and hierarchization, which it ensures by the *measuring* of subjects. To the former corresponds the faculty of judgement known as common sense; to the latter the faculty known as good sense (or first sense). Both constitute just measure or 'justice' as a value of judgement. In this sense, every philosophy of categories takes judgement for its model – as we see in the case of Kant, and still even in the case of Hegel. With its common sense and first sense, however, the analogy of judgement allows the identity of a concept to subsist, either in implicit and confused form or in virtual form. Analogy is itself the analogue of identity within judgement. Analogy is the essence of judgement, but the analogy within judgement is the analogy of the identity of concepts. That is why we cannot expect that generic or categorial difference, any more than specific difference, will deliver us a proper concept of difference. Whereas specific difference is content to inscribe difference in the identity of the indeterminate concept in general, generic (distributive and hierarchical) difference is content in turn to inscribe difference in the quasi-identity of the most general determinable concepts; that is, in the analogy within judgement itself. The entire Aristotelian philosophy of difference is contained in this complementary double inscription, both grounded in the same postulate and together drawing the arbitrary boundaries of the propitious moment.

Generic and specific differences are tied together by their complicity in representation. Not that they in any way share the same nature: genus is determinable only by specific difference from without; and the identity of the genus in relation to the species contrasts with the impossibility for Being of forming a similar identity in relation to the genera themselves. However, it is precisely the nature of the specific differences (the fact that they *are*) which grounds that impossibility, preventing generic differences from being related to being as if to a common genus (if being were a genus, its differences would be assimilable to specific differences, but then one could no longer say that they 'are', since a genus is not in itself attributed to its differences). In this sense, the univocity of species in a common genus refers back to the equivocity of being in the various genera: the one reflects the other. We see this clearly in the requirements of the ideal of classification: at once the large units – *genē megista*, which will eventually be called branches – are determined according to relations of analogy, which suppose a choice of characters carried out by judgement in the abstract representation, and the small units, the little genera or species, are determined by a direct perception of *resemblances*, which suppose a continuity of sensible intuition in the concrete representation. Even neo-evolutionism will rediscover these two related aspects of the categories of the Large and the Small, when it distinguishes the large precocious embryological differenciations from the small, tardy, adult, species or intraspecies differenciations. Alternatively, these two aspects enter into conflict according to whether the large genera or the species are taken to be concepts of Nature, both constituting the limits of organic representation, and the *requisites* equally necessary for classification: methodological continuity in the perception of resemblances is no less indispensable than systematic distribution in the judgement of analogy. However, from one point of view as from the other, Difference appears only as a *reflexive concept*. In effect, difference allows the passage from similar neighbouring species to the identity of a genus which subsumes them – that is, the extraction or cutting out of generic identities from the flux of a continuous perceptible series. At the other pole, it allows the passage from respectively identical genera to the relations of analogy which obtain between them in the intelligible. As a concept of reflection, difference testifies to its full submission to all the requirements of representation, which becomes thereby 'organic representation'. In the concept of reflection, mediating and mediated difference is in effect fully subject to the identity of the concept, the opposition of predicates, the analogy of judgement and the resemblance of perception. Here we rediscover the necessarily quadripartite character of representation. The question is to know whether, under all these reflexive aspects, difference does not lose both its own concept and its own reality. In effect, difference ceases to be reflexive and recovers an effectively real concept only to the extent that it designates catastrophes: either breaks of continuity in the series of resemblances or impassable fissures between the analogical structures. It ceases to be reflexive only in order to become catastrophic. No doubt it cannot be the one without the other. But does not difference as catastrophe precisely bear witness to an irreducible ground which continues to act under the apparent equilibrium of organic representation?

There has only ever been one ontological proposition: Being is univocal. There has only ever been one ontology, that of Duns Scotus, which gave being a single voice. We say Duns Scotus because he was the one who elevated univocal being to the highest point of subtlety, albeit at the price of abstraction. However, from Parmenides to Heidegger it is the same voice which is taken up, in an echo which itself forms the whole deployment of the univocal. A single voice raises the clamour of being. We have no difficulty in understanding that Being, even if it is absolutely common, is nevertheless not a genus. It is enough to replace the model of judgement with that of the proposition. In the proposition understood as a complex entity we distinguish: the sense, or what is expressed in the proposition; the designated (what expresses itself in the proposition); the expressors or designators, which are numerical modes – that is to say, differential factors characterising the elements endowed with sense and designation. We can conceive that names or propositions do not have the same sense even while they designate exactly the same thing (as in the case of the celebrated examples: morning star – evening star, Israel–Jacob, *p*lan–*b*lanc). The distinction between these senses is indeed a real distinction [*distinctio realis*], but there is nothing numerical – much less ontological – about it: it is a formal, qualitative or semiological distinction. The question whether categories are directly assimilable to such senses, or – more probably – derive from them, must be left aside for the moment. What is important is that we can conceive of several formally distinct senses which none the less refer to being as if to a single designated entity, ontologically one. It is true that such a point of view is not sufficient to prevent us from considering these senses as analogues and this unity of being as an analogy. We must add that being, this common designated, in so far as it expresses itself, is said in turn *in a single and same sense* of all the numerically distinct designators and expressors. In the ontological proposition, not only is that which is designated ontologically the same for qualitatively distinct senses, but also the sense is ontologically the same for individuating modes, for numerically distinct designators or expressors: the ontological proposition involves a circulation of this kind (expression as a whole).

In effect, the essential in univocity is not that Being is said in a single and same sense, but that it is said, in a single and same sense, *of* all its individuating differences or intrinsic modalities. Being is the same for all these modalities, but these modalities are not the same. It is 'equal' for all, but they themselves are not equal. It is said of all in a single sense, but they themselves do not have the same sense. The essence of univocal being is to include individuating differences, while these differences do not have the same essence and do not change the essence of being – just as white includes various intensities, while remaining essentially the same white. There are not two 'paths', as Parmenides' poem suggests, but a single 'voice' of Being which includes all its modes, including the most diverse, the most varied, the most differenciated. Being is said in a single and same sense of everything of which it is said, but that of which it is said differs: it is said of difference itself.

No doubt there is still hierarchy and distribution in univocal being, in relation to the individuating factors and their sense, but distribution and even hierarchy have two completely different, irreconcilable acceptations. Similarly for the expressions *logos* and *nomos*, in so far as these refer to problems of distribution. We must first of all distinguish a type of distribution which implies a dividing up of that which is distributed: it is a matter of dividing up the distributed as such. It is here that in judgement the rules of analogy are all-powerful. In so far as common sense and good sense are qualities of judgement, these are presented as principles of division which declare themselves *the best distributed*. A distribution of this type proceeds by fixed and proportional determinations which may be assimilated to 'properties' or limited territories within representation. The agrarian question may well have been very important for this organisation of judgement as the faculty which distinguishes parts ('on the one hand and on the other hand'). Even among the gods, each has his domain, his category, his attributes, and all distribute limits and lots to mortals in accordance with destiny. Then there is a completely other distribution which must be called nomadic, a nomad *nomos*, without property, enclosure or measure. Here, there is no longer a division of that which is distributed but rather a division among those who distribute *themselves* in an open space – a space which is unlimited, or at least without precise limits.[6] Nothing pertains or belongs to any person, but all persons are arrayed here and there in such a manner as to cover the largest possible space. Even when it concerns the serious business of life, it is more like a space of play, or a rule of play, by contrast with sedentary space and *nomos*. To fill a space, to be distributed within it, is very different from distributing the space. It is an errant and even 'delirious' distribution, in which things are deployed across the entire extensity of a univocal and undistributed Being. It is not a matter of being which is distributed according to the requirements of representation, but of all things being divided up within being in the univocity of simple presence (the One – All). Such a distribution is demonic rather than divine, since it is a peculiarity of demons to operate in the intervals between the gods' fields of action, as it is to leap over the barriers or the enclosures, thereby confounding the boundaries between properties. Oedipus' chorus cries: 'Which demon has leapt further than the longest leap?' The leap here bears witness to the unsettling difficulties that nomadic distributions introduce into the sedentary structures of representation. The same goes for hierarchy. There is a hierarchy which measures beings according to their limits, and according to their degree of proximity or distance from a principle. But there is also a hierarchy which considers things and beings from the point of view of power: it is not a question of considering absolute degrees of power, but only of knowing whether a being eventually 'leaps over' or transcends its limits in going to the limit of what it can do, whatever its degree. 'To the limit', it will be argued, still presupposes a limit. Here, limit [*peras*] no longer refers to what maintains the thing under a law, nor to what delimits or separates it from other things. On the contrary, it refers to that on the basis of which it is deployed and deploys all its power; hubris ceases to be simply condemnable and *the smallest becomes equivalent to the largest* once it is not separated from what it can do. This enveloping measure is the same for all things, the same also for substance, quality, quantity, etc., since it forms a single maximum at which the developed diversity of all degrees touches the equality which envelops them. This ontological measure is closer to the immeasurable state of things than to the first kind of measure; this ontological hierarchy is closer to the hubris and anarchy of beings than to the first hierarchy. It is the monster which combines all the demons. The words 'everything is equal' may therefore resound joyfully, on condition that they are said *of* that which is not equal in this equal, univocal Being: equal being is immediately present in everything, without mediation or intermediary, even though things reside unequally in this equal being. There, however, where they are borne by hubris, all things are in absolute proximity, and whether they are large or small, inferior or superior, none of them participates more or less in being, nor receives it by analogy. Univocity of being thus also signifies equality of being. Univocal Being is at one and the same time nomadic distribution and crowned anarchy.

Nevertheless, can we not conceive a reconciliation between analogy and univocity? For if being, as being, is univocal in itself, is it not 'analogous' in relation to its intrinsic modes or individuating factors (what we called above expressors or designators)? If it is equal in relation to itself, is it not unequal in relation to the modalities which reside within it? If it designates a common entity, is this not for existents which have nothing 'really' in common? If its metaphysical state is univocal, does it not have a physical state of analogy? Finally, if analogy recognises an identical quasi-concept, does not univocity recognise a quasi-judgement of analogy, if only in order to relate being to these particular existents?[7] However, such questions risk distorting the two theses they attempt to bring together. For analogy, as we have seen, rests essentially upon a certain complicity between generic and specific differences (despite their difference in kind): being cannot be supposed a common genus without destroying the reason for which it was supposed thus; that is, the possibility of *being* for specific differences. ... It is not, therefore, surprising that from the standpoint of analogy, everything happens in the middle regions of genus and species in terms of mediation and generality – identity of the concept in general and analogy of the most general concepts. It is henceforth inevitable that analogy falls into an unresolvable difficulty: it must essentially relate being to particular existents, but at the same time it cannot say what constitutes their individuality. For it retains in the particular only that which conforms to the general (matter and form), and seeks the principle of individuation in this or that element of the fully constituted individuals. By contrast, when we say that univocal being is related immediately and essentially to individuating factors, we certainly do not mean by the latter individuals constituted in experience, but that which acts in them as a transcendental principle: as a plastic, anarchic and nomadic principle, contemporaneous with the process of individuation, no less capable of dissolving and destroying individuals than of constituting them temporarily; intrinsic modalities of being, passing from one 'individual' to another, circulating and communicating underneath matters and forms. The individuating is not the simple individual. In these conditions, it is not enough to say that individuation differs in kind from the determination of species. It is not even enough to say this in the manner of Duns Scotus, who was nevertheless not content to analyse the elements of an individual but went as far as the conception of individuation as the 'ultimate actuality of form'. We must show not only how individuating difference differs in kind from specific difference, but primarily and above all how individuation properly *precedes* matter and form, species and parts, and every other element of the constituted individual. Univocity of being, in so far as it is immediately related to difference, demands that we show how individuating difference precedes generic, specific and even individual differences within being; how a prior field of individuation within being conditions at once the determination of species of forms, the determination of parts and their individual variations. If individuation does not take place either by form or by matter, neither qualitatively nor extensionally, this is not only because it differs in kind but because it is already presupposed by the forms, matters and extensive parts.

Thus it is not at all in the same manner that in the analogy of being, generic and specific differences are in general mediated in relation to individuating differences, and that in univocity, univocal being is said immediately of individual differences or the universal is said of the most singular independently of any mediation. If it is true that analogy denies being the status of a common genus because the (specific) differences 'are', then conversely, univocal being is indeed common in so far as the (individuating) differences 'are not' and must not be. No doubt we shall see that they are not, in a very particular sense: if in univocal being they are not, it is because they depend upon a non-being without negation. With univocity, however, it is not the differences which are and must be: it is being which is Difference, in the sense that it is said of difference. Moreover, it is not we who are univocal in a Being which is not; it is we and our individuality which remains equivocal in and for a univocal Being.

There are three principal moments in the history of the philosophical elaboration of the univocity of being. The first is represented by Duns Scotus. In the greatest book of pure ontology, the *Opus Oxoniense*, being is understood as univocal, but univocal being is understood as neutral, *neuter*, indifferent to the distinction between the finite and the infinite, the singular and the universal, the created and the uncreated. Scotus therefore deserves the name 'subtle doctor' because he saw being on this side of the intersection between the universal and the singular. In order to neutralise the forces of analogy in judgement, he took the offensive and neutralised being itself in an abstract concept. That is why he only *thought* univocal being. Moreover, we can see the enemy he tried to escape in accordance with the requirements of Christianity: pantheism, into which he would have fallen if the common being were not neutral. Nevertheless, he was able to define two types of distinction which relate that indifferent, neutral being to difference. *Formal distinction* is, in effect, a real distinction, since it is grounded in being or in the object; but it is not necessarily a numerical distinction because it is established between essences or senses, between 'formal reasons' which may allow the persistence of the unity of the subject to which they are attributed. In this manner, not only is the univocity of being (in relation to God and to creatures) extended in the univocity of its 'attributes', but, given his infinity, God can possess his formally distinct univocal attributes without losing anything of his unity. The other type of distinction, *modal distinction*, is established between being or the attributes on the one hand, and the intensive variations of which these are capable on the other. These variations, like degrees of whiteness, are individuating modalities of which the finite and the infinite constitute precisely singular intensities. From the point of view of its own neutrality, univocal being therefore does not only implicate distinct attributes or qualitative forms which are themselves univocal, it also relates these and itself to intensive factors or individuating degrees which vary the mode of these attributes or forms without modifying their essence in so far as this is being. If it is true that distinction in general relates being to difference, formal distinction and modal distinction are two types under which univocal being is related, by itself, to difference in itself.

With the second moment, Spinoza marks a considerable progress. Instead of understanding univocal being as neutral or indifferent, he makes it an object of pure affirmation. Univocal being becomes identical with unique, universal and infinite substance: it is proposed as *Deus sive Natura.* Moreover, the struggle undertaken against Descartes by Spinoza is not unrelated to that which Duns Scotus led against Saint Thomas. Against the Cartesian theory of substances thoroughly imbued with analogy, and against the Cartesian conception of distinctions which runs together the ontological, the formal and the numerical (substance, quality and quantity), Spinoza organises a remarkable division into substance, attributes and modes. From the opening pages of the *Ethics*, he shows that real distinctions are never numerical but only formal – that is, qualitative or essential (essential attributes of the unique substance); and conversely, that numerical distinctions are never real, but only modal (intrinsic modes of the unique substance and its attributes). The attributes behave like real qualitatively different senses which relate to substance as if to a single and same designated; and substance in turn behaves like an ontologically unique sense in relation to the modes which express it, and inhabit it like individuating factors or intrinsic and intense degrees. From this follows a determination of modes as degrees of power, and a single 'obligation' for such modes: to deploy all their power or their being *within* the limit itself. Attributes are thus absolutely common to substance and the modes, even though modes and substance do not have the same essence. Being itself is said in a single unique sense of substance and the modes, even though the modes and substance do not have the same sense or do not have that being in the same manner [*in se* and *in alio*]. Any hierarchy or pre-eminence is denied in so far as substance is equally designated by all the attributes in accordance with their essence, and equally expressed by all the modes in accordance with their degree of power. With Spinoza, univocal being ceases to be neutralised and becomes expressive; it becomes a truly expressive and affirmative proposition.

Nevertheless, there still remains a difference between substance and the modes: Spinoza's substance appears independent of the modes, while the modes are dependent on substance, but as though on something other than themselves. Substance must itself be said *of* the modes and only *of* the modes. Such a condition can be satisfied only at the price of a more general categorical reversal according to which being is said of becoming, identity of that which is different, the one of the multiple, etc. That identity not be first, that it exist as a principle but as a second principle, as a principle *become*; that it revolve around the Different: such would be the nature of a Copernican revolution which opens up the possibility of difference having its own concept, rather than being maintained under the domination of a concept in general already understood as identical. Nietzsche meant nothing more than this by eternal return. Eternal return cannot mean the return of the Identical because it presupposes a world (that of the will to power) in which all previous identities have been abolished and dissolved. Returning is being, but only the being of becoming. The eternal return does not bring back 'the same', but returning constitutes the only Same of that which becomes. Returning is the becoming-identical of becoming itself. Returning is thus the only identity, but identity as a secondary power; the identity of difference, the identical which belongs to the different, or turns around the different. Such an identity, produced by difference, is determined as 'repetition'. Repetition in the eternal return, therefore, consists in conceiving the same on the basis of the different. However, this conception is no longer merely a theoretical representation: it carries out a practical selection among differences according to their capacity to produce – that is, to return or to pass the test of the eternal return. The selective character of eternal return appears clearly in Nietzsche's idea: it is not the Whole, the Same or the prior identity in general which returns. Nor is it the small or the large, either as parts of the whole or as elements of the same. Only the extreme forms return – those which, large or small, are deployed within the limit and extend to the limit of their power, transforming themselves and changing one into another. Only the extreme, the excessive, returns; that which passes into something else and becomes identical. That is why the eternal return is said only of the theatrical world of the metamorphoses and masks of the Will to power, of the pure intensities of that Will which are like mobile individuating factors unwilling to allow themselves to be contained within the factitious limits of this or that individual, this or that Self. Eternal return or returning expresses the common being of all these metamorphoses, the measure and the common being of all that is extreme, of all the realised degrees of power. It is the being-equal of all that is unequal and has been able to fully realise its inequality. All that is extreme and becoming the same communicates in an equal and common Being which determines its return. That is why the Overman is defined as the superior form of everything that 'is'. We must discover what Nietzsche means by noble: he borrows the language of energy physics and calls noble that energy which is capable of transforming itself. When Nietzsche says that hubris is the real problem of every Heraclitan, or that hierarchy is the problem of free spirits, he means one – and only one – thing: that it is in hubris that everyone finds the being which makes him return, along with that sort of crowned anarchy, that overturned hierarchy which, in order to ensure the selection of difference, begins by subordinating the identical to the different.[8] In all these respects, eternal return is the univocity of being, the effective realisation of that univocity. In the eternal return, univocal being is not only thought and even affirmed, but effectively realised. Being is said in a single and same sense, but this sense is that of eternal return as the return or repetition of that of which it is said. The wheel in the eternal return is at once both production of repetition on the basis of difference and selection of difference on the basis of repetition.

The test of the Small and the Large seemed to us to misconstrue selection because it renounced any concept of difference itself in favour of the requirements of the identity of the concept in general. By inscribing itself within the identical concept or within analogous concepts (minimum and maximum), it only fixed the limits within which determination became difference. That is why the selection which consists of 'making the difference' seemed to us to have another sense: to allow the extreme forms to appear and be deployed in the simple presence of a univocal Being, rather than to measure and to divide up the average forms according to the requirements of organic representation. Even so, can it be said that we have exhausted all the resources of the Small and the Large in so far as they apply to difference? Or will we not rediscover them as an alternative characteristic of the extreme forms themselves? For it seems that the extreme can be defined by the infinite, in the small or in the large. The infinite, in this sense, even signifies the identity of the small and the large, the identity of extremes. When representation discovers the infinite within itself, it no longer appears as *organic* representation but as *orgiastic* representation: it discovers within itself the limits of the organised; tumult, restlessness and passion underneath apparent calm. It rediscovers monstrosity. Henceforth it is no longer a question of a propitious moment which marks determination's entrance into and exit from the concept in general, the relative maximum and minimum, the *punctum proximum* and the *punctum remotem*. On the contrary, a short-sighted and a long-sighted eye are required in order for the concept to take upon itself all moments: the concept is now the Whole, either in the sense that it extends its benediction to all parts or in the sense that the division between the parts and their misery are reflected back on the Whole, granting them a kind of absolution. The concept thus follows and espouses determination in all its metamorphoses, from one end to the other, and represents it as pure difference in delivering it up to a *ground* in relation to which it no longer matters whether one is before a relative minimum or maximum, a large or a small, nor before a beginning or an end, since the two coincide in this ground which is like a single and unique 'total' moment, simultaneously the moment of the evanescence and production of difference, of disappearance and appearance.

In this sense, it is noticeable how far Hegel, no less than Leibniz, attaches importance to the infinite movement of evanescence as such – that is, to the moment at which difference both vanishes and is produced. The signification of the very notion of limit changes completely: it no longer refers to the limits of finite representation, but on the contrary to the womb in which finite determination never ceases to be born and to disappear, to be enveloped and deployed within orgiastic representation. It no longer refers to the limitation of a form, but to the *convergence* towards a ground; no longer to the distinction of forms but to the correlation of the grounded and the ground; no longer to the arrestation of power but to the element in which power is effectuated, on which it is grounded. In effect, differential calculus no less than the dialectic is a matter of 'power' and of the power of the limit. If we consider the limits of finite representation to be two abstract mathematical determinations, the Small and the Large, we notice that it is a matter of complete indifference to Leibniz (as to Hegel) to know whether the determined is large or small, the largest or the smallest. By subjecting it to an architectonic element which discovers the most perfect or the best grounded in every case, consideration of the infinite renders the determined independent of that question.[9] It is in this sense that orgiastic representation must be said to *make* the difference, because it selects it by introducing this infinite which relates it to the ground (either grounding by the Good which functions as a rule of the game or principle of choice, or grounding by negativity which functions as suffering and labour). Moreover, if the limits of finite representation, the Small and the Large, are considered with regard to the character or the concrete content given to them by the genus and species, then here again the introduction of the infinite into representation renders the determined independent of the genus as determinable and the species as determination, by retaining in a middle term both the true universality which escapes the genus and the authentic singularity which escapes the species. In short, orgiastic representation has the ground as its principle and the infinite as its element, by contrast with organic representation which retains form as its principle and the finite as its element. It is the infinite which renders determination conceivable and selectable: difference thus appears as the orgiastic representation of determination and no longer as its organic representation.

Instead of animating judgements about things, orgiastic representation makes things themselves so many expressions or so many propositions: infinite analytic or synthetic propositions. Why, then, is there a choice within orgiastic representation, given that the two points, the small and the large, the maximum and the minimum, have become indifferent or identical in the infinite, while difference has become completely independent of them in the ground? It is because the infinite is not the point at which finite determination disappears (that would be to project a mistaken conception of limit on to the infinite). Orgiastic representation can discover the infinite within itself only by allowing finite determination to subsist: better, by saying the infinite *of* that finite determination itself, by representing it not as having vanished and disappeared but as vanishing and on the point of disappearing, thus as also being engendered in the infinite. This representation is such that the infinite and the finite have here the same 'restlessness', which is precisely what allows the one to be represented in the other. However, when the infinite is said of the finite itself under the conditions of representation, there are two ways in which it can be said: either as infinitely small or as infinitely large. These two ways, these two 'differences', are by no means symmetrical. Thus duality is reintroduced into orgiastic representation, no longer in the form of a complementarity or a reflection of two finite assignable moments (as was the case for specific difference and generic difference) but in the form of a choice between two infinite, unassignable processes – in the form of a choice between Leibniz and Hegel. If it is true that the small and the large become identical in the infinite, the infinitely small and the infinitely large separate once more, even more sharply in so far as the infinite is said of the finite. Leibniz and Hegel separately both escape the choice between the Large and the Small, but together they fall back into the choice between the infinitely small and the infinitely large. That is why orgiastic representation involves a duality which only increases its restlessness, or is even the real reason for it, and divides it into two kinds.

It seems that, according to Hegel, 'contradiction' poses very few problems. It serves a quite different purpose: contradiction resolves itself and, in resolving itself, resolves difference by relating it to a ground. Difference is the only problem. The criticism that Hegel addresses to his predecessors is that they stopped at a purely relative maximum without reaching the absolute maximum of difference, namely contradiction; they stopped before reaching the infinite (as infinitely large) of contradiction. They dared not go all the way:

> Difference as such is already *implicitly* contradiction. ... Only when the manifold terms have been driven to the point of contradiction do they become active and lively towards one another, receiving in contradiction the negativity which is the indwelling pulsation of self-movement and spontaneous activity. ... More precisely, when the difference of reality is taken into account, it develops from difference into opposition, and from this into contradiction, so that in the end the sum total of all realities simply becomes absolute contradiction within itself.[10]

Like Aristotle, Hegel determines difference by the opposition of extremes or of contraries. However, opposition remains abstract so long as it does not extend to the infinite, and the infinite remains abstract every time it is posed outside of finite oppositions: the introduction of the infinite here entails the identity of contraries, or makes the contrary of the Other a contrary of the Self. It is true that contrariety represents only the movement of interiority in the infinite. This movement allows indifference to subsist, since each determination, in so far as it contains the other, is independent of the other as though of a relation with the outside. Each contrary must further expel its other, therefore expel itself, and become the other it expels. Such is the movement of contradiction as it constitutes the true pulsation of the infinite, the movement of exteriority or real objectivation. This goes beyond the simple identity of contraries as the identity of the positive and negative. For it is not in the same manner that the positive and the negative are the Same: the negative is now at once both the becoming of the positive when the positive is denied, and the return of the positive when it denies or excludes itself. No doubt each of the contraries determined as positive and negative was already contradiction, 'But the Positive is only *implicitly* this contradiction, whereas the negative is the contradiction *posited. ...*'[11] Difference finds its own concept in the posited contradiction: it is here that it becomes pure, intrinsic, essential, qualitative, synthetic and productive; here that it no longer allows indifference to subsist. To maintain or to raise contradiction is the selective test which 'makes' the difference (between the effectively real and the passing or contingent phenomenon). In this manner, difference is pushed to the limit – that is, to the ground which is no less its return or its reproduction than its annihilation.

Even though it is said of opposition or of finite determination, this Hegelian infinite remains the infinitely large of theology, of the *Ens quo nihil majus*. We should even consider that the nature of real contradiction, in so far as it distinguishes a thing from *everything that it is not*, was formulated for the first time by Kant, under the name of 'complete determination'. He made it depend upon the positing of a whole of reality as an *Ens summum*. There is therefore no reason to expect a mathematical treatment of this theological infinitely large, this sublime of the infinitely large. This is not the case with Leibniz. For in order to avoid any admixture of God and his creatures, for the modesty of those creatures, Leibniz introduces the infinite into the finite only in the form of the infinitely small. Nevertheless, we hesitate to say that he does not go as far as Hegel in this sense. He too goes beyond organic representation towards orgiastic representation, albeit by another route. If Hegel discovers in serene representation the intoxication and restlessness of the infinitely large, Leibniz discovers in the clear, finite idea the restlessness of the infinitely small, a restlessness also made up of intoxication, giddiness, evanescence and even death. It seems, therefore, that the difference between Hegel and Leibniz is a matter of two ways of going beyond the organic. Certainly, the essential and the inessential are inseparable: they are like the one and the many, the equal and the unequal, the identical and the different. However, Hegel begins with the essential as a genus, and treats the infinite as that which divides the genus and suppresses division in the species. The genus is thus itself and the species, the whole is itself and the part. Henceforth, it contains the other essentially, it contains it *in essence.*[12] Leibniz, on the other hand, begins with the inessential so far as phenomena are concerned, with movement, inequality and difference. By virtue of the infinitely small, it is the inessential which is now posed as species and genus, and terminates as such in the 'opposing quasi-species'. This implies that it does not contain the other in essence but only with respect to properties, in *cases*. It is a mistake to impose upon infinitesimal analysis the alternative of being either a language of essences or a convenient fiction. For the subsumption under 'cases', or the language of properties, has its own originality. This procedure of the infinitely small, which maintains the distinction between essences (to the extent that one plays the role of inessential to the other), is quite different to contradiction. We should therefore give it a special name, that of 'vice-diction'. In the infinitely large, the equal contradicts the unequal to the extent that it possesses it in essence, and contradicts itself to the extent that it denies itself in denying the unequal. In the infinitely small, however, the unequal vice-dicts the equal and vice-dicts itself to the extent that it includes in the case what it excludes in essence. The inessential includes the essential in the case, whereas the essential contains the inessential in essence.

Must we say that vice-diction does not go as far as contradiction, on the grounds that it concerns only properties? In reality, the expression 'infinitely small difference' does indeed indicate that the difference vanishes so far as intuition is concerned. Once it finds its concept, however, it is rather intuition itself which disappears in favour of the differential relation, as is shown by saying that dx is minimal in relation to x, as dy is in relation to y, but that dy/dx is the internal qualitative relation, expressing the universal of a function independently of its particular numerical values. However, if this relation has no numerical determinations, it does have degrees of variation corresponding to diverse forms and equations. These degrees are themselves like the relations of the universal, and the differential relations, in this sense, are caught up in a process of reciprocal determination which translates the interdependence of the variable coefficients.[13] But once again, *reciprocal determination* expresses only the first aspect of a veritable principle of reason; the second aspect is *complete determination.* For each degree or relation, regarded as the universal of a given function, determines the existence and distribution of distinctive points on the corresponding curve. We must take great care here not to confuse 'complete' with 'completed'. The difference is that, for the equation of a curve, for example, the differential relation refers only to straight lines determined by the nature of the curve. It is already a complete determination of the object, yet it expresses only a part of the entire object, namely the part regarded as 'derived' (the other part, which is expressed by the so-called primitive function, can be found only by integration, which is not simply the inverse of differentiation. Similarly, it is integration which defines the nature of the previously determined distinctive points). That is why an object can be completely determined – *ens omni modo determinatum* – without, for all that, possessing the integrity which alone constitutes its actual existence. Under the double aspect of reciprocal determination and complete determination, however it appears already as if the limit coincides with the power itself. The limit is defined by convergence. The numerical values of a function find their limit in the differential relation; the differential relations find their limit in the degrees of variation; and at each degree the distinctive points are the limits of series which are analytically continued one into the other. Not only is the differential relation the pure element of potentiality, but the limit is the power of the continuous, as continuity is the power of these limits themselves. Difference thus finds its concept in a negative, but a negative of pure limitation, a *nihil respectivum* (dx is nothing in relation to x). From all these points of view, the distinction between the distinctive and the ordinary, the singular and the regular, forms the two categories of the inessential in the continuous. They inform the whole language of limits and properties, they constitute the structure of phenomena as such. We see in this sense all that philosophy must expect from a distribution of distinctive points and ordinary points for the description of experience. But already the two kinds of point prepare and determine, in the inessential, the constitution of the essences themselves. The inessential here refers not to that which lacks importance but, on the contrary, to the most profound, to the universal matter or continuum from which the essences are finally made.

In effect, Leibniz, for his part, never saw any contradiction between the law of continuity and the principle of indiscernibles. The one governs properties, affections or complete cases; the other rules essences understood as completed individual notions. We know that each one of these completed notions (monads) expresses the totality of the world: but it expresses it precisely under a certain differential relation and around certain distinctive points which correspond to this relation.[14] It is in this sense that the differential relations and distinctive points already indicate centres of envelopment within the continuum, centres of possible implication or involution which are brought about by individual essences. It suffices to show that the continuum of affections and properties in a sense precedes the constitution of these individual essences (which amounts to saying that the distinctive points are themselves pre-individual singularities; this in no way contradicts the idea that individuation precedes the actual determination of species, even though it is preceded by the whole differential continuum). This condition is fulfilled in Leibniz's philosophy in the following manner: the world, as that which is expressed in common by all monads, pre-exists its expressions. It is nevertheless true that it does not *exist* apart from that which expresses it, apart from the monads themselves; but these expressions refer to the expressed as though to the *requisite* of their constitution. It is in this sense (as Leibniz constantly reminds us in his letters to Arnauld) that the inherence of predicates in each subject supposes the compossibility of the world expressed by all these subjects: God did not create Adam as a sinner, but rather the world in which Adam sinned. It is undoubtedly continuity which defines the compossibility of each world; and if the real world is the best, this is to the extent that it presents a maximum of continuity in a maximum number of cases, in a maximum number of relations and distinctive points. That is to say: for each world a series which converges around a distinctive point is capable of being continued in all directions in other series converging around other points, while the incompossibility of worlds, by contrast, is defined by the juxtaposition of points which would make the resultant series diverge. We can see why the notion of incompossibility in no way reduces to contradiction and does not even imply real opposition: it implies only divergence, while compossibility is only an analytic continuation which translates the originality of the process of vice-diction. In the continuum of a compossible world, differential relations and distinctive points thus determine expressive centres (essences or individual substances) in which, at each moment, the entire world is contained from a certain point of view. Conversely, the action and unfolding of these centres restores the world in which they themselves play the role of simple distinctive points and of 'cases' in the expressed continuum. The law of continuity appears here as a law of properties or cases of the world, a law of development which applies to the expressed world, but also to the monads in the world themselves. The principle of indiscernibles is a principle of essences and a principle of envelopment which applies to expressions – that is, to monads and to the world within the monads. The two languages continually translate into one another. Together they relate difference, both as infinitely small difference and as finite difference, to sufficient reason as the foundation which selects or chooses the best world – in this sense, the best of all worlds does indeed imply a comparison, but it is not a comparative: since each world is finite, it is a superlative which carries difference to an absolute maximum through the very test of the infinitely small. Finite difference is determined in a monad as that part of the world clearly expressed, infinitely small difference as the confused ground which underpins that clarity. In these two ways, orgiastic representation mediates determination and makes it a concept of difference by assigning it a 'reason'.

Finite representation is that of a form which contains a matter, but a secondary matter in so far as it is defined by contraries. We have seen that it represented difference by mediating it, by subordinating it to identity as the genus, and by ensuring that subordination by means of analogy among the genera themselves, by means of the logical opposition of determinations and the resemblance of properly material contents. It is not the same with infinite representation, since this includes the Whole or ground as primary matter and the essence as subject, absolute form or Self. Infinite representation relates at once both the essence and the ground, and the difference between the two, to a foundation or sufficient reason. Mediation itself has become foundation. However, in the one case the ground is the infinite continuity of the properties of the universal which is itself contained in finite particular Selves considered as essences. In the other case, particulars are only properties or figures which are developed in the infinite universal ground, but refer to essences as the true determinations of a pure Self, or rather a 'Self' enveloped by this ground. In both cases, infinite representation is the object of a double discourse: that of properties and that of essences – that of physical points and metaphysical points or points of view in the case of Leibniz; that of figures and moments or categories in the case of Hegel. It cannot be said that Leibniz does not go as far as Hegel: there is even a greater depth in his case, more orgiastic or bacchanalian delirium, in the sense that the ground plays a greater role. In both cases, as well, it seems that infinite representation does not suffice to render the thought of difference independent of the simple analogy of essences, or the simple similarity of properties. The point is that in the last resort *infinite representation does not free itself from the principle of identity as a presupposition of representation.* That is why it remains subject to the condition of the convergence of series in the case of Leibniz and to the condition of the monocentring of circles in the case of Hegel. Infinite representation invokes a foundation. While this foundation is not the identical itself, it is nevertheless a way of taking the principle of identity particularly seriously, giving it an infinite value and rendering it coextensive with the whole, and in this manner allowing it to reign over existence itself. It matters little whether identity (as the identity of the world and the self) be considered analytic, in the form of the infinitely small, or synthetic, in the form of the infinitely large. In the former case, the foundation or sufficient reason is that which vice-dicts identity; in the latter case, it is that which contradicts it. In all cases, however, the foundation or sufficient reason employs the infinite only to lead the identical to *exist* in its very identity. Moreover, what is apparent here with Leibniz is no less so with Hegel. Hegelian contradiction does not deny identity or non-contradiction: on the contrary, it consists in inscribing the double negation of *non*-contradiction within the existent in such a way that identity, under that condition or on that basis, is sufficient to think the existent as such. Those formulae according to which 'the object denies what it is not', or 'distinguishes itself from everything that it is not', are logical monsters (the Whole of everything which is not the object) in the service of identity. It is said that difference is negativity, that it extends or must extend to the point of contradiction once it is taken to the limit. This is true only to the extent that difference is already placed on a path or along a thread laid out by identity. It is true only to the extent that it is identity that pushes it to that point. Difference is the ground, but only the ground for the demonstration of the identical. Hegel's circle is not the eternal return, only the infinite circulation of the identical by means of negativity. Hegel's innovation is the final and most powerful homage rendered to the old principle. Between Leibniz and Hegel it matters little whether the supposed negative of difference is understood as a vice-dicting limitation or a contradicting limitation, any more than it matters whether infinite identity be considered analytic or synthetic. In either case, difference remains subordinated to identity, reduced to the negative, incarcerated within similitude and analogy. That is why, in infinite representation, the delirium is only a pre-formed false delirium which poses no threat to the repose or serenity of the identical. Infinite representation, therefore, suffers from the same defect as finite representation: that of confusing the concept of difference in itself with the inscription of difference in the identity of the concept in general (even though it treats identity as a pure infinite principle instead of treating it as a genus, and extends the rights of the concept in general to the whole instead of fixing their limits).

There is a crucial experience of difference and a corresponding experiment: every time we find ourselves confronted or bound by a limitation or an opposition, we should ask what such a situation presupposes. It presupposes a swarm of differences, a pluralism of free, wild or untamed differences; a properly differential and original space and time; all of which persist alongside the simplifications of limitation and opposition. A more profound real element must be defined in order for oppositions of forces or limitations of forms to be drawn, one which is determined as an abstract and potential multiplicity. Oppositions are roughly cut from a delicate milieu of overlapping perspectives, of communicating distances, divergences and disparities, of heterogeneous potentials and intensities. Nor is it primarily a question of dissolving tensions in the identical, but rather of distributing the disparities in a multiplicity. Limitations correspond to a simple first-order power – in a space with a single dimension and a single direction, where, as in Leibniz's example of boats borne on a current, there may be collisions, but these collisions necessarily serve to limit and to equalise, but not to neutralise or to oppose. As for opposition, it represents in turn the second-order power, where it is as though things were spread out upon a flat surface, polarised in a single plane, and the synthesis itself took place only in a false depth – that is, in a fictitious third dimension added to the others which does no more than double the plane. In any case, what is missing is the original, intensive depth which is the matrix of the entire space and the first affirmation of difference: here, that which only afterwards appears as linear limitation and flat opposition lives and simmers in the form of free differences. Everywhere, couples and polarities presuppose bundles and networks, organised oppositions presuppose radiations in all directions. Stereoscopic images form no more than an even and flat opposition, but they depend upon something quite different: an arrangement of coexistent, tiered, mobile planes, a 'disparateness' within an original depth. Everywhere, the depth of difference is primary. It is no use rediscovering depth as a third dimension unless it has already been installed at the beginning, enveloping the other two and enveloping itself as third. Space and time display oppositions (and limitations) only on the surface, but they presuppose in their real depth far more voluminous, affirmed and distributed differences which cannot be reduced to the banality of the negative. It is as though we were in Lewis Carroll's mirror where everything is contrary and inverted on the surface, but 'different' in depth. We shall see that it is the same with every space: geometrical, physical, biophysical, social and linguistic (in this respect, how unlikely Trubetzkoy's declaration of principle appears: 'the idea of difference presupposes the idea of opposition ...'). There is a false profundity in conflict, but underneath conflict, the space of the play of differences. The negative is the image of difference, but a flattened and inverted image, like the candle in the eye of the ox – the eye of the dialectician dreaming of a futile combat?

In this sense, too, Leibniz goes further or deeper than Hegel when he distributes the distinctive points and the differential elements of a multiplicity throughout the ground, and when he discovers a play in the creation of the world. It seems, therefore, as though the first dimension, that of the limit, despite all its imperfection, remains closest to the original depth. Leibniz's only error was to have linked difference to the negative of limitation, because he maintained the dominance of the old principle, because he linked the series to a principle of convergence, without seeing that divergence itself was an object of affirmation, or that the incompossibles belonged to the same world and were affirmed as the greatest crime and the greatest virtue of the one and only world, that of the eternal return.

It is not difference which presupposes opposition but opposition which presupposes difference, and far from resolving difference by tracing it back to a foundation, opposition betrays and distorts it. Our claim is not only that difference in itself is not 'already' contradiction, but that it cannot be reduced or traced back to contradiction, since the latter is not more but less profound than difference. On what condition is difference traced or projected on to a flat space? Precisely when it has been forced into a previously established identity, when it has been placed on the slope of the identical which makes it reflect or desire identity, and necessarily takes it where identity wants it to go – namely, into the negative.[15] The imprint of the Hegelian dialectic on the beginnings of Phenomenology has often been noted: the here and the now are posited as empty identities, as abstract universalities which claim to draw difference along with them, when in fact difference does not by any means follow and remains attached in the depths of its own space, in the here-now of a differential reality always made up of singularities. It is said that there were thinkers who explained that movement was impossible, but that this did not prevent movement from occurring. With Hegel it is the other way round: he creates movement, even the movement of the infinite, but because he creates it with words and representations it is a false movement, and nothing follows. It is the same every time there is mediation or representation. The representant says: 'Everyone recognises that ...', but there is always an unrepresented singularity who does not recognise precisely because it is not everyone or the universal. 'Everyone' recognises the universal because it is itself the universal, but the profound sensitive conscience which is nevertheless presumed to bear the cost, the singular, does not recognise it. The misfortune in speaking is not speaking, but speaking *for others* or representing something. The sensitive conscience (that is, the particular, difference or *ta alla*) refuses. One can always mediate, pass over into the antithesis, combine the synthesis, but the thesis does not follow: it subsists in its immediacy, in its difference which itself constitutes the true movement. Difference is the true content of the thesis, the persistence of the thesis. The negative and negativity do not even capture the phenomenon of difference, only the phantom or the epiphenomenon. The whole of Phenomenology is an epiphenomenology.

This is what the philosophy of difference refuses: *omnis determinatio negatio*. ... We refuse the general alternative proposed by infinite representation: the indeterminate, the indifferent, the undifferenciated or a difference already determined as negation, implying and enveloping the negative (by the same token, we also refuse the particular alternative: negative of limitation or negative of opposition). In its essence, difference is the object of affirmation or affirmation itself. In its essence, affirmation is itself difference. At this point, does the philosophy of difference not risk appearing as a new version of the beautiful soul? The beautiful soul is in effect the one who sees differences everywhere and appeals to them only as respectable, reconcilable or federative differences, while history continues to be made through bloody contradictions. The beautiful soul behaves like a justice of the peace thrown on to a field of battle, one who sees in the inexpiable struggles only simple 'differends' or perhaps misunderstandings. Conversely, however, it is not enough to harden oneself and invoke the well-known complementarities between affirmation and negation, life and death, creation and destruction (as if these were sufficient to ground a dialectic of negativity) in order to throw the taste for pure differences back at the beautiful soul, and to weld the fate of real differences to that of the negative and contradiction. For such complementarities as yet tell us nothing about the relation between one term and the other (does the determined affirmation result from an already negative and negating difference, or does the negative result from an already differential affirmation?). In very general terms, we claim that there are two ways to appeal to 'necessary destructions': that of the poet, who speaks in the name of a creative power, capable of overturning all orders and representations in order to affirm Difference in the state of permanent revolution which characterizes eternal return; and that of the politician, who is above all concerned to deny that which 'differs', so as to conserve or prolong an established historical order, or to establish a historical order which already calls forth in the world the forms of its representation. The two may coincide in particularly agitated moments, but they are never the same. No one passes less for a beautiful soul than Nietzsche. His soul is extremely beautiful, but not in the sense of the beautiful soul: no one is more endowed than he with a sense for cruelty or a taste for destruction. Moreover, throughout his work he never ceases to contrast two conceptions of the affirmation–negation relation.

In one case, it is negation which is the motor and driving force. Affirmation results from it – like an ersatz, as it were. It may well be that two negations are not too many to produce a phantom of affirmation. But how would affirmation result from negation unless it conserved that which is denied? Accordingly, Nietzsche indicates the terrifying conservatism of such a conception. Affirmation is indeed produced, but in order to say yes to all that is negative and negating, to all that *can be denied.* Thus Zarathustra's Ass says yes, but for him to affirm is to bear, to assume or to shoulder a burden. He bears everything: the burdens with which he is laden (divine values), those which he assumes himself (human values), and the weight of his tired muscles when he no longer has anything to bear (the absence of values).[16] This Ass and the dialectical ox leave a moral aftertaste. They have a terrifying taste for responsibility, as though one could affirm only by expiating, as though it were necessary to pass through the misfortunes of rift and division in order to be able to say yes. It is as though Difference were evil and already negative, so that it could produce affirmation only by expiation – that is, by assuming at once both the weight of that which is denied and negation itself. Always the same old malediction which resounds from the heights of the principle of identity: alone will be saved not that which is simply represented, but the infinite representation (the concept) which conserves all the negative finally to deliver difference up to the identical. Of all the senses of *Aufheben*, none is more important than that of 'raise up'. There is indeed a dialectical circle, but this infinite circle has everywhere only a single centre; it retains within itself all the other circles, all the other momentary centres. The reprises or repetitions of the dialectic express only the conservation of the whole, all the forms and all the moments, in a gigantic Memory. Infinite representation is a memory which conserves. In this case, repetition is no more than a conservatory, a power of memory itself. There is indeed a circular dialectical selection, but one which always works to the advantage of that which is conserved in infinite representation – that which bears and that which is borne. The selection works in reverse, and mercilessly eliminates whatever would render the circle tortuous or shatter the transparence of memory. In infinite representation, the bearer and the borne incessantly enter, leaving only to re-enter, like the shadows in the cave, and by this means they claim to have assumed themselves the properly dialectical power.

According to the other conception, difference is primary: it affirms difference and distance. Difference is light, aerial and affirmative. To affirm is not to bear but, on the contrary, to discharge and to lighten. It is no longer the negative which produces a phantom of affirmation like an ersatz, but rather a No which results from affirmation. This is also in turn a shadow, but rather in the sense of a consequence – one could say a *Nachfolge*. The negative is an epiphenomenon. Negation, like the ripples in a pond, is the effect of an affirmation which is too strong or too different. Perhaps two affirmations are necessary in order to produce the shadow of negation as a *Nachfolge*. Moreover, perhaps there are two moments at which the shadow disappears: difference as midnight and as noon. It is in this sense that Nietzsche opposes the Yes *and* the No of the Ass to the Yes *and* the No of Dionysus–Zarathustra: the point of view of the slave who draws from 'No' the phantom of an affirmation, and the point of view of the 'master' who draws from 'Yes' a consequence of negation and destruction; the point of view of the conservers of old values and that of the creators of new values.[17] Those whom Nietzsche calls masters are certainly powerful men, but not men of power, since power is in the gift of the values of the day. A slave does not cease to be a slave by taking power, and it is even the way of the world, or the law of its surface, to be led by slaves. Nor must the distinction between established values and creation be understood as implying an historical relativism, as though the established values were new in their day, while the new ones had to be established once their time had come. On the contrary, the difference is one of kind, like the difference between the conservative order of representation and a creative disorder or inspired chaos which can only ever coincide with a historical moment but never be confused with it. The most profound difference in kind is between the average forms and the extreme forms (new values): the extreme is not reached by carrying the average forms to infinity or by using their opposition in the finite to affirm their identity in the infinite. Pseudo-affirmation in infinite representation does not escape the average forms. Thus Nietzsche reproaches all those selection procedures based upon opposition or conflict with working to the advantage of the average forms and operating to the benefit of the 'large number'. Eternal return alone effects the true selection, because it eliminates the average forms and uncovers 'the superior form of everything that is'. The extreme is not the identity of opposites, but rather the univocity of the different; the superior form is not the infinite, but rather the eternal formlessness of the eternal return itself, throughout its metamorphoses and transformations. Eternal return 'makes' the difference because it creates the superior form. Eternal return employs negation like a *Nachfolge* and invents a new formula for the negation of the negation: *everything which can be denied* is and must be denied. The genius of eternal return lies not in memory but in waste, in active forgetting. All that is negative and all that denies, all those average affirmations which bear the negative, all those pale and unwelcome 'Yeses' which come from 'Nos', *everything which cannot pass the test of eternal return* – all these must be denied. If eternal return is a wheel, then it must be endowed with a violent centrifugal movement which expels everything which 'can' be denied, everything which cannot pass the test. Nietzsche announces only a light punishment for those who do not 'believe' in eternal return: they will have, and be aware of, only an ephemeral life! They will be aware of themselves and know themselves for what they are: epiphenomena. This will be their absolute Knowledge. In this manner, negation as a consequence, as the result of full affirmation, consumes all that is negative, and consumes itself at the mobile centre of eternal return. For if eternal return is a circle, then Difference is at the centre and the Same is only on the periphery: it is a constantly decentred, continually tortuous circle which revolves only around the unequal.

Negation is difference, but difference seen from its underside, seen from below. Seen the right way up, from top to bottom, difference is affirmation. This proposition, however, means many things: that difference is an object of affirmation; that affirmation itself is multiple; that it is creation but also that it must be created, as affirming difference, as being difference in itself. It is not the negative which is the motor. Rather, there are positive differential elements which determine the genesis of both the affirmation and the difference affirmed. It is precisely the fact that there is a genesis of affirmation as such which escapes us every time we leave affirmation in the undetermined, or put determination in the negative. Negation results from affirmation: this means that negation arises in the wake of affirmation or beside it, *but only as the shadow of the more profound genetic element* – of that power or 'will' which engenders the affirmation and the difference in the affirmation. Those who bear the negative know not what they do: they take the shadow for the reality, they encourage phantoms, they uncouple consequences from premisses and they give epiphenomena the value of phenomena and essences.

Representation fails to capture the affirmed world of difference. Representation has only a single centre, a unique and receding perspective, and in consequence a false depth. It mediates everything, but mobilises and moves nothing. Movement, for its part, implies a plurality of centres, a superposition of perspectives, a tangle of points of view, a coexistence of moments which essentially distort representation: paintings or sculptures are already such 'distorters', forcing us to create movement – that is, to combine a superficial and a penetrating view, or to ascend and descend within the space as we move through it. Is it enough to multiply representations in order to obtain such effects? Infinite representation includes precisely an infinity of representations – either by ensuring the convergence of all points of view on the same object or the same world, or by making all moments properties of the same Self. In either case it maintains a unique centre which gathers and represents all the others, like the unity of a series which governs or organises its terms and their relations once and for all. The fact is that infinite representation is indissociable from a law which renders it possible: the form of the concept as a form of identity which constitutes on the one hand the in-itself of the represented (A is A) and on the other the for-itself of the representant (Self = Self). The prefix RE- in the word representation signifies this conceptual form of the identical which subordinates differences. The immediate, defined as 'sub-representative', is therefore not attained by multiplying representations and points of view. On the contrary, each composing representation must be distorted, diverted and torn from its centre. Each point of view must itself be the object, or the object must belong to the point of view. The object must therefore be in no way identical, but torn asunder in a difference in which the identity of the object as seen by a seeing subject vanishes. Difference must become the element, the ultimate unity; it must therefore refer to other differences which never identify it but rather differenciate it. Each term of a series, being already a difference, must be put into a variable relation with other terms, thereby constituting other series devoid of centre and convergence. Divergence and decentring must be affirmed in the series itself. Every object, every thing, must see its own identity swallowed up in difference, each being no more than a difference between differences. Difference must be shown *differing*. We know that modern art tends to realise these conditions: in this sense it becomes a veritable *theatre* of metamorphoses and permutations. A theatre where nothing is fixed, a labyrinth without a thread (Ariadne has hung herself). The work of art leaves the domain of representation in order to become 'experience', transcendental empiricism or science of the sensible.

It is strange that aesthetics (as the science of the sensible) could be founded on what *can* be represented in the sensible. True, the inverse procedure is not much better, consisting of the attempt to withdraw the pure sensible from representation and to determine it as that which remains once representation is removed (a contradictory flux, for example, or a rhapsody of sensations). Empiricism truly becomes transcendental, and aesthetics an apodictic discipline, only when we apprehend directly in the sensible that which can only be sensed, the very being *of* the sensible: difference, potential difference and difference in intensity as the reason behind qualitative diversity. It is in difference that movement is produced as an 'effect', that phenomena flash their meaning like signs. The intense world of differences, in which we find the reason behind qualities and the being of the sensible, is precisely the object of a superior empiricism. This empiricism teaches us a strange 'reason', that of the multiple, chaos and difference (nomadic distributions, crowned anarchies). It is always differences which resemble one another, which are analogous, opposed or identical: difference is behind everything, but behind difference there is nothing. Each difference passes through all the others; it must 'will' itself or find itself through all the others. That is why eternal return does not appear second or come after, but is already present in every metamorphosis, contemporaneous with that which it causes to return. Eternal return relates to a world of differences implicated one in the other, to a complicated, properly chaotic world *without identity*. Joyce presented the *vicus of recirculation* as causing a *chaosmos* to turn; and Nietzsche had already said that chaos and eternal return were not two distinct things but a single and same *affirmation*. The world is neither finite nor infinite as representation would have it: it is completed and unlimited. Eternal return is the unlimited of the finished itself, the univocal being which is said of difference. With eternal return, chao-errancy is opposed to the coherence of representation; it excludes both the coherence of a subject which represents itself and that of an object represented. *Re*-petition opposes *re*-presentation: the prefix changes its meaning, since in the one case difference is said only in relation to the identical, while in the other it is the univocal which is said of the different. Repetition is the formless being of all differences, the formless power of the ground which carries every object to that extreme 'form' in which its representation comes undone. The ultimate element of repetition is the disparate [*dispars*], which stands opposed to the identity of representation. Thus, the circle of eternal return, difference and repetition (which undoes that of the identical and the contradictory) is a tortuous circle in which Sameness is said only of that which differs. The poet Blood expresses transcendental empiricism's profession of faith as a veritable aesthetic:

> Nature is contingent, excessive and mystical essentially. ... We have realised the highest divine thought of itself, and there is in it as much of wonder as of certainty. ... Not unfortunately the universe is wild – game flavoured as a hawk's wing. Nature is miracle all. She knows no laws; the same returns not, save to bring the different. The slow round of the engraver's lathe gains but the breadth of a hair, but the difference is distributed back over the whole curve, never an instant true – ever not quite.[18]

It is sometimes argued that a considerable philosophical change took place between pre- and post-Kantianism – the former being defined by the negative of limitation, the latter by the negative of opposition; the one by analytic identity, the other by synthetic identity; the one from the point of view of infinite substance, the other from the point of view of the finite Self. In the grand Leibnizian analysis, it is the finite Self which is introduced into the development of the infinite, whereas in the grand Hegelian synthesis, it is the infinite which is reintroduced into the operation of the finite Self. However, the importance of such changes is open to question. For a philosophy of difference, it matters little whether the negative is understood in terms of limitation or opposition, or whether identity is taken to be analytic or synthetic, once difference is already reduced to the negative and subordinated to identity. The oneness and identity of the divine substance are in truth the only guarantee of a unique and identical Self, and God is retained so long as the Self is preserved. Finite synthetic Self or divine analytic substance: it amounts to the same thing. That is why the Man–God permutations are so disappointing, and do not advance matters one step. Nietzsche seems to have been the first to see that the death of God becomes effective only with the dissolution of the Self. What is then revealed is being, which is said of differences which are neither in substance nor in a subject: so many subterranean affirmations. If eternal return is the highest, the most intense thought, this is because its own extreme coherence, at the highest point, excludes the coherence of a thinking subject, of a world which is thought of as a guarantor God.[19] Rather than being concerned with what happens before and after Kant (which amounts to the same thing), we should be concerned with a precise moment within Kantianism, a furtive and explosive moment which is not even continued by Kant, much less by post-Kantianism – except, perhaps, by Hölderlin in the experience and the idea of a 'categorical abduction'. For when Kant puts rational theology into question, *in the same stroke* he introduces a kind of disequilibrium, a fissure or crack in the pure Self of the 'I think', an alienation in principle, insurmountable in principle: the subject can henceforth represent its own spontaneity only as that of an Other, and in so doing invoke a mysterious coherence in the last instance which excludes its own – namely, that of the world and God. A Cogito for a dissolved Self: the Self of 'I think' includes in its essence a receptivity of intuition in relation to which *I* is already an other. It matters little that synthetic identity – and, following that, the morality of practical reason – restore the integrity of the self, of the world and of God, thereby preparing the way for post-Kantian syntheses: for a brief moment we enter into that schizophrenia in principle which characterises the highest power of thought, and opens Being directly on to difference, despite all the mediations, all the reconciliations, of the concept.

The task of modern philosophy has been defined: to overturn Platonism. That this overturning should conserve many Platonic characteristics is not only inevitable but desirable. It is true that Platonism already represents the subordination of difference to the powers of the One, the Analogous, the Similar and even the Negative. It is like an animal in the process of being tamed, whose final resistant movements bear witness better than they would in a state of freedom to a nature soon to be lost: the Heraclitan world still growls in Platonism. With Plato, the issue is still in doubt: mediation has not yet found its ready-made movement. The Idea is not yet the concept of an object which submits the world to the requirements of representation, but rather a brute presence which can be invoked in the world only in function of that which is not 'representable' in things. The Idea has therefore not yet chosen to relate difference to the identity of a concept in general: it has not given up hope of finding a pure concept of difference in itself. The labyrinth or chaos is untangled, but without thread or the assistance of a thread. Aristotle indeed saw what is irreplaceable in Platonism, even though he made it precisely the basis of a criticism of Plato: the dialectic of difference has its own method – division – but this operates without mediation, without middle term or reason; it acts in the immediate and is inspired by the Ideas rather than by the requirements of a concept in general. It is true that division is a capricious, incoherent procedure which jumps from one singularity to another, by contrast with the supposed identity of a concept. Is this not its strength from the point of view of the Idea? Far from being one dialectical procedure among others which must be completed or relayed by others, is not division the one which replaces all the other procedures from the moment it appears, and gathers up all the dialectical power in favour of a genuine philosophy of difference? Is it not simultaneously the measure of both Platonism and the possibility of overturning Platonism?

Our mistake lies in trying to understand Platonic division on the basis of Aristotelian requirements. According to Aristotle, it is a question of dividing a genus into opposing species: but then this procedure not only lacks 'reason' by itself, it lacks a reason in terms of which we could decide whether something falls into one species rather than another. For example, we divide art into arts of production and arts of acquisition: but then why is fishing among the arts of acquisition? What is missing here is mediation – that is, the identity of a concept capable of serving as middle term. However, this objection clearly fails if Platonic division in no way proposes to determine the species of a genus – or if, rather, it proposes to do so, but superficially and even ironically, the better to hide under this mask its true secret.[20] Division is not the inverse of a 'generalisation'; it is not a determination of species. It is in no way a method of determining species, but one of selection. It is not a question of dividing a determinate genus into definite species, but of dividing a confused species into pure lines of descent, or of selecting a pure line from material which is not. We could speak of 'Platons' as opposed to 'Aristotelons', in the same manner that biologists oppose 'Jordanons' and 'Linnaeons', since Aristotelian species are large, whereas Platonic division deals with small species or lines of descent. Even the indivisible, *infima species* in Aristotle remains a large species, while Platonic division operates in a quite different domain. Its point of departure can therefore be either a genus or a species, but this genus or this large species is understood as an undifferenciated logical matter, an indifferent material, a mixture, an indefinite representing multiplicity which must be eliminated in order to bring to light the Idea which constitutes a pure line of descent. The search for gold provides the model for this process of division. Difference is not between species, between two determinations of a genus, but entirely on one side, within the chosen line of descent: there are no longer contraries within a single genus, but pure and impure, good and bad, authentic and inauthentic, in a mixture which gives rise to a large species. Pure difference, the pure concept of difference, not difference mediated within the concept in general, in the genus and the species. The meaning and the goal of the method of division is selection among rivals, the testing of claimants – not *antiphasis* but *antisbetesis* (we can see this clearly in Plato's two principal examples of division: in *The Statesman*, where the statesman is defined as the one who knows 'the pastoral care of men', but many introduce themselves by saying 'I am the true shepherd of men', including merchants, farmers, bakers, as well as athletes and the entire medical profession; and in the *Phaedrus*, where it is a question of defining the good madness and the true lover, but many claimants cry: 'I am love, I am the lover'). There is no question here of species, except ironically. There is nothing in common with the concerns of Aristotle: it is a question not of identifying but of authenticating. The one problem which recurs throughout Plato's philosophy is the problem of measuring rivals and selecting claimants. This problem of distinguishing between *things and their simulacra* within a pseudo-genus or a large species presides over his classification of the arts and sciences. It is a question of making the difference, thus of operating in the depths of the immediate, a dialectic of the immediate. It is a dangerous trial without thread and without net, for according to the ancient custom of myth and epic, false claimants must die.

Our question is not yet that of knowing whether the selective difference is indeed between the true and false claimants, as Plato says it is, but rather of knowing how Plato establishes the difference thanks to the method of division. To the reader's great surprise, he does so by introducing a 'myth'. It is as though division, once it abandons the mask of determining species and discloses its true goal, nevertheless renounces the realisation of this goal and is instead relayed by the simple 'play' of a myth. In effect, once the question of the claimants is reached, *The Statesman* invokes the image of an ancient God who ruled the world and men: strictly speaking, only this God deserves the name of shepherd–King of mankind. None of the claimants is his equal, but there is a certain 'care' of the human community which devolves to the statesman *par excellence*, since he is closest to the model of the archaic shepherd–God. The claimants find themselves in a sense measured according to an order of elective participation, and among the statesman's rivals we can distinguish (according to the ontological measure afforded by the myth) parents, servants, auxiliaries and, finally, charlatans and counterfeits.[21] The procedure in the *Phaedrus* is the same: when it becomes a question of distinguishing the different 'madnesses', Plato suddenly invokes a myth. He describes the circulation of souls before their incarnation, along with the memory which they carry of the Ideas they have been able to contemplate. It is the nature and degree of this mythic contemplation, but also the kind of occasions necessary for remembering, which determine the value and the order of different types of present madness. We can determine who is the false lover and who is the true lover. We can even determine which – lover, poet, priest, soothsayer or philosopher – is elected to participation in reminiscence and contemplation: which is the true claimant, the true participant, and in what order the others follow. (It will be objected that the third important text concerning division, the *Sophist*, presents no such myth. The point is that in this text, by a paradoxical utilisation of the method, a counter-utilisation, Plato proposes to isolate the false claimant *par excellence*, the one who lays claim to everything without any right: the 'sophist'.)

This introduction of myth appears, however, to confirm all Aristotle's objections: in the absence of any mediation, division lacks probative force; it has to be relayed by a myth which provides an imaginary equivalent of mediation. Here again, however, we betray the sense of this so-mysterious method. For if it is true that, within Platonism in general, myth and dialectic are distinct forces, this distinction no longer matters once dialectic discovers its true method in division. Division overcomes this duality and integrates myth into the dialectic; it makes myth an element of the dialectic itself. The structure of this myth in Plato is clear: it is a circle, with two dynamic functions – namely, turning and returning, distributing and allocation: the allocation of lots is carried out by the turning wheel of an eternally recurring metempsychosis. The reasons which establish that Plato is certainly not a protagonist of eternal return do not concern us here. It is nevertheless true that in the *Phaedrus* – as in *The Statesman* and elsewhere – myth establishes the model of a partial circulation in which appears a suitable ground on which to base the difference, on which to measure the roles or claims. In the *Phaedrus*, this ground appears as the Ideas, such as these are contemplated by the souls which circulate above the celestial vault. In *The Statesman*, it appears in the form of the shepherd–God who presides over the circular movement of the universe. The ground may be either the centre or the motor of the circle. It is constituted by the myth as the principle of a test or selection which imparts meaning to the method of division by fixing the degrees of an elective participation. Thus, in accordance with the oldest tradition, the circular myth is indeed the story-repetition of a foundation. Division demands such a foundation as the ground capable of making the difference. Conversely, the foundation demands division as the state of difference in that which must be grounded. Division is the true unity of dialectic and mythology, of the myth as foundation and of the logos as *logos tomeus*.

This role of the ground appears in all clarity in the Platonic conception of participation. (And no doubt it is this foundation which provides division with the mediation it seems to lack and, at the same time, relates difference to the One, but in such a peculiar manner...). To participate means to have part in, to have after, to have in second place. What possesses in first place is the ground itself. Justice alone is just, says Plato. As for those whom we call the just, they possess the quality of being just in second, third or fourth place ... or in simulacral fashion. That justice alone should be just is not a simple analytic proposition. It is the designation of the Idea as the ground which possesses in first place. The function of the ground is then to allow participation, to give in second place. Thus, that which participates more or less in varying degrees is necessarily a claimant. The claimant calls for a ground; the claim must be grounded (or denounced as groundless). Laying claim is not one phenomenon among others, but the nature of every phenomenon. The ground is a test which permits claimants to participate in greater or lesser degree in the object of the claim. In this sense the ground measures and makes the difference. We must therefore distinguish between Justice, which is the ground; the quality of justice, which is the object of the claim possessed by that which grounds; and the just, who are the claimants who participate unequally in the object. That is why the Neo-Platonists provide us with such a profound understanding of Platonism in setting out their sacred triad: the Imparticipable, the Participated, and the Participants. The grounding principle is imparticipable but nevertheless provides something to be participated in, which it gives to the participant, who is the possessor in second place, the claimant who has been able to pass the grounding test. One could say: the father, the daughter and the suitor. Moreover, since the triad is reproduced throughout a whole series of participations, and since the claimants participate within an order and in degrees which represent difference in action, the Neo-Platonists indeed saw the essential point: that the aim of division was not the broad distinction among species but the establishment of a serial dialectic, of series or lines of descent in depth which mark the operations of a selective foundation or an elective participation (Zeus I, Zeus II, etc.). It seems, then, that contradiction, far from signifying the founding test itself, represents instead the state of an ungrounded claim at the limit of participation. If the true claimant (the first grounded, the well grounded, the authentic) has rivals who are like parents, auxiliaries or servants, all participating in his claim in various capacities, he also has simulacra or counterfeits who would be exposed by the test. Such, according to Plato, is the 'sophist', the buffoon, centaur or satyr who lays claim to everything, and who, in laying such claims to everything, is never grounded but contradicts everything, including himself ...

However, in what, exactly, does the grounding test consist? Myth tells us that it always involves a further task to be performed, an enigma to be resolved. The oracle is questioned, but the oracle's response is itself a problem. The dialectic is ironic, but irony is the art of problems and questions. Irony consists in treating things and beings as so many responses to hidden questions, so many cases for problems yet to be resolved. We recall that Plato defined the dialectic as proceeding by 'problems', by means of which one attains the pure grounding principle – that is, the principle which measures the problems as such and distributes the corresponding solutions. Memory is discussed in the *Meno* only in connection with a geometric problem which must be understood before it can be resolved, and must have the solution it deserves according to the manner in which the rememberer has understood it. We are not concerned at the moment with the distinction which should be drawn between the two instances of the problem and the question, but rather with the essential role which both together play in the Platonic dialectic – a role comparable to that which the negative will play later, for example in the Hegelian dialectic. However, it is precisely *not* the negative which plays this role in Plato – so much so that we must consider whether or not the celebrated thesis of the *Sophist*, despite certain ambiguities, should be understood as follows: 'non' in the expression 'non-being' expresses *something other than the negative.* On this point, the mistake of the traditional accounts is to impose upon us a dubious alternative: in seeking to dispel the negative, we declare ourselves satisfied if we show that being is full positive reality which admits no non-being; conversely, in seeking to ground negation, we are satisfied if we manage to posit, in being itself or in relation to being, some sort of non-being (it seems to us that this non-being is necessarily the being of the negative or the ground of negation). The alternative is thus the following: either there is no non-being and negation is illusory and ungrounded, or there is non-being, which puts the negative in being and grounds negation. Perhaps, however, we have reasons to say *both* that there is non-being *and* that the negative is illusory.

Neither the problem nor the question is a subjective determination marking a moment of insufficiency in knowledge. Problematic structure is part of objects themselves, allowing them to be grasped as signs, just as the questioning or problematising instance is a part of knowledge allowing its positivity and its specificity to be grasped in the act of *learning.* More profoundly still, Being (what Plato calls the Idea) 'corresponds' to the essence of the problem or the question as such. It is as though there were an 'opening', a 'gap', an ontological 'fold' which relates being and the question to one another. In this relation, being is difference itself. Being is also non-being, *but non-being is not the being of the negative*; rather, it is the being of the problematic, the being of problem and question. Difference is not the negative; on the contrary, non-being is Difference: *heteron,* not *enantion.* For this reason non-being should rather be written (non)-being or, better still, ?-being. In this sense, it turns out that the infinitive, the *esse*, designates less a proposition than the interrogation to which the proposition is supposed to respond. This (non)-being is the differential element in which affirmation, as multiple affirmation, finds the principle of its genesis. As for negation, this is only the shadow of the highest principle, the shadow of the difference alongside the affirmation produced. Once we confuse (non)-being with the negative, contradiction is inevitably carried into being; but contradiction is only the appearance or the epiphenomenon, the illusion projected by the problem, the shadow of a question which remains open and of a being which corresponds as such to that question (before it has been given a response). Is it not already in this sense that for Plato contradiction characterises only the so-called aporetic dialogues? Beyond contradiction, difference – beyond *non*-being, (non)-being; beyond the negative, problems and questions.

Note on Heidegger's Philosophy of Difference

It seems that the principal misunderstandings which Heidegger denounced as misreadings of his philosophy after *Being and Time* and 'What is Metaphysics?' have to do with the following: the Heideggerian *Not* refers not to the negative in Being but to Being as difference; it refers not to negation but to questioning. When Sartre analysed interrogation at the beginning of *Being and Nothingness*, he made it a preliminary to the discovery of the negative and negativity. This was, in a sense, the opposite of Heidegger's procedure. None the less, it involved no misunderstanding, since Sartre did not set out to write a commentary on Heidegger. Merleau-Ponty, on the other hand, undoubtedly followed a more thoroughly Heideggerian inspiration in speaking of 'folds' and 'pleating' (by contrast with Sartrean 'holes' and 'lakes of non-being') from *The Phenomenology of Perception* onwards, and in returning to an ontology of difference and questioning in his posthumous book *The Visible and the Invisible*.

It seems that Heidegger's theses may be summarised as follows:

1. The *not* expresses not the negative but the difference between Being and being. See the preface to *The Essence of Reasons*, 3rd edn, 1949, transl.

Terrence Malick, Evanston, IL: Northwestern University Press, 1969, p. 3: 'The Ontological Difference is the Not between being and Being'; and the postscript to 'What is Metaphysics?', in *Existence and Being*, London: Vision Press, 1949, p. 384, where Heidegger asks: 'whether that which never and nowhere "is" discloses itself as that which differs from everything that "is", i.e. what we call "Being"'.

2. This difference is not 'between' in the ordinary sense of the word. It is the Fold, *Zwiefalt*. It is constitutive of Being and of the manner in which Being constitutes being, in the double movement of 'clearing' and 'veiling'. Being is truly the differenciator of difference – whence the expression 'ontological difference'. See 'Overcoming Metaphysics', transl. Joan Stambaugh, in *The End of Philosophy*, New York: Harper & Row, 1973, pp. 91 ff.
3. Ontological Difference corresponds to questioning. It is the being of questions, which become problems, marking out the determinant fields of existence. See *The Essence of Reasons*.
4. Understood in this manner, difference is not an object of representation. As the element of metaphysics, representation subordinates difference to identity, if only in relating it to a third term as the centre of a comparison *between* two supposedly different terms (Being and being). Heidegger recognises that this point of view of metaphysical representation is still present in *The Essence of Reasons* (see the French translation, p. 59, where the third term is found in the 'transcendence of being-there'). But metaphysics is unable to think difference in itself, or the importance of that which separates as much as of that which unites (the differenciator). There is no synthesis, mediation or reconciliation in difference, but rather a stubborn differenciation. This is the 'turning' beyond metaphysics: 'Being itself can open out in its truth the difference of Being and beings preserved in itself only when the difference explicitly takes place' ('Overcoming Metaphysics', p. 91). On this point, see Beda Alleman, *Hölderlin et Heidegger*, French translation, Paris: Presses Universitaires de France, pp. 157–62, 168–72; Jean Beaufret, Introduction to *Poème de Parménide*, Paris: Presses Universitaires de France, 1955, pp. 69–72, 455.
5. Difference cannot, therefore, be subordinated to the Identical or the Equal but must be thought as the Same, in the Same. See *Identity and Difference*, transl. Joan Stambaugh, New York: Harper & Row, 1969; and 'Poetically Man Dwells...' in *Poetry, Language, Thought*, transl. Albert Hofstadter, New York: Harper & Row, 1971, pp. 218–19:

The same never coincides with the equal, not even in the empty indifferent oneness of what is merely identical. The equal or identical always moves toward the absence of difference, so that everything may be reduced to a common denominator. The same, by contrast, is the belong-

> ing together of what differs, through a gathering by way of the difference. We can only say 'the same' if we think difference. ... The same banishes all zeal always to level what is different into the equal or identical. The same gathers what is distinct into an original being-at-one. The equal, on the contrary, disperses them into the dull unity of mere uniformity.

We regard as fundamental this 'correspondence' between difference and questioning, between ontological difference and the being of the question. It can nevertheless be asked whether Heidegger did not himself encourage the misunderstandings, by his conception of 'Nothing' as well as by his manner of 'striking through' Being instead of parenthesising the (non) of non-Being. Moreover, is it enough to oppose the Same and the Identical in order to think original difference and to disconnect this from all mediations? If it is true that some commentators have found Thomist echos in Husserl, Heidegger, by contrast, follows Duns Scotus and gives renewed splendour to the Univocity of Being. But does he effectuate the conversion after which univocal Being belongs only to difference and, in this sense, revolves around being? Does he conceive of *being* in such a manner that it will be truly disengaged from any subordination in relation to the identity of representation? It would seem not, given his critique of the Nietzschean eternal return.

The four figures of the Platonic dialectic are therefore: the selection of difference, the installation of a mythic circle, the establishment of a foundation, and the position of a question–problem complex. However, difference is still related to the Same or to the One through these figures. No doubt the *same* should not be confused with the identity of the concept in general: rather, it characterises the Idea as the thing itself. Nevertheless, to the extent that it plays the role of a true ground, it is difficult to see what its effect is if not to make that which is grounded 'identical', to use difference in order to make the identical exist. In reality, the distinction between the same and the identical bears fruit only if one subjects the Same to a conversion which relates it to the different, while at the same time the things and beings which are distinguished in the different suffer a corresponding radical destruction of their *identity*. Only on this condition is difference thought in itself, neither represented nor mediated. The whole of Platonism, by contrast, is dominated by the idea of drawing a distinction between 'the thing itself' and the simulacra. Difference is not thought in itself but related to a ground, subordinated to the same and subject to mediation in mythic form. Overturning Platonism, then, means denying the primacy of original over copy, of model over image; glorifying the reign of simulacra and reflections. Pierre Klossowski has clearly noted this point in the articles referred to above: taken in its strict sense, eternal return means that each thing exists only in returning, copy of an infinity of copies which allows neither original nor origin to subsist. That is why the eternal return is called 'parodic': it qualifies as simulacrum that which it causes to be (and to return).[22] When eternal return is the power of (formless) Being, the simulacrum is the true character or form – the 'being' – of that which is. When the identity of things dissolves, being escapes to attain univocity, and begins to revolve around the different. That which is or returns has no prior constituted identity: things are reduced to the difference which fragments them, and to all the differences which are implicated in it and through which they pass. In this sense, the simulacrum and the symbol are one; in other words, the simulacrum is the sign in so far as the sign interiorises the conditions of its own repetition. The simulacrum seizes upon a constituent *disparity* in the thing from which it strips the rank of model. If, as we have seen, eternal return serves to establish a difference in kind between the average and the superior forms, then there is also a difference in kind between the average or moderate positions of the eternal return (whether these involve partial cycles or approximate global return *in specie*) and its strict or categorical position. For eternal return, affirmed in all its power, allows no installation of a foundation–ground. On the contrary, it swallows up or destroys every ground which would function as an instance responsible for the difference between the original and the derived, between things and simulacra. It makes us party to a universal *ungrounding*. By 'ungrounding' we should understand the freedom of the non-mediated ground, the discovery of a ground behind every other ground, the relation between the groundless and the ungrounded, the immediate reflection of the formless and the superior form which constitutes the eternal return. Every thing, animal or being assumes the status of simulacrum; so that the thinker of eternal return – who indeed refuses to be drawn out of the cave, finding instead another cave beyond, always another in which to hide – can rightly say that he is himself burdened with the superior form of everything that is, like the poet 'burdened with humanity, even that of the animals'. These words themselves have their echo in the superposed caves. Moreover, that cruelty which at the outset seemed to us monstrous, demanding expiation, and could be alleviated only by representative mediation, now seems to us to constitute the pure concept or Idea of difference within overturned Platonism: the most innocent difference, the state of innocence and its echo.

Plato gave the establishment of difference as the supreme goal of dialectic. However, difference does not lie between things and simulacra, models and copies. Things are simulacra themselves, simulacra are the superior forms, and the difficulty facing everything is to become its own simulacrum, to attain the status of a sign in the coherence of eternal return. Plato opposed eternal return to chaos as though chaos were a contradictory state which must be subject to order or law from outside, as it is when the Demiurge subjugates a rebellious matter. He reduced the Sophist to contradiction, to that supposed state of chaos, the lowest power and last degree of participation. In reality the 'nth' power does not pass through two, three or four: it is immediately affirmed in order to constitute the highest power; it is affirmed of chaos itself and, as Nietzsche said, chaos and eternal return are not two different things. The sophist is not the being (or the non-being) of contradiction, but the one who raises everything to the level of simulacra and maintains them in that state. Was it not inevitable that Plato should push irony to that point – to parody? Was it not inevitable that Plato should be the first to overturn Platonism, or at least to show the direction such an overturning should take? We are reminded of the grand finale of the *Sophist*: difference is displaced, division turns back against itself and begins to function in reverse, and, as a result of being applied to simulacra themselves (dreams, shadows, reflections, paintings), shows the impossibility of distinguishing them from originals or from models. The Eleatic Stranger gives a definition of the sophist such that he can no longer be distinguished from Socrates himself: the ironic imitator who proceeds by brief arguments (questions and problems). Each moment of difference must then find its true figure: selection, repetition, ungrounding, the question–problem complex.

We have contrasted representation with a different kind of formation. The elementary concepts of representation are the categories defined as the conditions of possible experience. These, however, are too general or too large for the real. The net is so loose that the largest fish pass through. No wonder, then, that aesthetics should be divided into two irreducible domains: that of the theory of the sensible which captures only the real's conformity with possible experience; and that of the theory of the beautiful, which deals with the reality of the real in so far as it is thought. Everything changes once we determine the conditions of real experience, which are not larger than the conditioned and which differ in kind from the categories: the two senses of the aesthetic become one, to the point where the being of the sensible reveals itself in the work of art, while at the same time the work of art appears as experimentation. The fault of representation lies in not going beyond the form of identity, in relation to both the object seen and the seeing subject. Identity is no less conserved in each component representation than in the whole of infinite representation as such. Infinite representation may well multiply points of view and organise these in series; these series are no less subject to the condition of converging upon the same object, upon the same world. Infinite representation may well multiply figures and moments and organise these into circles endowed with self-movement; these circles no less turn around a single centre which is that of the great circle of consciousness. By contrast, when the modern work of art develops its permutating series and its circular structures, it indicates to philosophy a path leading to the abandonment of representation. It is not enough to multiply perspectives in order to establish perspectivism. To every perspective or point of view there must correspond an autonomous work with its own self-sufficient sense: what matters is the divergence of series, the decentring of circles, 'monstrosity'. The totality of circles and series is thus a formless *ungrounded* chaos which has no law other than its own repetition, its own reproduction in the development of that which diverges and decentres. We know how these conditions are already satisfied in such works as Mallarmé's *Book* or Joyce's *Finnegans Wake*: these are by nature problematic works.[23] The identity of the object read really dissolves into divergent series defined by esoteric words, just as the identity of the reading subject is dissolved into the decentred circles of possible multiple readings. Nothing, however, is lost; each series exists only by virtue of the return of the others. Everything has become simulacrum, for by simulacrum we should not understand a simple imitation but rather the act by which the very idea of a model or privileged position is challenged and overturned. The simulacrum is the instance which includes a difference within itself, such as (at least) two divergent series on which it plays, all resemblance abolished so that one can no longer point to the existence of an original and a copy. It is in this direction that we must look for the conditions, not of possible experience, but of real experience (selection, repetition, etc.). It is here that we find the lived reality of a sub-representative domain. If it is true that representation has identity as its element and similarity as its unit of measure, then pure presence such as it appears in the simulacrum has the 'disparate' as its unit of measure – in other words, always a difference of difference as its immediate element.

Chapter II
Repetition for Itself

Repetition changes nothing in the object repeated, but does change something in the mind which contemplates it. Hume's famous thesis takes us to the heart of a problem: since it implies, in principle, a perfect independence on the part of each presentation, how can repetition change something in the case of the repeated element? The rule of discontinuity or instantaneity in repetition tells us that one instance does not appear unless the other has disappeared – hence the status of matter as *mens momentanea*. However, given that repetition disappears even as it occurs, how can we say 'the second', 'the third' and 'it is the same'? It has no in-itself. On the other hand, it does change something in the mind which contemplates it. This is the essence of modification. Hume takes as an example the repetition of cases of the type AB, AB, AB, A ... . Each case or objective sequence AB is independent of the others. The repetition (although we cannot yet properly speak of repetition) changes nothing in the object or the state of affairs AB. On the other hand, a change is produced in the mind which contemplates: a difference, something new *in* the mind. Whenever A appears, I expect the appearance of B. Is this the for-itself of repetition, an originary subjectivity which necessarily enters into its constitution? Does not the paradox of repetition lie in the fact that one can speak of repetition only by virtue of the change or difference that it introduces into the mind which contemplates it? By virtue of a difference that the mind *draws from* repetition?

What does this change comprise? Hume explains that the independent identical or similar cases are grounded in the imagination. The imagination is defined here as a contractile power: like a sensitive plate, it retains one case when the other appears. It contracts cases, elements, agitations or homogeneous instants and grounds these in an internal qualitative impression endowed with a certain weight. When A appears, we expect B with a force corresponding to the qualitative impression of all the contracted ABs. This is by no means a memory, nor indeed an operation of the understanding: contraction is not a matter of reflection. Properly speaking, it forms a synthesis of time. A succession of instants does not constitute time any more than it causes it to disappear; it indicates only its constantly aborted moment of birth. Time is constituted only in the originary synthesis which operates on the repetition of instants. This synthesis contracts the successive independent instants into one another, thereby constituting the lived, or living, present. It is in this present that time is deployed. To it belong both the past and the future: the past in so far as the preceding instants are retained in the contraction; the future because its expectation is anticipated in this same contraction. The past and the future do not designate instants distinct from a supposed present instant, but rather the dimensions of the present itself in so far as it is a contraction of instants. The present does not have to go outside itself in order to pass from past to future. Rather, the living present goes from the past to the future which it constitutes in time, which is to say also from the particular to the general: from the particulars which it envelops by contraction to the general which it develops in the field of its expectation (the difference produced in the mind is generality itself in so far as it forms a living rule for the future). In any case, this synthesis must be given a name: passive synthesis. Although it is constitutive it is not, for all that, active. It is not carried out by the mind, but occurs *in* the mind which contemplates, prior to all memory and all reflection. Time is subjective, but in relation to the subjectivity of a passive subject. Passive synthesis or contraction is essentially asymmetrical: it goes from the past to the future in the present, thus from the particular to the general, thereby imparting direction to the arrow of time.

In considering repetition in the object, we remain within the conditions which make possible an idea of repetition. But in considering the change in the subject, we are already beyond these conditions, confronting the general form of difference. The ideal constitution of repetition thus implies a kind of retroactive movement between these two limits. It is woven between the two. This is the movement which Hume so profoundly analyses when he shows that the cases contracted or grounded in the imagination remain no less distinct in the memory or in the understanding. Not that we return to the state of matter which produces one case only when the other has disappeared. Rather, on the basis of the qualitative impression in the imagination, memory reconstitutes the particular cases as distinct, conserving them in its own 'temporal space'. The past is then no longer the immediate past of retention but the reflexive past of representation, of reflected and reproduced particularity. Correlatively, the future also ceases to be the immediate future of anticipation in order to become the reflexive future of prediction, the reflected generality of the understanding (the understanding weights the expectation in the imagination in proportion to the number of distinct similar cases observed and recalled). In other words, the active syntheses of memory and understanding are superimposed upon and supported by the passive synthesis of the imagination. The constitution of repetition already implies three instances: the in-itself which causes it to disappear as it appears, leaving it unthinkable; the for-itself of the passive synthesis; and, grounded upon the latter, the reflected representation of a 'for-us' in the active syntheses. Associationism possesses an irreplaceable subtlety. It is not surprising that Bergson rediscovers Hume's analyses once he encounters an analogous problem: four o'clock strikes ... each stroke, each disturbance or excitation, is logically independent of the other, *mens momentanea*. However, quite apart from any memory or distinct calculation, we contract these into an internal qualitative impression within this living present or *passive synthesis* which is duration. Then we restore them in an auxiliary space, a derived time in which we may reproduce them, reflect on them or count them like so many quantifiable external-impressions.[1]

No doubt Bergson's example is not the same as Hume's. One refers to a closed repetition, the other to an open one. Moreover, one refers to a repetition of elements of the type A A A A ... (tick, tick, tick, tick ...), the other to a repetition of cases such as AB AB AB A ... (tick-tock, tick-tock, tick-tock, tick ...). The principal distinction between these two forms rests upon the fact that in the second case difference not only appears in the contraction of the elements in general but also occurs in each particular case, between two elements which are both determined and joined together by a relation of opposition. The function of opposition here is to impose a limit on the elementary repetition, to enclose it upon the simplest group, to reduce it to a minimum of two (tock being the inverse of tick). Difference therefore appears to abandon its first figure of generality and to be distributed in the repeating particular, but in such a way as to give rise to new living generalities. Repetition finds itself enclosed in the 'case', reduced to the pair, while a new infinity opens up in the form of the repetition of the cases themselves. It would be wrong, therefore, to believe that every repetition of cases is open by nature, while every repetition of elements is closed. The repetition of cases is open only by virtue of the closure of a binary opposition between elements. Conversely, the repetition of elements is closed only by virtue of a reference to structures of cases in which as a whole it plays itself the role of one of the two opposed elements: not only is four a generality in relation to four strokes, but 'four o'clock' enters into a duality with the preceding or the following half-hour, or even, on the horizon of the perceptual universe, with the corresponding four o'clock in the morning or afternoon. In the case of passive synthesis, the two forms of repetition always refer back to one another: repetition of cases presupposes that of elements, but that of elements necessarily extends into that of cases (whence the natural tendency of passive synthesis to experience tick-tick as tick-tock).

That is why what matters even more than the distinction between the two forms is the distinction between the levels on which *both* operate, separately and in combination. Hume's example no less than Bergson's leaves us at the level of sensible and perceptual syntheses. The sensed quality is indistinguishable from the contraction of elementary excitations, but the object perceived implies a contraction of cases such that one quality may be read in the other, and a structure in which the form of the object allies itself with the quality at least as an intentional part. However, in the order of constituent passivity, perceptual syntheses refer back to organic syntheses which are like the sensibility of the senses; they refer back to a primary sensibility that we *are*. We are made of contracted water, earth, light and air – not merely prior to the recognition or representation of these, but prior to their being sensed. Every organism, in its receptive and perceptual elements, but also in its viscera, is a sum of contractions, of retentions and expectations. At the level of this primary vital sensibility, the lived present constitutes a past and a future in time. Need is the manner in which this future appears, as the organic form of expectation. The retained past appears in the form of cellular heredity. Furthermore, by combining with the perceptual syntheses built upon them, these organic syntheses are redeployed in the active syntheses of a psycho-organic memory and intelligence (instinct and learning). We must therefore distinguish not only the forms of repetition in relation to passive synthesis but also the levels of passive synthesis and the combinations of these levels with one another and with active syntheses. All of this forms a rich domain of *signs* which always envelop heterogeneous elements and animate behaviour. Each contraction, each passive synthesis, constitutes a sign which is interpreted or deployed in active syntheses. The signs by which an animal 'senses' the presence of water do not resemble the elements which its thirsty organism lacks. The manner in which sensation and perception – along with need and heredity, learning and instinct, intelligence and memory – participate in repetition is measured in each case by the combination of forms of repetition, by the levels on which these combinations take place, by the relationships operating between these levels and by the interference of active syntheses with passive syntheses.

What is in question throughout this domain that we have had to extend to include the organic as such? Hume says precisely that it is a question of the problem of habit. However, how are we to explain the fact that – in the case of Bergson's clock-strokes no less than with Hume's causal sequences – we feel ourselves in effect so close to the mystery of habit, yet recognise nothing of what is 'habitually' called habit? Perhaps the reason lies in the illusions of psychology, which made a fetish of activity. Its unreasonable fear of introspection allowed it to observe only that which moved. It asks how we acquire habits in acting, but the entire theory of learning risks being misdirected so long as the prior question is not posed – namely, whether it is through acting that we acquire habits ... *or whether, on the contrary, it is through contemplating*? Psychology regards it as established that the self cannot contemplate itself. This, however, is not the question. The question is whether or not the self itself is a contemplation, whether it is not in itself a contemplation, and whether we can learn, form behaviour and form ourselves other than through contemplation.

Habit *draws* something new from repetition – namely, difference (in the first instance understood as generality). In essence, habit is contraction.

Language testifies to this in allowing us to speak of 'contracting' a habit, and in allowing the verb 'to contract' only in conjunction with a complement capable of constituting a habitude. It will be objected that the heart no more has (or no more is) a habit when it contracts than when it dilates. This, however, is to confuse two quite different kinds of contraction: contraction may refer to one of the two active elements, one of the two opposing moments in a tick-tock type series, the other element being relaxation or dilation. But contraction also refers to the fusion of successive tick-tocks in a contemplative soul. Passive synthesis is of the latter kind: it constitutes our habit of living, our expectation that 'it' will continue, that one of the two elements will appear after the other, thereby assuring the perpetuation of our *case*. When we say that habit is a contraction we are speaking not of an instantaneous action which combines with another to form an element of repetition, but rather of the fusion of that repetition in the contemplating mind. A soul must be attributed to the heart, to the muscles, nerves and cells, but a contemplative soul whose entire function is to contract a habit. This is no mystical or barbarous hypothesis. On the contrary, habit here manifests its full generality: it concerns not only the sensory–motor habits that we have (psychologically), but also, before these, the primary habits that we are; the thousands of passive syntheses of which we are organically composed. It is simultaneously through contraction that we are habits, but through contemplation that we contract. We are contemplations, we are imaginations, we are generalities, claims and satisfactions. The phenomenon of claiming is nothing but the contracting contemplation through which we affirm our right and our expectation in regard to that which we contract, along with our self-satisfaction in so far as we contemplate. We do not contemplate ourselves, but we exist only in contemplating – that is to say, in contracting that from which we come. Whether pleasure is itself a contraction or a tension, or whether it is always tied to a process of relaxation, is not a well-formed question: elements of pleasure may be found in the active succession of relaxations and contractions produced by excitants, but it is a quite different question to ask why pleasure is not simply an element or a case within our psychic life, but rather a *principle* which exercises sovereign rule over the latter in every case. Pleasure is a principle in so far as it is the emotion of a fulfilling contemplation which contracts in itself cases of relaxation *and* contraction. There is a beatitude associated with passive synthesis, and we are all Narcissus in virtue of the pleasure (auto-satisfaction) we experience in contemplating, even though we contemplate things quite apart from ourselves. We are always Actaeon by virtue of what we contemplate, even though we are Narcissus in relation to the pleasure we take from it. To contemplate is to draw something from. We must always first contemplate something else – the water, or Diana, or the woods – in order to be filled with an image of ourselves.

No one has shown better than Samuel Butler that there is no continuity apart from that of habit, and that we have no other continuities apart from those of our thousands of component habits, which form within us so many superstitious and contemplative selves, so many claimants and satisfactions: 'for even the corn in the fields grows upon a superstitious basis as to its own existence, and only turns the earth and moisture into wheat through the conceit of its own ability to do so, without which faith it were powerless ...'.[2] Only an empiricist can happily risk such formulae. What we call wheat is a contraction of the earth and humidity, and this contraction is both a contemplation and the auto-satisfaction of that contemplation. By its existence alone, the lily of the field sings the glory of the heavens, the goddesses and gods – in other words, the elements that it contemplates in contracting. What organism is not made of elements and cases of repetition, of contemplated and contracted water, nitrogen, carbon, chlorides and sulphates, thereby intertwining all the habits of which it is composed? Organisms awake to the sublime words of the third *Ennead*: all is contemplation! Perhaps it is irony to say that everything is contemplation, even rocks and woods, animals and men, even Actaeon and the stag, Narcissus and the flower, even our actions and our needs. But irony in turn is still a contemplation, nothing but a contemplation. ... Plotinus says that one determines one's own image, and appreciates it, only by turning back to contemplate that from which one comes.

It is easy to multiply reasons which make habit independent of repetition: to act is never to repeat, whether it be an action in process or an action already completed. As we have seen, action has, rather, the particular as its variable and generality as its element. However, while generality may well be quite different from repetition, it nevertheless refers to repetition as the hidden basis on which it is constructed. Action is constituted, in the order of generality and in the field of variables which correspond to it, only by the contraction of elements of repetition. This contraction, however, takes place not in the action itself, but in a contemplative self which doubles the agent. Moreover, in order to integrate actions within a more complex action, the primary actions must in turn play the role of elements of repetition within a 'case', but always in relation to a contemplative soul adjacent to the subject of the compound action. Underneath the self which acts are little selves which contemplate and which render possible both the action and the active subject. We speak of our 'self' only in virtue of these thousands of little witnesses which contemplate within us: it is always a third party who says 'me'. These contemplative souls must be assigned even to the rat in the labyrinth and to each muscle of the rat. Given that contemplation never appears at any moment during the action – since it is always hidden, and since it 'does' nothing (even though something is done through it, something completely novel) – it is easy to forget it and to interpret the entire process of excitation and reaction without any reference to repetition – the more so since this reference appears only in the relation in which both excitations and reactions stand to the contemplative souls.

The role of the imagination, or the mind which contemplates in its multiple and fragmented states, is to draw something new from repetition, to draw difference from it. For that matter, repetition is itself in essence imaginary, since the imagination alone here forms the 'moment' of the *vis repetitiva* from the point of view of constitution: it makes that which it contracts appear as elements or cases of repetition. Imaginary repetition is not a false repetition which stands in for the absent true repetition: true repetition takes place in imagination. Between a repetition which never ceases to unravel itself and a repetition which is deployed and conserved for us in the space of representation there was difference, the for-itself of repetition, the imaginary. Difference inhabits repetition. On the one hand – lengthwise, as it were – difference allows us to pass from one order of repetition to another: from the instantaneous repetition which unravels itself to the actively represented repetition through the intermediary of passive synthesis. On the other hand – in depth, as it were – difference allows us to pass from one order of repetition to another and from one generality to another within the passive syntheses themselves. The nods of the chicken's head accompany its cardiac pulsations in an organic synthesis before they serve as pecks in the perceptual synthesis with grain. And already in the series of passive syntheses, the generality originally formed by the contraction of 'ticks' is redistributed in the form of particularities in the more complex repetition of 'tick-tocks', which are in turn contracted. In every way, material or bare repetition, so-called repetition of the same, is like a skin which unravels, the external husk of a kernel of difference and more complicated internal repetitions. *Difference lies between two repetitions*. Is this not also to say, conversely, that repetition lies between two differences, that it allows us to pass from one order of difference to another? Gabriel Tarde described dialectical development in this manner: a process of repetition understood as the passage from a state of general differences to singular difference, from external differences to internal difference – in short, repetition as the differenciator of difference.[3]

The synthesis of time constitutes the present in time. It is not that the present is a dimension of time: the present alone exists. Rather, synthesis constitutes time as a living present, and the past and the future as dimensions of this present. This synthesis is none the less intratemporal, which means that this present passes. We could no doubt conceive of a perpetual present, a present which is coextensive with time: it would be sufficient to consider contemplation applied to the infinite succession of instants. But such a present is not physically possible: the contraction implied in any contemplation always qualifies an order of repetition according to the elements or cases involved. It necessarily forms a present which may be exhausted and which passes, a present of a certain duration which varies according to the species, the individuals, the organisms and the parts of organisms under consideration. Two successive presents may be contemporaneous with a third present, more extended by virtue of the number of instants it contracts. The duration of an organism's present, or of its various presents, will vary according to the natural contractile range of its contemplative souls. In other words, fatigue is a real component of contemplation. It is correctly said that those who do nothing tire themselves most. Fatigue marks the point at which the soul can no longer contract what it contemplates, the moment at which contemplation and contraction come apart. We are made up of fatigues as much as of contemplations. That is why a phenomenon such as need can be understood in terms of 'lack', from the point of view of action and the active syntheses which it determines, but as an extreme 'satiety' or 'fatigue' from the point of view of the passive synthesis by which it is conditioned. More precisely, need marks the limits of the variable present. The present extends between two eruptions of need, and coincides with the duration of a contemplation. The *repetition of need*, and of everything which depends upon it, expresses the time which belongs to the synthesis of time, the intratemporal character of that synthesis. Repetition is essentially inscribed in need, since need rests upon an instance which essentially involves repetition: which forms the for-itself of repetition and the for-itself of a certain duration. All our rhythms, our reserves, our reaction times, the thousand intertwinings, the presents and fatigues of which we are composed, are defined on the basis of our contemplations. The rule is that one cannot go faster than one's own present – or rather, one's presents. *Signs* as we have defined them – as habitudes or contractions referring to one another – always belong to the present. One of the great strengths of Stoicism lies in having shown that every sign is a sign of the present, from the point of view of the passive synthesis in which past and future are precisely only dimensions of the present itself. A scar is the sign not of a past wound but of 'the present fact of having been wounded': we can say that it is the contemplation of the wound, that it contracts all the instants which separate us from it into a living present. Or rather, that we find here the true meaning of the distinction between natural and artificial: natural signs are signs founded upon passive synthesis; they are signs of the present, referring to the present in which they signify. Artificial signs, by contrast, are those which refer to the past or the future as distinct dimensions of the present, dimensions on which the present might in turn depend. Artificial signs imply active syntheses – that is to say, the passage from spontaneous imagination to the active faculties of reflective representation, memory and intelligence.

Need itself is therefore very imperfectly understood in terms of negative structures which relate it to activity. It is not even enough to invoke activity in the process of occurring or taking place, so long as the contemplative base on which it occurs has not been determined. Here again, with regard to this base, we cannot avoid seeing in the negative (need as lack) the shadow of a higher instance. Need expresses the openness of a question before it expresses the non-being or the absence of a response. To contemplate is to question. Is it not the peculiarity of questions to 'draw' a response? Questions present at once both the stubbornness or obstinacy and the lassitude or fatigue which correspond to need. 'What difference is there...?' This is the question the contemplative soul puts to repetition, and to which it draws a response from repetition. Contemplations are questions, while the contractions which occur in them and complete them are so many finite affirmations produced in the same way as presents are produced out of the perpetual present by means of the passive synthesis of time. Conceptions of the negative come from our haste to understand need in relation to active syntheses, which in fact are elaborated only on this basis. Moreover, if we reconsider the active syntheses themselves in the light of this basis which they presuppose, we see that they signify rather the constitution of problematic fields in relation to questions. The whole domain of behaviour, the intertwining of artificial and natural signs, the intervention of instinct and learning, memory and intelligence, shows how the questions involved in contemplation are developed in the form of active problematic fields. To the first synthesis of time there corresponds a first question–problem complex as this appears in the living present (the urgency of life). This living present, and with it the whole of organic and psychic life, rests upon habit. Following Condillac, we must regard habit as the foundation from which all other psychic phenomena derive. All these other phenomena either rest upon contemplations or are themselves contemplations: even need, even questions, even 'irony'.

These thousands of habits of which we are composed – these contractions, contemplations, pretensions, presumptions, satisfactions, fatigues; these variable presents – thus form the basic domain of passive syntheses. The passive self is not defined simply by receptivity – that is, by means of the capacity to experience sensations – but by virtue of the contractile contemplation which constitutes the organism itself before it constitutes the sensations. This self, therefore, is by no means simple: it is not enough to relativise or pluralise the self, all the while retaining for it a simple attenuated form. Selves are larval subjects; the world of passive syntheses constitutes the system of the self, under conditions yet to be determined, but it is the system of a dissolved self. There is a self wherever a furtive contemplation has been established, whenever a contracting machine capable of drawing a difference from repetition functions somewhere. The self does not undergo modifications, it is itself a modification – this term designating precisely the difference drawn. Finally, one is only what one *has*: here, being is formed or the passive self *is*, by having. Every contraction is a presumption, a claim – that is to say, it gives rise to an expectation or a right in regard to that which it contracts, and comes undone once its object escapes. In all his novels, Samuel Beckett has traced the inventory of peculiarities pursued with fatigue and passion by larval subjects: Molloy's series of stones, Murphy's biscuits, Malone's possessions – it is always a question of drawing a small difference, a weak generality, from the repetition of elements or the organisation of cases. It is undoubtedly one of the more profound intentions of the 'new novel' to rediscover, below the level of active syntheses, the domain of passive syntheses which constitute us, the domain of modifications, tropisms and little peculiarities. In all its component fatigues, in all its mediocre auto-satisfactions, in all its derisory presumptions, in its misery and its poverty, the dissolved self still sings the glory of God – that is, of that which it contemplates, contracts and possesses.

Although it is originary, the first synthesis of time is no less intratemporal. It constitutes time as a present, but a present which passes. Time does not escape the present, but the present does not stop moving by leaps and bounds which encroach upon one another. This is the paradox of the present: to constitute time while passing in the time constituted. We cannot avoid the necessary conclusion – *that there must be another time in which the first synthesis of time can occur*. This refers us to a second synthesis. By insisting upon the finitude of contraction, we have shown the effect; we have by no means shown why the present passes, or what prevents it from being coextensive with time. The first synthesis, that of habit, is truly the foundation of time; but we must distinguish the foundation from the ground. The foundation concerns the soil: it shows how something is established upon this soil, how it occupies and possesses it; whereas the ground comes rather from the sky, it goes from the summit to the foundations, and measures the possessor and the soil against one another according to a title of ownership. Habit is the foundation of time, the moving soil occupied by the passing present. The claim of the present is precisely that it passes. However, it is what causes the present to pass, that to which the present and habit belong, which must be considered the ground of time. It is memory that grounds time. We have seen how memory, as a derived active synthesis, depended upon habit: in effect, everything depends upon a foundation. But this does not tell us what constitutes memory. At the moment when it grounds itself upon habit, memory must be grounded by another passive synthesis distinct from that of habit. The passive synthesis of habit in turn refers to this more profound passive synthesis of memory:

Habitus and Mnemosyne, the alliance of the sky and the ground. Habit is the originary synthesis of time, which constitutes the life of the passing present; Memory is the fundamental synthesis of time which constitutes the being of the past (that which causes the present to pass).

At first sight, it is as if the past were trapped between two presents: the one which it has been and the one in relation to which it is past. The past is not the former present itself but the element in which we focus upon the latter. Particularity, therefore, now belongs to that on which we focus – in other words, to that which 'has been'; whereas the past itself, the 'was', is by nature general. The past in general is the element in which each former present is focused upon in particular and as a particular. In accordance with Husserlian terminology, we must distinguish between retention and reproduction. However, what we earlier called the retention of habit was the state of successive instants contracted in a present present of a certain duration. These instants formed a particularity – in other words, an immediate past naturally belonging to the present present, while the present itself, which remains open to the future in the form of expectation, constitutes the general. By contrast, from the point of view of the reproduction involved in memory, it is the past (understood as the mediation of presents) which becomes general while the (present as well as former) present becomes particular. To the degree to which the past in general is the element in which each former present preserves itself and may be focused upon, the former present finds itself 'represented' in the present one. The limits of this representation or reproduction are in fact determined by the variable relations of resemblance and contiguity known as forms of association. In order to be represented the former present must resemble the present one, and must be broken up into partially simultaneous presents with very different durations which are then contiguous with one another and, even at the limit, contiguous with the present present. The great strength of associationism lies in having founded a whole theory of artificial signs on these relations of association.

Now the former present cannot be represented in the present one without the present one itself being represented in that representation. It is of the essence of representation not only to represent something but to represent its own representativity. The present and former presents are not, therefore, like two successive instants on the line of time; rather, the present one necessarily contains an extra dimension in which it represents the former and also represents itself. The present present is treated not as the future object of a memory but as that which reflects itself at the same time as it forms the memory of the former present. Active synthesis, therefore, has two correlative – albeit non-symmetrical – aspects: reproduction and reflection, remembrance and recognition, memory and understanding. It has often been pointed out that reflection implies something more than reproduction: this something more is only this supplementary dimension in which every present reflects itself as present while at the same time representing the former. 'Every conscious state requires a dimension in addition to the one of which it implies the memory.'[4] As a result, the active synthesis of memory may be regarded as the principle of representation under this double aspect: reproduction of the former present *and* reflection of the present present. This active synthesis of memory is founded upon the passive synthesis of habit, since the latter constitutes the general possibility of any present. But the two syntheses are profoundly different: the asymmetry here follows from the constant augmentation of dimensions, their infinite proliferation. The passive synthesis of habit constituted time as a *contraction* of instants with respect to a present, but the active synthesis of memory constitutes it as the *embedding* of presents themselves. The whole problem is: with respect to what? It is with respect to the pure element of the past, understood as the past in general, as an *a priori* past, that a given former present is reproducible and the present present is able to reflect itself. Far from being derived from the present or from representation, the past is presupposed by every representation. In this sense, the active synthesis of memory may well be founded upon the (empirical) passive synthesis of habit, but on the other hand it can be grounded only by another (transcendental) passive synthesis which is peculiar to memory itself. Whereas the passive synthesis of habit constitutes the living present in time and makes the past and the future two asymmetrical elements of that present, the passive synthesis of memory constitutes the pure past in time, and makes the former and the present present (thus the present in reproduction and the future in reflection) two asymmetrical elements of this past as such. However, what do we mean in speaking of the pure, *a priori* past, the past in general or as such? If *Matter and Memory* is a great book, it is perhaps because Bergson profoundly explored the domain of this transcendental synthesis of a pure past and discovered all its constitutive paradoxes.

It is futile to try to reconstitute the past from the presents between which it is trapped, either the present which it was or the one in relation to which it is now past. In effect, we are unable to believe that the past is constituted after it has been present, or because a new present appears. If a new present were required for the past to be constituted as past, then the former present would never pass and the new one would never arrive. No present would ever pass were it not past 'at the same time' as it is present; no past would ever be constituted unless it were first constituted 'at the same time' as it was present. This is the first paradox: the contemporaneity of the past with the present that it *was*. It gives us the reason for the passing of the present. Every present passes, in favour of a new present, because the past is contemporaneous with itself as present. A second paradox emerges: the paradox of coexistence. If each past is contemporaneous with the present that it was, then *all* of the past coexists with the new present in relation to which it is now past. The past is no more 'in' this second present than it is 'after' the first – whence the Bergsonian idea that each present present is only the entire past in its most contracted state. The past does not cause one present to pass without calling forth another, but itself neither passes nor comes forth. For this reason the past, far from being a dimension of time, is the synthesis of all time of which the present and the future are only dimensions. We cannot say that it was. It no longer exists, it does not exist, but it insists, it consists, it *is*. It insists with the former present, it consists with the new or present present. It is the in-itself of time as the final ground of the passage of time. In this sense it forms a pure, general, *a priori* element of all time. In effect, when we say that it is contemporaneous with the present that it *was*, we necessarily speak of a past which never *was* present, since it was not formed 'after'. Its manner of being contemporaneous with itself as present is that of being posed as already-there, presupposed by the passing present and causing it to pass. Its manner of coexisting with the new present is one of being posed in itself, conserving itself in itself and being presupposed by the new present which comes forth only by contracting this past. The paradox of pre-existence thus completes the other two: each past is contemporaneous with the present it was, the whole past coexists with the present in relation to which it is past, but the pure element of the past in general pre-exists the passing present.[5] There is thus a substantial temporal element (the Past which was never present) playing the role of ground. This is not itself represented. It is always the former or present present which is represented. The transcendental passive synthesis bears upon this pure past from the triple point of view of contemporaneity, coexistence and pre-existence. By contrast, the active synthesis is the representation of the present under the dual aspect of the reproduction of the former and the reflection of the new. The latter synthesis is founded upon the former, and if the new present is always endowed with a supplementary dimension, this is because it is reflected *in* the element of the pure past in general, whereas it is only *through* this element that we focus upon the former present as a particular.

If we compare the passive synthesis of habit and the passive synthesis of memory, we see how much the distribution of repetition and contraction changes from one to the other. No doubt, in either case, the present appears to be the result of a contraction, but this relates to quite different dimensions. In one case, the present is the most contracted state of successive elements or instants which are in themselves independent of one another. In the other case, the present designates the most contracted degree of an entire past, which is itself like a coexisting totality. Let us suppose, in effect, in accordance with the conditions of the second paradox, that the past is not conserved in the present in relation to which it is past, but is conserved in itself, the present present being only the maximal contraction of all this past which coexists with *it*. It must first be the case that this whole past coexists with *itself*, in varying degrees of relaxation ... and of contraction. The present can be the most contracted degree of the past which coexists with it only if the past first coexists with itself in an infinity of diverse degrees of relaxation and contraction at an infinity of levels (this is the meaning of the famous Bergsonian metaphor of the cone, the fourth paradox in relation to the past).[6] Consider what we call repetition within a life – more precisely, within a spiritual life. Presents succeed, encroaching upon one another. Nevertheless, however strong the incoherence or possible opposition between successive presents, we have the impression that each of them plays out 'the same life' at different levels. This is what we call destiny. Destiny never consists in step-by-step deterministic relations between presents which succeed one another according to the order of a represented time. Rather, it implies between successive presents non-localisable connections, actions at a distance, systems of replay, resonance and echoes, objective chances, signs, signals and roles which transcend spatial locations and temporal successions. We say of successive presents which express a destiny that they always play out the same thing, the same story, but at different levels: here more or less relaxed, there more or less contracted. This is why destiny accords so badly with determinism but so well with freedom: freedom lies in choosing the levels. The succession of present presents is only the manifestation of something more profound – namely, the manner in which each continues the whole life, but at a different level or degree to the preceding, since all levels and degrees coexist and present themselves for our choice on the basis of a past which was never present. What we call the empirical character of the presents which make us up is constituted by the relations of succession and simultaneity between them, their relations of contiguity, causality, resemblance and even opposition. What we call their noumenal character is constituted by the relations of virtual coexistence between the levels of a pure past, each present being no more than the actualisation or represention of one of these levels. In short, what we live empirically as a succession of different presents from the point of view of active synthesis is also *the ever-increasing coexistence of levels of the past within passive synthesis*. Each present contracts a level of the whole, but this level is already one of relaxation or contraction. In other words, the sign of the present is a *passage* to the limit, a maximal contraction which comes to sanction the choice of a particular level as such, which is in itself contracted or relaxed among an infinity of other possible levels. Moreover, what we say of a life may be said of several lives. Since each is a passing present, one life may replay another at a different level, as if the philosopher and the pig, the criminal and the saint, played out the same past at different levels of a gigantic cone. This is what we call metempsychosis. Each chooses his pitch or his tone, perhaps even his lyrics, but the tune remains the same, and underneath all the lyrics the same tra-la-la, in all possible tones and all pitches.

Between the two repetitions, the material and the spiritual, there is a vast difference. The former is a repetition of successive independent elements or instants; the latter is a repetition of the Whole on diverse coexisting levels (as Leibniz said, 'everything can be said to be the same at all times and places except in degrees of perfection'[7]). As a result, the two repetitions stand in very different relations to 'difference' itself. Difference is drawn from one in so far as the elements or instants are contracted within a living present. It is included in the other in so far as the Whole includes the difference between its levels. One is bare, the other clothed; one is repetition of parts, the other of the whole; one involves succession, the other coexistence; one is actual, the other virtual; one is horizontal, the other vertical. The present is always contracted difference, but in one case it contracts indifferent instants; in the other case, by passing to the limit, it contracts a differential level of the whole which is itself a matter of relaxation and contraction. In consequence, the difference between presents themselves is that between the two repetitions: that of the elementary instants from which difference is subtracted, and that of the levels of the whole in which difference is included. And following the Bergsonian hypothesis, the bare repetition must be understood as the external envelope of the clothed: that is, the repetition of successive instants must be understood as the most relaxed of the coexistent levels, matter as a dream or as mind's most relaxed past. Neither of these two repetitions is, strictly speaking, representable. Material repetition comes undone even as it occurs, and can be represented only by the active synthesis which projects its elements into a space of conservation and calculation. At the same time, however, once it has become an object of representation, this repetition is subordinated to the identity of the elements or to the resemblance of the conserved and added cases. Spiritual repetition unfolds in the being in itself of the past, whereas representation concerns and reaches only those presents which result from active synthesis, thereby subordinating all repetition, to the identity of the present present in reflection, or to the resemblance of the former present in reproduction.

The passive syntheses are obviously sub-representative. The question for us, however, is whether or not we can penetrate the passive synthesis of memory; whether we can in some sense live the being in itself of the past in the same way that we live the passive synthesis of habit. The entire past is conserved in itself, but how can we save it for ourselves, how can we penetrate that in-itself without reducing it to the former present that it was, or to the present present in relation to which it is past? How can we save it *for ourselves*? It is more or less at this point that Proust intervenes, taking up the baton from Bergson. Moreover, it seems that the response has long been known: reminiscence. In effect, this designates a passive synthesis, an involuntary memory which differs in kind from any active synthesis associated with voluntary memory. Combray reappears, not as it was or as it could be, but in a splendour which was never lived, like a pure past which finally reveals its double irreducibility to the two presents which it telescopes together: the present that it was, but also the present present which it could be. Former presents may be represented beyond forgetting by active synthesis, in so far as forgetting is empirically overcome. Here, however, it is *within* Forgetting, as though immemorial, that Combray reappears in the form of a past which was never present: the in-itself of Combray. If there is an in-itself of the past, then reminiscence is its noumenon or the thought with which it is invested. Reminiscence does not simply refer us back from a present present to former ones, from recent loves to infantile ones, from our lovers to our mothers. Here again, the relation between passing presents does not account for the pure past which, with their assistance, takes advantage of their passing in order to reappear underneath representation: beyond the lover and beyond the mother, coexistent with the one and contemporary with the other, lies the never-lived reality of the Virgin. The present exists, but the past alone insists and provides the element in which the present passes and successive presents are telescoped. The echo of the two presents forms only a persistent question, which unfolds within representation like a field of problems, with the rigorous imperative to search, to respond, to resolve. However, the response always comes from elsewhere: every reminiscence, whether of a town or a woman, is erotic. It is always Eros, the noumenon, who allows us to penetrate this pure past in itself, this virginal repetition which is Mnemosyne. He is the companion, the fiancé, of Mnemosyne. Where does he get this power? Why is the exploration of the pure past erotic? Why is it that Eros holds both the secret of questions and answers, and the secret of an insistence in all our existence? Unless we have not yet found the last word, unless there is a third synthesis of time ... .

Temporally speaking – in other words, from the point of view of the theory of time – nothing is more instructive than the difference between the Kantian and the Cartesian Cogito. It is as though Descartes's Cogito operated with two logical values: determination and undetermined existence. The determination (I think) implies an undetermined existence (I am, because 'in order to think one must exist') – and determines it precisely as the existence of a thinking subject: I think therefore I am, I am a thing which thinks. The entire Kantian critique amounts to objecting against Descartes that it is impossible for determination to bear directly upon the undetermined. The determination ('I think') obviously implies something undetermined ('I am'), but nothing so far tells us how it is that this undetermined is determinable by the '*I think*': 'in the consciousness of myself in mere thought I am the *being itself*, although nothing in myself is thereby given for thought.'[8] Kant therefore adds a third logical value: the determinable, or rather the form in which the undetermined is determinable (by the determination). This third value suffices to make logic a transcendental instance. It amounts to the discovery of Difference – no longer in the form of an empirical difference between two determinations, but in the form of a transcendental Difference between the Determination as such and what it determines; no longer in the form of an external difference which separates, but in the form of an internal Difference which establishes an *a priori* relation between thought and being. Kant's answer is well known: the form under which undetermined existence is determinable by the 'I think' is that of time ...[9] The consequences of this are extreme: my undetermined existence can be determined only *within time* as the existence of a phenomenon, of a passive, receptive phenomenal subject *appearing within time*. As a result, the spontaneity of which I am conscious in the 'I think' cannot be understood as the attribute of a substantial and spontaneous being, but only as the affection of a passive self which experiences its own thought – its own intelligence, that by virtue of which it can say *I* – being exercised in it and upon it but not by it. Here begins a long and inexhaustible story: *I* is an other, or the paradox of inner sense. The activity of thought applies to a receptive being, to a passive subject which represents that activity to itself rather than enacts it, which experiences its effect rather than initiates it, and which lives it like an Other within itself. To 'I think' and 'I am' must be added the self – that is, the passive position (what Kant calls the receptivity of intuition); to the determination and the undetermined must be added the form of the determinable, namely time. Nor is 'add' entirely the right word here, since it is rather a matter of establishing the difference and interiorising it within being and thought. It is as though the *I* were fractured from one end to the other: fractured by the pure and empty form of time. In this form it is the correlate of the passive self which appears in time. Time signifies a fault or a fracture in the *I* and a passivity in the self, and the correlation between the passive self and the fractured I constitutes the discovery of the transcendental, the element of the Copernican Revolution.

Descartes could draw his conclusion only by expelling time, by reducing the Cogito to an instant and entrusting time to the operation of continuous creation carried out by God. More generally, the supposed identity of the I has no other guarantee than the unity of God himself. For this reason, the substitution of the point of view of the 'I' for the point of view of 'God' has much less importance than is commonly supposed, so long as the former retains an identity that it owes precisely to the latter. God survives as long as the I enjoys a subsistence, a simplicity and an identity which express the entirety of its resemblance to the divine. Conversely, the death of God does not leave the identity of the I intact, but installs and interiorises within it an essential dissimilarity, a 'demarcation' in place of the mark or the seal of God. This is what Kant saw so profoundly in the *Critique of Pure Reason*, at least at one point: the manner in which the speculative death of God entails the fracture of the I, the simultaneous disappearance of rational theology and rational psychology. If the greatest initiative of transcendental philosophy was to introduce the form of time into thought as such, then this pure and empty form in turn signifies indissolubly the death of God, the fractured I and the passive self. It is true that Kant did not pursue this initiative: both God and the I underwent a practical resurrection. Even in the speculative domain, the fracture is quickly filled by a new form of identity – namely, active synthetic identity; whereas the passive self is defined only by receptivity and, as such, endowed with no power of synthesis. On the contrary, we have seen that receptivity, understood as a capacity for experiencing affections, was only a consequence, and that the passive self was more profoundly constituted by a synthesis which is itself passive (contemplation–contraction). The possibility of receiving sensations or impressions follows from this. It is impossible to maintain the Kantian distribution, which amounts to a supreme effort to save the world of representation: here, synthesis is understood as active and as giving rise to a new form of identity in the I, while passivity is understood as simple receptivity without synthesis. The Kantian initiative can be taken up, and the form of time can support both the death of God and the fractured I, but in the course of a quite different understanding of the passive self. In this sense, it is correct to claim that neither Fichte nor Hegel is the descendant of Kant – rather, it is Hölderlin, who discovers the emptiness of pure time and, in this emptiness, simultaneously the continued diversion of the divine, the prolonged fracture of the I and the constitutive passion of the self.[10] Hölderlin saw in this form of time both the essence of tragedy and the adventure of Oedipus, as though these were complementary figures of the same death instinct. Is it possible that Kantian philosophy should thus be the heir of Oedipus?

Nevertheless, is it really Kant's prestigious contribution to have introduced time into thought as such? Platonic reminiscence would seem already to have implied this. Innateness is a myth, no less so than reminiscence, but it is a myth of instantaneity, which is why it suited Descartes. When Plato expressly opposes reminiscence and innateness, he means that the latter represents only the abstract image of knowledge, whereas the real movement of learning implies a distinction within the soul between a 'before' and an 'after'; in other words, it implies the introduction of a first time, in which we forget what we knew, since there is a second time in which we recover what we have forgotten.[11] But the question is: In what form does reminiscence introduce time? Even for the soul, it is a matter of physical time, of a periodic or circular time which is that of the *Physis* and is subordinate to events which occur within it, to movements which it measures or to events which punctuate it. This time undoubtedly finds its ground in an in-itself – that is, in the pure past of the Ideas which arranges the order of presents in a circle according to their decreasing or increasing resemblances to the ideal, but also removes from the circle those souls which have been able to preserve or recover the realm of the in-itself. The Ideas none the less remain the ground on which the successive presents are organised into the circle of time, so that the pure past which defines them is itself still necessarily expressed in terms of a present, as an ancient *mythical* present. This equivocation, all the ambiguity of Mnemosyne, was already implicit in the second synthesis of time. For the latter, from the height of its pure past, surpassed and dominated the world of representation: it is the ground, the in-itself, noumenon and Form. However, it still remains relative to the representation that it grounds. It elevates the principles of representation – namely, identity, which it treats as an immemorial model, and resemblance, which it treats as a present image: the Same and the Similar. It is irreducible to the present and superior to representation, yet it serves only to render the representation of presents circular or infinite (even with Leibniz or Hegel, it is still Mnemosyne which grounds the deployment of representation in the infinite). The shortcoming of the ground is to remain relative to what it grounds, to borrow the characteristics of what it grounds, and to be proved by these. It is in this sense that it creates a circle: it introduces movement into the soul rather than time into thought. Just as the ground is in a sense 'bent' and must lead us towards a beyond, so the second synthesis of time points beyond itself in the direction of a third which denounces the illusion of the in-itself as still a correlate of representation. The in-itself of the past and the repetition in reminiscence constitute a kind of 'effect', like an optical effect, or rather the erotic effect of memory itself.

What does this mean: the empty form of time or third synthesis? The Northern Prince says 'time is out of joint'. Can it be that the Northern philosopher says the same thing: that he should be Hamletian because he is Oedipal? The joint, *cardo*, is what ensures the subordination of time to those properly cardinal points through which pass the periodic movements which it measures (time, number of the movement, for the soul as much as for the world). By contrast, time out of joint means demented time or time outside the curve which gave it a god, liberated from its overly simple circular figure, freed from the events which made up its content, its relation to movement overturned; in short, time presenting itself as an empty and pure form. Time itself unfolds (that is, apparently ceases to be a circle) instead of things unfolding within it (following the overly simple circular figure). It ceases to be cardinal and becomes ordinal, a pure *order* of time.

Hölderlin said that it no longer 'rhymed', because it was distributed unequally on both sides of a 'caesura', as a result of which beginning and end no longer coincided. We may define the order of time as this purely formal distribution of the unequal in the function of a caesura. We can then distinguish a more or less extensive past and a future in inverse proportion, but the future and the past here are not empirical and dynamic determinations of time: they are formal and fixed characteristics which follow *a priori* from the order of time, as though they comprised a static synthesis of time. The synthesis is necessarily static, since time is no longer subordinated to movement; time is the most radical form of change, but the form of change does not change. The caesura, along with the before and after which it ordains once and for all, constitutes the fracture in the I (the caesura is exactly the point at which the fracture appears).

Having abjured its empirical content, having overturned its own ground, time is defined not only by a formal and empty order but also by a totality and a series. In the first place, the idea of a totality of time must be understood as follows: the caesura, of whatever kind, must be determined in the image of a unique and tremendous event, an act which is adequate to time as a whole. This image itself is divided, torn into two unequal parts. Nevertheless, it thereby draws together the totality of time. It must be called a symbol by virtue of the unequal parts which it subsumes and draws together, but draws together as unequal parts. Such a symbol adequate to the totality of time may be expressed in many ways: to throw time out of joint, to make the sun explode, to throw oneself into the volcano, to kill God or the father. This symbolic image constitutes the totality of time to the extent that it draws together the caesura, the before and the after. However, in so far as it carries out their distribution within inequality, it creates the possibility of a temporal series. In effect, there is always a time at which the imagined act is supposed 'too big for me'. This defines *a priori* the past or the before. It matters little whether or not the event itself occurs, or whether the act has been performed or not: past, present and future are not distributed according to this empirical criterion. Oedipus has already carried out the act, Hamlet has not yet done so, but in either case the first part of the symbol is lived in the past, they are in the past and live themselves as such so long as they experience the image of the act as too big for them. The second time, which relates to the caesura itself, is thus the present of metamorphosis, a becoming-equal to the act and a doubling of the self, and the projection of an ideal self in the image of the act (this is marked by Hamlet's sea voyage and by the outcome of Oedipus's enquiry: the hero becomes 'capable' of the act). As for the third time in which the future appears, this signifies that the event and the act possess a secret coherence which excludes that of the self; that they turn back against the self which has become their equal and smash it to pieces, as though the bearer of the new world were carried away and dispersed by the shock of the multiplicity to which it gives birth: what the self has become equal to is the unequal in itself. In this manner, the I which is fractured according to the order of time and the Self which is divided according to the temporal series correspond and find a common descendant in the man without name, without family, without qualities, without self or I, the 'plebeian' guardian of a secret, the already-Overman whose scattered members gravitate around the sublime image.

All is repetition in the temporal series, in relation to this symbolic image. The past itself is repetition by default, and it prepares this other repetition constituted by the metamorphosis in the present. Historians sometimes look for empirical correspondences between the present and the past, but however rich it may be, this network of historical correspondences involves repetition only by analogy or similitude. In truth, the past is in itself repetition, as is the present, but they are repetition in two different modes which repeat each other. Repetition is never a historical fact, but rather the historical condition under which something new is effectively produced. It is not the historian's reflection which demonstrates a resemblance between Luther and Paul, between the Revolution of 1789 and the Roman Republic, etc. Rather, it is in the first place for themselves that the revolutionaries are determined to lead their lives as 'resuscitated Romans', before becoming capable of the act which they have begun by repeating in the mode of a proper past, therefore under conditions such that they necessarily identify with a figure from the historical past. *Repetition is a condition of action before it is a concept of reflection.* We produce something new only on condition that we repeat – once in the mode which constitutes the past, and once more in the present of metamorphosis. Moreover, what is produced, the absolutely new itself, is in turn nothing but repetition: the third repetition, this time by excess, the repetition of the future as eternal return. For even though the doctrine of eternal return may be expounded as though it affected the whole series or the totality of time, the past and the present no less than the future, such an exposition remains purely introductory. It has no more than a problematic and indeterminate value, no function beyond that of posing the problem of eternal return. Eternal return, in its esoteric truth, concerns – and can concern – only the third time of the series. Only there is it determined. That is why it is properly called a belief of the future, a belief in the future. Eternal return affects only the new, what is produced under the condition of default and by the intermediary of metamorphosis. However, it causes neither the *condition* nor the *agent* to return: on the contrary, it repudiates these and expels them with all its centrifugal force. It constitutes the autonomy of the product, the independence of the work. It is repetition by excess which leaves intact nothing of the default or the becoming-equal. It is itself the new, complete novelty. It is by itself the third time in the series, the future as such. As Klossowski says, it is the secret coherence which establishes itself only by excluding my own coherence, my own identity, the identity of the self, the world and God. It allows only the plebeian to return, the man without a name. It draws into its circle the dead god and the dissolved self. It does not allow the sun to return, since it presupposes its explosion; it concerns only the nebulae, for which alone it moves and from which it becomes indistinguishable. For this reason, as Zarathustra says at one point to the demon, we simplify matters in expounding the doctrine of eternal return as though it affected the totality of time; we make a hurdy-gurdy song of it, as he says at another point to his animals. In other words, we rely upon the overly simple circle which has as its content the passing present and as its shape the past of reminiscence. However, the order of time, time as a pure and empty form, has precisely undone that circle. It has undone it in favour of a less simple and much more secret, much more tortuous, more nebulous circle, an eternally excentric circle, the decentred circle of difference which is re-formed uniquely in the third time of the series. The order of time has broken the circle of the Same and arranged time in a series only in order to re-form a circle of the Other at the end of the series. The 'once and for all' of the order is there only for the 'every time' of the final esoteric circle. The form of time is there only for the revelation of the formless in the eternal return. The extreme formality is there only for an excessive formlessness (Hölderlin's *Unförmliche*). In this manner, the ground has been superseded by a groundlessness, a universal ungrounding which turns upon itself and causes only the yet-to-come to return.

Note on the Three Repetitions

Marx's theory of historical repetition, as it appears notably in *The Eighteenth Brumaire of Louis Bonaparte*, turns on the following principle which does not seem to have been sufficiently understood by historians: historical repetition is neither a matter of analogy nor a concept produced by the reflection of historians, but above all a condition of historical action itself. Harold Rosenberg illuminates this point in some fine pages: historical actors or agents can create only on condition that they identify themselves with figures from the past. In this sense, history is theatre: 'their action became a spontaneous repetition of an old role. ... It is the revolutionary crisis, the compelled striving for "something entirely new", that causes history to become veiled in myth ...' (Harold Rosenberg, *The Tradition of the New*, London: Thames & Hudson, 1962, ch.12, 'The Resurrected Romans', pp. 155–6).

According to Marx, repetition is comic when it falls short – that is, when instead of leading to metamorphosis and the production of something new, it forms a kind of involution, the opposite of an authentic creation. Comic travesty replaces tragic metamorphosis. However, it appears that for Marx this comic or grotesque repetition necessarily comes *after* the tragic, evolutive and creative repetition ('all great events and historical personages occur, as it were, twice ... the first time as tragedy, the second as farce'). This temporal order does not, however, seem to be absolutely justified. Comic repetition works by means of some defect, in the mode of the past properly so called. The hero necessarily confronts this repetition so long as 'the act is too big for him': Polonius's murder by mistake is comic, as is Oedipus's enquiry. The moment of metamorphosis, tragic repetition, follows. It is true that these two moments are not independent, existing as they do only for the third moment beyond the comic and the tragic: the production of something new entails a dramatic repetition which excludes even the hero. However, once the first two elements acquire an abstract independence or become genres, then the comic succeeds the tragic as though the failure of metamorphosis, raised to the absolute, presupposed an earlier metamorphosis already completed.

Note that the three-stage structure of repetition is no less that of Hamlet than that of Oedipus. Hölderlin showed this with incomparable rigour in the case of Oedipus: the before, the caesura and the after. He indicated that the relative dimensions of the before and after could vary according to the position of the caesura (for example, the sudden death of Antigone by contrast with Oedipus's long wandering). The essential point, however, is the persistence of the triadic structure. In this regard, Rosenberg interprets Hamlet in a manner which conforms completely to Hölderlin's schema, the caesura being constituted by the the sea voyage: Rosenberg, *The Tradition of the New*, ch. 11, 'Character Change and the Drama', pp. 135–53. Hamlet resembles Oedipus by virtue of not only the content but also the dramatic form.

Drama has but a single form involving all three repetitions. Nietzsche's *Zarathustra* is clearly a drama, a theatrical work. The largest part of the book is taken up with the before, in the mode of a defect or of the past: this act is too big for me (compare the idea of 'criminal blame', or the whole comic story of the death of God, or Zarathustra's fear before the revelation of eternal return – 'your fruits are ripe but you are not ripe for your fruits'). Then comes the moment of the caesura or the metamorphosis, 'The Sign', when Zarathustra becomes *capable*. The third moment remains absent: this is the moment of the revelation and affirmation of eternal return, and implies the death of Zarathustra. We know that Nietzsche did not have time to write this projected part. That is why it has been constantly supposed that the Nietzschean doctrine of eternal return was never stated but reserved for a future work: Nietzsche gave us only the past condition and the present metamorphosis, but not the unconditioned which was to have resulted as the 'future'.

We rediscover, or find already, this theme of three temporal stages in most *cyclical* conceptions, such as the three Testaments of Joachim of Flora, or the three ages of Vico: the age of gods, the age of heroes and the age of men. The first is necessarily by default, and as though closed upon itself; the second is open and witness to a heroic metamorphosis; but the most important and mysterious lies in the third, which plays the role of 'signified' in relation to the other two (thus Joachim wrote: 'There are two signifying things and one signified': *L'Evangile éternel*, transl. Aegester, Paris: Editions Rieder, 1928, p. 42). Pierre Ballanche, who owes much to both Joachim and Vico together, attempts to specify this third age as that of the plebeian, of Ulysses or 'no one', 'the man without name', the regicide or the modern Oedipus who 'searches for the scattered members of the great victim' (see his strange *Essais de palingénésie sociale*, Paris: Didot, 1827).

From this point of view, we must distinguish several possible repetitions which cannot be exactly reconciled:

1. An intracyclic repetition, which involves the manner in which the first two ages repeat one another – or rather, repeat one and the same 'thing', act or event yet to come. This is above all the thesis of Joachim, who establishes a table of concordances between the Old Testament and the New; but it is a thesis which cannot go beyond simple analogies of reflection.
2. A cyclic repetition in which it is supposed that, at the end of the third age and at the end of a process of dissolution, everything recommences with the first age: here, the analogies are drawn between two cycles (Vico).
3. The problem remains: isn't there a repetition peculiar to the third age, which alone merits the name of eternal return? For the two first ages do no more than repeat something which appears for itself only in the third, but in the third this 'thing' repeats itself. The two 'significations' are already repetitive, but the signified itself is pure repetition. This superior repetition, understood as an eternal return *in* the third state, is precisely what is needed both to correct the intracyclical hypothesis and to contradict the cyclical hypothesis. In effect, on the one hand, the repetition in the first two moments no longer expresses analogies of reflection, but the conditions under which eternal return is effectively produced by means of some action or other; on the other hand, these first two moments do not return, being on the contrary eliminated by the reproduction of the eternal return in the third. From these two points of view, Nietzsche is profoundly correct to oppose 'his' conception to every cyclical conception (see Kröner, XII, part 1, para. 106).

We see, then, that in this final synthesis of time, the present and future are in turn no more than dimensions of the future: the past as condition, the present as agent. The first synthesis, that of habit, constituted time as a living present by means of a passive foundation on which past and future depended. The second synthesis, that of memory, constituted time as a pure past, from the point of view of a ground which causes the passing of one present and the arrival of another. In the third synthesis, however, the present is no more than an actor, an author, an agent destined to be effaced; while the past is no more than a condition operating by default. The synthesis of time here constitutes a future which affirms at once both the unconditioned character of the product in relation to the conditions of its production, and the independence of the work in relation to its author or actor. In all three syntheses, present, past and future are revealed as Repetition, but in very different modes. The present is the repeater, the past is repetition itself, but the future is that which is repeated. Furthermore, the secret of repetition as a whole lies in that which is repeated, in that which is twice signified. The future, which subordinates the other two to itself and strips them of their autonomy, is the royal repetition. The first synthesis concerns only the content and the foundation of time; the second, its ground; but beyond these, the third ensures the order, the totality of the series and the final end of time. A philosophy of repetition must pass through all these 'stages', condemned to repeat repetition itself. However, by traversing these stages it ensures its programme of making repetition the category of the future: making use of the repetition of habit and that of memory, but making use of them as stages and leaving them in its wake; struggling on the one hand against Habitus, on the other against Mnemosyne; refusing the content of a repetition which is more or less able to 'draw off' difference (Habitus); refusing the form of a repetition which includes difference, but in order once again to subordinate it to the Same and the Similar (Mnemosyne); refusing the overly simple cycles, the one followed by a habitual present (customary cycle) as much as the one described by a pure past (memorial or immemorial cycle); changing the ground of memory into a simple condition by default, but also the foundation of habit into a failure of 'habitus', a metamorphosis of the agent; expelling the agent and the condition in the name of the work or product; making repetition, not that from which one 'draws off' a difference, nor that which includes difference as a variant, but making it the thought and the production of the 'absolutely different'; making it so that repetition is, for itself, difference in itself.

The majority of these points stimulated a research programme which was both Protestant and Catholic: that of Kierkegaard and Péguy. No one opposed his 'own' repetition to that of habit and that of memory more than these two authors. No one more ably denounced the inadequacy of a past or present repetition, the simplicity of cycles, the trap of reminiscences, the status of differences that one was supposed to 'draw' from repetition – or, on the contrary, understand as simple variants. No one appealed to repetition as the category of the future more than these two. No one more surely rejected the ancient ground, Mnemosyne, and with it Platonic reminiscence. The ground is no more than a condition by default, one lost in sin which must be recovered in Christ. The present foundation of Habitus is no less rejected: it does not escape the metamorphosis of the actor or the agent in the modern world, in which he may well lose his coherence, his life, his habits.[12]

However, although Kierkegaard and Péguy may be the great repeaters, they were not ready to pay the necessary price. They entrusted this supreme repetition, repetition as a category of the future, to faith. Undoubtedly, faith possesses sufficient force to undo habit and reminiscence, and with them the habitual self and the god of reminiscences, as well as the foundation and the ground of time. However, faith invites us to rediscover *once and for all* God and the self in a common resurrection. Kierkegaard and Péguy are the culmination of Kant, they realise Kantianism by entrusting to faith the task of overcoming the speculative death of God and healing the wound in the self. This is their problem, from Abraham to Joan of Arc: the betrothal of a self rediscovered and a god recovered, in such a manner that it is no longer possible truly to escape from either the condition or the agent. Even further: habit is renovated and memory is refreshed. However, there is an adventure of faith, according to which one is always the clown of one's own faith, the comedian of one's ideal. For faith has its own Cogito which in turn conditions the sentiment of grace, like an interior light. Moreover, it is in this very particular Cogito that faith reflects upon itself and discovers by experiment that its condition can be given to it only as 'recovered', and that it is not only separated from that condition but doubled in it. Hence the believer does not lead his life only as a tragic sinner in so far as he is deprived of the condition, but as a comedian and clown, a simulacrum of himself in so far as he is doubled in the condition. Two believers cannot observe each other without laughing. Grace excludes no less when it is given than when it is lacking. Indeed, Kierkegaard said that he was a poet of the faith rather than a knight – in short, a 'humorist'. This was not his fault but that of the concept of faith; and Gogol's terrible adventure is perhaps more exemplary still. How could faith not be its own habit and its own reminiscence, and how could the repetition it takes for its object – a repetition which, paradoxically, takes place *once and for all* – not be comical? Beneath it rumbles another, Nietzschean, repetition: that of eternal return. Here, a different and more mortuary betrothal between the dead God and the dissolved self forms the true condition by default and the true metamorphosis of the agent, both of which disappear in the unconditioned character of the product. Eternal return is not a faith, but the truth of faith: it has isolated the double or the simulacrum, it has liberated the comic in order to make this an element of the superhuman. That is why – again as Klossowski says – it is not a doctrine but the simulacrum of every doctrine (the highest irony); it is not a belief but the parody of every belief (the highest humour): a belief and a doctrine eternally yet to come. We have too often been invited to judge the atheist from the viewpoint of the belief or the faith that we suppose still drives him – in short, from the viewpoint of grace; not to be tempted by the inverse operation – to judge the believer by the violent atheist by which he is inhabited, the Antichrist eternally given 'once and for all' within grace.

Biopsychical life implies a field of individuation in which differences in intensity are distributed here and there in the form of excitations. The quantitative and qualitative process of the resolution of such differences is what we call pleasure. A totality of this kind – a mobile distribution of differences and local resolutions within an intensive field – corresponds to what Freud called the Id, or at least the primary layer of the Id. The word 'id' [*Ça*] in this sense is not only a pronoun referring to some formidable unknown, but also an adverb referring to a mobile place, a 'here and there' [*Ça et là*] of excitations and resolutions. It is here that Freud's problem begins: it is a question of knowing how pleasure ceases to be a process in order to become a principle, how it ceases to be a local process in order to assume the value of an empirical principle which tends to organise biopsychical life in the Id. Obviously pleasure is pleasing, but this is not a reason for its assuming a systematic value according to which it is what we seek 'in principle'. This is the primary concern of *Beyond the Pleasure Principle*: not the exceptions to this principle, but rather the determination of the conditions under which pleasure effectively becomes a principle. The Freudian answer is that excitation in the form of free difference must, in some sense, be 'invested', 'tied' or bound in such a manner that its resolution becomes systematically possible. This binding or investment of difference is what makes possible in general, not pleasure itself, but the value taken on by pleasure as a principle: we thereby pass from a state of scattered resolution to a state of integration, which constitutes the second layer of the Id and the beginnings of an organisation.

This binding is a genuine reproductive synthesis, a Habitus. An animal forms an eye for itself by causing scattered and diffuse luminous excitations to be reproduced on a privileged surface of its body. The eye binds light, it is itself a bound light. This example is enough to show the complexity of synthesis. For there is indeed an activity of reproduction which takes as its object the difference to be bound; but there is more profoundly a passion of repetition, from which emerges a new difference (the formed eye or the seeing subject). Excitation as a difference was *already* the contraction of an elementary repetition. To the extent that the excitation becomes in turn the element of a repetition, the contracting synthesis is raised to a second power, one precisely represented by this binding or investment.

Investments, bindings or integrations are passive syntheses or contemplations–contractions in the second degree. Drives are nothing more than bound excitations. At the level of each binding, an ego is formed in the Id; a passive, partial, larval, contemplative and contracting ego. The Id is populated by local egos which constitute the time peculiar to the Id, the time of the living present there where the binding integrations are carried out. The fact that these egos should be immediately narcissistic is readily explained if we consider narcissism to be not a contemplation of oneself but the fulfilment of a self-image through the contemplation of something else: the eye or the seeing ego is filled with an image of itself in contemplating the excitation that it binds. It produces itself or 'draws itself' from what it contemplates (and from what it contracts and invests by contemplation). This is why the satisfaction which flows from binding is necessarily a 'hallucinatory' satisfaction of the ego itself, even though hallucination here in no way contradicts the effectivity of the binding. In all these senses, binding represents a pure passive synthesis, a Habitus which confers on pleasure the value of being a principle of satisfaction in general. Habit underlies the organisation of the Id.

The problem of habit is therefore badly framed so long as it is subordinated to pleasure. On the one hand, the repetition involved in habit is supposed to be explained by the desire to reproduce a pleasure obtained; on the other hand, it is supposed to concern tensions which are disagreeable in themselves, but may be mastered with a view to obtaining pleasure. Clearly, both hypotheses already presuppose the pleasure principle: the *idea* of pleasure obtained and the *idea* of pleasure to be obtained act only under this principle to form the two applications, past and future. On the contrary, habit, in the form of a passive binding synthesis, precedes the pleasure principle and renders it possible. The idea of pleasure follows from it in the same way that, as we have seen, past and future follow from the synthesis of the living present. The effect of binding is to install the pleasure principle; it cannot have as its object something which presupposes that principle. When pleasure acquires the dignity of a principle, then and only then does the idea of pleasure act in accordance with that principle, in memory or in projects. Pleasure then exceeds its own instantaneity in order to assume the allure of satisfaction in general (the attempts to substitute 'objective' concepts for the instance of pleasure considered too subjective, such as those of achievement or success, only bear witness to this extension conferred by the principle, here under conditions such that the idea of pleasure is merely transposed into the mind of the experimenter). Occasionally we may empirically experience repetition as subordinated to a pleasure obtained or to be obtained, but in the order of conditions the relation is reversed. Binding synthesis cannot be explained by the intention or the effort to *master* an excitation, even though it may have that effect.[13] Once again, we must beware of confusing the activity of reproduction with the passion for repetition which underlies it. The repetition of an excitation has as its true object the elevation of the passive synthesis to a power which implies the pleasure principle along with its future and past applications. Repetition in habit or the passive synthesis of binding is thus 'beyond' the principle.

This first beyond already constitutes a kind of Transcendental Aesthetic. If this aesthetic appears more profound to us than that of Kant, it is for the following reasons: Kant defines the passive self in terms of simple receptivity, thereby assuming sensations already formed, then merely relating these to the *a priori* forms of their representation which are determined as space and time. In this manner, not only does he unify the passive self by ruling out the possibility of composing space step by step, not only does he deprive this passive self of all power of synthesis (synthesis being reserved for activity), but moreover he cuts the Aesthetic into two parts: the objective element of sensation guaranteed by space and the subjective element which is incarnate in pleasure and pain. The aim of the preceding analyses, on the contrary, has been to show that receptivity must be defined in terms of the formation of local selves or egos, in terms of the passive syntheses of contemplation or contraction, thereby accounting simultaneously for the possibility of experiencing sensations, the power of reproducing them and the value that pleasure assumes as a principle.

On the basis of passive synthesis, however, a twofold development appears, in two very different directions. On the one hand, an active synthesis is established upon the foundation of the passive syntheses: this consists in relating the bound excitation to an object supposed to be both real and the end of our actions (synthesis of recognition, supported by the passive synthesis of reproduction). Active synthesis is defined by the test of reality in an 'objectal' relation, and it is precisely according to the reality principle that the Ego tends to 'be activated', to be actively unified, to unite all its small composing and contemplative passive egos, and to be topologically distinguished from the Id. The passive egos were already integrations, but only local integrations, as mathematicians say; whereas the active self is an attempt at global integration. It would be completely wrong to consider the positing of reality to be an effect induced by the external world, or even the result of failures encountered by passive syntheses. On the contrary, the test of reality mobilises, drives and inspires all the activity of the ego: not so much in the form of a negative judgement, but in moving beyond the binding in the direction of a 'substantive' which serves as a support for the connection. It would also be wrong to suppose that the reality principle is opposed to the pleasure principle, limiting it and imposing renunciations upon it. The two principles are on the same track, even though one goes further than the other. The renunciations of immediate pleasure are already implicit in the role of principle which pleasure assumes, in the role that the idea of pleasure assumes in relation to a past and a future. A principle is not without duties. Reality and the renunciations that it inspires within us only populate the margins, they work only within the extensions acquired by the pleasure principle; and the reality principle determines an active synthesis only in so far as it is founded upon the preceding passive syntheses.

However, the real objects, the objects proposed as reality or as support for the connection, are not the only objects of the ego, any more than they exhaust the totality of so-called objectal relations. We can distinguish two simultaneous dimensions in such a way that there is no movement beyond the passive synthesis towards an active synthesis without the former also being extended in another direction, one in which it utilises the bound excitation in order to attain something else – albeit in a manner different from the reality principle – even while it remains a passive and contemplative synthesis. Moreover, it seems that active syntheses would never be erected on the basis of passive syntheses unless these persisted simultaneously, unless they did not develop on their own account at the same time, finding new formulae at once both dissymmetrical and complementary with the activity. A child who begins to walk does not only bind excitations in a passive synthesis, even supposing that these were endogenous excitations born of its own movements. No one has ever walked endogenously. On the one hand, the child goes beyond the bound excitations towards the supposition or the intentionality of an object, such as the mother, as the goal of an effort, the end to be actively reached 'in reality' and in relation to which success and failure may be measured. But *on the other hand and at the same time*, the child constructs for itself another object, a quite different kind of object which is a *virtual* object or centre and which then governs and compensates for the progresses and failures of its real activity: it puts several fingers in its mouth, wraps the other arm around this virtual centre, and appraises the whole situation from the point of view of this virtual mother. The fact that the child's glance may be directed at the real mother and that the virtual object may be the goal of an apparent activity (for example, sucking) may inspire an erroneous judgement on the part of the observer. Sucking occurs only in order to provide a virtual object to contemplate in the context of extending the passive synthesis; conversely, the real mother is contemplated only in order to provide a goal for the activity, and a criterion by which to evaluate the activity, in the context of an active synthesis. There is no need to speak of an egocentrism on the part of the child. The child who begins to handle a book by imitation, without being able to read, invariably holds it back to front. It is as though the book were being held out to the other, the real end of the activity, even though the child seizing the book back to front is the virtual centre of its passion, of its own extended contemplation. Widely diverse phenomena, such as left-handedness, mirror-writing, certain forms of stuttering, certain stereotypes, may be explained on the basis of this duality of centres in the infant world. What is important, however, is that neither one of these two centres is the ego. The same lack of understanding leads to the interpretation of the child's behaviour as stemming from a supposed 'egocentrism' and to the interpretation of infantile narcissism as excluding the contemplation of other things. In fact the child is constructed within a double series: on the basis of the passive synthesis of connection and on the basis of the bound excitations. Both series are objectal: one series comprises real objects which serve as correlates of active synthesis; the other virtual objects which serve as correlates of an extension of passive synthesis. The extended passive ego fulfils itself with a narcissistic image in contemplating the virtual centres. One series would not exist without the other, yet they do not resemble one another. For this reason, Henri Maldiney is correct to say, in analysing children's movement, that the infantile world is in no way circular or egocentric but elliptical; that it has two centres and that these differ in kind, both nevertheless being objective or objectal.[14] In virtue of their dissimilarity, perhaps a crossing, a twist, a helix or a figure 8 is even formed between the two centres. What, then, would be the ego, where would it be, given its topological distinction from the Id, if not at the crossing of the 8, at the point of connection between these two intersecting asymmetrical circles, the circle of real objects and that of the virtual objects or centres?

The differenciation between self-preservative and sexual drives must be related to this duality between two correlative series. The self-preservative drives are, after all, inseparable from the constitution of the reality principle, from the foundation of active synthesis and the active global ego, and from the relations with the real object perceived as satisfying or menacing. The sexual drives are no less inseparable from the constitution of virtual centres, or the extension of passive syntheses and the passive egos which correspond to them: in pre-genital sexuality, actions are always observations or contemplations, but it is always the virtual which is contemplated or observed. The fact that the two series cannot exist without each other indicates not only that they are complementary, but that by virtue of their dissimilarity and their difference in kind they borrow from and feed into one another. We see both that the virtuals are deducted from the series of reals and that they are incorporated in the series of reals. This derivation implies, first, an isolation or suspension which freezes the real in order to extract a pose, an aspect or a part. This isolation, however, is qualitative: it does not consist simply in subtracting a part of the real object, since the subtracted part acquires a new nature in functioning as a virtual object. The virtual object is a *partial* object – not simply because it lacks a part which remains in the real, but in itself and for itself because it is cleaved or doubled into two virtual parts, one of which is always missing from the other. In short, the virtual is never subject to the global character which affects real objects. It is – not only by its origin but by its own nature – a fragment, a shred or a remainder. It lacks its own identity. The good and the bad mother – or, in terms of the paternal duality, the serious and the playful father – are not two partial objects but the same object in so far as it has lost its identity in the double. Whereas active synthesis points beyond passive synthesis towards global integrations and the supposition of identical totalisable objects, passive synthesis, as it develops, points beyond itself towards the contemplation of partial objects which remain non-totalisable. These partial or virtual objects are encountered under various names, such as Melanie Klein's good *and* bad object, the 'transitional' object, the fetish-object, and above all Lacan's object *a*. Freud definitively showed how pre-genital sexuality consisted of partial drives deducted from the exercise of self-preservative drives; such a derivation presupposes the constitution of objects which are themselves partial and which function as so many virtual centres, so many poles always doubled with sexuality.

Conversely, these virtual objects are incorporated in the real objects. In this sense they can correspond to parts of the subject's body, to another person, or even to very special objects such as toys or fetishes. This incorporation is in no way an identification, or even an introjection, since it exceeds the limits of the subject. Far from opposing itself to the process of isolation, it complements it. Whatever the reality in which the virtual object is incorporated, it does not become integrated: it remains planted or stuck there, and does not find in the real object the half which completes it, but rather testifies to the other virtual half which the real continues to lack. When Melanie Klein shows how many virtual objects the maternal body contains, it must not be thought that it totalises or englobes them, or possesses them, but rather that they are planted in it like trees from another world, like Gogol's nose or Deucalion's stones. Incorporation nevertheless remains the condition under which the self-preservative drives and the active synthesis which corresponds to them can – in turn, and with their own resources – fold sexuality back on to the series of real objects and, from without, integrate it into the domain ruled by the reality principle.

Virtual objects belong essentially to the past. In *Matter and Memory*, Bergson proposed the schema of a world with two centres, one real and the other virtual, from which emanate on the one hand a series of 'perception-images', and on the other a series of 'memory-images', the two series collaborating in an endless circuit. The virtual object is not a former present, since the quality of the present and the modality of its passing here affect exclusively the series of the real as this is constituted by active synthesis. However, the pure past as it was defined above does qualify the virtual object; that is, the past as contemporaneous with its own present, as pre-existing the passing present and as that which causes the present to pass. Virtual objects are shreds of pure past. It is from the height of my contemplation of virtual centres that I am present at and preside over my passing present, along with the succession of real objects in which those centres are incorporated. The reason for this may be found in the nature of these centres. Although it is deducted from the present real object, the virtual object differs from it in kind: not only does it lack something in relation to the real object from which it is subtracted, it lacks something in itself, since it is always half of itself, the other half being different as well as absent. This absence, as we shall see, is the opposite of a negative. Eternal half of itself, it is where it is only on condition that it is not where it should be. It is where we find it only on condition that we search for it where it is not. It is at once not possessed by those who have it and had by those who do not possess it. *It is always a 'was.'* In this sense, Lacan's pages assimilating the virtual object to Edgar Allan Poe's purloined letter seem to us exemplary. Lacan shows that real objects are subjected to the law of being *or* not being somewhere, by virtue of the reality principle; whereas virtual objects, by contrast, have the property of being *and* not being where they are, wherever they go:

> what is hidden is never but what is *missing from its place*, as the call slip puts it when speaking of a volume lost in the library. And even if the book be on an adjacent shelf or in the next slot, it would be hidden there, however visibly it may appear. For it can *literally* be said that something is missing from its place only of what can change it: the symbolic. For the real, whatever upheaval we subject it to, is always in its place; it carries it glued to its heel, ignorant of what might exile it from it.[15]

The passing present which bears itself away has never been better opposed to the pure past which perpetually differs from itself and whose universal mobility and universal ubiquity cause the present to pass. The virtual object is never past in relation to a new present, any more than it is past in relation to a present which it was. It is past as the contemporary of the present which it is, in a frozen present; as though lacking on the one hand the part which, on the other hand, it is at the same time; as though displaced while still in place. This is why virtual objects exist only as fragments of themselves: they are found only as lost; they exist only as recovered. Loss or forgetting here are not determinations which must be overcome; rather, they refer to the objective nature of that which we recover, as lost, at the heart of forgetting. Contemporaneous with itself as present, being itself its own past, pre-existing every present which passes in the real series, the virtual object belongs to the pure past. It is pure fragment and fragment of itself. As in a physical experiment, however, the incorporation of this pure fragment changes the quality and causes the present to pass into the series of real objects.

This is the link between Eros and Mnemosyne. Eros tears virtual objects out of the pure past and gives them to us in order that they may be lived. Lacan discovers the 'phallus', understood as a symbolic organ, behind all these virtual or partial objects. He is able to give this extension to the concept of the phallus (such that it subsumes all the virtual objects) because the concept effectively comprises the preceding characteristics: testifying to its own absence and to itself as past, being essentially displaced in relation to itself, being found only as lost, being possessed of an always fragmentary identity which loses its identity in the double; since it may be searched for and discovered only on the side of the mother, and since it has the paradoxical property of changing its place, not being possessed by those who have a 'penis', yet being *possessed* by those who do not have one, as the theme of castration shows. The symbolic phallus signifies no less the erotic mode of the pure past than the immemorial of sexuality. The symbol is the always-displaced fragment, standing for a past which was never present: the object = x. But what is the meaning of this idea that virtual objects refer, in the last instance, to an element which is itself symbolic?

Undoubtedly, the whole psychoanalytic – or, in other words, amorous – game of repetition is at issue here. The question is whether repetition may be understood as operating from one present to another in the real series, from a present to a former present. In this case, the former present would play the role of a complex point, like an ultimate or original term which would remain in place and exercise a power of attraction: it would be the one which provides the *thing* that is to be repeated, the one which conditions the whole process of repetition, and in this sense would remain independent of it. The concepts of fixation and regression, along with trauma and the primal scene, express this first element. As a consequence, repetition would in principle conform to the model of a material, bare and brute repetition, understood as the repetition of the same: the idea of an 'automatism' in this context expresses the modality of a fixated drive, or rather, of repetition conditioned by fixation or regression. And if this material model is in fact perturbed and covered over with all kinds of disguises, with a thousand and one forms of disguise or displacement, then these are only secondary even if they are necessary: the distortion in the majority of cases does not belong to the fixation, or even to the repetition, but is added or superimposed on to these; it necessarily clothes them, but from without, and may be explained by the repression which translates the conflict (within the repetition) between the repeater and what is repeated. The three very different concepts of fixation, automatic repetition and repression testify to this distribution between a supposed last or first term in relation to repetition, a repetition which is supposed to be bare underneath the disguises which cover it, and the disguises which are necessarily added by the force of a conflict. Even – and above all – the Freudian conception of the death instinct, understood as a return to inanimate matter, remains inseparable from the positing of an ultimate term, the model of a material and bare repetition and the conflictual dualism between life and death. It matters little whether or not the former present acts in its objective reality, or rather, in the form in which it was lived or imagined. For imagination intervenes here only in order to gather up the resonances and ensure the disguises between the two presents in the series of the real as lived reality. Imagination gathers the traces of the former present and models the new present upon the old. The traditional theory of the compulsion to repeat in psychoanalysis remains essentially realist, materialist and subjective or individualist. It is realist because everything 'happens' between presents. It is materialist because the model of a brute, automatic repetition is presupposed. It is individualist, subjective, solipsistic or monadic because both the former present – in other words, the repeated or disguised element – and the new present – in other words, the present terms of the disguised repetition – are considered to be only the conscious or unconscious, latent or manifest, repressed or repressing *representations* of the subject. The whole theory of repetition is thereby subordinated to the requirements of simple representation, from the standpoint of its realism, materialism and subjectivism. Repetition is subjected to a principle of identity in the former present and a rule of resemblance in the present one. Nor do we believe that the Freudian discovery of a phylogenesis or the Jungian discovery of archetypes can correct the weaknesses of such a conception. Even if the rights of the imaginary as a whole are opposed to the facts of reality, it remains a question of a 'psychic' reality considered to be ultimate or original; even if we oppose spirit and matter, it remains a question of a bare, uncovered spirit resting upon its own identity and supported by its derived analogies; even if we oppose a collective or cosmic unconscious to the individual unconscious, the former can act only through its power to inspire representations in a solipsistic subject, whether this be the subject of a culture or a world.

The difficulties of conceptualising the process of repetition have often been emphasized. Consider the two presents, the two scenes or the two events (infantile and adult) in their reality, separated by time: how can the former present act at a distance upon the present one? How can it provide a model for it, when all its effectiveness is retrospectively received from the later present? Furthermore, if we invoke the indispensable imaginary operations required to fill the temporal space, how could these operations fail ultimately to absorb the entire reality of the two presents, leaving the repetition to subsist only as the illusion of a solipsistic subject? However, while it may seem that the two presents are successive, at a variable distance apart in the series of reals, in fact they form, rather, *two real series which coexist in relation to a virtual object of another kind*, one which constantly circulates and is displaced in them (even if the characters, the subjects which give rise to the positions, the terms and the relations of each series, remain, for their part, temporally distinct). Repetition is constituted not from one present to another, but between the two coexistent series that these presents form in function of the virtual object (object = x). It is because this object constantly circulates, always displaced in relation to itself, that it determines transformations of terms and modifications of imaginary relations within the two real series in which it appears, and therefore between the two presents. The displacement of the virtual object is not, therefore, one disguise among others, but the principle from which, in reality, repetition follows in the form of disguised repetition. Repetition is constituted only with and through the *disguises* which affect the terms and relations of the real series, but it is so because it depends upon the virtual object as an immanent instance which operates above all by *displacement*. In consequence, we cannot suppose that disguise may be explained by repression. On the contrary, it is because repetition is necessarily disguised, by virtue of the characteristic displacement of its determinant principle, that repression occurs in the form of a consequence in regard to the representation of presents. Freud, no doubt, was aware of this, since he did search for a more profound instance than that of repression, even though he conceived of it in similar terms as a so-called 'primary' repression. We do not repeat because we repress, we repress because we repeat. Moreover – which amounts to the same thing – we do not disguise because we repress, we repress because we disguise, and we disguise by virtue of the determinant centre of repetition. Repetition is no more secondary in relation to a supposed ultimate or originary fixed term than disguise is secondary in relation to repetition. For if the two presents, the former and the present one, form two series which coexist in the function of the virtual object which is displaced in them and in relation to itself, *neither of these two series can any longer be designated as the original or the derived.* They put a variety of terms and subjects into play in a complex intersubjectivity in which each subject owes its role and function in the series to the timeless position that it occupies in relation to the virtual object.[16] As for this object itself, it can no longer be treated as an ultimate or original term: this would be to assign it a fixed place and an identity repugnant to its whole nature. If it can be 'identified' with the phallus, this is only to the extent that the latter, in Lacan's terms, is always missing from its place, from its own identity and from its representation. In short, there is no ultimate term – our loves do not refer back to the mother; it is simply that the mother occupies a certain place in relation to the virtual object in the series which constitutes our present, a place which is necessarily filled by another character in the series which constitutes the present of another subjectivity, always taking into account the displacements of that object = x. In somewhat the same manner, by loving his mother the hero of *In Search of Lost Time* repeats Swann's love for

Odette. The parental characters are not the ultimate terms of individual subjecthood but the middle terms of an intersubjectivity, forms of communication and disguise from one series to another for different subjects, to the extent that these forms are determined by the displacement of the virtual object. Behind the masks, therefore, are further masks, and even the most hidden is still a hiding place, and so on to infinity. The only illusion is that of unmasking something or someone. The symbolic organ of repetition, the phallus, is no less a mask than it is itself hidden. For the mask has two senses. 'Give me, please, give me ... what then? another mask.' In the first place, the mask means the *disguise* which has an imaginary effect on the terms and relations of the two real series which properly coexist. More profoundly, however, it signifies the *displacement* which essentially affects the virtual symbolic object, both in its series and in the real series in which it endlessly circulates. (Thus, the displacement which makes the eyes of the bearer correspond with the mouth of the mask, or shows the face of the bearer only as a headless body, allowing that a head may none the less, in turn, appear upon that body.)

Repetition is thus in essence symbolic, spiritual, and intersubjective or monadological. A final consequence follows with regard to the nature of the unconscious. The phenomena of the unconscious cannot be understood in the overly simple form of opposition or conflict. For Freud, it is not only the theory of repression but the dualism in the theory of drives which encourages the primacy of a conflictual model. However, the conflicts are the result of more subtle differential mechanisms (displacements and disguises). And if the *forces* naturally enter into relations of opposition, this is on the basis of differential elements which express a more profound instance. The negative, under its double aspect of limitation and opposition, seemed to us in general secondary in relation to the instance of problems and questions: in other words, the negative expresses only within consciousness the shadow of fundamentally unconscious questions and problems, and owes its apparent power to the inevitable place of the 'false' in the natural positing of these problems and questions. It is true that the unconscious desires, and only desires. However, just as desire finds the principle of its difference from need in the virtual object, so it appears neither as a power of negation nor as an element of an opposition, but rather as a questioning, problematising and searching force which operates in a different domain than that of desire and satisfaction. Questions and problems are not speculative acts, and as such completely provisional and indicative of the momentary ignorance of an empirical subject. On the contrary, they are the living acts of the unconscious, investing special objectivities and destined to survive in the provisional and partial state characteristic of answers and solutions. The problems 'correspond' to the reciprocal disguise of the terms and relations which constitute the reality series. The questions or sources of problems correspond to the displacement of the virtual object which causes the series to develop. The phallus as virtual object is always located by enigmas and riddles in a place where it is not, because it is indistinguishable from the space in which it is displaced. Even Oedipus's conflicts depend upon the Sphinx's question. Birth and death, and the difference between the sexes, are the complex themes of problems before they are the simple terms of an opposition. (Before the opposition between the sexes, determined by the possession or lack of the penis, there is the 'question' of the phallus which determines the differential position of sexed characters in each series.) It may be that there is necessarily something mad in every question and every problem, as there is in their transcendence in relation to answers, in their insistence through solutions and the manner in which they maintain their own openness.[17]

It is enough that the question be posed with sufficient force, as it is by Dostoyevsky or Shestov, in order to quell rather than incite any response. It is here that it discovers its properly ontological import, the (non)-being of the question which cannot be reduced to the non-being of the negative. There are no ultimate or original responses or solutions, there are only problem–questions, in the guise of a mask behind every mask and a displacement behind every place. It would be naive to think that the problems of life and death, love and the difference between the sexes are amenable to their scientific solutions and positings, even though such positings and solutions necessarily arise without warning, even though they must necessarily emerge at a certain moment in the unfolding process of the development of these problems. The problems concern the eternal disguise; questions, the eternal displacement. Neuropaths and psychopaths perhaps explore this original ultimate ground, at the cost of their suffering, the former asking *how to shift the problem*, the latter *where to pose the question*. Precisely their suffering, their pathos, is the only response to a question which in itself is endlessly shifted, to a problem which in itself is endlessly disguised. It is not what they say or what they think but their life which is exemplary, and is larger than they are. They bear witness to that transcendence, and to the most extraordinary play of the true and the false which occurs not at the level of answers and solutions but at the level of the problems themselves, in the questions themselves – in other words, in conditions under which the false becomes the mode of exploration of the true, the very space of its essential disguises or its fundamental displacement: the *pseudos* here becomes the pathos of the True. The power of the questions always comes from somewhere else than the answers, and benefits from a free depth which cannot be resolved. The insistence, the transcendence and the ontological bearing of questions and problems is expressed not in the form of the finality of a sufficient reason (to what end? why?) but in the discrete form of difference and repetition: what difference is there? and 'repeat a little'. There is never any difference – not because it comes down to the same in the answer, but because it is never anywhere but in the question, and in the repetition of the question, which ensures its movement and its disguise. Problems and questions thus belong to the unconscious, but as a result the unconscious is differential and iterative by nature; it is serial, problematic and questioning. To ask whether the unconscious is ultimately oppositional or differential, an unconscious of great forces in conflict or one of little elements in series, one of opposing great representations or differenciated little perceptions, appears to resuscitate earlier hesitations and earlier polemics between the Leibnizian tradition and the Kantian tradition. However, if Freud was completely on the side of an Hegelian post-Kantianism – in other words, of an unconscious of opposition – why did he pay so much homage to the Leibnizian Fechner and to his 'symptomologist's' differential finesse? In truth, it is not at all a question of knowing whether the unconscious implies a non-being of logical limitation or a non-being of real opposition. Both these two forms of non-being are, in any case, figures of the negative. The unconscious is neither an unconscious of degradation nor an unconscious of contradiction; it involves neither limitation nor opposition; it concerns, rather, problems and questions in their difference in kind from answers–solutions: the (non)-being of the problematic which rejects equally the two forms of negative non-being which govern only propositions of consciousness. The celebrated phrase 'the unconscious knows no negative', must be taken literally. Partial objects are the elements of little perceptions. The unconscious is differential, involving little perceptions, and as such it is different in kind from consciousness. It concerns problems and questions which can never be reduced to the great oppositions or the overall effects that are felt in consciousness (we shall see that Leibnizian theory already indicated this path).

We have thus encountered a second beyond the pleasure principle, a second synthesis of time in the unconscious itself. The first passive synthesis, that of Habitus, presented repetition as a binding, in the constantly renewed form of a living present. It ensured the foundation of the pleasure principle in two complementary senses, since it led both to the general value of pleasure as an instance to which psychic life was henceforth subordinated in the Id, and to the particular hallucinatory satisfaction which filled each passive ego with a narcissistic image of itself. The second synthesis, that of Eros–Mnemosyne, posits repetition as *displacement* and *disguise*, and functions as the ground of the pleasure principle: in effect, it is then a question of knowing how this principle applies to what it governs, under what conditions of use and at the cost of what limitations and what extensions. The answer is given in two directions: one is that of a general law of reality, according to which the first synthesis points beyond itself in the direction of an active synthesis and ego; in the other direction, by contrast, the first synthesis is extended in the form of a second passive synthesis which gathers up the particular narcissistic satisfaction and relates it to the contemplation of virtual objects. The pleasure principle here receives new conditions, as much in regard to a produced reality as to a constituted sexuality. Drives, which are defined only as bound excitation, now appear in differenciated form: as self-preservative drives following the active line of reality, as sexual drives in this new passive extension. If the first passive synthesis constitutes an 'aesthetic', the second may properly be defined as the equivalent of an 'analytic'. If the first passive synthesis concerns the present, the second concerns the past. If the first makes use of repetition in order to draw off a difference, the second passive synthesis includes difference at the heart of repetition, since the two figures of difference, movement and disguise – the displacement which symbolically affects the virtual object and the disguises which affect, in imaginary fashion, the real objects in which it is incorporated – have become the elements of repetition itself. This is why Freud experienced some difficulty in distributing difference and repetition from the point of view of Eros, to the extent that he maintains the opposition between these two factors and understands repetition on the material model of cancelled difference, while defining Eros by the introduction, or even the production, of new differences.[18] In fact, Eros's force of repetition derives directly from a power of difference – one which Eros borrows from Mnemosyne, one which affects virtual objects like so many fragments of a pure past. As Janet in some ways suspected, it is not amnesia but rather a hypernesia which explains the role of erotic repetition and its combination with difference. The 'never-seen' which characterises an always displaced and disguised object is immersed in the 'already-seen' of the pure past in general, from which that object is extracted. We do not know *when* or *where* we have seen it, in accordance with the objective nature of the problematic; and ultimately, it is only the strange which is familiar and only difference which is repeated.

It is true that the synthesis of Eros and Mnemosyne still suffers from an ambiguity. In relation to the first passive synthesis of Habitus, the series of the real (or the presents which pass in the real) and the series of the virtual (or of a past which differs in kind from any present) form two divergent circular lines, two circles or even two arcs of the same circle. But in relation to the object = x taken as the immanent limit of the series of virtuals, and as the principle of the second passive synthesis, these are the successive presents of the reality which now forms coexistent series, circles or even arcs of the same circle. It is inevitable that the two references become confused, the pure past assuming thereby the status of a former present, albeit mythical, and reconstituting the illusion it was supposed to denounce, resuscitating the illusion of an original and a derived, of an identity in the origin and a resemblance in the derived. Moreover, Eros leads its life as a cycle, or as an element within a cycle, where the opposing element can only be Thanatos at the base of memory, the two combining like love and hate, construction and destruction, attraction and repulsion. Always the same ambiguity on the part of the ground: to represent itself in the circle that it imposes on what it grounds, to return as an element in the circuit of representation that it determines in principle.

The essentially lost character of virtual objects and the essentially disguised character of real objects are powerful motivations of narcissism. However, it is by interiorising the difference between the two lines and by experiencing itself as perpetually displaced in the one, perpetually disguised in the other, that the libido returns or flows back into the ego and the passive ego becomes entirely narcissistic. The narcissistic ego is inseparable not only from a constitutive wound but from the disguises and displacements which are woven from one side to the other, and constitute its modification. The ego is a mask for other masks, a disguise under other disguises. Indistinguishable from its own clowns, it walks with a limp on one green and one red leg. Nevertheless, the importance of the reorganisation which takes place at this level, in opposition to the preceding stage of the second synthesis, cannot be overstated. For while the passive ego becomes narcissistic, the activity must be *thought.* This can occur only in the form of an affection, in the form of the very modification that the narcissistic ego passively *experiences* on its own account. Thereafter, the narcissistic ego is related to the form of an I which operates upon it as an 'Other'. This active but fractured I is not only the basis of the superego but the correlate of the passive and wounded narcissistic ego, thereby forming a complex whole that Paul Ricoeur aptly named an 'aborted cogito'.[19] Moreover, there is only the aborted Cogito, only the larval subject. We saw above that the fracture of the I was no more than the pure and empty form of time, separated from its content. The narcissistic ego indeed appears in time, but does not constitute a temporal content: the narcissistic libido, the reflux of the libido into the ego, abstracts from all content. The narcissistic ego is, rather, the phenomenon which corresponds to the empty form of time without filling it, the spatial phenomenon of that form in general (it is this phenomenon of space which is presented in a different manner in neurotic castration and psychotic fragmentation). The form of time in the I determines an order, a whole and a series. The formal static order of before, during and after marks the division of the narcissistic ego in time, or the conditions of its contemplation. The whole of time is gathered in the image of the formidable action as this is simultaneously presented, forbidden and predicted by the superego: the action = x. The temporal series designates the confrontation of the divided narcissistic ego with the whole of time or the image of the action. The narcissistic ego repeats once in the form of the before or lack, in the form of the *Id* (this action is too big for me); a second time in the form of an infinite becoming-equal appropriate to the *ego ideal*; a third time in the form of the after which realises the prediction of the *superego* (the id and the ego, the condition and the agent, will themselves be annihilated)! For the practical law itself signifies nothing other than that empty form of time.

When the narcissistic ego takes the place of the virtual and real objects, when it assumes the displacement of the former and the disguise of the latter, it does not replace one content of time with another. On the contrary, we enter into the third synthesis. It is as though time had abandoned all possible mnemic content, and in so doing had broken the circle into which it was lead by Eros. It is as though it had unrolled, straightened itself and assumed the ultimate shape of the labyrinth, the straight-line labyrinth which is, as Borges says, 'invisible, incessant'. Time empty and out of joint, with its rigorous formal and static order, its crushing unity and its irreversible series, is precisely the death instinct. The death instinct does not enter into a cycle with Eros, but testifies to a completely different synthesis. It is by no means the complement or antagonist of Eros, nor in any sense symmetrical with him. The correlation between Eros and Mnemosyne is replaced by that between a narcissistic ego without memory, a great amnesiac, and a death instinct desexualised and without love. The narcissistic ego has no more than a dead body, having lost the body at the same time as the objects. It is by means of the death instinct that it is reflected in the ego ideal and has a presentiment of its end in the superego, as though in two fragments of the fractured I. It is this relation between the narcissistic ego and the death instinct that Freud indicated so profoundly in saying that there is no reflux of the libido on to the ego without it becoming *desexualised* and forming a neutral *displaceable* energy, essentially capable of serving Thanatos.[20] Why, however, did Freud thus propose a death instinct existing prior to that desexualised energy, independent of it in principle? Undoubtedly for two reasons – one relating to the persistance of a dualistic and conflictual model which inspired the entire theory of drives; the other to the material model which presided over the theory of repetition. That is why Freud insisted on the one hand on the difference in kind between Eros and Thanatos, according to which Thanatos should be addressed in his own terms in opposition to Eros; and on the other hand on a difference in rhythm or amplitude, as though Thanatos had returned to the state of inanimate matter, thereby becoming identified with that power of bare or brute repetition that the vital differences arising from Eros are supposed only to cover or contradict. In any case, determined as the qualitative and quantitative return of the living to inanimate matter, death has only an extrinsic, scientific and objective definition. Freud strangely refused any other dimension to death, any prototype or any presentation of death in the unconscious, even though he conceded the existence of such prototypes for birth and castration.[21] This reduction of death to an objective determination of matter displays the same prejudice according to which repetition must find its ultimate principle in an undifferenciated material model, beyond the displacements and disguises of a secondary or opposed difference. In truth, the structure of the unconscious is not conflictual, oppositional or contradictory, but questioning and problematising. Nor is repetition a bare and brute power behind the disguises, the latter affecting it only secondarily, like so many variations: on the contrary, it is woven from disguise and displacement, without any existence apart from these constitutive elements. Death does not appear in the objective model of an indifferent inanimate matter to which the living would 'return'; it is present in the living in the form of a subjective and differenciated experience endowed with its prototype. It is not a material state; on the contrary, having renounced all matter, it corresponds to a pure form – the empty form of time. (As a means of filling time, it makes no difference whether repetition is subordinated to the extrinsic identity of a dead matter or to the intrinsic identity of an immortal soul.) For death cannot be reduced to negation, neither to the negative of opposition nor to the negative of limitation. It is neither the limitation imposed by matter upon mortal life, nor the opposition between matter and immortal life, which furnishes death with its prototype. Death is, rather, the last form of the problematic, the source of problems and questions, the sign of their persistence over and above every response, the 'Where?' and 'When?' which designate this (non)-being where every affirmation is nourished.

Blanchot rightly suggests that death has two aspects. One is personal, concerning the I or the ego, something which I can confront in a struggle or meet at a limit, or in any case encounter in a present which causes everything to pass. The other is strangely impersonal, with no relation to 'me', neither present nor past but always coming, the source of an incessant multiple adventure in a persistent question:

> It is the fact of dying that includes a radical reversal, through which the death that was the extreme form of my power not only becomes what loosens my hold upon myself by casting me out of my power to begin and even to finish, but also becomes that which is without any relation to me, without power over me – that which is stripped of all possibility – the unreality of the indefinite. I cannot represent this reversal to myself, I cannot even conceive of it as definitive. It is not the irreversible step beyond which there would be no return, for it is that which is not accomplished, the interminable and the incessant. ... It is inevitable but inaccessible death; it is the abyss of the present, time without a present, with which I have no relationships; it is that toward which I cannot go forth, for in it *I* do not die, I have fallen from the power to die. In it *they* die; they do not cease, and they do not finish dying ... not the term, but the interminable, not proper but featureless death, and not true death but, as Kafka says, "the sneer of its capital error".[22]

In confronting these two aspects, it is apparent that even suicide does not make them coincide with one another or become equivalent. The first signifies the personal disappearance of the person, the annihilation of *this* difference represented by the I or the ego. This is a difference which existed only in order to die, and the disappearance of which can be objectively represented by a return to inanimate matter, as though calculated by a kind of entropy. Despite appearances, this death always comes from without, even at the moment when it constitutes the most personal possibility, and from the past, even at the moment when it is most present. The other death, however, the other face or aspect of death, refers to the state of free differences when they are no longer subject to the form imposed upon them by an I or an ego, when they assume a shape which excludes *my* own coherence no less than that of any identity whatsoever. There is always a 'one dies' more profound than 'I die', and it is not only the gods who die endlessly and in a variety of ways; as though there appeared worlds in which the individual was no longer imprisoned within the personal form of the I and the ego, nor the singular imprisoned within the limits of the individual – in short, the insubordinate multiple, which cannot be 'recognised' in the first aspect. The Freudian conception refers to this first aspect, and for that reason fails to discover the death instinct, along with the corresponding experience and prototype.

We see no reason to propose a death instinct which would be distinguishable from Eros, either by a difference in kind between two forces, or by a difference in rhythm or amplitude between two movements. In both cases, the difference would already be given and Thanatos would be independent as a result. It seems to us, on the contrary, that Thanatos is completely indistinguishable from the desexualisation of Eros, with the resultant formation of that neutral and displaceable energy of which Freud speaks. This energy does not serve Thanatos, it constitutes him: there is no analytic difference between Eros and Thanatos, no already given difference such that the two would be combined or made to alternate within the same 'synthesis'. It is not that the difference is any less. On the contrary, being synthetic, it is greater precisely because Thanatos stands for a synthesis of time quite unlike that of Eros; all the more exclusive because it is drawn from him, constructed upon his remains. It is all in the same movement that there is a reflux of Eros on to the ego, that the ego takes upon itself the disguises and displacements which characterise the objects in order to construct its own fatal affection, that the libido loses all mnemic content and Time loses its circular shape in order to assume a merciless and straight form, and that the death instinct appears, indistinguishable from that pure form, the desexualised energy *of* that narcissistic libido. The complementarity between the narcissistic libido and the death instinct defines the third synthesis as much as Eros and Mnemosyne defined the second. Moreover, when Freud says that perhaps the process of *thought* in general should be attached to that desexualised energy which is the correlative of the libido become narcissistic, we should understand that, contrary to the old dilemma, it is no longer a question of knowing whether thought is innate or acquired. It is neither innate nor acquired but genital – *in other words*, desexualised and drawn from that reflux which opens us on to empty time. In order to indicate this genesis of thought in an always fractured I, Artaud said: 'I am an innate genital', meaning equally thereby a 'desexualised acquisition'. It is not a question of acquiring thought, nor of exercising it as though it were innate, but of engendering the act of thinking within thought itself, perhaps under the influence of a violence which causes the reflux of libido on to the narcissistic ego, and in the same movement both extracting Thanatos from Eros and abstracting time from all content in order to separate out the pure form. There is an experience of death which corresponds to this third synthesis.

Freud supposes the unconscious to be ignorant of three important things: Death, Time and No. Yet it is a question only of time, death and no in the unconscious. Does this mean merely that they are acted [*agis*] without being represented? Furthermore, the unconscious is ignorant of no because it lives off the (non)-being of problems and questions, rather than the non-being of the negative which affects only consciousness and its representations. It is ignorant of death because every representation of death concerns its inadequate aspect, whereas the unconscious discovers and seizes upon the other side, the other face. It is ignorant of time because it is never subordinated to the empirical contents of a present which passes in representation, but rather carries out the passive syntheses of an original time. *It is these three syntheses which must be understood as constitutive of the unconscious.* They correspond to the figures of repetition which appear in the work of a great novelist: the binding, the ever renewed fine cord; the ever displaced stain on the wall; the ever erased eraser. The repetition–binding, the repetition–stain, the repetition–eraser: the three beyonds of the pleasure principle. The first synthesis expresses the foundation of time upon the basis of a living present, a foundation which endows pleasure with its value as a general empirical principle to which is subject the content of the psychic life in the Id. The second synthesis expresses the manner in which time is grounded in a pure past, a ground which conditions the application of the pleasure principle to the contents of the Ego. The third synthesis, however, refers to the absence of ground into which we are precipitated by the ground itself: Thanatos appears in third place as this groundlessness, beyond the ground of Eros and the foundation of Habitus. He therefore has a disturbing kind of relation with the pleasure principle which is often expressed in the unfathomable paradoxes of a pleasure linked to pain (when in fact it is a question of something else altogether: the desexualisation which operates in this third synthesis, in so far as it inhibits the application of the pleasure principle as the prior directive idea in order then to proceed to a resexualisation in which pleasure is invested only in a pure, cold, apathetic and frozen thought, as we see in the cases of sadism and masochism). In one sense the third synthesis unites all the dimensions of time, past, present and future, and causes them to be played out in the pure form. In another sense it involves their reorganisation, since the past is treated in function of a totality of time as the condition by default which characterises the Id, while the present is defined by the metamorphosis of the agent in the ego ideal. In a third sense, finally, the ultimate synthesis concerns only the future, since it announces in the superego the destruction of the Id and the ego, of the past as well as the present, of the condition and the agent. At this extreme point the straight line of time forms a circle again, a singularly tortuous one; or alternatively, the death instinct reveals an unconditional truth hidden in its 'other' face – namely, the eternal return in so far as this does not cause everything to come back but, on the contrary, affects a world which has rid itself of the default of the condition and the equality of the agent in order to affirm only the excessive and the unequal, the interminable and the incessant, the formless as the product of the most extreme formality. This is how the story of time ends: by undoing its too well centred natural or physical circle and forming a straight line which then, led by its own length, reconstitutes an eternally decentred circle.

The eternal return is a force of affirmation, but it affirms everything of the multiple, everything of the different, everything of chance *except* what subordinates them to the One, to the Same, to necessity, everything *except* the One, the Same and the Necessary. It is said that the One subjugated the multiple once and for all. But is this not the face of death? And does not the other face cause to die in turn, once and for all, everything which operates once and for all? If there is an essential relation between eternal return and death, it is because it promises and implies 'once and for all' the death of that which is one. If there is an essential relation with the future, it is because the future is the deployment and explication of the multiple, of the different and of the fortuitous, for themselves and 'for all times'. Repetition in the eternal return excludes two determinations: the Same or the identity of a subordinating concept, and the negative of the condition which would relate the repeated to the same, and thereby ensure the subordination. Repetition in the eternal return excludes both the becoming-equal or the becoming-similar in the concept, and being conditioned by lack of such a becoming. It concerns instead excessive systems which link the different with the different, the multiple with the multiple, the fortuitous with the fortuitous, in a complex of affirmations always coextensive with the questions posed and the decisions taken. It is claimed that man does not know how to *play*: this is because, even when he is given a situation of chance or multiplicity, he understands his affirmations as destined to impose limits upon it, his decisions as destined to ward off its effects, his reproductions as destined to bring about the return of the same, given a winning hypothesis. This is precisely a losing game, one in which we risk losing as much as winning because we do not affirm the *all* of chance: the pre-established character of the rule which fragments has as its correlate the condition by default in the player, who never knows which fragment will emerge. The system of the future, by contrast, must be called a divine game, since there is no pre-existing rule, since the game bears already upon its own rules and since the child-player can only win, all of chance being affirmed each time and for all times. Not restrictive or limiting affirmations, but affirmations coextensive with the questions posed and with the decisions from which these emanate: such a game entails the repetition of the necessarily winning move, since it wins by embracing all possible combinations and rules in the system of its own return. On this question of the game of repetition and difference as governed by the death instinct, no one has gone further than Borges, throughout his astonishing work:

> if the lottery is an intensification of chance, a periodic infusion of chaos into the cosmos, would it not be desirable for chance to intervene at all stages of the lottery and not merely in the drawing? Is it not ridiculous for chance to dictate the death of someone, while the circumstances of his death – its silent reserve or publicity, the time limit of one hour or one century – should remain immune to hazard? ... The ignorant suppose that an infinite number of drawings require an infinite amount of time; in reality, it is quite enough that time be infinitely subdivisible. ... In all fiction, when a man is faced with alternatives he chooses one at the expense of the others. In the almost unfathomable Ts'ui Pên, he chooses – simultaneously – all of them. He thus *creates* various futures, various times which start others that will in their turn branch out and bifurcate in other times. This is the cause of the contradictions in the novel. 'Fang, let us say, has a secret. A stranger knocks at his door. Fang makes up his mind to kill him. Naturally there are various possible outcomes. Fang can kill the intruder, the intruder can kill Fang, both can be saved, both can die and so on and so on. In Ts'ui Pên's work, all the possible solutions occur, each one being the point of departure for other bifurcations.'[23]

What are these systems constituted by the eternal return? Consider the two propositions: only that which is alike differs; and only differences are alike.[24] The first formula posits resemblance as the condition of difference. It therefore undoubtedly demands the possibility of an identical concept for the two things which differ on condition that they are alike; and implies an analogy in the relation each thing has to this concept; and finally leads to the reduction of the difference between them to an opposition determined by these three moments. According to the other formula, by contrast, resemblance, identity, analogy and opposition can no longer be considered anything but effects, the products of a primary difference or a primary system of differences. According to this other formula, difference must immediately relate the differing terms to one another. In accordance with Heidegger's ontological intuition, difference must be articulation and connection in itself; it must relate different to different without any mediation whatsoever by the identical, the similar, the analogous or the opposed. There must be a differenciation of difference, an in-itself which is like a *differenciator*, a *Sich-unterscheidende*, by virtue of which the different is gathered all at once rather than represented on condition of a prior resemblance, identity, analogy or opposition. As for these latter instances, since they cease to be conditions, they become no more than effects of the primary difference and its differenciation, overall or surface effects which characterise the distorted world of representation, and express the manner in which the in-itself of difference hides itself by giving rise to that which covers it. The question is whether these two formulae are simply two manners of speaking which do not change things very much, or whether they apply to completely different systems; or indeed whether, while applying to the same systems (and ultimately to the world system), they do not signify two incompatible interpretations of unequal value, one of which is capable of changing everything.

It is under the same conditions that the in-itself of difference is hidden, and that difference falls into the categories of representation. Under what other conditions does difference develop this in-itself as a 'differenciator', and gather the different outside of any possible representation? The first characteristic seems to us to be organisation in series. A system must be constituted on the basis of two or more series, each series being defined by the differences between the terms which compose it. If we suppose that the series communicate under the impulse of a force of some kind, then it is apparent that this communication relates differences to other differences, constituting differences between differences within the system. These second-degree differences play the role of the 'differenciator' – in other words, they relate the first-degree differences to one another. This state of affairs is adequately expressed by certain physical concepts: *coupling* between heterogeneous systems, from which is derived an *internal resonance* within the system, and from which in turn is derived a *forced movement* the amplitude of which exceeds that of the basic series themselves. The nature of these elements whose value is determined at once both by their difference in the series to which they belong, and by the difference of their difference from one series to another, can be determined: these are intensities, the peculiarity of intensities being to be constituted by a difference which itself refers to other differences (E-E' where E refers to *e-e*' and *e* to ε-ε' ...). The intensive character of the systems considered should not prejudice their being characterized as mechanical, physical, biological, psychic, social, aesthetic or philosophical, etc. Each type of system undoubtedly has its own particular conditions, but these conform to the preceding characteristics even while they give them a structure appropriate in each case: for example, words are genuine intensities within certain aesthetic systems; concepts are also intensities from the point of view of philosophical systems. Note, too, that according to the celebrated 1895 Freudian *Project for a Scientific Psychology*, biophysical life is presented in the form of such an intensive field in which differences determinable as excitations, and differences of differences determinable as cleared paths, are distributed. Above all, however, the syntheses of the Psyche incarnate on their own account the three dimensions of these systems in general: psychic connection (Habitus) effects a coupling of series of excitations; Eros designates the specific state of internal resonance which results; and the death instinct amounts to the forced movement whose psychic amplitude exceeds that of the resonating series themselves (whence the difference in amplitude between the death instinct and the resonating Eros).

Once communication between heterogeneous series is established, all sorts of consequences follow within the system. Something 'passes' between the borders, events explode, phenomena flash, like thunder and lightning. Spatio–temporal dynamisms fill the system, expressing simultaneously the resonance of the coupled series and the amplitude of the forced movement which exceeds them. The system is populated by subjects, both larval subjects and passive selves: passive selves because they are indistinguishable from the contemplation of couplings and resonances; larval subjects because they are the supports or the patients of the dynamisms. In effect, a pure spatio–temporal dynamism, with its necessary participation in the forced movement, can be experienced only at the borders of the livable, under conditions beyond which it would entail the death of any well-constituted subject endowed with independence and activity. Embryology already displays the truth that there are systematic vital movements, torsions and drifts, that only the embryo can sustain: an adult would be torn apart by them. There are movements for which one can only be a patient, but the patient in turn can only be a larva. Evolution does not take place in the open air, and only the involuted evolves. A nightmare is perhaps a psychic dynamism that could be sustained neither awake *nor even in dreams*, but only in profound sleep, in a dreamless sleep. In this sense, it is not even clear that thought, in so far as it constitutes the dynamism peculiar to philosophical systems, may be related to a substantial, completed and well-constituted subject, such as the Cartesian Cogito: thought is, rather, one of those terrible movements which can be sustained only under the conditions of a larval subject. These systems admit only such subjects as these, since they alone can undertake the forced movement by becoming the patient of the dynamisms which express it. Even the philosopher is a larval subject of his own system. Thus we see that these systems are not defined only by the heterogeneous series which border them, nor by the coupling, the resonance and the forced movement which constitute their dimensions, but also by the subjects which populate them and the dynamisms which fill them, and finally by the qualities and extensities which develop on the basis of such dynamisms.

The most important difficulty, however, remains: is it really difference which relates different to different in these intensive systems? Does the difference between differences relate difference to itself without any other intermediary? When we speak of communication between heterogeneous systems, of coupling and resonance, does this not imply a minimum of resemblance between the series, and an identity in the agent which brings about the communication? Would not 'too much' difference between the series render any such operation impossible? Are we not condemned to rediscover a privileged point at which difference can be understood only by virtue of a resemblance between the things which differ and the identity of a third party? Here we must pay the greatest attention to the respective roles of difference, resemblance and identity. To begin with, what is this agent, this force which ensures communication? Thunderbolts explode between different intensities, but they are preceded by an invisible, imperceptible *dark precursor*, which determines their path in advance but in reverse, as though intagliated. Likewise, every system contains its dark precursor which ensures the communication of peripheral series. As we shall see, given the variety among systems, this role is fulfilled by quite diverse determinations. The question is to know in any given case how the precursor fulfils this role. There is no doubt that *there is* an identity belonging to the precursor, and a resemblance between the series which it causes to communicate. This 'there is', however, remains perfectly indeterminate. Are identity and resemblance here the preconditions of the functioning of this dark precursor, or are they, on the contrary, its effects? If the latter, might it necessarily project upon itself the illusion of a fictive identity, and upon the series which it relates the illusion of a retrospective resemblance? Identity and resemblance would then be no more than inevitable illusions – in other words, concepts of reflection which would account for our inveterate habit of thinking difference on the basis of the categories of representation. All that, however, would be possible only because the invisible precursor conceals itself and its functioning, and at the same time conceals the in-itself or true nature of difference. Given two heterogeneous series, two series of differences, the precursor plays the part of the differenciator of these differences. In this manner, by virtue of its own power, it puts them into immediate relation to one another: it is the in-itself of difference or the 'differently different' – in other words, difference in the second degree, the self-different which relates different to different by itself. Because the path it traces is invisible and becomes visible only in reverse, to the extent that it is travelled over and covered by the phenomena it induces within the system, it has no place other than that from which it is 'missing', no identity other than that which it lacks: it is precisely the object = *x*, the one which 'is lacking in its place' as it lacks its own identity. As a result, the logical identity abstractly imputed to it by reflection, along with the physical resemblance which reflection imputes to the series which it relates, express only the statistical effect of its functioning upon the system as a whole. In other words, these express only the manner in which it conceals itself under its own effects, because of the way it perpetually *displaces* itself within itself and perpetually *disguises* itself in the series. We cannot, therefore, suppose that the identity of a third party and the resemblance of the parties in question are a condition of the being and thought of difference. These are only a condition of its representation, which expresses a distortion of that being and that thought, like an optical effect which disturbs the true, in-itself status of the condition.

We call this dark precursor, this difference in itself or difference in the second degree which relates heterogeneous systems and even completely disparate things, the *disparate*. In each case, the space in which it is displaced and its process of disguise determine a relative size of the differences brought into relation. It is well known that in certain cases (in certain systems), the difference between the differences brought into play may be 'very large'; in other systems it must be 'very small'.[25] It would be wrong, however, to see in this second case the pure expression of a prior requirement of resemblance, which would then be relaxed in the first case only by being extended to the world scale. For example, it is insisted that disparate series must necessarily be almost similar, or that the frequencies be neighbouring (w neighbour of w0) – in short, that the difference be small. If, however, the identity of the agent which causes the different things to communicate is presupposed, then there are no differences which will not be 'small', even on the world scale. We have seen that small and large apply badly to difference, because they judge it according to the criteria of the Same and the similar. If difference is related to its differenciator, and if we refrain from attributing to the differenciator an identity that it cannot and does not have, then the difference will be small or large according to its possibilities of fractionation – that is, according to the displacements and disguise of the differenciator. In no case will it be possible to claim that a small difference testifies to a strict condition of resemblance, any more than a large difference testifies to the persistence of a resemblance which is simply relaxed. Resemblance is in any case an effect, a functional product, an external result – an illusion which appears once the agent arrogates to itself an identity that it lacked. The important thing is not that the difference be small or large, and ultimately always small in relation to a greater resemblance. The important thing, for the in-itself, is that the difference, whether small or large, be internal. There are systems with large external resemblance and small internal difference. The contrary is also possible: systems with small external resemblance and large internal difference. What is impossible, however, is the contradictory: resemblance is always exterior and difference, whether small or large, forms the kernel of the system.

Take the following examples borrowed from very diverse literary systems. In the work of Raymond Roussel, we find verbal series: the role of precursor is filled by a homonym or quasi-homonym (*b*illard–*p*illard), but this dark precursor is all the less visible and noticeable to the extent that one or other of the two series remains hidden. Strange stories fill in the difference between the two series in such a manner as to induce an effect of resemblance and external identity. The precursor, however, by no means acts by virtue of its identity, whether this be a nominal or a homonymic identity: we see this clearly in the case of the quasi-homonym which functions only by becoming indistinguishable from the differential character which separates two words (*b* and *p*). Similarly, the homonym appears here not as the nominal identity of a signifier but as the differenciator of distinct signifieds which then produces secondarily an effect of resemblance between the signifieds along with an effect of identity in the signifier. It would therefore be inadequate to say that the system is grounded upon a certain negative determination – namely, the default in which words stand in relation to things and as a result of which single words are condemned to designate several things. The same illusion leads us to conceive of difference on the basis of a supposed prior resemblance and identity, and makes it appear as negative. In fact, it is not by the poverty of its vocabulary that language invents the form in which it plays the role of dark precursor, but by its excess, by its most positive syntactic and semantic power. In playing this role it differenciates the differences between the different things spoken of, relating these immediately to one another in series which it causes to resonate. For the same reason, as we have seen, the repetition of words cannot be explained negatively, cannot be presented as a bare repetition without difference. Joyce's work obviously appeals to quite different procedures. However, it remains a question of drawing together a maximum of disparate series (ultimately, all the divergent series constitutive of the cosmos) by bringing into operation linguistic dark precursors (here, esoteric words, portmanteau words) which rely upon no prior identity, which are above all not 'identifiable' in principle, but which induce a maximum of resemblance and identity into the system as a whole, as though this were the result of the process of differenciation of difference in itself (see the cosmic letter in *Finnegans Wake*). What takes place in the system between resonating series under the influence of the dark precursor is called 'epiphany'. The cosmic extension coincides with the amplitude of a forced movement which sweeps aside and overruns the series, ultimately a death instinct, Stephen's 'No' which is not the non-being of the negative but the (non)-being of a persistent question to which the cosmic 'Yes' of Mrs Bloom corresponds, without being a response, since it alone adequately occupies and fills that space.

Note on the Proustian experiences

These clearly have a quite different structure than Joyce's epiphanies. However, it is still a question of two series, that of a former present (Combray as it was lived) and that of a present present. No doubt, to remain at a first dimension of the experience, there is a resemblance between the two series (the madeleine, breakfast), and even an identity (the taste as a quality which is not only similar but self-identical across the two moments). Nevertheless, the secret does not lie there. The taste possesses a power only because it *envelops* something = x, something which can no longer be defined by an identity: it envelops Combray *as it is in itself*, as a fragment of the pure past, in its double irreducibility to the present that it has been (perception) and to the present present in which it might reappear or be reconstituted (voluntary memory). This Combray in itself is defined by its own essential difference, that 'qualitative difference' which, according to Proust, does not exist 'on the surface of the earth', but only at a particular depth. It is this difference which, by enveloping itself, produces the identity of the quality which constitutes the resemblance between the series. Identity and resemblance are therefore once again the result of a differenciator. And if the two series succeed one another, they nevertheless coexist in relation to Combray in itself as the object = x which causes them to resonate. Moreover, the resonance of the series may give rise to a death instinct which overruns them both: for example, the ankle-boot and the memory of the grandmother. Eros is constituted by the resonance, but overcomes itself in the direction of the death instinct which is constituted by the amplitude of a forced movement (this death instinct finds its glorious issue in the work of art, over and above the erotic experiences of the involuntary memory). The Proustian formula 'a little time in its pure state' refers first to the pure past, the in-itself of the past or the erotic synthesis of time, but more profoundly to the pure and empty form of time, the ultimate synthesis, that of the death instinct which leads to the eternity of the return in time.

The question of whether psychic experience is structured like a language, or even whether the physical world may be regarded as a book, depends upon the nature of the dark precursors. A linguistic precursor or an esoteric word does not have an identity by itself, not even a nominal one, any more than its significations have a resemblance, even an infinitely relaxed one: it is not just a complex word or a simple gathering of words, but a word about words which is indistinguishable from the 'differenciator' of first-degree words and from the 'dissembler' of their significations. Its value, therefore, lies not in the extent to which it claims to say something but in the extent to which it claims to state the sense of what it says. The law of language which operates within representation excludes that possibility: the sense of a word can be stated only by another word which takes the first as its object. Whence the following paradoxical situation: the linguistic precursor belongs to a kind of metalanguage and can be incarnated only within a word devoid of sense from the point of view of the series of first-degree verbal representations. It is the *refrain*. This double status of esoteric words, which state their own sense but do so only by representing it and themselves as nonsense, clearly expresses the perpetual displacement of sense and its disguise among the series. In consequence, esoteric words are properly linguistic cases of the object = *x*, while the object = *x* structures psychic experience like a language on condition that the perpetual, invisible and silent displacement of linguistic sense is taken into account. In a sense, everything speaks and has sense, on condition that speech is also that which does not speak – or rather, speech is the sense which does not speak in speech. Gombrowicz, in his fine novel *Cosmos*, shows how two series of heterogeneous differences (that of hangings and that of mouths) call forth their own communication through various signs, until the inauguration of a dark precursor (the murder of the cat) which plays the role of differenciator of their differences. This is like the sense, nevertheless incarnated in an absurd representation, but on the basis of which dynamisms will be unleashed and events produced in the Cosmos system which will culminate in a death instinct which points beyond the series.[26] In this manner, the conditions under which a book is a cosmos or the cosmos is a book appear, and through a variety of very different techniques the ultimate Joycean identity emerges, the one we find in Borges and in Gombrowicz: chaos = cosmos.

Each series tells a story: not different points of view on the same story, like the different points of view on the town we find in Leibniz, but completely distinct stories which unfold simultaneously. The basic series are divergent: not relatively, in the sense that one could retrace one's path and find a point of convergence, but absolutely divergent in the sense that the point or horizon of convergence lies in a chaos or is constantly displaced within that chaos. This chaos is itself the most positive, just as the divergence is the object of affirmation. It is indistinguishable from the great work which contains all the *complicated* series, which affirms and complicates all the series at once. (It is not surprising that Joyce should have been so interested in Bruno, the theoretician of *complicatio*.) The trinity complication–explication–implication accounts for the totality of the system – in other words, the chaos which contains all, the divergent series which lead out and back in, and the differenciator which relates them one to another. Each series explicates or develops itself, but *in* its difference from the other series which it implicates and which implicate it, which it envelops and which envelop it; *in* this chaos which complicates everything. The totality of the system, the unity of the divergent series as such, corresponds to the objectivity of a 'problem'. Hence the method of questions–problems by means of which Joyce animates his work, and before that the manner in which Lewis Carroll linked portmanteau words to the status of the problematic.

The essential point is the simultaneity and contemporaneity of all the divergent series, the fact that all coexist. From the point of view of the presents which pass in representation, the series are certainly successive, one 'before' and the other 'after'. It is from this point of view that the second is said to *resemble* the first. However, this no longer applies from the point of view of the chaos which contains them, the object = x which runs through them, the precursor which establishes communication between them or the forced movement which points beyond them: the differenciator always makes them coexist. We have encountered several times the paradox of presents which succeed one another, or series which succeed one another in reality, but coexist symbolically in relation to the pure past or the virtual object. When Freud shows that a *phantasy* is constituted on the basis of at least two series, one infantile and pre-genital, the other genital and post-pubescent, it is clear that the series succeed one another in time from the point of view of the solipsistic unconscious of the subject in question. The question then arises how to explain the phenomenon of 'delay' which is involved in the time it takes for the supposedly original infantile scene to produce its effect at a distance, in an adult scene which resembles it and which we call 'derived'.[27] It is indeed a problem of resonance between two series, but the problem is not well formulated so long as we do not take into account the instance in relation to which the two series coexist in an intersubjective unconscious. In fact the two series – one infantile, the other adult – are not distributed within the same subject. The childhood event is not one of the two real series but, rather, the dark precursor which establishes communication between the basic series, that of the adults we knew as a child and that of the adult we are among other adults and other children. So it is with the hero of *In Search of Lost Time*: his infantile love for the mother is the agent of communication between two adult series, that of Swann with Odette and that of the hero become adult with Albertine – and always the same secret in both cases, the eternal displacement, the eternal disguise of the prisoner, which thereby indicates the point at which the series coexist in the intersubjective unconscious. There is no question as to how the childhood event acts only with a delay. It *is* this delay, but this delay itself is the pure form of time in which before and after coexist. When Freud discovers that phantasy is perhaps the ultimate reality and that it implicates something which points beyond the series, we should not conclude that the childhood scene is unreal or imaginary, but rather that the empirical condition of succession in time gives way in the phantasy to the coexistence of the two series, that of the adult that we will be along with the adults that we 'have been' (compare what Ferenczi called the identification of the child with the aggressor). The phantasy is the manifestation of the child as dark precursor. Moreover, what is originary in the phantasy is not one series in relation to the other, but the difference between series in so far as this relates one series of differences to another series of differences, in abstraction from their empirical succession in time.

If it is no longer possible in the system of the unconscious to establish an order of succession between series – in other words, if all series coexist – then it is no longer possible to regard one as originary and the other as derived, one as model and the other as copy. For it is in the same movement that the series are understood as coexisting, outside any condition of succession in time, and as *different*, outside any condition under which one would enjoy the identity of a model and the other the resemblance of a copy. When two divergent stories unfold simultaneously, it is impossible to privilege one over the other: it is a case in which everything is equal, but 'everything is equal' is said of the difference, and is said only of the difference between the two. *However small* the internal difference between the two series, the one story does not reproduce the other, one does not serve as model for the other: rather, resemblance and identity are only functional effects of that difference which alone is originary within the system. It is therefore proper to say that the system excludes the assignation of an originary and a derived as though these were a first and second occurrence, because the sole origin is difference, and it causes the differents which it relates to other differents to coexist independently of any resemblance.[28] It is under this aspect, without doubt, that the eternal return is revealed as the groundless 'law' of this system. The eternal return does not cause the same and the similar to return, but is itself derived from a world of pure difference. Each series returns, not only in the others which imply it, but for itself, since it is not implied by the others without being in turn fully restored as that which implies them. The eternal return has no other sense but this: the absence of any assignable origin – in other words, the assignation of difference as the origin, which then relates different to different in order to make it (or them) return as such. In this sense, the eternal return is indeed the consequence of a difference which is originary, pure, synthetic and in-itself (which Nietzsche called will to power). If difference is the in-itself, then repetition in the eternal return is the for-itself of difference. Yet how can it be denied that the eternal return is inseparable from the Same? Is it not itself the eternal return *of* the Same? However, we must be aware of the (at least three) different senses of the terms 'the same', 'the identical' and 'the similar'.

In the first sense, the Same designates a supposed subject of the eternal return. In this case it designates the identity of the One as a principle. Precisely this, however, constitutes the greatest and the longest *error*. Nietzsche correctly points out that if it were the One which returned, it would have begun by being unable to leave itself; if it were supposed to determine the many to resemble it, it would have begun by not losing its identity in that degradation of the similar. Repetition is no more the permanence of the One than the resemblance of the many. The subject of the eternal return is not the same but the different, not the similar but the dissimilar, not the one but the many, not necessity but chance. Moreover, repetition in the eternal return implies the destruction of all forms which hinder its operation, all the categories of representation incarnated in the primacy of the Same, the One, the Identical and the Like. Alternatively, in the second sense, the same and the similar are only an effect of the operation of systems subject to eternal return. By this means, an identity would be found to be necessarily projected, or rather retrojected, on to the originary difference and a resemblance interiorised within the divergent series. We should say of this identity and this resemblance that they are 'simulated': they are products of systems which relate different to different by means of difference (which is why such systems are themselves simulacra). The same and the similar are fictions engendered by the eternal return. This time, there is no longer error but *illusion*: inevitable illusion which is the source of error, but may nevertheless be distinguished from it. Finally, in the third sense, the same and the similar are indistinguishable from the eternal return itself. They do not exist prior to the eternal return: it is not the same or the similar which returns but the eternal return which is the only same and the only resemblance of that which returns. Nor can they be abstracted from the eternal return in order to react upon the cause. The same is said of that which differs and remains different. The eternal return is the same of the different, the one of the multiple, the resemblant of the dissimilar. Although it is the source of the preceding illusion, it engenders and maintains it only in order to rejoice in it, and to admire itself in it as though in its own optical effect, without ever falling into the adjoining error.

These differential systems with their disparate and resonating series, their dark precursor and forced movements, are what we call simulacra or phantasms. The eternal return concerns only simulacra, it causes only such phantasms to return. Perhaps we find here the most significant point of Platonism and anti-Platonism, the touchstone of both Platonism and the overturning of Platonism. In Chapter I, we suggested that Plato's thought turned upon a particularly important distinction: that between the original and the image, the model and the copy. The model is supposed to enjoy an originary superior identity (the Idea alone is nothing other than what it is:

only Courage is courageous, Piety pious), whereas the copy is judged in terms of a derived internal resemblance. Indeed, it is in this sense that difference comes only in third place, behind identity and resemblance, and can be understood only in terms of these prior notions. Difference is understood only in terms of the comparative play of two similitudes: the exemplary similitude of an identical original and the imitative similitude of a more or less accurate copy. This is the measure or test which decides between claimants. More profoundly, however, the true Platonic distinction lies elsewhere: it is of another nature, not between the original and the image but between two kinds of images [*idoles*], of which copies [*icônes*] are only the first kind, the other being simulacra [*phantasmes*]. The model–copy distinction is there only in order to found and apply the copy–simulacra distinction, since the copies are selected, justified and saved in the name of the identity of the model and owing to their internal resemblance to this ideal model. The function of the notion of the model is not to oppose the world of images in its entirety but to select the good images, the icons which resemble from within, and eliminate the bad images or simulacra. Platonism as a whole is erected on the basis of this wish to hunt down the phantasms or simulacra which are identified with the Sophist himself, that devil, that insinuator or simulator, that always disguised and displaced false pretender. For this reason it seems to us that, with Plato, a philosophical decision of the utmost importance was taken: that of subordinating difference to the supposedly initial powers of the Same and the Similar, that of declaring difference unthinkable in itself and sending it, along with the simulacra, back to the bottomless ocean. However, precisely because Plato did not yet have at his disposition the constituted categories of representation (these appeared with Aristotle), he had to base his decision on a theory of Ideas. What appears then, in its purest state, before the logic of representation could be deployed, is a moral vision of the world. It is in the first instance for these moral reasons that simulacra must be exorcized and difference thereby subordinated to the same and the similar. For this reason, however, because Plato *makes* the decision, and because with him the victory is not assured as it will be in the established world of representation, the rumbling of the enemy can still be heard. Insinuated throughout the Platonic cosmos, difference resists its yoke. Heraclitus and the Sophists make an infernal racket. It is as though there were a strange *double* which dogs Socrates' footsteps and haunts even Plato's style, inserting itself into the repetitions and variations of that style.[29]

Simulacra or phantasms are not simply copies of copies, degraded *icônes* involving infinitely relaxed relations of resemblance. The catechism, so heavily influenced by the Platonic Fathers, has made us familiar with the idea of an image without likeness: man is in the image and likeness of God, but through sin we have lost the likeness while remaining in the image ... simulacra are precisely demonic images, stripped of resemblance. Or rather, in contrast to *icônes*, they have externalised resemblance and live on difference instead. If they produce an external effect of resemblance, this takes the form of an illusion, not an internal principle; it is itself constructed on the basis of a disparity, having interiorised the dissimilitude of its constituent series and the divergence of its points of view to the point where it shows several things or tells several stories at once. This is its first characteristic. Does this not mean, however, that if simulacra themselves refer to a model, it is one which is not endowed with the ideal identity of the Same but, on the contrary, is a model of the Other, an other model, the model of difference in itself from which flows that interiorised dissimilitude? Among the most extraordinary pages in Plato, demonstrating the anti-Platonism at the heart of Platonism, are those which suggest that the different, the dissimilar, the unequal – in short, becoming – may well be not merely defects which affect copies like a ransom paid for their secondary character or a counterpart to their resemblance, but rather models themselves, terrifying models of the *pseudos* in which unfolds the power of the false.[30] This hypothesis is quickly put aside, silenced and banished. Nevertheless it did appear, if only momentarily, like a flash of lightning in the night, testifying to a persistent activity on the part of simulacra, to their underground work and to the possibility of a world of their own. Does this not mean, thirdly, that simulacra provide the means of challenging *both* the notion of the copy *and* that of the model? The model collapses into difference, while the copies disperse into the dissimilitude of the series which they interiorise, such that one can never say that the one is a copy and the other a model. Such is the ending of the *Sophist*, where we glimpse the possibility of the triumph of the simulacra. For Socrates distinguishes himself from the Sophist, but the Sophist does not distinguish himself from Socrates, placing the legitimacy of such a distinction in question. Twilight of the *icônes*. Is this not to indicate the point at which the identity of the model and the resemblance of the copy become errors, the same and the similar no more than illusions born of the functioning of simulacra? Simulacra function by themselves, passing and repassing the decentred centres of the eternal return. It is no longer the Platonic project of opposing the cosmos to chaos, as though the Circle were the imprint of a transcendent Idea capable of imposing its likeness upon a rebellious matter. It is indeed the very opposite: the immanent identity of chaos and cosmos, being in the eternal return, a thoroughly tortuous circle. Plato attempted to discipline the eternal return by making it an effect of the Ideas – in other words, making it copy a model. However, in the infinite movement of degraded likeness from copy to copy, we reach a point at which everything changes nature, at which copies themselves flip over into simulacra and at which, finally, resemblance or spiritual imitation gives way to repetition.

Chapter III

The Image of Thought

Where to begin in philosophy has always – rightly – been regarded as a very delicate problem, for beginning means eliminating all presuppositions. However, whereas in science one is confronted by objective presuppositions which axiomatic rigour can eliminate, presuppositions in philosophy are as much subjective as objective. By objective presuppositions we mean concepts explicitly presupposed by a given concept. Descartes, for example, in the *Second Meditation*, does not want to define man as a rational animal because such a definition explicitly presupposes the concepts of rationality and animality: in presenting the Cogito as a definition, he therefore claims to avoid all the objective presuppositions which encumber those procedures that operate by genus and difference. It is clear, however, that he does not escape presuppositions of another kind – subjective or implicit presuppositions contained in opinions rather than concepts: it is presumed that everyone knows, independently of concepts, what is meant by self, thinking, and being. The pure self of 'I think' thus appears to be a beginning only because it has referred all its presuppositions back to the empirical self. Moreover, while Hegel criticized Descartes for this, he does not seem, for his part, to proceed otherwise: pure being, in turn, is a beginning only by virtue of referring all its presuppositions back to sensible, concrete, empirical being. The same attitude of refusing objective presuppositions, but on condition of assuming just as many subjective presuppositions (which are perhaps the same ones in another form), appears when Heidegger invokes a pre-ontological understanding of Being. We may conclude that there is no true beginning in philosophy, or rather that the true philosophical beginning, Difference, is in-itself already Repetition. However, this formula, and the evocation of the idea of philosophy as a Circle, are subject to so many interpretations that we cannot be too prudent. For if it is a question of rediscovering at the end what was there in the beginning, if it is a question of recognising, of bringing to light or into the conceptual or the explicit, what was simply known implicitly without concepts – whatever the complexity of this process, whatever the differences between the procedures of this or that author – the fact remains that all this is still too simple, and that this circle is truly not tortuous enough. The circle image would reveal instead that philosophy is powerless truly to begin, or indeed authentically to repeat.

We would do better to ask what is a subjective or implicit presupposition: it has the form of 'Everybody knows ...'. Everybody knows, in a pre-philosophical and pre-conceptual manner ... everybody knows what it means to think and to be. ... As a result, when the philosopher says 'I think therefore I am', he can assume that the universality of his premisses – namely, what it means to be and to think ... – will be implicitly understood, and that no one can deny that to doubt is to think, and to think is to be. ... *Everybody knows, no one can deny*, is the form of representation and the discourse of the representative. When philosophy rests its beginning upon such implicit or subjective presuppositions, it can claim innocence, since it has kept nothing back – except, of course, the essential – namely, the form of this discourse. It then opposes the 'idiot' to the pedant, *Eudoxus* to *Epistemon*, good will to the overfull understanding, the individual man endowed only with his natural capacity for thought to the man perverted by the generalities of his time.[1] The philosopher takes the side of the idiot as though of a man without presuppositions. In fact, *Eudoxus* has no fewer presuppositions than *Epistemon*, he simply has them in another, implicit or subjective form, 'private' and not 'public'; in the form of a natural capacity for thought which allows philosophy to claim to begin, and to begin without presuppositions.

But here and there isolated and passionate cries are raised. How could they not be isolated when they deny what 'everybody knows...'? And passionate, since they deny that which, it is said, nobody can deny? Such protest does not take place in the name of aristocratic prejudices: it is not a question of saying what few think and knowing what it means to think. On the contrary, it is a question of someone – if only one – with the necessary modesty not managing to know what everybody knows, and modestly denying what everybody is supposed to recognise. Someone who neither allows himself to be represented nor wishes to represent anything. Not an individual endowed with good will and a natural capacity for thought, but an individual full of ill will who does not manage to think, either naturally or conceptually. Only such an individual is without presuppositions. Only such an individual effectively begins and effectively repeats. For this individual the subjective presuppositions are no less prejudices than the objective presuppositions: *Eudoxus* and *Epistemon* are one and the same misleading figure who should be mistrusted. At the risk of playing the idiot, do so in the Russian manner: that of an underground man who recognises himself no more in the subjective presuppositions of a natural capacity for thought than in the objective presuppositions of a culture of the times, and lacks the compass with which to make a circle. Such a one is the Untimely, neither temporal nor eternal. Ah Shestov, with the questions he poses, the ill will he manifests, the powerlessness to think he puts into thought and the double dimension he develops in these demanding questions concerning at once both the most radical beginning and the most stubborn repetition.

Many people have an interest in saying that everybody knows 'this', that everybody recognises this, or that nobody can deny it. (They triumph easily so long as no surly interlocutor appears to reply that he does not wish to be so represented, and that he denies or does not recognise those who speak in his name.) The philosopher, it is true, proceeds with greater disinterest: all that he proposes as universally recognised is what is meant by thinking, being and self – in other words, not a particular this or that but the form of representation or recognition in general. This form, nevertheless, has a matter, but a pure matter or element. This element consists only of the supposition that thought is the natural exercise of a faculty, of the presupposition that there is a natural capacity for thought endowed with a talent for truth or an affinity with the true, under the double aspect of a *good will on the part of the thinker* and an *upright nature on the part of thought.* It is because everybody naturally thinks that everybody is supposed to know implicitly what it means to think. The most general form of representation is thus found in the element of a common sense understood as an upright nature and a good will (*Eudoxus* and orthodoxy). The implicit presupposition of philosophy may be found in the idea of a common sense as *Cogitatio natura universalis*. On this basis, philosophy is able to begin. There is no point in multiplying the declarations of philosophers, from 'Everybody has by nature the desire to know' to 'Good sense is of all things in the world the most equally distributed', in order to verify the existence of this presupposition, for its importance lies less in the explicit declarations that it inspires than in its persistence among those philosophers who precisely leave it hidden. Postulates in philosophy are not propositions the acceptance of which the philosopher demands; but, on the contrary, propositional themes which remain implicit and are understood in a pre-philosophical manner. In this sense, conceptual philosophical thought has as its implicit presupposition a pre-philosophical and natural Image of thought, borrowed from the pure element of common sense. According to this image, thought has an affinity with the true; it formally possesses the true and materially wants the true. It is *in terms of* this image that everybody knows and is presumed to know what it means to think. Thereafter it matters little whether philosophy begins with the object or the subject, with Being or with beings, as long as thought remains subject to this Image which already prejudges everything: the distribution of the object and the subject as well as that of Being and beings.

We may call this image of thought a dogmatic, orthodox or moral image. It certainly has variant forms: 'rationalists' and 'empiricists' do not presume its construction in the same fashion. Moreover, as we shall see, philosophers often have second thoughts and do not accept this implicit image without adding further traits drawn from explicit reflection on conceptual thought which react against it and tend to overturn it. In the realm of the implicit, it nevertheless holds fast, even if the philosopher specifies that truth is not, after all, 'an easy thing to achieve and within reach of all'. For this reason, we do not speak of this or that image of thought, variable according to the philosophy in question, but of a single Image in general which constitutes the subjective presupposition of philosophy as a whole. When Nietzsche questions the most general presuppositions of philosophy, he says that these are essentially moral, since Morality alone is capable of persuading us that thought has a good nature and the thinker a good will, and that only the good can ground the supposed affinity between thought and the True. Who else, in effect, but Morality, and this Good which gives thought to the true, and the true to thought? ... As a result, the conditions of a philosophy which would be without any kind of presuppositions appear all the more clearly: instead of being supported by the moral Image of thought, it would take as its point of departure a radical critique of this Image and the 'postulates' it implies. It would find its difference or its true beginning, not in an agreement with the *pre-philosophical* Image but in a rigorous struggle against this Image, which it would denounce as *non-philosophical*.[2] As a result, it would discover its authentic repetition in a thought without Image, even at the cost of the greatest destructions and the greatest demoralisations, and a philosophical obstinacy with no ally but paradox, one which would have to renounce both the form of representation and the element of common sense. As though thought could begin to think, and continually begin again, only when liberated from the Image and its postulates. It is futile to claim to reformulate the doctrine of truth without first taking stock of the postulates which project this distorting image of thought.

It cannot be regarded as a *fact* that thinking is the natural exercise of a faculty, and that this faculty is possessed of a good nature and a good will. 'Everybody' knows very well that in fact men think rarely, and more often under the impulse of a shock than in the excitement of a taste for thinking. Moreover, Descartes's famous suggestion that good sense (the capacity for thought) is of all things in the world the most equally distributed[3] rests upon no more than an old saying, since it amounts to reminding us that men are prepared to complain of lack of memory, imagination or even hearing, but they always find themselves well served with regard to intelligence and thought. What makes Descartes a philosopher is that he makes use of that saying in order to erect an image of thought as it is *in principle*: good nature and an affinity with the true belong in principle to thought, whatever the difficulty of translating this principle into fact or rediscovering it behind the facts. Natural good sense or common sense are thus taken to be determinations of pure thought. Sense is able to adjudicate with regard to its own universality, and to suppose itself universal and communicable in principle. In order to impose or rediscover this principle – in other words, to *apply* the mind so endowed – there must be an explicit method. There is no doubt, therefore, that in fact it is difficult to think, but the most difficult in fact may still be the easiest in principle. This is why the method itself is said to be easy from the point of view of the nature of thought (it is no exaggeration to say that this notion of ease poisons the whole of Cartesianism). When the presupposition of philosophy is found in an Image of thought which is claimed to hold in principle, we can no longer be content to oppose it with contrary facts. The discussion must be carried out on the level of principle itself, in order to see whether this image does not betray the very essence of thought as pure thought. To the extent that it holds in principle, this image presupposes a certain distribution of the empirical and the transcendental, and it is this distribution or transcendental model implied by the image that must be judged.

There is indeed a model, in effect: that of recognition. Recognition may be defined by the harmonious exercise of all the faculties upon a supposed same object: the same object may be seen, touched, remembered, imagined or conceived. ... As Descartes says of the piece of wax: 'It is of course the same wax which I see, which I touch, which I picture in my imagination, in short the same wax which I thought it to be from the start.'[4] No doubt each faculty – perception, memory, imagination, understanding ... – has its own particular given and its own style, its peculiar ways of acting upon the given. An object is recognised, however, when one faculty locates it as identical to that of another, or rather when all the faculties together relate their given and relate themselves to a form of identity in the object. Recognition thus relies upon a subjective principle of collaboration of the faculties for 'everybody' – in other words, a common sense as a *concordia facultatum*; while simultaneously, for the philosopher, the form of identity in objects relies upon a ground in the unity of a thinking subject, of which all the other faculties must be modalities. This is the meaning of the Cogito as a beginning: it expresses the unity of all the faculties in the subject; it thereby expresses the possibility that all the faculties will relate to a form of object which reflects the subjective identity; it provides a philosophical concept for the presupposition of a common sense; it is the common sense become philosophical. For Kant as for Descartes, it is the identity of the Self in the 'I think' which grounds the harmony of all the faculties and their agreement on the form of a supposed Same object. The objection will be raised that we never confront a formal, unspecified, universal object but only this or that object delimited and specified by a determinate contribution from the faculties. At this point, however, we must refer to the precise difference between these two complementary instances, *common sense* and *good sense*. For while common sense is the norm of identity from the point of view of the pure Self and the form of the unspecified object which corresponds to it, good sense is the norm of distribution from the point of view of the empirical selves and the objects qualified as this or that kind of thing (which is why it is considered to be universally distributed). Good sense determines the contribution of the faculties in each case, while common sense contributes the form of the Same. Furthermore, if the unspecified object exists only in so far as it is qualified in a particular way, then conversely, qualification operates only given the supposition of the unspecified object. We will see below how – in an entirely necessary manner – good sense and common sense complete each other in the image of thought: together they constitute the two halves of the *doxa*. For the moment, it suffices to note the precipitation of the postulates themselves: the image of a naturally upright thought, which knows what it means to think; the pure element of common sense which follows from this 'in principle'; and the model of recognition – or rather, the form of recognition – which follows in turn. Thought is supposed to be naturally upright because it is not a faculty like the others but the unity of all the other faculties which are only modes of the supposed subject, and which it aligns with the form of the Same in the model of recognition. The model of recognition is necessarily included in the image of thought, and whether one considers Plato's *Theaetetus*, Descartes's *Meditations* or Kant's *Critique of Pure Reason*, this model remains sovereign and defines the orientation of the philosophical analysis of what it means to think.

Such an orientation is a hindrance to philosophy. The supposed three levels – a naturally upright thought, an in principle natural common sense, and a transcendental model of recognition – can constitute only an ideal orthodoxy. Philosophy is left without means to realise its project of breaking with *doxa*. No doubt philosophy refuses every particular *doxa*; no doubt it upholds no particular propositions of good sense or common sense. No doubt it recognises nothing in particular. Nevertheless, it retains the essential aspect of *doxa* – namely, the form; and the essential aspect of common sense – namely, the element; and the essential aspect of recognition – namely, the model itself (harmony of the faculties grounded in the supposedly universal thinking subject and exercised upon the unspecified object). The image of thought is only the figure in which *doxa* is universalised by being elevated to the rational level. However, so long as one only abstracts from the empirical content of *doxa*, while maintaining the operation of the faculties which corresponds to it and implicitly retains the essential aspect of the content, one remains imprisoned by it. We may well discover a supra-temporal form or even a sub-temporal primary matter, an underground or Ur-*doxa*: we have not advanced a single step, but remain imprisoned by the same cave or ideas of the times which we only flatter ourselves with having 'rediscovered', by blessing them with the sign of philosophy. The form of recognition has never sanctioned anything but the recognisable and the recognised; form will never inspire anything but conformities. Moreover, while philosophy refers to a common sense as its implicit presupposition, what need has common sense of philosophy? Common sense shows every day – unfortunately – that it is capable of producing philosophy in its own way. Therein lies a costly double danger for philosophy. On the one hand, it is apparent that acts of recognition exist and occupy a large part of our daily life: this is a table, this is an apple, this the piece of wax, Good morning Theaetetus. But who can believe that the destiny of thought is at stake in these acts, and that when we recognise, we are thinking? Like Bergson, we may well distinguish between two kinds of recognition – that of the cow in the presence of grass, and that of a man summoning his memories: the second can serve no more than the first as a model for what it means to think. We said above that the Image of thought must be judged on the basis of what it claims in principle, not on the basis of empirical objections. However, the criticism that must be addressed to this image of thought is precisely that it has based its supposed principle upon extrapolation from certain facts, particularly insignificant facts such as Recognition, everyday banality in person; as though thought should not seek its models among stranger and more compromising adventures. Take the example of Kant: of all philosophers, Kant is the one who discovers the prodigious domain of the transcendental. He is the analogue of a great explorer – not of another world, but of the upper or lower reaches of this one. However, what does he do? In the first edition of the *Critique of Pure Reason* he describes in detail three syntheses which measure the respective contributions of the thinking faculties, all culminating in the third, that of recognition, which is expressed in the form of the unspecified object as correlate of the 'I think' to which all the faculties are related. It is clear that, in this manner, Kant traces the so-called transcendental structures from the empirical acts of a psychological consciousness: the transcendental synthesis of apprehension is directly induced from an empirical apprehension, and so on. In order to hide this all too obvious procedure, Kant suppressed this text in the second edition. Although it is better hidden, the tracing method, with all its 'psychologism', nevertheless subsists.

In the second place, recognition is insignificant only as a speculative model. It ceases to be so with regard to the ends which it serves and to which it leads us. What is recognised is not only an object but also the values attached to an object (values play a crucial role in the distributions undertaken by good sense). In so far as the practical finality of recognition lies in the 'established values', then on this model the whole image of thought as *Cogitatio natura* bears witness to a disturbing complacency. As Nietzsche says, Truth may well seem to be 'a more modest being from which no disorder and nothing extraordinary is to be feared: a self-contented and happy creature which is continually assuring all the powers that be that no one needs to be the least concerned on its account; for it is, after all, only "pure knowledge"....'[5] What is a thought which harms no one, neither thinkers nor anyone else? Recognition is a sign of the celebration of monstrous nuptials, in which thought 'rediscovers' the State, rediscovers 'the Church' and rediscovers all the current values that it subtly presented in the pure form of an eternally blessed unspecified eternal object. Nietzsche's distinction between the creation of new values and the recognition of established values should not be understood in a historically relative manner, as though the established values were new in their time and the new values simply needed time to become established. In fact it concerns a difference which is both formal and in kind. The new, with its power of beginning and beginning again, remains forever new, just as the established was always established from the outset, even if a certain amount of empirical time was necessary for this to be recognised. What becomes established with the new is precisely not the new. For the new – in other words, difference – calls forth forces in thought which are not the forces of recognition, today or tomorrow, but the powers of a completely other model, from an unrecognised and unrecognisable *terra incognita*. What forces does this new bring to bear upon thought, from what central bad nature and ill will does it spring, from what central ungrounding which strips thought of its 'innateness', and treats it every time as something which has not always existed, but begins, forced and under constraint? By contrast, how derisory are the voluntary struggles for recognition. Struggles occur only on the basis of a common sense and established values, for the attainment of current values (honours, wealth and power). A strange struggle among consciousnesses for the conquest of the trophy constituted by the *Cogitatio natura universalis*, the trophy of pure recognition and representation. Nietzsche laughed at the very idea that what he called will to power could be concerned with this. He called both Kant and Hegel 'philosophical labourers' because their philosophy remained marked by this indelible model of recognition.

Kant, however, seemed equipped to overturn the Image of thought. For the concept of error, he substituted that of illusion: internal illusions, interior to reason, instead of errors from without which were merely the effects of bodily causes. For the substantial self, he substituted a self profoundly fractured by a line of time; while in the same movement God and the self encountered a kind of speculative death. However, in spite of everything, and at the risk of compromising the conceptual apparatus of the three Critiques, Kant did not want to renounce the implicit presuppositions. Thought had to continue to enjoy an upright nature, and philosophy could go no further than – nor in directions other than those taken by – common sense or 'common popular reason'. At most, therefore, Critique amounts to giving civil rights to thought considered from the point of view of its *natural law*: Kant's enterprise multiplies common senses, making as many of them as there are natural interests of rational thought. For while it is true that in general common sense always implies a collaboration of the faculties upon a form of the Same or a model of recognition, it is no less true that, depending upon the case, one active faculty among others is charged with the task of providing that form or that model, along with the contribution of the other faculties subjected to it. Thus, imagination, reason and the understanding collaborate in the case of knowledge and form a 'logical common sense'. Here, understanding is the legislative faculty which provides the speculative model on which the other two are summoned to collaborate. In the case of the practical model of recognition, by contrast, reason legislates with regard to the moral common sense. There remains a third model involving a properly aesthetic common sense in which the faculties attain a free accord. While it is true that in general all the faculties collaborate in recognition, the formulae of that collaboration differ according to the nature of that which is to be recognised: object of knowledge, moral value, aesthetic effect. ... Far from overturning the form of common sense, Kant merely multiplied it. (Must not the same be said of phenomenology? Does it not discover a fourth common sense, this time grounded upon sensibility as a passive synthesis – one which, even though it constitutes an Ur-*doxa*, remains no less prisoner of the form of *doxa*?[6]) We see to what degree the Kantian Critique is ultimately respectful: knowledge, morality, reflection and faith are supposed to correspond to natural interests of reason, and are never themselves called into question; only the use of the faculties is declared legitimate or not in relation to one or other of these interests. Throughout, the variable model of recognition fixes good usage in the form of a harmony between the faculties determined by a dominant faculty under a given common sense. For this reason, illegitimate usage (illusion) is explained solely in the following manner: in its natural *state*, thought confuses its interests and allows its various domains to encroach upon one another. This does not prevent thought from having at its base a good natural *law*, on which Critique bestows its civil sanction; nor does it mean that the domains, interests, limits and properties are not sacred and grounded upon inalienable right. Critique has everything – a tribunal of justices of the peace, a registration room, a register – except the power of a new politics which would overturn the image of thought. Even the dead God and the fractured I are no more than a passing bad moment, the speculative moment: they are resuscitated in a more integrated and certain form than ever, more sure of themselves, but with other, practical or moral, interests.

Such is the world of *representation* in general. We said above that representation was defined by certain elements: identity with regard to concepts, opposition with regard to the determination of concepts, analogy with regard to judgement, resemblance with regard to objects. The identity of the unspecified concept constitutes the form of the Same with regard to recognition. The determination of the concept implies the comparison between possible predicates and their opposites in a regressive and progressive double series, traversed on the one side by remembrance and on the other by an imagination the aim of which is to rediscover or re-create (memorial–imaginative reproduction). Analogy bears either upon the highest determinable concepts or on the relations between determinate concepts and their respective objects. It calls upon the power of distribution present in judgement. As for the object of the concept, in itself or in relation to other objects, it relies upon resemblance as a requirement of perceptual continuity. Each element thus appeals to one particular faculty, but is also established across different faculties within the context of a given common sense (for example, the resemblance between a perception and a remembrance). The 'I think' is the most general principle of representation – in other words, the source of these elements and of the unity of all these faculties: I conceive, I judge, I imagine, I remember and I perceive – as though these were the four branches of the Cogito. On precisely these branches, difference is crucified. They form quadripartite fetters under which only that which is identical, similar, analogous or opposed can be considered different: *difference becomes an object of representation always in relation to a conceived identity, a judged analogy, an imagined opposition or a perceived similitude.*[7] Under these four coincident figures, difference acquires a sufficient reason in the form of a *principium comparationis.* For this reason, the world of representation is characterised by its inability to conceive of difference in itself; and by the same token, its inability to conceive of repetition for itself, since the latter is grasped only by means of recognition, distribution, reproduction and resemblance in so far as these alienate the prefix RE in simple generalities of representation. The postulate of recognition was therefore a first step towards a much more general postulate of representation.

'... some reports of our perceptions do not provoke thought to reconsideration because the judgment of them by sensation seems adequate, while others always invite the intellect to reflection because the sensation yields nothing that can be trusted. – You obviously mean distant appearances, or things drawn in perspective. – You have quite missed my meaning ...'.[8] This text distinguishes two kinds of things: those which do not disturb thought and (as Plato will later say) those which *force* us to think. The first are objects of recognition: thought and all its faculties may be fully employed therein, thought may busy itself thereby, but such employment and such activity have nothing to do with thinking. Thought is thereby filled with no more than an image of itself, one in which it recognises itself the more it recognises things: this is a finger, this is a table, Good morning Theaetetus. Whence the question of Socrates' interlocutor: is it when we do not recognise, when we have difficulty in recognising, that we truly think?

The interlocutor seems already Cartesian. It is clear, however, that the dubitable will not allow us to escape from the point of view of recognition. Moreover, it will only give rise to a local scepticism – or, indeed, to a generalised method – on condition that thought already has the will to recognise what essentially distinguishes doubt from certitude. The same goes for dubitable as for certain things: they presuppose the good will of the thinker along with the good nature of thought, where these are understood to include an ideal form of recognition as well as a claimed affinity with the true, that *philia* which predetermines at once both the image of thought and the concept of philosophy. Certainties force us to think no more than doubts. To realise that three angles of a triangle should be equal to two right angles does suppose thought, it supposes the will to think, to think of triangles and even to think of their angles: Descartes remarked that we cannot deny this equality should we think of it, but we can indeed think, even of triangles, without thinking of that equality. All truths of that kind are hypothetical, since they presuppose all that is in question and are incapable of giving birth in thought to the act of thinking. In fact, concepts only ever designate possibilities. They lack the claws of absolute necessity – in other words, of an original violence inflicted upon thought; the claws of a strangeness or an enmity which alone would awaken thought from its natural stupor or eternal possibility: there is only involuntary thought, aroused but constrained within thought, and all the more absolutely necessary for being born, illegitimately, of fortuitousness in the world. Thought is primarily trespass and violence, the enemy, and nothing presupposes philosophy: everything begins with misosophy. Do not count upon thought to ensure the relative necessity of what it thinks. Rather, count upon the contingency of an encounter with that which forces thought to raise up and educate the absolute necessity of an act of thought or a passion to think. The conditions of a true critique and a true creation are the same: the destruction of an image of thought which presupposes itself and the genesis of the act of thinking in thought itself.

Something in the world forces us to think. This something is an object not of recognition but of a fundamental *encounter*. What is encountered may be Socrates, a temple or a demon. It may be grasped in a range of affective tones: wonder, love, hatred, suffering. In whichever tone, its primary characteristic is that it can only be sensed. In this sense it is opposed to recognition. In recognition, the sensible is not at all that which can only be sensed, but that which bears directly upon the senses in an object which can be recalled, imagined or conceived. The sensible is referred to an object which may not only be experienced other than by sense, but may itself be attained by other faculties. It therefore presupposes the exercise of the senses and the exercise of the other faculties in a common sense. The object of encounter, on the other hand, really gives rise to sensibility with regard to a given sense. It is not an *aisthēton* but an *aisthēteon*. It is not a quality but a sign. It is not a sensible being but the being *of* the sensible. It is not the given but that by which the given is given. It is therefore in a certain sense the imperceptible [*insensible*]. It is imperceptible precisely from the point of view of recognition – in other words, from the point of view of an empirical exercise of the senses in which sensibility grasps only that which also could be grasped by other faculties, and is related within the context of a common sense to an object which also must be apprehended by other faculties. Sensibility, in the presence of that which can only be sensed (and is at the same time imperceptible) finds itself before its own limit, the sign, and raises itself to the level of a transcendental exercise: to the 'nth' power. Common sense is there only in order to limit the specific contribution of sensibility to the conditions of a joint labour: it thereby enters into a discordant play, its organs become metaphysical.

Second character: that which can only be sensed (the *sentiendum* or the being of the sensible) moves the soul, 'perplexes' it – in other words, forces it to pose a problem: as though the object of encounter, the sign, were the bearer of a problem – as though it were a problem.[9] Must problems or questions be identified with singular objects of a transcendental Memory, as other texts of Plato suggest, so that there is the possibility of a training aimed at grasping what can only be recalled? Everything points in this direction: it is indeed true that Platonic reminiscence claims to grasp the immemorial being *of* the past, the *memorandum* which is at the same time afflicted with an essential forgetting, in accordance with that law of transcendental exercise which insists that what can only be recalled should also be empirically impossible to recall. There is a considerable difference between this essential forgetting and an empirical forgetting. Empirical memory is addressed to those things which can and even must be grasped: what is recalled must have been seen, heard, imagined or thought. That which is forgotten, in the empirical sense, is that which cannot be grasped a second time by the memory which searches for it (it is too far removed; forgetting has effaced or separated us from the memory). Transcendental memory, by contrast, grasps that which from the outset can only be recalled, even the first time: not a contingent past, but the being of the past as such and the past of every time. In this manner, the *forgotten* thing *appears* in person to the memory which essentially apprehends it. It does not address memory without addressing the forgetting within memory. The *memorandum* here is both unrememberable and immemorial. Forgetting is no longer a contingent incapacity separating us from a memory which is itself contingent: it exists within essential memory as though it were the 'nth' power of memory with regard to its own limit or to that which can only be recalled. It was the same with sensibility: the contingently imperceptible, that which is too small or too far for the empirical exercise of our senses, stands opposed to an essentially imperceptible which is indistinguishable from that which can be sensed only from the point of view of a transcendental exercise. Thus sensibility, forced by the encounter to sense the *sentiendum*, forces memory in its turn to remember the *memorandum*, that which can only be recalled. Finally, the third characteristic of transcendental memory is that, in turn, it forces thought to grasp that which can only be thought, the *cogitandum* or *noēteon*, the Essence: not the intelligible, for this is still no more than the mode in which we think that which might be something other than thought, but the being of the intelligible as though this were both the final power of thought and the unthinkable. The violence of that which forces thought develops from the *sentiendum* to the *cogitandum*. Each faculty is unhinged, but what are the hinges if not the form of a common sense which causes all the faculties to function and converge? Each one, in its own order and on its own account, has broken the form of common sense which kept it within the empirical element of *doxa*, in order to attain both its 'nth' power and the paradoxical element within transcendental exercise. Rather than all the faculties converging and contributing to a common project of recognising an object, we see divergent projects in which, with regard to what concerns it essentially, each faculty is in the presence of that which is its 'own'. Discord of the faculties, chain of force and fuse along which each confronts its limit, receiving from (or communicating to) the other only a violence which brings it face to face with its own element, as though with its disappearance or its perfection.

Let us pause, however, at the manner in which Plato determines the nature of the limits in each case. The text of *The Republic* defines that which is essentially encountered, and must be distinguished from all recognition as the object of a 'contradictory perception'. Whereas a finger always calls for recognition and is never more than a finger, that which is hard is never hard without also being soft, since it is inseparable from a becoming or a relation which includes the opposite within it (the same is true of the large and the small, the one and the many). The sign or point of departure for that which forces thought is thus the coexistence of contraries, the coexistence of more and less in an unlimited qualitative becoming. Recognition, by contrast, measures and limits the quality by relating it to something, thereby interrupting the mad-becoming. In defining the first instance by that *form of qualitative opposition or contrariety*, however, does not Plato already confuse the being of the sensible with a simple sensible being, with a pure qualitative being [*aisthēton*]? The suspicion is reinforced when we consider the second instance, reminiscence. For reminiscence only appears to break with the recognition model when in fact it is content to complicate the schema: whereas recognition bears upon a perceptible or perceived object reminiscence bears upon another object, supposed to be associated with or rather enveloped within the first, which demands to be recognised for itself independently of any distinct perception. This other thing, enveloped within the sign, must be at once never-seen and yet already-recognised, a disturbing unfamiliarity. It is then tempting to say poetically that this has been seen, but in another life, in a mythical present: You are the image of ... . By this means, however, everything is betrayed: first, the nature of the encounter in so far as this does not merely propose a particularly difficult test for recognition, an envelopment that is particularly difficult to unfold, but instead opposes all possible recognition; second, the nature of the transcendental memory and of that which can only be recalled. For this second instance is only conceived in the *form of similitude in the reminiscence*, to the point where the same objection arises: reminiscence confuses the being of the past with a past being, and since it is unable to assign an empirical moment at which this past was present, it invokes an original or mythical present. The importance of the concept of reminiscence (and the reason why it must be radically distinguished from the Cartesian concept of innateness) consists in its manner of introducing time or the duration of time into thought as such. By this means, it establishes an opacity peculiar to thought, and testifies to the existence of both a bad nature and an ill will which must be shaken by signs from without. As we have seen, however, because time is introduced here only in the form of a physical cycle, and not in its pure or essential form, thought is still supposed to possess a good nature and a resplendent clarity which are merely obscured or waylaid amidst the misadventures of the natural cycle. Reminiscence is still a refuge for the recognition model, and Plato no less than Kant traces the operation of the transcendental memory from the outlines of its empirical exercise (we see this clearly in the account of the *Phaedo*).

As for the third instance, that of pure thought or that which can only be thought, Plato determines this instance in terms of separated contraries. Thus, under the pressure of reminiscence, we are forced to think such things as Largeness which is nothing but large, Smallness which is nothing but small, Heaviness which is nothing but heavy, or Unity which is nothing but one. According to Plato, therefore, the essence is defined by the *form of real Identity* (the Same understood as *auto kath' hauto*). Everything culminates in the great principle: that there is – before all else, and despite everything – an affinity or a filiation – or perhaps it should be called a philiation – of thought with the true; in short, a good nature and a good desire, grounded in the last instance upon the *form of analogy in the Good*. As a result, the Plato who wrote the passage from *The Republic* cited above was also the first to erect the dogmatic and moralising image of thought which neutralises that text and allows it to function only as a 'repentance'. Having discovered the superior or transcendent exercise of the faculties, Plato subordinated this to the forms of opposition in the sensible, similitude in reminiscence, identity in the essence and analogy in the Good. In this manner he prepared the way for the world of representation, carrying out a first distribution of its elements and already covering the exercise of thought with a dogmatic image which both presupposes and betrays it.

The transcendental form of a faculty is indistinguishable from its disjointed, superior or transcendent exercise. Transcendent in no way means that the faculty addresses itself to objects outside the world but, on the contrary, that it grasps that in the world which concerns it exclusively and brings it into the world. The transcendent exercise must not be traced from the empirical exercise precisely because it apprehends that which cannot be grasped from the point of view of common sense, that which measures the empirical operation of all the faculties according to that which pertains to each, given the form of their collaboration. That is why the transcendental is answerable to a superior empiricism which alone is capable of exploring its domain and its regions. Contrary to Kant's belief, it cannot be induced from the ordinary empirical forms in the manner in which these appear under the determination of common sense. Despite the fact that it has become discredited today, the doctrine of the faculties is an entirely necessary component of the system of philosophy. Its discredit may be explained by the misrecognition of this properly transcendental empiricism, for which was substituted in vain a tracing of the transcendental from the empirical. Each faculty must be borne to the extreme point of its dissolution, at which it falls prey to triple violence: the violence of that which forces it to be exercised, of that which it is forced to grasp and which it alone is able to grasp, yet also that of the ungraspable (from the point of view of its empirical exercise). This is the threefold limit of the final power. Each faculty discovers at this point its own unique passion – in other words, its radical difference and its eternal repetition, its differential and repeating element along with the instantaneous engendering of its action and the eternal replay of its object, its manner of coming into the world already repeating. We ask, for example: What forces sensibility to sense? What is it that can only be sensed, yet is imperceptible at the same time? We must pose this question not only for memory and thought, but also for the imagination – is there an *imaginandum*, a *phantasteon*, which would also be the limit, that which is impossible to imagine?; for language – is there a *loquendum*, that which would be silence at the same time?; and for the other faculties which would find their place in a complete doctrine – vitality, the transcendent object of which would include monstrosity; and sociability, the transcendent object of which would include anarchy – and even for faculties yet to be discovered, whose existence is not yet suspected.[10] For nothing can be said in advance, one cannot prejudge the outcome of research: it may be that some well-known faculties – too well known – turn out to have no proper limit, no verbal adjective, because they are imposed and have an exercise only under the form of common sense. It may turn out, on the other hand, that new faculties arise, faculties which were repressed by that form of common sense. For a doctrine in general, there is nothing regrettable in this uncertainty about the outcome of research, this complexity in the study of the particular case of each faculty: on the contrary, transcendental empiricism is the only way to avoid tracing the transcendental from the outlines of the empirical.

Our concern here is not to establish such a doctrine of the faculties. We seek only to determine the nature of its requirements. In this regard, the Platonic determinations cannot be satisfactory. For it is not figures already mediated and related to representation that are capable of carrying the faculties to their respective limits but, on the contrary, free or untamed states of difference in itself; not qualitative opposition within the sensible, but an element which is in itself difference, and creates at once both the quality in the sensible and the transcendent exercise within sensibility. This element is intensity, understood as pure difference in itself, as that which is at once both imperceptible for empirical sensibility which grasps intensity only already covered or mediated by the quality to which it gives rise, and at the same time that which can be perceived only from the point of view of a transcendental sensibility which apprehends it immediately in the encounter. Moreover, when sensibility transmits its constraint to the imagination, when the imagination in turn is raised to the level of transcendent exercise, it is the phantasm, the disparity within the phantasm, which constitutes the *phantasteon*, which is both that which can only be imagined and the empirically unimaginable. With regard to memory, it is not similitude in the reminiscence but, on the contrary, the dissimilar in the pure form of time which constitutes the immemorial of a transcendent memory. Finally, it is an I fractured by this form of time which finds itself constrained to think that which can only be thought; not the Same, but that transcendent 'aleatory point', always Other by nature, in which all the essences are enveloped like so many differentials of thought, and which signifies the highest power of thought only by virtue of also designating the unthinkable or the inability to think at the empirical level. We recall Heidegger's profound texts showing that as long as thought continues to presuppose its own good nature and good will, in the form of a common sense, a *ratio*, a *Cogitatio natura universalis*, it will think nothing at all but remain a prisoner to opinion, frozen in an abstract possibility ... : 'Man can think in the sense that he possesses the possibility to do so. This possibility alone, however, is no guarantee to us that we are capable of thinking.'[11] It is true that on the path which leads to that which is to be thought, all begins with sensibility. Between the intensive and thought, it is always by means of an intensity that thought comes to us. The privilege of sensibility as origin appears in the fact that, in an encounter, what forces sensation and that which can only be sensed are one and the same thing, whereas in other cases the two instances are distinct. In effect, the intensive or difference in intensity is at once both the object of the encounter and the object to which the encounter raises sensibility. It is not the gods which we encounter: even hidden, the gods are only the forms of recognition. What we encounter are the demons, the sign-bearers: powers of the leap, the interval, the intensive and the instant; powers which only cover difference with more difference. What is most important, however, is that – between sensibility and imagination, between imagination and memory, between memory and thought – when each disjointed faculty communicates to another the violence which carries it to its own limit, every time it is a free form of difference which awakens the faculty, and awakens it as the different within that difference. So it is with difference in intensity, disparity in the phantasm, dissemblance in the form of time, the differential in thought. *Opposition, resemblance, identity and even analogy are only effects produced by these presentations of difference*, rather than being conditions which subordinate difference and make it something represented. There is no *philia* which testifies to a desire, love, good nature or good will by virtue of which the faculties already possess or tend towards the object to which they are raised by violence, and by virtue of which they would enjoy an analogy with it or a homology among themselves. Each faculty, including thought, has only involuntary adventures: involuntary operation remains embedded in the empirical. The Logos breaks up into hieroglyphics, each one of which speaks the transcendent language of a faculty. Even the point of departure – namely, sensibility in the encounter with that which forces sensation – presupposes neither affinity nor predestination. On the contrary, it is the fortuitousness or the contingency of the encounter which guarantees the necessity of that which it forces to be thought. There is no *amicability*, such as that between the similar and the Same or even that which unites opposites, to link sensibility to a *sentiendum*. The dark precursor is sufficient to enable communication between difference as such, and to make the different communicate with difference: the dark precursor is not a friend. President Schreber reformulates Plato's three moments, in his own way and in restoring them to their original communicative violence: the nerves and the annexation of nerves, examined souls and the murder of souls, constrained thought and the constraint to think.

The very principle of communication, even if this should be violence, seems to maintain the form of a common sense. However, it is nothing of the sort. There is indeed a serial connection between the faculties and an order in that series. But neither the order nor the series implies any collaboration with regard to the form of a supposed same object or to a subjective unity in the nature of an 'I think'. It is a forced and broken connection which traverses the fragments of a dissolved self as it does the borders of a fractured I. The transcendental operation of the faculties is a properly paradoxical operation, opposed to their exercise under the rule of a common sense. In consequence, the harmony between the faculties can appear only in the form of a *discordant harmony*, since each communicates to the other only the violence which confronts it with its own difference and its divergence from the others.[12] Kant was the first to provide the example of such a discordant harmony, the relation between imagination and thought which occurs in the case of the sublime. There is, therefore, something which is communicated from one faculty to another, but it is metamorphosed and does not form a common sense. We could just as well say that there are Ideas which traverse all the faculties, but are the object of none in particular. Perhaps in effect, as we shall see, it will be necessary to reserve the name of Ideas not for pure *cogitanda* but rather for those instances which go from sensibility to thought and from thought to sensibility, capable of engendering in each case, according to their own order, the limit- or transcendent-object of each faculty. Ideas are problems, but problems only furnish the conditions under which the faculties attain their superior exercise. Considered in this light, Ideas, far from having as their milieu a good sense or a common sense, refer to a para-sense which determines only the communication between disjointed faculties. Neither are they illuminated by a natural light: rather, they shine like differential flashes which leap and metamorphose. The very conception of a natural light is inseparable from a certain value supposedly attached to the Idea – namely, 'clarity and distinctness'; and from a certain supposed origin – namely, 'innateness'. Innateness, however, only represents the good nature of thought from the point of view of a Christian theology or, more generally, the requirements of creation (which is why Plato opposed reminiscence to innateness, criticising the latter for ignoring the role of a form of time in the soul as a consequence of pure thought, or the necessity of a formal distinction between a Before and an After capable of grounding forgetting in that which forces thought). The 'clear and distinct' itself is inseparable from the model of recognition which serves as the instrument of every orthodoxy, even when it is rational. Clarity and distinctness form the logic of recognition, just as innateness is the theology of common sense: both have already pushed the Idea over into representation. The restitution of the Idea in the doctrine of the faculties requires the explosion of the clear and distinct, and the discovery of a Dionysian value according to which *the Idea is necessarily obscure in so far as it is distinct*, all the more obscure the more it is distinct. Distinction-obscurity becomes here the true tone of philosophy, the symphony of the discordant Idea.

Nothing is more exemplary in this respect than the exchange of letters between Jacques Rivière and Antonin Artaud. Rivière defended the image of an autonomous thinking function, endowed in principle with its own nature and will. In fact, we are confronted with great difficulties in thinking: lack of method, technique or application, and even lack of health.

These, however, are fortunate difficulties: not only because they prevent the nature of thought from devouring our own nature, not only because they bring thought into relation with obstacles which are so many 'facts' without which it would not manage to orientate itself, but also because our efforts to overcome these obstacles allow us to maintain an ideal of the self as it exists in pure thought, like a 'superior degree of identity with ourselves', which persists through the factual variations, differences and inequalities which constantly affect us. The reader notes with astonishment that the more Rivière believes himself to be close to an understanding of Artaud, the further away he is, and the more he speaks of something altogether different. Rarely has there been such misunderstanding. Artaud does not simply talk about his own 'case', but already in his youthful letters shows an awareness that his case brings him into contact with a generalised thought process which can no longer be covered by the reassuring dogmatic image but which, on the contrary, amounts to the complete destruction of that image. The difficulties he describes himself as experiencing must therefore be understood as not merely in fact but as difficulties in principle, concerning and affecting the essence of what it means to think. Artaud said that the problem (for him) was not to orientate his thought, or to perfect the expression of what he thought, or to acquire application and method or to perfect his poems, but simply to manage to think something. For him, this was the only conceivable 'work': it presupposes an impulse, a compulsion to think which passes through all sorts of bifurcations, spreading from the nerves and being communicated to the soul in order to arrive at thought. Henceforth, thought is also forced to think its central collapse, its fracture, its own natural 'powerlessness' which is indistinguishable from the greatest power – in other words, from those unformulated forces, the *cogitanda*, as though from so many thefts or trespasses in thought. Artaud pursues in all this the terrible revelation of a thought without image, and the conquest of a new principle which does not allow itself to be represented. He knows that *difficulty* as such, along with its cortège of problems and questions, is not a *de facto* state of affairs but a *de jure* structure of thought; that there is an acephalism in thought just as there is an amnesia in memory, an aphasia in language and an agnosia in sensibility. He knows that thinking is not innate, but must be engendered in thought. He knows that the problem is not to direct or methodically apply a thought which pre-exists in principle and in nature, but to bring into being that which does not yet exist (there is no other work, all the rest is arbitrary, mere decoration). To think is to create – there is no other creation – but to create is first of all to engender 'thinking' in thought. For this reason Artaud opposes *genitality* to innateness in thought, but equally to reminiscence, and thereby proposes the principle of a transcendental empiricism:

> I am innately genital. ... There are some fools who think of themselves as beings, as innately being. I am he who, in order to be, must whip his innateness. One who innately must be a being, that is always whipping this sort of non-existent kennel, O bitches of impossibility! ... Underneath grammar there lies thought, an infamy harder to conquer, an infinitely more shrewdish maid, rougher to overcome when taken as an innate fact. For thought is a matron who has not always existed.[13]

It is not a question of opposing to the dogmatic image of thought another image borrowed, for example, from schizophrenia, but rather of remembering that schizophrenia is not only a human fact but also a possibility for thought – one, moreover, which can only be revealed as such can through the abolition of that image. It is noteworthy that the dogmatic image, for its part, recognises only *error* as a possible misadventure of thought, and reduces everything to the form of error. This, indeed, is the fifth postulate that we should take into account: taking error to be the sole 'negative' of thought. Without doubt this postulate belongs to the others as much as they belong to it: what can befall a *Cogitatio natura universalis* which presupposes a good will on the part of the thinker along with a good nature on the part of thought except that it be mistaken – in other words, that it take the false for the true (the false according to nature for the true according to the will)? Does not error itself testify to the form of a common sense, since one faculty alone cannot be mistaken but two faculties can be, at least from the point of view of their collaboration, when an object of one is confused with *another* object of the other? What is error if not always false recognition? Whence does it come if not from a false distribution of the elements of representation, from a false evaluation of opposition, analogy, resemblance and identity? Error is only the reverse of a rational orthodoxy, still testifying on behalf of that from which it is distanced – in other words, on behalf of an honesty, a good nature and a good will on the part of the one who is said to be mistaken. Error, therefore, pays homage to the 'truth' to the extent that, lacking a form of its own, it gives the form of the true to the false. It is in this sense that in the *Theaetetus*, under the sway of an apparently quite different inspiration from that in *The Republic*, Plato presents simultaneously both a positive model of recognition or common sense, and a negative model of error. Not only does thought appropriate the ideal of an 'orthodoxy', not only does common sense find its object in the categories of opposition, similitude, analogy and identity, but error itself implies this transcendence of a common sense with regard to sensations, and of a soul with regard to all the faculties whose collaboration [*syllogismos*] in relation to the form of the Same it determines. For if I cannot confuse two things that I perceive or conceive, I can always confuse something I see with something I conceive or remember – when, for example, I slip the present object of my sensation into the engram of *another* object of my memory – as in the case of 'Good morning Theodorus' when it is Theaetetus who passes by. Error in all its misery, therefore, still testifies to the transcendence of the *Cogitatio natura*. It is as though error were a kind of failure of good sense within the form of a common sense which remains integral and intact. It thereby confirms the preceding postulates of the dogmatic image as much as it derives from them, proving them by *reductio ad absurdum*.

It is true that this proof is completely ineffectual, since it operates in the same element as the postulates themselves. Yet it is perhaps easier to reconcile the *Theaetetus* and the text from the *Republic* than it may at first seem. It is not by chance that the *Theaetetus* is an aporetic dialogue, and the aporia on which it closes is that of difference or *diaphora* (to the same extent that thought requires that difference transcend 'opinion', opinion requires for itself an immanence of difference). *Theaetetus* is the first great theory of common sense, of recognition, representation and error as their correlate. However, the aporia of difference exposes its failure from the outset, along with the need to search in a quite different direction for a doctrine of thought: perhaps the one indicated by Book VII of the *Republic*? ... Always with the reservation that the *Theaetetus* model continues to act in a subterranean manner, and that the persistent elements of representation still compromise the new vision of the *Republic*.

According to the hypothesis of the *Cogitatio natura universalis*, error is the 'negative' which develops naturally. Nevertheless, the dogmatic image does not ignore the fact that thought has other misadventures besides error: humiliations more difficult to overcome, negatives much more difficult to unravel. It does not overlook the fact that the terrible Trinity of madness, stupidity and malevolence can no more be reduced to error than they can be reduced to any form of the same. Once again, however, these are no more than *facts* for the dogmatic image. Stupidity, malevolence and madness are regarded as facts occasioned by external causes, which bring into play external forces capable of subverting the honest character of thought from without – all this to the extent that we are not only thinkers. The sole effect of these forces in thought is then assimilated precisely to error, which is supposed in principle to include all the effects of factual external causes. The reduction of stupidity, malevolence and madness to the single figure of error must therefore be understood to occur in principle – whence the hybrid character of this weak concept which would not have a place within pure thought if thought were not diverted from without, and would not be occasioned by this outside if the outside were not within pure thought. For this reason, we cannot be content to invoke certain facts against the in-principle dogmatic image of thought. As in the case of recognition, we must pursue the discussion at the level of principle itself, by questioning the legitimacy of the distribution of the empirical and the transcendental carried out by the dogmatic image. For it rather seems to us that there are facts with regard to error, but which facts? Who says 'Good morning Theodorus' when Theaetetus passes, 'It is three o'clock' when it is three-thirty, and that 7 + 5 = 13? Answer: the myopic, the distracted and the young child at school. These are effective examples of errors, but examples which, like the majority of such 'facts', refer to thoroughly artificial or puerile situations, and offer a grotesque image of thought because they relate it to very simple questions to which one can and must respond by independent propositions.[14] Error acquires a sense only once the play of thought ceases to be speculative and becomes a kind of radio quiz. Everything must therefore be inverted: error is a fact which is then arbitrarily extrapolated and arbitrarily projected into the transcendental. As for the true transcendental structures of thought and the 'negative' in which these are enveloped, perhaps these must be sought elsewhere, and in figures other than those of error?

In one way or another, philosophers have always had a lively awareness of this necessity. There are few who did not feel the need to enrich the concept of error by means of determinations of a quite different kind. (To cite some examples: the notion of superstition as this is elaborated by Lucretius, Spinoza and the eighteenth-century *philosophes*, in particular Fontanelle. It is clear that the 'absurdity' of a superstition cannot be reduced to its kernel of error. Similarly, Plato's ignorance or forgetting are distinguished from error as much as from innateness and reminiscence itself. The Stoic notion of *stultitia* involves at once both madness and stupidity. The Kantian idea of inner illusion, internal to reason, is radically different from the extrinsic mechanism of error. The Hegelian idea of alienation supposes a profound restructuring of the true–false relation. The Schopenhauerian notions of vulgarity and stupidity imply a complete reversal of the will–understanding relation.) What prevents these richer determinations from being developed on their own account, however, is the maintenance, despite everything, of the dogmatic image, along with the postulates of common sense, recognition and representation which comprise its cortège. The correctives can thus appear only as 'repentances' which complicate or inconvenience the image without overturning its implicit principle.

Stupidity [*bêtise*] is not animality. The animal is protected by specific forms which prevent it from being 'stupid' [*bête*]. Formal correspondences between the human face and the heads of animals have often been composed; in other words, correspondences between individual differences peculiar to humans and the specific differences of animals. Such correspondences, however, take no account of stupidity as a specifically human form of bestiality. When satirical poets proceed through the various degrees of insult, they do not stop with animal forms but continue on to more profound regressions, passing from carnivores to herbivores and ending with cloaca as though with a universal leguminous and digestive ground. The internal process of digestion is more profound than the external gesture of attack or voracious movement: stupidity with peristaltic movements. This is why tyrants have the heads not only of beasts but also of pears, cauliflowers or potatoes. One is neither superior nor external to that from which one benefits: a tyrant institutionalises stupidity, but he is the first servant of his own system and the first to be installed within it. Slaves are always commanded by another slave. Here too, how could the concept of error account for this unity of stupidity and cruelty, of the grotesque and the terrifying, which doubles the way of the world? Cowardice, cruelty, baseness and stupidity are not simply corporeal capacities or traits of character or society; they are structures of thought as such. The transcendental landscape comes to life: places for the tyrant, the slave and the imbecile must be found within it – without the place resembling the figure who occupies it, and without the transcendental ever being traced from the empirical figures which it makes possible. It is always our belief in the postulates of the *Cogitatio* which prevents us from making stupidity a transcendental problem. Stupidity can then be no more than an empirical determination, referring back to psychology or to the anecdotal – or worse, to polemic and insults – and to the especially atrocious pseudo-literary genre of the *sottisier*. But whose fault is this? Does not the fault lie first with philosophy, which has allowed itself to be convinced by the concept of error even though this concept is itself borrowed from facts, relatively insignificant and arbitrary facts? The worst literature produces *sottisiers*, while the best (Flaubert, Baudelaire, Bloy) was haunted by the problem of stupidity. By giving this problem all its cosmic, encyclopaedic and gnoseological dimensions, such literature was able to carry it as far as the entrance to philosophy itself. Philosophy could have taken up the problem with its own means and with the necessary modesty, by considering the fact that stupidity is never that of others but the object of a properly transcendental question: how is stupidity (not error) possible?

It is possible by virtue of the link between thought and individuation. This link is much more profound than that which appears in the 'I think': it is established in a field of intensity which already constitutes the sensibility of the thinking subject. For the I and the Self are perhaps no more than indices of the species: of humanity as a species with divisions. The species has undoubtedly reached an implicit state in man. As a result, the form of the *I* can serve as a universal principle for recognition and representation, whereas the specific explicit forms are recognised only by means of this I, and the determination of species is only the rule of one of the elements of representation. The I is therefore not a species; rather – since it implicitly contains what the species and kinds explicitly develop, in particular the represented becoming of the form – they have a common fate, *Eudoxus* and *Epistemon*. Individuation, by contrast, has nothing to do with even the continued process of determining species. Not only does it differ in kind from all determination of species but, as we shall see, it precedes and renders the latter possible. It involves fields of fluid intensive factors which no more take the form of an I than of a Self. Individuation as such, as it operates beneath all forms, is inseparable from a pure ground that it brings to the surface and trails with it. It is difficult to describe this ground, or the terror and attraction it excites. Turning over the ground is the most dangerous occupation, but also the most tempting in the stupefied moments of an obtuse will. For this ground, along with the individual, rises to the surface yet assumes neither form nor figure. It is there, staring at us, but without eyes. The individual distinguishes itself from it, but it does not distinguish itself, continuing rather to cohabit with that which divorces itself from it. It is the indeterminate, but the indeterminate in so far as it continues to embrace determination, as the ground does the shoe. Animals are in a sense forewarned against this ground, protected by their explicit forms. Not so for the I and the Self, undermined by the fields of individuation which work beneath them, defenceless against a rising of the ground which holds up to them a distorted or distorting mirror in which all presently thought forms dissolve. Stupidity is neither the ground nor the individual, but rather this relation in which individuation brings the ground to the surface without being able to give it form (this ground rises by means of the I, penetrating deeply into the possibility of thought and constituting the unrecognised in every recognition). All determinations become bad and cruel when they are grasped only by a thought which invents and contemplates them, flayed and separated from their living form, adrift upon this barren ground. Everything becomes violence on this passive ground. Everything becomes attack on this digestive ground. Here the Sabbath of stupidity and malevolence takes place. Perhaps this is the origin of that melancholy which weighs upon the most beautiful human faces: the presentiment of a hideousness peculiar to the human face, of a rising tide of stupidity, an evil deformity or a thought governed by madness. For from the point of view of a philosophy of nature, madness arises at the point at which the individual contemplates itself in this free ground – and, as a result, stupidity in stupidity and cruelty in cruelty – to the point that it can no longer stand itself. 'A pitiful faculty then emerges in their minds, that of being able to see stupidity and no longer tolerate it...'.[15] It is true that this most pitiful faculty also becomes the royal faculty when it animates philosophy as a philosophy of mind – in other words, when it leads all the other faculties to that transcendent exercise which renders possible a violent reconciliation between the individual, the ground and thought. At this point, the intensive factors of individuation take themselves as objects in such a manner as to constitute the highest element of a transcendent sensibility, the *sentiendum*; and from faculty to faculty, the ground is borne within thought – still as the unthought and unthinking, but this unthought has become the necessary empirical form in which, in the fractured I (Bouvard *and* Pécuchet), thought at last thinks the *cogitandum*; in other words, the transcendent element which can only be thought ('the fact that we do not yet think' or 'What is stupidity?').

Teachers already know that errors or falsehoods are rarely found in homework (except in those exercises where a fixed result must be produced, or propositions must be translated one by one). Rather, what is more frequently found – and worse – are nonsensical sentences, remarks without interest or importance, banalities mistaken for profundities, ordinary 'points' confused with singular points, badly posed or distorted problems – all heavy with dangers, yet the fate of us all. We doubt whether, when mathematicians engage in polemic, they criticize one another for being mistaken in the results of their calculations. Rather, they criticize one another for having produced an insignificant theorem or a problem devoid of sense. Philosophy must draw the conclusions which follow from this. The element of sense is well known to philosophy; it has even become very familiar to philosophers. Nevertheless, this is perhaps not enough. Sense is defined as the condition of the true, but since it is supposed that the condition must retain an extension larger than that which is conditioned, sense does not ground truth without also allowing the possibility of error. A false proposition remains no less a proposition endowed with sense. Non-sense would then be the characteristic of that which can be neither true nor false. Two dimensions may be distinguished in a proposition: *expression*, in which a proposition says or expresses some idea; and *designation*, in which it indicates or designates the objects to which what is said or expressed applies. One of these would then be the dimension of sense, the other the dimension of truth and falsity. However, in this manner sense would only found the truth of a proposition while remaining indifferent to what it founds. Truth and falsity would be matters of designation (as Russell says: 'The question of truth and falsehood has to do with what words and sentences indicate, not with what they express.'[16]). We are then in a strange situation: having discovered the domain of sense, we refer it only to a psychological trait or a logical formalism. If need be, a new value, that of the nonsensical or the absurd, is added to the classical values of truth and falsity. However, the true and the false are supposed to continue in the same state as before – in other words, as if they were independent of the condition assigned to them or of the new value which is added to them. Either too much is said, or not enough: too much, because the search for a ground forms the essential step of a 'critique' which should inspire in us new ways of thinking; not enough, because so long as the ground remains larger than the grounded, this critique serves only to justify traditional ways of thinking. The true and the false are supposed to remain unaffected by the condition which grounds the one only by rendering the other possible. By referring the true and the false back to the relation of designation within the proposition, we acquire a sixth postulate: the postulate of designation or of the proposition itself, which both incorporates and follows from the preceding postulates (the relation of designation is only the logical form of recognition).

In fact, the condition must be a condition of real experience, not of possible experience. It forms an intrinsic genesis, not an extrinsic conditioning. In every respect, truth is a matter of production, not of adequation. It is a matter of genitality, not of innateness or reminiscence. We cannot accept that the grounded remains the same as it was before, the same as when it was not grounded, when it had not passed the test of grounding. If sufficient reason or the ground has a 'twist', this is because it relates what it grounds to that which is truly groundless. At this point, it must be said, there is no longer recognition. To ground is to metamorphose. Truth and falsity do not concern a simple designation, rendered possible by a sense which remains indifferent to it. The relation between a proposition and what it designates must be established within sense itself: the nature of ideal sense is to point beyond itself towards the object designated. Designation, in so far as it is achieved in the case of a true proposition, would never be grounded unless it were understood as the limit of the genetic series or the ideal connections which constitute sense. If sense points beyond itself towards the object, the latter can no longer be posited in reality exterior to sense, but only at the limit of its process. Moreover, the proposition's relation to what it designates, in so far as this relation is established, is constituted within the unity of sense, along with the object which realises this unity. There is only a single case where the designated stands alone and remains external to sense: precisely the case of those singular propositions arbitrarily detached from their context and employed as examples.[17] Here too, however, how can we accept that such puerile and artificial textbook examples justify an image of thought? Every time a proposition is replaced in the context of living thought, it is apparent that it has exactly the truth it deserves according to its sense, and the falsity appropriate to the non-sense that it implies. We always have as much truth as we deserve in accordance with the sense of what we say. Sense is the genesis or the production of the true, and truth is only the empirical result of sense. We rediscover in all the postulates of the dogmatic image the same confusion: elevating a simple empirical figure to the status of a transcendental, at the risk of allowing the real structures of the transcendental to fall into the empirical.

Sense is what is expressed by a proposition, but what is this *expressed*? It cannot be reduced either to the object designated or to the lived state of the speaker. Indeed, we must distinguish sense and signification in the following manner: signification refers only to concepts and the manner in which they relate to the objects conditioned by a given field of representation; whereas sense is like the Idea which is developed in the sub-representative determinations. It is not surprising that it should be easier to say what sense is not than to say what it is. In effect, we can never formulate simultaneously both a proposition and its sense; we can never say what is the sense of what we say. From this point of view, sense is the veritable *loquendum*, that which in its empirical operation cannot be said, even though it can be said only in its transcendental operation. The Idea which runs throughout all the faculties nevertheless cannot be reduced to sense, since in turn it is also non-sense. Nor is there any difficulty in reconciling this double aspect by means of which the Idea is constituted of structural elements which have no sense themselves, while it constitutes the sense of all that it produces (structure and genesis). There is only one kind of word which expresses both itself and its sense – precisely the nonsense word: abraxas, snark or blituri. If sense is necessarily a nonsense for the empirical function of the faculties, then conversely, the nonsenses so frequent in the empirical operation are like the secret of sense for the conscientious observer, all of whose faculties point towards a transcendent limit. As so many authors have recognised in diverse ways (Flaubert, Lewis Carroll), the mechanism of nonsense is the highest finality of sense, just as the mechanism of stupidity is the highest finality of thought. While it is true that we cannot express the sense of what we say, we can at least take the sense of a proposition – in other words, the *expressed*, as the *designated* of another proposition – of which in turn we cannot express the sense, and so on to infinity. As a result, if we call each proposition of consciousness a 'name', it is caught in an indefinite nominal regress, each name referring to another name which designates the sense of the preceding. However, the inability of empirical consciousness here corresponds to the 'nth' power of the language and its transcendent repetition to be able to speak infinitely of or about words themselves. In any case, thought is betrayed by the dogmatic image and by the postulate of propositions according to which philosophy would find a beginning in a first proposition of consciousness: Cogito. But perhaps Cogito is the name which has no sense and no object other than the power of reiteration in indefinite regress (I think that I think that I think ...). Every proposition of consciousness implies an unconscious of pure thought which constitutes the sphere of sense in which there is infinite regress.

The first paradox of sense, therefore, is that of proliferation, in which that which is expressed by one 'name' is designated by another name which doubles the first. No doubt this paradox may be avoided, but at the risk of falling into another: this time, the proposition is suspended, immobilised, just long enough to extract from it a double which retains only the ideal content, the immanent given. The paradoxical repetition essential to language then no longer consists in a redoubling but in a doubling; no longer in a precipitation but in a suspension. This double of the proposition appears distinct at once from the proposition itself, the formulator of the proposition and the object which it concerns. It is distinguished from the subject and the object because it does not exist outside of the proposition which expresses it. It is distinguished from the proposition itself because it relates to the object as though it were its logical attribute, its 'statable' or 'expressible'. It is the *complex theme* of the proposition and, as such, the first term of knowledge. In order to distinguish it at once both from the object (God or the sky, for example) and from the proposition (God is, the sky is blue), it is stated in infinitive or participial form: to-be-God or God-being, the being-blue of the sky. This complex is an ideal event. It is an objective entity, but one of which we cannot say that it exists in itself: it insists or subsists, possessing a quasi-being or an extra-being, that minimum of being common to real, possible and even impossible objects. In this way, however, we fall into a nest of secondary difficulties, for how are we to avoid the consequence that contradictory propositions have the same sense, given that affirmation and negation are only propositional modes? Or how are we to avoid the consequence that an impossible object, one which is self-contradictory, has a sense even though it has no 'signification' (the being-square of a circle)? Or again, how are we to reconcile the transience of an object with the eternity of its sense? Finally, how are we to avoid the following play of mirrors: a proposition must be true because its expressible is true, while the expressible is true only when the proposition itself is true? All these difficulties stem from a common source: in extracting a double from the proposition we have evoked a simple phantom. Sense so defined is only a vapour which plays at the limit of things and words. Sense appears here as the outcome of the most powerful logical effort, but as Ineffectual, a sterile incorporeal deprived of its generative power.[18] Lewis Carroll gave a marvellous account of all these paradoxes: that of the neutralising doubling appears in the form of the smile without a cat, while that of the proliferating redoubling appears in the form of the knight who always gives a new name to the name of the song – and between these two extremes lie all the secondary paradoxes which form Alice's adventures.[19]

Is anything gained by expressing sense in the interrogative rather than the infinitive or participial form ('Is God?' rather than to-be-God or the being of God)? At first glance the gain is slight. It is slight because a question is always traced from givable, probable or possible responses. It is therefore itself the neutralised double of a supposedly pre-existent proposition which may or must serve as response. All the orator's art goes into constructing questions in accordance with the responses he wishes to evoke or the propositions of which he wants to convince us. Even when we do not know the answer, we question only in supposing that in principle it is already given, or that it already exists in another consciousness. That is why – in accordance with its etymology – interrogation always takes place within the framework of a community: to interrogate implies not only a common sense but a good-sense, a distribution of knowledge and of the given with respect to empirical consciousnesses in accordance with their situations, their points of view, their positions and their skills, in such a way that a given consciousness is supposed to know already what the other does not (What time is it? – You who have a watch or are close to a clock. When was Caesar born? – You who know Roman history). Despite this weakness, the interrogative formula has at least one advantage: at the same time as it invites us to consider the corresponding proposition as a response, it opens up a new path for us. A proposition conceived as a response is always a particular solution, a case considered for itself, abstractly and apart from the superior synthesis which relates it, along with other cases, to a problem as problem. Therefore interrogation, in turn, expresses the manner in which a problem is dismembered, cashed out and revealed, in experience and for consciousness, according to its diversely apprehended cases of solution. Even though it gives us an insufficient idea, it thereby inspires in us the presentiment of that which it dismembers.

Sense is located in the problem itself. Sense is constituted in the complex theme, but the complex theme is that set of problems and questions in relation to which the propositions serve as elements of response and cases of solution. This definition, however, requires us to rid ourselves of an illusion which belongs to the dogmatic image of thought: problems and questions must no longer be traced from the corresponding propositions which serve, or can serve, as responses. We know the agent of this illusion: it is interrogation which, within the framework of a community, dismembers problems and questions, and reconstitutes them in accordance with the propositions of the common empirical consciousness – in other words, according to the probable truths of a simple *doxa*. The great logical dream of a combinatory or calculus of problems is compromised as a result. It was believed that problems or questions were only the neutralisation of a corresponding proposition. Consequently, how could it not be believed that the theme or sense is only an ineffectual double, traced from the type of proposition that it subsumes or even from an element supposed to be common to all propositions (the indicative thesis)? The failure to see that sense or the problem is extra-propositional, that it differs in kind from every proposition, leads us to miss the essential: the genesis of the act of thought, the operation of the faculties. Dialectic is the art of problems and questions, the combinatory or calculus of problems as such. However, dialectic loses its peculiar power when it remains content to trace problems from propositions: thus begins the history of the long perversion which places it under the power of the negative. Aristotle writes:

> The difference between a problem and a proposition is a difference in the turn of phrase. For if it be put in this way, 'Is two-footed terrestrial animal the definition of man?' or 'Is animal the genus of man?' the result is a proposition; but if thus, 'Is two-footed terrestrial animal the definition of man or not?' and 'Is animal the genus of man or not?' the result is a problem. Similarly too in other cases. Naturally, then, problems and propositions are equal in number; for out of every proposition you will make a problem if you change the turn of phrase.

(The illusion wends its way into contemporary logic where the calculus of problems is presented as extra-mathematical, which is true, since it is essentially logical or dialectical. It is still inferred, however, from a simple calculus of propositions, copied or traced from the propositions themselves.)[20]

We are led to believe that problems are given ready-made, and that they disappear in the responses or the solution. Already, under this double aspect, they can be no more than phantoms. We are led to believe that the activity of thinking, along with truth and falsehood in relation to that activity, begins only with the search for solutions, that both of these concern only solutions. This belief probably has the same origin as the other postulates of the dogmatic image: puerile examples taken out of context and arbitrarily erected into models. According to this infantile prejudice, the master sets a problem, our task is to solve it, and the result is accredited true or false by a powerful authority. It is also a social prejudice with the visible interest of maintaining us in an infantile state, which calls upon us to solve problems that come from elsewhere, consoling or distracting us by telling us that we have won simply by being able to respond: the problem as obstacle and the respondent as Hercules. Such is the origin of the grotesque image of culture that we find in examinations and government referenda as well as in newspaper competitions (where everyone is called upon to choose according to his or her taste, on condition that this taste coincides with that of everyone else). Be yourselves – it being understood that this self must be that of others. As if we would not remain slaves so long as we do not control the problems themselves, so long as we do not possess a right to the problems, to a participation in and management of the problems. The dogmatic image of thought supports itself with psychologically puerile and socially reactionary examples (cases of recognition, error, simple propositions and solutions or responses) in order to prejudge what should be the most valued in regard to thought – namely, the genesis of the act of thinking and the *sense* of truth and falsehood. There is, therefore, a seventh postulate to add to the others: the postulate of responses and solutions according to which truth and falsehood only begin with solutions or only qualify responses. When, however, a false problem is 'set' in a science examination, this propitious scandal serves only to remind families that problems are not ready-made but must be constituted and invested in their proper symbolic fields; and that the master text necessarily requires a (necessarily fallible) master in order to be written. Pedagogic experiments are proposed in order to allow pupils, even very young pupils, to participate in the fabrication of problems, in their constitution and their being posed as problems. Moreover, everyone 'recognises' after a fashion that problems are the most important thing. Yet it is not enough to recognise this in fact, as though problems were only provisional and contingent movements destined to disappear in the formation of knowledge, which owed their importance only to the negative empirical conditions imposed upon the knowing subject. On the contrary, this discovery must be raised to the transcendental level, and problems must be considered not as 'givens' (data) but as ideal 'objecticities' possessing their own sufficiency and implying acts of constitution and investment in their respective symbolic fields. Far from being concerned with solutions, truth and falsehood primarily affect problems. A solution always has the truth it deserves according to the problem to which it is a response, and the problem always has the solution it deserves in proportion to *its own* truth or falsity – in other words, in proportion to its sense. This is what is meant by such famous formulae as: 'The really great problems are posed only once they are solved' or 'Mankind always sets itself only such tasks as it can solve' – not because practical or speculative problems are only the shadow of pre-existing solutions but, on the contrary, because the solution necessarily follows from the complete conditions under which the problem is determined as a problem, from the means and the terms which are employed in order to pose it. The problem or sense is at once both the site of an originary truth and the genesis of a derived truth. The notions of nonsense, false sense and misconstrual [*contresens*] must be related to problems themselves (there are problems which are false through indetermination, others through overdetermination, while stupidity, finally, is the faculty for false problems; it is evidence of an inability to constitute, comprehend or determine a problem as such). Philosophers and savants dream of applying the test of truth and falsity to problems: this is the aim of dialectics as a superior calculus or combinatory. However, as long as the transcendental consequences are not explicitly drawn and the dogmatic image of thought subsists in principle, this dream also functions as no more than a 'repentance'.

The natural illusion (which involves tracing problems from propositions) is in effect extended into a philosophical illusion. The critical requirement is recognised, and the attempt is made to apply the test of truth and falsity to problems themselves, but it is maintained that the truth of a problem consists only in the possibility that it receive a solution. The new form of the illusion and its technical character comes this time from the fact that the form of problems is modelled upon the *form of possibility* of propositions. This is already the case with Aristotle. Aristotle assigned the dialectic its real task, its only effective task: the art of problems and questions. Whereas Analytics gives us the means to solve a problem already given, or to respond to a question, Dialectics shows how to pose a question legitimately. Analytics studies the process by which the syllogism necessarily leads to a conclusion, while Dialectics invents the subjects of syllogisms (precisely what Aristotle calls 'problems') and engenders the elements of syllogisms concerning a given subject ('propositions'). However, in order to judge a problem, Aristotle invites us to consider 'the opinions accepted by all men or by the majority among them, or by the wise' in order to relate these to general (predicable) points of view, and thereby form the *places* which allow them to be established or refuted in discussion. The common places are thus the test of common sense itself: every problem the corresponding proposition of which contains a logical fault in regard to accident, genus, property or definition will be considered a false proposition. If the dialectic appears devalued in Aristotle, reduced to the simple probabilities of opinion or the *doxa*, this is not because he misunderstood the essential task but, on the contrary, because he conceived the realisation of that task badly. In the grip of the natural illusion, he traced problems from the propositions of common sense; in the grip of the philosophical illusion, he made the truth of problems depend upon the common places – in other words, upon the logical possibility of finding a solution (the propositions themselves designate cases of possible solutions).

At most, the form of possibility varies throughout the history of philosophy. Thus, while the partisans of a mathematical method claim to be opposed to the dialectic, they nevertheless retain the essential – namely, the ideal of a combinatory or a calculus of problems. Instead of having recourse to the logical form of the possible, however, they separate out another, properly mathematical form of possibility – be it geometric or algebraic. Problems, therefore, continue to be traced from the corresponding propositions, and to be evaluated according to the possibility of their finding a solution. More precisely, from a geometric and synthetic point of view, problems are inferred from a particular type of proposition known as theorems. Greek geometry has a general tendency on the one hand to limit problems to the benefit of theorems, on the other to subordinate problems to theorems themselves. The reason is that theorems seem to express and to develop the properties of simple essences, whereas problems concern only events and affections which show evidence of a deterioration or projection of essences in the imagination. As a result, however, the genetic point of view is forcibly relegated to an inferior rank: proof is given that something cannot not be rather than that it is and why it is (hence the frequency in Euclid of negative, indirect and *reductio* arguments, which serve to keep geometry under the domination of the principle of identity and prevent it from becoming a geometry of sufficient reason). Nor do the essential aspects of the situation change with the shift to an algebraic and analytic point of view. Problems are now traced from algebraic equations and evaluated according to the possibility of carrying out a series of operations on the coefficients of the equation which provide the roots. However, just as in geometry we imagine the problem solved, so in algebra we operate upon unknown quantities as if they were known: this is how we pursue the hard work of reducing problems to the form of propositions capable of serving as cases of solution. We see this clearly in Descartes. The Cartesian method (the search for the clear and distinct) is a method for solving supposedly given problems, not a method of invention appropriate to the constitution of problems or the understanding of questions. The rules concerning problems and questions have only an expressly secondary and subordinate role. While combating the Aristotelian dialectic, Descartes has nevertheless a decisive point in common with it: the calculus of problems and questions remains inferred from a calculus of supposedly prior 'simple propositions', once again the postulate of the dogmatic image.[21]

The variations succeed one another, but all within the same perspective. What do the empiricists do but invent a new form of possibility: probability or the physical possibility of finding a solution? And Kant himself? More than anyone, however, Kant wanted to apply the test of truth and falsehood to problems and questions: he even defined Critique in these terms. His profound theory of Ideas as problematising and problematic allowed him to rediscover the real source of the dialectic, and even to introduce problems into the geometrical exposition of Practical Reason. However, because the Kantian critique remains dominated by common sense or the dogmatic image, Kant still defines the truth of a problem in terms of the possibility of its finding a solution: this time it is a question of a transcendental form of possibility, in accordance with a legitimate use of the faculties as this is determined in each case by this or that organisation of common sense (to which the problem corresponds). We always find the two aspects of the illusion: the natural illusion which involves tracing problems from supposedly pre-existent propositions, logical opinions, geometrical theorems, algebraic equations, physical hypotheses or transcendental judgements; and the philosophical illusion which involves evaluating problems according to their 'solvability' – in other words, according to the extrinsic and variable form of the possibility of their finding a solution. It is then fatal that the ground should itself be no more than a simple external conditioning. A strange leap on the spot or vicious circle by which philosophy, claiming to extend the truth of solutions to problems themselves but remaining imprisoned by the dogmatic image, refers the truth of problems to the possibility of their solution. What is missed is the internal character of the problem as such, the imperative internal element which decides in the first place its truth or falsity and measures its intrinsic genetic power: that is, the very object of the dialectic or combinatory, the 'differential'. Problems are tests and selections. What is essential is that there occurs at the heart of problems a genesis of truth, a production of the true in thought. Problems are the differential elements in thought, the genetic elements in the true. We can therefore substitute for the simple point of view of conditioning a point of view of effective genesis. The true and the false do not suffer the indifference of the conditioned with regard to its condition, nor does the condition remain indifferent with regard to what it renders possible. The only way to take talk of 'true and false problems' seriously is in terms of a production of the true and the false by means of problems, and in proportion to their sense. To do so, it is sufficient to renounce copying problems from possible propositions, and defining the truth of problems in terms of the possibility of their finding a solution. On the contrary, 'solvability' must depend upon an internal characteristic: it must be determined by the conditions of the problem, engendered in and by the problem along with the real solutions. Without this reversal, the famous Copernican Revolution amounts to nothing. Moreover, there is no revolution so long as we remain tied to Euclidean geometry: we must move to a geometry of sufficient reason, a Riemannian-type differential geometry which tends to give rise to discontinuity on the basis of continuity, or to ground solutions in the conditions of the problems.

Not only is sense ideal, but problems are Ideas themselves. There is always a difference in kind between problems and propositions, an essential hiatus. A proposition by itself is particular, and represents a determinate *response*. A series of propositions can be distributed in such a way that the responses they represent constitute a general *solution* (as in the case of the values of an algebraic equation). But precisely, propositions, whether general or particular, find their sense only in the subjacent problem which inspires them. Only the Idea or problem is universal. It is not the solution which lends its generality to the problem, but the problem which lends its universality to the solution. It is never enough to solve a problem with the aid of a series of simple cases playing the role of analytic elements: the conditions under which the problem acquires a maximum of comprehension and extension must be determined, conditions capable of communicating to a given case of solution the ideal continuity appropriate to it. Even for a problem which has only a single case of solution, the proposition which designates this case would acquire its sense only within a complex capable of comprehending imaginary situations and integrating an ideal of continuity. To solve a problem is always to give rise to discontinuities on the basis of a continuity which functions as Idea. Once we 'forget' the problem, we have before us no more than an abstract general solution, and since there is no longer anything to support that generality, there is nothing to prevent the solution from fragmenting into the particular propositions which constitute its cases. Once separated from the problem, the propositions fall back into the status of particular propositions whose sole value is designatory. Consciousness then attempts to reconstitute the problem, but by way of the neutralised double of particular propositions (interrogations, doubts, likelihoods, hypotheses) and the empty form of general propositions (equations, theorems, theories ...).[22] So begins the double confusion which assimilates problems to the series of *hypotheticals* and subordinates them to the series of *categories*. The nature of the universal is lost, but with it equally the nature of the singular, for the problem or the Idea is a concrete singularity no less than a true universal. Corresponding to the relations which constitute the universality of the problem is the distribution of singular points and distinctive points which determine the conditions of the problem. Proclus, even while maintaining the primacy of theorems over problems, rigorously defined the conditions of the problem in terms of an order of events and affections.[23] Leibniz, too, clearly stated what separates problems and propositions: all kinds of events, 'the how and the circumstances', from which propositions draw their sense. These events, however, are ideal events, more profound than and different in nature from the real events which they determine in the order of solutions. Underneath the large noisy events lie the small events of silence, just as underneath the natural light there are the little glimmers of the Idea. Singularity is beyond particular propositions no less than universality is beyond general propositions. Problematic Ideas are not simple essences, but multiplicities or complexes of relations and corresponding singularities. From the point of view of thought, the problematic distinction between the ordinary and the singular, and the nonsenses which result from a bad distribution among the conditions of the problem, are undoubtedly more important than the hypothetical or categorical duality of truth and falsehood along with the 'errors' which only arise from their confusion in cases of solution.

A problem does not exist, apart from its solutions. Far from disappearing in this overlay, however, it insists and persists in these solutions. A problem is determined at the same time as it is solved, but its determination is not the same as its solution: the two elements differ in kind, the determination amounting to the genesis of the concomitant solution. (In this manner the distribution of singularities belongs entirely to the conditions of the problem, while their specification already refers to solutions constructed under these conditions.) The problem is at once both transcendent and immanent in relation to its solutions. Transcendent, because it consists in a system of ideal liaisons or differential relations between genetic elements. Immanent, because these liaisons or relations are incarnated in the actual relations which do not resemble them and are defined by the field of solution. Nowhere better than in the admirable work of Albert Lautman has it been shown how problems are first Platonic Ideas or ideal liaisons between dialectical notions, relative to 'eventual situations of the existent'; but also how they are realised within the real relations constitutive of the desired solution within a *mathematical*, *physical* or other field. It is in this sense, according to Lautman, that science always participates in a dialectic which points beyond it – in other words, in a meta-mathematical and extra-propositional power – even though the liaisons of this dialectic are incarnated only in effective scientific propositions and theories.[24] Problems are always dialectical. This is why, whenever the dialectic 'forgets' its intimate relation with Ideas in the form of problems, whenever it is content to trace problems from propositions, it loses its true power and falls under the sway of the power of the negative, necessarily substituting for the ideal objecticity of the *problematic* a simple confrontation between opposing, contrary or contradictory, propositions. This long perversion begins with the dialectic itself, and attains its extreme form in Hegelianism. If it is true, however, that it is problems which are dialectical in principle, and their solutions which are scientific, we must distinguish completely between the following: the problem as transcendental instance; the symbolic field in which the immanent movement of the problem expresses its conditions; the field of scientific solvability in which the problem is incarnated, and in terms of which the preceding symbolism is defined. The relation between these elements will be specifiable by only a general theory of problems and the corresponding ideal synthesis.

Problems and their symbolic fields stand in a relationship with signs. It is the signs which 'cause problems' and are developed in a symbolic field. The paradoxical functioning of the faculties – including, in the first instance, sensibility with respect to signs – thus refers to the Ideas which run throughout all the faculties and awaken them each in turn. Conversely, the Idea which itself offers sense to language refers each case to the paradoxical functioning of the faculty. The exploration of Ideas and the elevation of each faculty to its transcendent exercise amounts to the same thing. These are two aspects of an essential apprenticeship or process of *learning*. For, on the one hand, an apprentice is someone who constitutes and occupies practical or speculative problems as such. Learning is the appropriate name for the subjective acts carried out when one is confronted with the objecticity of a problem (Idea), whereas knowledge designates only the generality of concepts or the calm possession of a rule enabling solutions. A well-known test in psychology involves a monkey who is supposed to find food in boxes of one particular colour amidst others of various colours: there comes a paradoxical period during which the number of 'errors' diminishes even though the monkey does not yet possess the 'knowledge' or 'truth' of a solution in each case: propitious moment in which the philosopher-monkey opens up to truth, himself producing the true, but only to the extent that he begins to penetrate the coloured thickness of a problem. We see here how the discontinuity among answers is engendered on the basis of the continuity of an ideal apprenticeship; how truth and falsity are distributed according to what one understands of a problem; and how the final truth, when it is obtained, emerges as though it were the limit of a problem completely determined and entirely understood, or the product of those genetic series which constitute the sense, or the outcome of a genesis which does not take place only in the head of a monkey. To learn is to enter into the universal of the relations which constitute the Idea, and into their corresponding singularities. The idea of the sea, for example, as Leibniz showed, is a system of liaisons or differential relations between particulars and singularities corresponding to the degrees of variation among these relations – the totality of the system being incarnated in the real movement of the waves. To learn to swim is to conjugate the distinctive points of our bodies with the singular points of the objective Idea in order to form a problematic field. This conjugation determines for us a threshold of consciousness at which our real acts are adjusted to our perceptions of the real relations, thereby providing a solution to the problem. Moreover, problematic Ideas are precisely the ultimate elements of nature and the subliminal objects of little perceptions. As a result, 'learning' always takes place in and through the unconscious, thereby establishing the bond of a profound complicity between nature and mind.

The apprentice, on the other hand, raises each faculty to the level of its transcendent exercise. With regard to sensibility, he attempts to give birth to that second power which grasps that which can only be sensed. This is the education of the senses. From one faculty to another is communicated a violence which nevertheless always understands the Other through the perfection of each. On the basis of which signs within sensibility, by which treasures of the memory, under torsions determined by the singularities of which Idea will thought be aroused? We never know in advance how someone will learn: by means of what loves someone becomes good at Latin, what encounters make them a philosopher, or in what dictionaries they learn to think. The limits of the faculties are encased one in the other in the broken shape of that which bears and transmits difference. There is no more a method for learning than there is a method for finding treasures, but a violent training, a culture or *paideïa* which affects the entire individual (an albino in whom emerges the act of sensing in sensibility, an aphasic in whom emerges the act of speech in language, an acephalous being in whom emerges the act of thinking in thought). Method is the means of that knowledge which regulates the collaboration of all the faculties. It is therefore the manifestation of a common sense or the realisation of a *Cogitatio natura*, and presupposes a good will as though this were a 'premeditated decision' of the thinker. Culture, however, is an involuntary adventure, the movement of learning which links a sensibility, a memory and then a thought, with all the cruelties and violence necessary, as Nietzsche said, precisely in order to 'train a "nation of thinkers" ' or to 'provide a training for the mind'.

Of course, the importance and dignity of learning are often recognised. However, this takes the form of a homage to the empirical conditions of knowledge: a nobility is discovered in this preparatory movement which must nevertheless disappear in the result. Moreover, even if we insist upon the specificity of learning and upon the time involved in apprenticeship, this is in order to appease the scruples of a psychological conscience which certainly does not allow itself to dispute the innate right of knowledge to represent the entire transcendental realm. Learning is only the intermediary between non-knowledge and knowledge, the living passage from one to the other. We may well say that learning is, after all, an infinite task: it is none the less cast with the circumstances and the acquisition of knowledge, outside the supposedly simple essence of knowledge in the form of an innate or *a priori* element, or even a regulative Idea. Finally, apprenticeship falls rather on the side of the rat in the maze, while the philosopher outside the cave carries off only the result – knowledge – in order to discover its transcendental principles. Even in Hegel, the extraordinary apprenticeship which we find in the *Phenomenology* remains subordinated, with regard to its result no less than its principle, to the ideal of knowledge in the form of absolute knowledge. It is true that, here again, Plato is the exception. For him, learning is truly the transcendental movement of the soul, irreducible as much to knowledge as to non-knowledge. It is from 'learning', not from knowledge, that the transcendental conditions of thought must be drawn. That is why Plato determines the conditions in the form of *reminiscence*, not innateness. In this manner, time is introduced into thought, – not in the form of the empirical time of the thinker subject to factual conditions, and for whom it takes time to think, but in the form of an in-principle condition or time of pure thought (time takes thought). Reminiscence then finds its proper object, its memorandum, in the specific material of apprenticeship – in other words, in questions and problems as such, in the urgency of problems independently of their solutions, in the realm of the Idea. Why should it be that so many fundamental principles concerning what it means to think are compromised by reminiscence itself? For as we have seen, Platonic time introduces difference, apprenticeship and heterogeneity into thought only in order to subject them again to the mythical form of resemblance and identity, and therefore to the image of thought itself. As a result, the whole Platonic theory of apprenticeship functions as a repentance, crushed by the emerging dogmatic image yet bringing forth a groundlessness that it remains incapable of exploring. A new Meno would say: it is knowledge that is nothing more than an empirical figure, a simple result which continually falls back into experience; whereas learning is the true transcendental structure which unites difference to difference, dissimilarity to dissimilarity, without mediating between them; and introduces time into thought – not in the form of a mythical past or former present, but in the pure form of an empty time in general. We always rediscover the necessity of reversing the supposed relations or divisions between the empirical and the transcendental. Moreover, we must regard the postulate of knowledge as the eighth postulate of the dogmatic image, one which incorporates and recapitulates all the others in a supposedly simple result.

We have listed eight postulates, each in two forms: (1) the postulate of the principle, or the *Cogitatio natura universalis* (good will of the thinker and good nature of thought); (2) the postulate of the ideal, or common sense (common sense as the *concordia facultatum* and good sense as the distribution which guarantees this concord); (3) the postulate of the model, or of recognition (recognition inviting all the faculties to exercise themselves upon an object supposedly the same, and the consequent possibility of error in the distribution when one faculty confuses one of its objects with a different object of another faculty); (4) the postulate of the element, or of representation (when difference is subordinated to the complementary dimensions of the Same and the Similar, the Analogous and the Opposed); (5) the postulate of the negative, or of error (in which error expresses everything which can go wrong *in* thought, but only as the product of *external* mechanisms); (6) the postulate of logical function, or the proposition (designation is taken to be the locus of truth, sense being no more than the neutralised double or the infinite doubling of the proposition); (7) the postulate of modality, or solutions (problems being materially traced from propositions or, indeed, formally defined by the possibility of their being solved); (8) the postulate of the end, or result, the postulate of knowledge (the subordination of learning to knowledge, and of culture to method). Each postulate has two forms, because they are both natural and philosophical, appearing once in the arbitrariness of examples, once in the presuppositions of the essence. The postulates need not be spoken: they function all the more effectively in silence, in this presupposition with regard to the essence as well as in the choice of examples. Together they form the dogmatic image of thought. They crush thought under an image which is that of the Same and the Similar in representation, but profoundly betrays what it means to think and alienates the two powers of difference and repetition, of philosophical commencement and recommencement. The thought which is born in thought, the act of thinking which is neither given by innateness nor presupposed by reminiscence but engendered in its genitality, is a thought without image. But what is such a thought, and how does it operate in the world?

Chapter IV

Ideas and the Synthesis of Difference

Kant never ceased to remind us that Ideas are essentially 'problematic'. Conversely, problems are Ideas. Undoubtedly, he shows that Ideas lead us into false problems, but this is not their most profound characteristic: if, according to Kant, reason does pose false problems and therefore itself gives rise to illusion, this is because in the first place it is the faculty of posing problems in general. In its natural state such a faculty lacks the means to distinguish what is true or false, what is founded or not, in any problem it poses. The aim of the critical operation is precisely to provide this means, since the science of metaphysics 'has to deal not with the objects of reason, the variety of which is inexhaustible, but only with itself and the problems which arise entirely from within itself ...'.[1] We are told that false problems result from an illegitimate employment of Ideas. It follows that not every problem is false: in accordance with their properly understood critical character, Ideas have a perfectly legitimate 'regulative' function in which they constitute true problems or pose well-founded problems. That is why 'regulative' means 'problematic'. Ideas are themselves problematic or problematising – and Kant tries to show the difference between, on the one hand, 'problematic' and, on the other, 'hypothetical', 'fictitious', 'general' or 'abstract', despite certain texts in which he assimilates the terms. In what sense, then, does Kantian reason, in so far as it is the faculty of Ideas, pose or constitute problems? The fact is that it alone is capable of drawing together the procedures of the understanding with regard to a set of objects.[2] The understanding by itself would remain entangled in its separate and divided procedures, a prisoner of partial empirical enquiries or researches in regard to this or that object, never raising itself to the level of a 'problem' capable of providing a systematic unity for all its operations. The understanding alone would obtain answers or results here and there, but these would never constitute a 'solution'. For every solution presupposes a problem – in other words, the constitution of a unitary and systematic field which orientates and subsumes the researches or investigations in such a manner that the answers, in turn, form precisely cases of solution. Kant even refers to Ideas as problems 'to which there is no solution'.[3] By that he does not mean that Ideas are necessarily false problems and thus insoluble but, on the contrary, that true problems are Ideas, and that these Ideas do not disappear with 'their' solutions, since they are the indispensable condition without which no solution would ever exist. Ideas have legitimate uses only in relation to concepts of the understanding; but conversely, the concepts of the understanding find the ground of their (maximum) full experimental use only in the degree to which they are related to problematic Ideas: either by being arranged upon lines which converge upon an ideal *focus* which lies outside the bounds of experience, or by being conceived on the basis of a common *horizon* which embraces them all.[4] Such focal points or horizons are Ideas – in other words, problems as such – whose nature is at once both immanent and transcendent.

Problems have an objective value, while Ideas in some sense have an object. 'Problematic' does not mean only a particularly important species of subjective acts, but a dimension of objectivity as such which is occupied by these acts. An object outside experience can be represented only in problematic form; this does not mean that Ideas have no real object, but that problems *qua* problems are the real objects of Ideas. The object of an Idea, Kant reminds us, is neither fiction nor hypothesis nor object of reason: it is an object which can be neither given nor known, but must be represented without being able to be directly determined. Kant likes to say that problematic Ideas are both objective and undetermined. The undetermined is not a simple imperfection in our knowledge or a lack in the object: it is a perfectly positive, objective structure which acts as a focus or horizon within perception. In effect, the undetermined object, or object as it exists in the Idea, allows us to represent other objects (those of experience) which it endows with a maximum of systematic unity. Ideas would not systematise the formal procedures of the understanding if their objects did not lend a similar unity to the matter or content of phenomena. In this manner, however, the undetermined is only the first objective moment of the Idea. For on the other hand, the object of the Idea becomes indirectly determined: it is determined by analogy with those objects of experience upon which it confers unity, but which in return offer it a determination 'analogous' to the relations it entertains with them. Finally, the object of the Idea carries with it the ideal of a complete and infinite determination, since it ensures a specification of the concepts of the understanding, by means of which the latter comprise more and more differences on the basis of a properly infinite field of continuity.

Ideas, therefore, present three moments: undetermined with regard to their object, determinable with regard to objects of experience, and bearing the ideal of an infinite determination with regard to concepts of the understanding. It is apparent that Ideas here repeat the three aspects of the Cogito: the *I am* as an indeterminate existence, *time* as the form under which this existence is determinable, and the *I think* as a determination. Ideas are exactly the thoughts of the Cogito, the differentials of thought. Moreover, in so far as the Cogito refers to a fractured I, an I split from end to end by the form of time which runs through it, it must be said that Ideas swarm in the fracture, constantly emerging on its edges, ceaselessly coming out and going back, being composed in a thousand different manners. It is not, therefore, a question of filling that which cannot be filled. Nevertheless, just as difference immediately reunites and articulates that which it distinguishes, and the fracture retains what it fractures, so Ideas contain their dismembered moments. It is for the Idea to interiorise the fracture and its antlike inhabitants. There is neither identification nor confusion within the Idea, but rather an internal problematic objective unity of the undetermined, the determinable and determination. Perhaps this does not appear sufficiently clearly in Kant: according to him, two of the three moments remain as extrinsic characteristics (if Ideas are in themselves undetermined, they are determinable only in relation to objects of experience, and bear the ideal of determination only in relation to concepts of the understanding). Furthermore, Kant incarnated these moments in distinct Ideas: the Self is above all undetermined, the World is determinable, and God is the ideal of determination. It is here, perhaps, that we should seek the real reasons for which, just as the post-Kantians objected, Kant held fast to the point of view of conditioning without attaining that of genesis. If the mistake of dogmatism is always to fill that which separates, that of empiricism is to leave external what is separated, and in this sense there is still too much empiricism in the *Critique* (and too much dogmatism among the post-Kantians). The 'critical' point, the horizon or focal point at which difference *qua* difference serves to reunite, has not yet been assigned.

Just as we oppose difference in itself to negativity, so we oppose *dx* to not-A, the symbol of difference [*Differenzphilosophie*] to that of contradiction. It is true that contradiction seeks its Idea on the side of the greatest difference, whereas the differential risks falling into the abyss of the infinitely small. This, however, is not the way to formulate the problem: it is a mistake to tie the value of the symbol *dx* to the existence of infinitesimals; but it is also a mistake to refuse it any ontological or gnoseological value in the name of a refusal of the latter. In fact, there is a treasure buried within the old so-called barbaric or pre-scientific interpretations of the differential calculus, which must be separated from its infinitesimal matrix. A great deal of heart and a great deal of truly philosophical naivety is needed in order to take the symbol *dx* seriously: for their part, Kant and even Leibniz renounced the idea. Nevertheless, in the esoteric history of differential philosophy, three names shine forth like bright stars: Salomon Maïmon – who, paradoxically, sought to ground post-Kantianism upon a Leibnizian reinterpretation of the calculus (1790); Hoëne Wronski, a profound mathematician who developed a positivist, messianic and mystical system which implied a Kantian interpretation of the calculus (1814); and Jean Bordas-Demoulin who, in the course of reflections upon Descartes, offered a Platonic interpretation of the calculus (1843). A Leibniz, a Kant and a Plato of the calculus: the many philosophical riches to be found here must not be sacrificed to modern scientific technique. The principle of a general differential philosophy must be the object of a rigorous exposition, and must in no way depend upon the infinitely small. The symbol *dx* appears as simultaneously undetermined, determinable and determination. Three principles which together form a sufficient reason correspond to these three aspects: a principle of determinability corresponds to the undetermined as such (*dx*, *dy*); a principle of reciprocal determination corresponds to the really determinable (dy/dx); a principle of complete determination corresponds to the effectively determined (values of dy/dx). In short, *dx* is the Idea – the Platonic, Leibnizian or Kantian Idea, the 'problem' and its being.

The Idea of fire subsumes fire in the form of a single continuous mass capable of increase. The Idea of silver subsumes its object in the form of a liquid continuity of fine metal. However, while it is true that continuousness must be related to Ideas and to their problematic use, this is on condition that it be no longer defined by characteristics borrowed from sensible or even geometric intuition, as it still is when one speaks of the interpolation of intermediaries, of infinite intercalary series or parts which are never the smallest possible. Continuousness truly belongs to the realm of Ideas only to the extent that an ideal cause of continuity is determined. Taken together with its cause, continuity forms the pure element of quantitability, which must be distinguished both from the fixed quantities of intuition [*quantum*] and from variable quantities in the form of concepts of the understanding [*quantitas*]. The symbol which expresses it is therefore completely undetermined: *dx* is strictly nothing in relation to *x*, as *dy* is in relation to *y*. The whole problem, however, lies in the signification of these zeros. Quanta as objects of intuition always have particular values; and even when they are united in a fractional relation, each maintains a value independently of the relation. As a concept of the understanding, *quantitas* has a general value; generality here referring to an infinity of possible particular values: as many as the variable can assume. However, there must always be a particular value charged with representing the others, and with standing for them: this is the case with the algebraic equation for the circle, $x^2 + y^2 - R^2 = 0$. The same does not hold for $ydy + xdx = 0$, which signifies 'the universal of the circumference or of the corresponding function'. The zeros involved in *dx* and *dy* express the annihilation of the quantum and the quantitas, of the general as well as the particular, in favour of 'the universal and its appearance'. The force of the interpretation given by Bordas-Demoulin is as follows: it is not the differential quantities which are cancelled in *dy*/*dx* or 0/0 but rather the individual and the individual relations within the function (by 'individual', Bordas means both the particular and the general). We have passed from one genus to another, as if to the other side of the mirror: having lost its mutable part or the property of variation, the function represents only the immutable along with the operation which uncovered it. 'That which is cancelled changes in it, and in being cancelled allows a glimpse beyond of that which does not change.'[5] In short, the limit must be conceived not as the limit of a function but as a genuine cut [*coupure*], a border between the changeable and the unchangeable within the function itself. Newton's mistake, therefore, is that of making the differentials equal to zero, while Leibniz's mistake is to identify them with the individual or with variability. In this respect, Bordas is already close to the modern interpretation of calculus: the limit no longer presupposes the ideas of a continuous variable and infinite approximation. On the contrary, the notion of limit grounds a new, static and purely ideal definition of continuity, while its own definition implies no more than number, or rather, the universal in number. Modern mathematics then specifies the nature of this universal of number as consisting in the 'cut' (in the sense of Dedekind): in this sense, it is the cut which constitutes the next genus of number, the ideal cause of continuity or the pure element of quantitability.

In relation to x, dx is completely undetermined, as dy is to y, but they are perfectly determinable in relation to one another. For this reason, a principle of determinability corresponds to the undetermined as such. The universal is not a nothing since there are, in Bordas's expression, 'relations of the universal'. dx and dy are completely undifferenciated [*indifferenciés*], in the particular and in the general, but completely differentiated [*differentiés*] in and by the universal. The relation dy/dx is not like a fraction which is established between particular quanta in intuition, but neither is it a general relation between variable algebraic magnitudes or quantities. Each term exists absolutely only in its relation to the other: it is no longer necessary, or even possible, to indicate an independent variable. For this reason, a principle of reciprocal determinability as such here corresponds to the determinability of the relation. The effectively synthetic function of Ideas is presented and developed by means of a reciprocal synthesis. The whole question, then, is: in what form is the differential relation determinable? It is determinable first in qualitative form, and in this connection it expresses a function which differs in kind from the so-called primitive function. When the primitive function expresses the curve, $dy/dx = -(x/y)$ expresses the trigonometric tangent of the angle made by the tangent of the curve and the axis of the abscissae. The importance of this qualitative difference or 'change of function' within the differential has often been emphasized. In the same way, the cut designates the irrational numbers which differ in kind from the terms of the series of rational numbers. This is only a first aspect, however, for in so far as it expresses another quality, the differential relation remains tied to the individual values or to the quantitative variations corresponding to that quality (for example, tangent). It is therefore differentiable in turn, and testifies only to the power of Ideas to give rise to Ideas of Ideas. The universal in relation to a quality must not, therefore, be confused with the individual values it takes in relation to another quality. In its universal function it expresses not simply that other quality but a pure element of qualitability. In this sense the Idea has the differential relation as its object: it then integrates variation, not as a variable determination of a supposedly constant relation ('variability') but, on the contrary, as a degree of variation of the relation itself ('variety') to which corresponds, for example, the qualified series of curves. If the Idea eliminates variability, this is in favour of what must be called variety or multiplicity. The Idea as concrete universal stands opposed to concepts of the understanding, and possesses a comprehension all the more vast as its extension is great. This is what defines the universal synthesis of the Idea (Idea of the Idea, etc.): the reciprocal dependence of the degrees of the relation, and ultimately the reciprocal dependence of the relations themselves.

It is Salomon Maïmon who proposes a fundamental reformulation of the *Critique* and an overcoming of the Kantian duality between concept and intuition. Such a duality refers us back to the extrinsic criterion of constructibility and leaves us with an external relation between the determinable (Kantian space as a pure given) and the determination (the concept in so far as it is thought). That the one should be adapted to the other by the intermediary of the schematism only reinforces the paradox introduced into the doctrine of the faculties by the notion of a purely external harmony: whence the reduction of the transcendental instance to a simple conditioning and the renunciation of any genetic requirement. In Kant, therefore, difference remains external and as such empirical and impure, suspended outside the construction 'between' the determinable intuition and the determinant concept. Maïmon's genius lies in showing how inadequate the point of view of conditioning is for a transcendental philosophy: both terms of the difference must equally be thought – in other words, determinability must itself be conceived as pointing towards a principle of reciprocal determination. The concepts of the understanding recognize reciprocal determination, if only in a completely formal and reflexive manner; for example, in the cases of causality and reciprocal influence. The reciprocal synthesis of differential relations as the source of the production of real objects – this is the substance of Ideas in so far as they bathe in the thought-element of qualitability. A triple genesis follows from this: that of qualities, produced in the form of differences between real objects of knowledge; that of space and time in the form of conditions for the knowledge of differences; that of concepts in the form of conditions for the difference or the distinction between knowledges themselves. Physical judgement thus tends to ensure its primacy over mathematical judgement, while the origin of extensity is inseparable from the origin of the objects which populate it. Ideas appear in the form of a system of ideal connections – in other words, a system of differential relations between reciprocally determined genetic elements. The Cogito incorporates all the power of a differential unconscious, an unconscious of pure thought which internalizes the difference between the determinable Self and the determining I, and injects into thought as such something unthought, without which its operation would always remain impossible and empty.

Maïmon writes:

> When I say, for example: red is different from green, the concept of the difference in so far as this is a pure concept of the understanding is not considered to be the relation between the sensible qualities (otherwise the Kantian question *quid juris* would still apply). Rather: either, in accordance with Kant's theory, it is considered to be the relation between their spaces as *a priori* forms, or, in accordance with my own theory, it is considered to be the relation between their differentials which are *a priori* Ideas. ... A particular object is the result of the particular rule of its production or the mode of its differential, and the relations between different objects result from the relations between their differentials.[6]

In order to understand better the alternative offered by Maïmon, let us return to a famous example: the straight line is the shortest path. 'Shortest' may be understood in two ways: from the point of view of conditioning, as a schema of the imagination which determines space in accordance with the concept (the straight line defined as that which in all parts may be superimposed upon itself) – in this case the difference remains external, incarnated in a rule of construction which is established 'between' the concept and the intuition. Alternatively, from the genetic point of view, the shortest may be understood as an Idea which overcomes the duality of concept and intuition, interiorises the difference between straight and curved, and expresses this internal difference in the form of a reciprocal determination and in the minimal conditions of an integral. The shortest is not a schema but an Idea; or it is an ideal schema and no longer the schema of a concept. In this sense, the mathematician Houël remarked that the shortest distance was not a Euclidean notion at all, but an Archimedean one, more physical than mathematical; that it was inseparable from a method of exhaustion, and that it served less to determine the straight line than to determine the length of a curve by means of the straight line – 'integral calculus performed unknowingly'.[7]

Finally, the differential relation presents a third element, that of pure potentiality. Power is the form of reciprocal determination according to which variable magnitudes are taken to be functions of one another. In consequence, calculus considers only those magnitudes where at least one is of a power superior to another. No doubt the first act of the calculus consists in a 'depotentialisation' of the equation (for example, instead of $2ax - x^2 = y^2$ we have $dy/dx = (a-x)/y$). However, the analogue may be found in the two preceding figures where the disappearance of the *quantum* and the *quantitas* was the condition for the appearance of the element of quantitability, and disqualification the condition for the appearance of the element of qualitability. This time, following Lagrange's presentation, the depotentialisation conditions pure potentiality by allowing an evolution of the function of a variable in a series constituted by the powers of i (undetermined quantity) and the coefficients of these powers (new functions of x), in such a way that the evolution function of that variable be comparable to that of the others. The pure element of potentiality appears in the first coefficient or the first derivative, the other derivatives and consequently all the terms of the series resulting from the repetition of the same operations. The whole problem, however, lies precisely in determining this first coefficient which is itself independent of i. It is on this point that Wronski's objection intervenes, being directed as much against Lagrange's presentation (Taylor's series) as against Carnot's (compensation of errors). Against Carnot, he objects that the so-called auxiliary equations are incorrect not because they imply dx and dy but because they neglect certain complementary quantities which diminish at the same time as dx and dy: far from explaining the nature of differential calculus, therefore, Carnot's presentation presupposes it. The same applies to Lagrange's series, where – from the point of view of the rigorous algorithm which, according to Wronski, characterises 'transcendental philosophy' – the discontinuous coefficients assume a signification only by virtue of the differential functions which compose them. If it is true that the understanding provides a 'discontinuous summation', this is only the matter for the generation of quantities: only 'graduation' or continuity constitutes their form, which belongs to Ideas of reason. That is why differentials certainly do not correspond to any engendered quantity, but rather constitute an unconditioned rule for the production of knowledge of quantity, and for the construction of series or the generation of discontinuities which constitute its material.[8] As Wronski says, the differential is 'an ideal difference' without which Lagrange's undetermined quantity could not carry out the determination expected of it. In this sense, the differential is indeed pure power, just as the differential relation is a pure element of potentiality.

A principle of complete determination corresponds to this element of potentiality. Complete determination must not be confused with reciprocal determination. The latter concerned the differential relations and their degrees or varieties in the Idea which correspond to diverse forms. The former concerns the values of a relation – in other words, the composition of a form or the distribution of singular points which characterise it: for example, when the relation becomes null, infinite, or 0/0. It is indeed a question of the complete determination of the parts of the object: it is now in the object, and therefore on the curve, that the elements which present the previously defined 'linear' relation must be found. Moreover, it is only here that the serial form within potentiality assumes its full meaning: it even becomes necessary to present what is a relation in the form of a sum. For a series of powers with numerical coefficients surround one singular point, and only one at a time. The interest and the necessity of the serial form appear in the plurality of series subsumed by it, in their dependence upon singular points, and in the manner in which we can pass from one part of the object where the function is represented by a series to another where it is expressed in a different series, whether the two series converge or extend one another or, on the contrary, diverge. Just as determinability pointed towards reciprocal determination, so the latter points towards complete determination. All three form the figure of sufficient reason in the threefold element of quantitability, qualitability and potentiality. Ideas are concrete universals in which extension and comprehension go together – not only because they include variety or multiplicity in themselves, but because they include singularity in all its varieties. They subsume the distribution of distinctive or singular points; their distinctive character – in other words, the *distinctness* of Ideas – consists precisely in the distribution of the ordinary and the distinctive, the singular and the regular, and in the extension of the singular across regular points into the vicinity of another singularity. There is no abstract universal beyond the individual or beyond the particular and the general: it is singularity itself which is 'pre-individual'.

The interpretation of the differential calculus has indeed taken the form of asking whether infinitesimals are real or fictive. From the beginning, however, other issues were also involved: is the fate of calculus tied to infinitesimals, or must it not be given a rigorous status from the point of view of finite representation? The real frontier defining modern mathematics lies not in the calculus itself but in other discoveries such as set theory which, even though it requires, for its own part, an axiom of infinity, gives a no less strictly finite interpretation of the calculus. We know in effect that the notion of limit has lost its phoronomic character and involves only static considerations; that variability has ceased to represent a progression through all the values of an interval and come to mean only the disjunctive assumption of one value within that interval; that the derivative and the integral have become ordinal rather than quantitative concepts; and finally that the differential designates only a magnitude left undetermined so that it can be made smaller than a given number as required. The birth of structuralism at this point coincides with the death of any genetic or dynamic ambitions of the calculus. It is precisely this alternative between infinite and finite representation that is at issue when we speak of the 'metaphysics' of calculus. Moreover, this alternative, and therefore the metaphysics, are strictly immanent to the techniques of the calculus itself.

That is why the metaphysical question was announced from the outset: why is it that, from a technical point of view, the differentials are negligible and must disappear in the result? It is obvious that to invoke here the infinitely small, and the infinitely small magnitude of the error (if there is 'error'), is completely lacking in sense and prejudges infinite representation. The rigorous response was given by Carnot in his famous *Reflections on the Metaphysics of Infinitesimal Calculus*, but precisely from the point of view of a finite interpretation: the differential equations are simple 'auxiliaries' expressing the conditions of the problem to which responds a desired equation; but a strict compensation of errors is produced between them such that no differentials persist in the result, since the latter can be arrived at only between fixed or finite quantities.

By invoking the notions of 'problem' and 'problem conditions', however, Carnot opened up for metaphysics a path which went beyond the frame of his own theory. Already Leibniz had shown that calculus was the instrument of a combinatory – in other words, that it expressed problems which could not hitherto be solved or, indeed, even posed (transcendent problems). One thinks in particular of the role of the regular and singular points which enter into the complete determination of a species of curve. No doubt the specification of the singular points (for example, dips, nodes, focal points, centres) is undertaken by means of the form of integral curves, which refers back to the solutions for the differential equation. There is nevertheless a complete determination with regard to the existence and distribution of these points which depends upon a completely different instance – namely, the field of vectors defined by the equation itself. The complementarity of these two aspects does not obscure their difference in kind – on the contrary. Moreover, if the specification of the points already shows the necessary immanence of the problem in the solution, its involvement in the solution which covers it, along with the existence and the distribution of points, testifies to the transcendence of the problem and its directive role in relation to the organisation of the solutions themselves. In short, the complete determination of a problem is inseparable from the existence, the number and the distribution of the determinant points *which precisely provide its conditions* (one singular point gives rise to two condition equations).[9] However, it then becomes more and more difficult to speak of error or the compensation of errors. The condition equations are not simply auxiliaries, nor are they imperfect equations, as Carnot suggested. They are constitutive of the problem, and of its synthesis. It is through lack of understanding of the ideal objective nature of the problematic that these are reduced to errors – albeit useful ones; or fictions – albeit well-founded ones; in any case, to a subjective moment of imperfect, approximative or erroneous knowledge. By 'problematic' we mean the ensemble of the problem and its conditions. If the differentials disappear in the result, this is to the extent that the problem-instance differs in kind from the solution-instance; it is in the movement by which the solutions necessarily come to conceal the problem; it is in the sense that the conditions of the problem are the object of a synthesis in the Idea which cannot be expressed in the analysis of the propositional concepts constituting cases of solution. As a result, the first alternative – real or fictive? – collapses. Neither real nor fictive, differentials express the nature of a problematic as such, its objective consistency along with its subjective autonomy.

Perhaps the other alternative collapses as well, that between infinite and finite representation. As we have seen, infinite and finite are indeed characteristics of a representation in so far as the concept that it implicates develops all its possible comprehension or, on the contrary, blocks it. In any case, the representation of difference refers to the identity of the concept as its principle. We can therefore treat representations like propositions of consciousness, designating cases of solution in relation to the concept in general. However, the problematic element, with its extra-propositional character, does not fall within representation. Neither particular nor general, neither finite nor infinite, it is the object of the Idea as a universal. This differential element is the play of difference as such, which can neither be mediated by representation nor subordinated to the identity of the concept. The antinomy of the finite and the infinite emerges precisely when Kant feels himself obliged, by virtue of the special nature of cosmology, to pour into representation the content corresponding to the Idea of the world. The antinomy is resolved, according to him, when on the one hand he discovers within representation an element irreducible to either infinity or finitude (regress); and when on the other he adds to this element the pure thought of another element which differs in kind from representation (noumena). However, to the extent that this pure thought remains undetermined – or is not determined as differential – representation, for its part, is not really overcome, any more than the propositions of consciousness which constitute the substance and the details of the antinomies. In a different manner, modern mathematics also leaves us in a state of antinomy, since the strict finite interpretation that it gives of the calculus nevertheless presupposes an axiom of infinity in the set theoretical foundation, even though this axiom finds no illustration in calculus. What is still missing is the extra-propositional or sub-representative element expressed in the Idea by the differential, precisely in the form of a problem.

We should speak of a dialectics of the calculus rather than a metaphysics. By 'dialectic' we do not mean any kind of circulation of opposing representations which would make them coincide in the identity of a concept, but the problem element in so far as this may be distinguished from the properly mathematical element of solutions. Following Lautman's general theses, a problem has three aspects: its difference in kind from solutions; its transcendence in relation to the solutions that it engenders on the basis of its own determinant conditions; and its immanence in the solutions which cover it, the problem *being* the better resolved the more *it is* determined. Thus the ideal connections constitutive of the problematic (dialectical) Idea are incarnated in the real relations which are constituted by mathematical theories and carried over into problems in the form of solutions. We have seen how all three of these aspects were present in the differential calculus: the solutions are like the discontinuities compatible with differential equations, engendered on the basis of an ideal continuity in accordance with the conditions of the problem. However, an important point must be specified. Differential calculus obviously belongs to mathematics, it is an entirely mathematical instrument. It would therefore seem difficult to see in it the Platonic evidence of a dialectic superior to mathematics. At least, it would be difficult if the immanent aspect of problems did not offer an adequate explanation. *Problems are always dialectical*: the dialectic has no other sense, nor do problems have any other sense. What is mathematical (or physical, biological, psychical or sociological) are the solutions. It is true, however, that on the one hand the nature of the solutions refers to different *orders* of problem within the dialectic itself; and on the other hand that problems – by virtue of their immanence, which is no less essential than their transcendence – express themselves technically in the domain of solutions to which they give rise by virtue of their dialectical order. Just as the right angle and the circle are duplicated by ruler and compass, so each dialectical problem is duplicated by a symbolic field in which it is expressed. That is why it must be said that there are mathematical, physical, biological, psychical and sociological problems, even though every problem is dialectical by nature and there are no non-dialectical problems. Mathematics, therefore, does not include only solutions to problems; it also includes the expression of problems relative to the field of solvability which they define, and define by virtue of their very dialectical order. That is why the differential calculus belongs entirely to mathematics, even at the very moment when it finds its sense in the revelation of a dialectic which points beyond mathematics.

We cannot even suppose that, from a technical point of view, differential calculus is the only mathematical expression of problems as such. The methods of exhaustion played this role in very diverse domains, as did analytic geometry. More recently, other procedures have fulfilled this role better. Recall the circle in which the theory of problems was caught: a problem is solvable only to the extent that it is 'true', but we always tend to define the truth of a problem in terms of its solvability. Instead of basing the extrinsic criterion of solvability upon the internal character of the problem (Idea), we make the internal character depend upon the simple external criterion. Now, the mathematician Abel was perhaps the first to break this circle: he elaborated a whole method according to which solvability must follow from the form of the problem. Instead of seeking to find out by trial and error whether a given equation is solvable in general, we must determine the conditions of the problem which progressively specify the fields of solvability in such a way that 'the statement contains the seeds of the solution'. This is a radical reversal in the problem–solution relation, a more considerable revolution than the Copernican. It has been said that Abel thereby inaugurated a new *Critique of Pure Reason*, in particular going beyond Kantian '*extrinsicism*'. This same judgement is confirmed in relation to the work of Galois: starting from a basic 'field' (R), successive adjunctions to this field (R', R", R'"...) allow a progressively more precise distinction of the roots of an equation, by the progressive limitation of possible substitutions. There is thus a succession of 'partial resolvents' or an embedding of 'groups' which make the solution follow from the very conditions of the problem: the fact that an equation cannot be solved algebraically, for example, is no longer discovered as a result of empirical research or by trial and error, but as a result of the characteristics of the groups and partial resolvents which constitute the synthesis of the problem and its conditions (an equation is solvable only by algebraic means – in other words, by radicals, when the partial resolvents are binomial equations and the indices of the groups are prime numbers). The theory of problems is completely transformed and at last grounded, since we are no longer in the classic master–pupil situation where the pupil understands and follows a problem only to the extent that the master already knows the solution and provides the necessary adjunctions. For, as Georges Verriest remarks, the group of an equation does not characterise at a given moment what we know about its roots, but the objectivity of what we do not know about them.[10] Conversely, this non-knowledge is no longer a negative or an insufficiency but a rule or something *to be learnt* which corresponds to a fundamental dimension of the object. The whole pedagogical relation is transformed – a new Meno – but many other things along with it, including knowledge and sufficient reason. Galois's 'progressive discernibility' unites in the same continuous movement the processes of reciprocal determination and complete determination (pairs of roots and the distinction between roots within a pair). It constitutes the total figure of sufficient reason, into which it introduces *time*. With Abel and Galois, the mathematical theory of problems is able to fulfil all its properly dialectical requirements, and to break the circle in which it was caught.

Modern mathematics is therefore regarded as based upon the theory of groups or set theory rather than upon differential calculus. Nevertheless, it is no accident that Abel's method concerned above all the integration of differential formulae. What matters to us is less the determination of this or that break [*coupure*] in the history of mathematics (analytic geometry, differential calculus, group theory ...) than the manner in which, at each moment of that history, dialectical problems, their mathematical expression and the simultaneous origin of their fields of solvability are interrelated. From this point of view, there is a continuity and a teleology in the development of mathematics which makes the differences in kind between differential calculus and other instruments merely secondary. Calculus recognises differentials of different orders. However, the notions of differential and order accord with the dialectic in a quite different manner. The problematic or dialectical Idea is a system of connections between differential elements, a system of differential relations between genetic elements. There are different orders of Ideas presupposed by one another according to the ideal nature of these relations and the elements considered (Ideas of Ideas, etc.). There is as yet nothing mathematical in these definitions. Mathematics appears with the fields of solution in which dialectical Ideas of the last order are incarnated, and with the expression of problems relative to these fields. Other orders of Ideas are incarnated in other fields and in other modes of expression corresponding to different sciences. In this manner, a genesis of diverse scientific domains takes place on the basis of dialectical problems and their orders. Differential calculus in the most precise sense is only a mathematical instrument which, even in its own domain, does not necessarily represent the most complete form of the expression of problems and the constitution of their solutions in relation to the order of dialectical Ideas which it incarnates. It nevertheless has a wider universal sense in which it designates the composite whole that includes Problems or dialectical Ideas, the Scientific expression of problems, and the Establishment of fields of solution. More generally, we must conclude that there is no difficulty with any supposed application of mathematics to other domains, in particular with regard to differential calculus or group theory. It is rather that each engendered domain, in which dialectical Ideas of this or that order are incarnated, possesses its own calculus. Ideas always have an element of quantitability, qualitability and potentiality; there are always processes of determinability, of reciprocal determination and complete determination; always distributions of distinctive and ordinary points; always adjunct fields which form the synthetic progression of a sufficient reason. There is no metaphor here, except the metaphor consubstantial with the notion of Ideas, that of the dialectical transport or '*diaphora*'. Herein lies the adventure of Ideas. It is not mathematics which is applied to other domains but the dialectic which establishes for its problems, by virtue of their order and their conditions, the direct differential calculus corresponding or appropriate to the domain under consideration. In this sense there is a *mathesis universalis* corresponding to the universality of the dialectic. If Ideas are the differentials of thought, there is a differential calculus corresponding to each Idea, an alphabet of what it means to think. Differential calculus is not the unimaginative calculus of the utilitarian, the crude arithmetic calculus which subordinates thought to other things or to other ends, but the algebra of pure thought, the superior irony of problems themselves – the only calculus 'beyond good and evil'. This entire adventurous character of Ideas remains to be described.

Ideas are multiplicities: every idea is a multiplicity or a variety. In this Reimannian usage of the word 'multiplicity' (taken up by Husserl, and again by Bergson) the utmost importance must be attached to the substantive form: multiplicity must not designate a combination of the many and the one, but rather an organisation belonging to the many as such, which has no need whatsoever of unity in order to form a system. The one and the many are concepts of the understanding which make up the overly loose mesh of a distorted dialectic which proceeds by opposition. The biggest fish pass through. Can we believe that the concrete is attained when the inadequacy of an abstraction is compensated for by the inadequacy of its opposite? We can say 'the one is multiple, the multiple one' for ever: we speak like Plato's young men who did not even spare the farmyard. Contraries may be combined, contradictions established, but at no point has the essential been raised: 'how many', 'how', 'in which cases'. The essence is nothing, an empty generality, when separated from this measure, this manner and this study of cases. Predicates may be combined, but the Idea is missed: the outcome is an empty discourse which lacks a substantive. 'Multiplicity', which replaces the one no less than the multiple, is the true substantive, substance itself. The variable multiplicity is the how many, the how and each of the cases. Everything is a multiplicity in so far as it incarnates an Idea. Even the many is a multiplicity; even the one is a multiplicity. That the one is *a* multiplicity (as Bergson and Husserl showed) is enough to reject back-to-back adjectival propositions of the one–many and many–one type. Everywhere the differences between multiplicities and the differences within multiplicities replace schematic and crude oppositions. Instead of the enormous opposition between the one and the many, there is only the variety of multiplicity – in other words, difference. It is, perhaps, ironic to say that everything is multiplicity, even the one, even the many. However, irony itself is a multiplicity – or rather, the art of multiplicities: the art of grasping the Ideas and the problems they incarnate in things, and of grasping things as incarnations, as cases of solution for the problems of Ideas.

An Idea is an *n*-dimensional, continuous, defined multiplicity. Colour – or rather, the Idea of colour – is a three-dimensional multiplicity. By dimensions, we mean the variables or co-ordinates upon which a phenomenon depends; by continuity, we mean the set of relations between changes in these variables – for example, a quadratic form of the differentials of the co-ordinates; by definition, we mean the elements reciprocally determined by these relations, elements which cannot change unless the multiplicity changes its order and its metric. When and under what conditions should we speak of a multiplicity? There are three conditions which together allow us to define the moment at which an Idea emerges: (1) the elements of the multiplicity must have neither sensible form nor conceptual signification, nor, therefore, any assignable function. They are not even actually existent, but inseparable from a potential or a virtuality. In this sense they imply no prior identity, no positing of a something that could be called one or the same. On the contrary, their indetermination renders possible the manifestation of difference freed from all subordination. (2) These elements must in effect be determined, but reciprocally, by reciprocal relations which allow no independence whatsoever to subsist. Such relations are precisely non-localisable ideal connections, whether they characterise the multiplicity globally or proceed by the juxtaposition of neighbouring regions. In all cases the multiplicity is intrinsically defined, without external reference or recourse to a uniform space in which it would be submerged. Spatio–temporal relations no doubt retain multiplicity, but lose interiority; concepts of the understanding retain interiority, but lose multiplicity, which they replace by the identity of an 'I think' or something thought. Internal multiplicity, by contrast, is characteristic of the Idea alone. (3) A multiple ideal connection, a differential *relation*, must be actualised in diverse spatio–temporal *relationships*, at the same time as its *elements* are actually incarnated in a variety of *terms* and forms. The Idea is thus defined as a structure. A structure or an Idea is a 'complex theme', an internal multiplicity – in other words, a system of multiple, non-localisable connections between differential elements which is incarnated in real relations and actual terms. In this sense, we see no difficulty in reconciling genesis and structure. Following Lautman and Vuillemin's work on mathematics, 'structuralism' seems to us the only means by which a genetic method can achieve its ambitions. It is sufficient to understand that the genesis takes place in time not between one actual term, however small, and another actual term, but between the virtual and its actualisation – in other words, it goes from the structure to its incarnation, from the conditions of a problem to the cases of solution, from the differential elements and their ideal connections to actual terms and diverse real relations which constitute at each moment the actuality of time. This is a genesis without dynamism, evolving necessarily in the element of a supra-historicity, a *static genesis* which may be understood as the correlate of the notion of *passive synthesis*, and which in turn illuminates that notion. Was not the mistake of the modern interpretation of calculus to condemn its genetic ambitions under the pretext of having discovered a 'structure' which dissociated calculus from any phoronomic or dynamic considerations? There are Ideas which correspond to mathematical relations and realities, others which correspond to physical laws and facts. There are others which, according to their order, correspond to organisms, psychic structures, languages and societies: these correspondences without resemblance are of a structural–genetic nature. Just as structure is independent of any principle of identity, so genesis is independent of a rule of resemblance. However, an Idea with all its adventures emerges in so far as it already satisfies certain structural and genetic conditions, and not others. The application of these criteria must therefore be sought in very different domains, by means of examples chosen almost at random.

First example: atomism as a physical Idea. Ancient atomism not only multiplied Parmenidean being, it also conceived of Ideas as multiplicities of atoms, atoms being the objective elements of thought. Thereafter it is indeed essential that atoms be related to other atoms at the heart of structures which are actualised in sensible composites. In this regard, the *clinamen* is by no means a change of direction in the movement of an atom, much less an indetermination testifying to the existence of a physical freedom. It is the original determination of the direction of movement, the synthesis of movement and its direction which relates one atom to another. '*Incerto tempore*' does not mean undetermined but non-assignable or non-localisable. If it is true that atoms, the elements of thought, move 'as rapidly as thought itself', as Epicurus says in his letter to Herodotus, then the *clinamen* is the reciprocal determination which is produced 'in a time smaller than the minimum continuous time thinkable'. It is not surprising that Epicurus makes use here of the vocabulary of exhaustion: there is something analogous in the *clinamen* to a relation between the differentials of atoms in movement. There is a declination here which also forms the language of thought; there is something here in thought which testifies to a limit of thought, but on the basis of which it thinks: faster than thought, 'in a time smaller...'. Nevertheless, the Epicurean atom still retains too much independence, a shape and an actuality. Reciprocal determination here still has too much of the aspect of a spatio–temporal relation. The question whether modern atomism, by contrast, fulfils all the conditions of a structure must be posed in relation to the differential equations which determine the laws of nature, in relation to the types of 'multiple and non-localisable connections' established between particles, and in relation to the character of the 'potentiality' expressly attributed to these particles.

Second example: the organism as biological Idea. Geoffroy Saint-Hilaire seems to be the first to have defended the consideration of elements that he called abstract, taken independently of their forms and their functions. This is why he criticised not only his predecessors but also his contemporaries (Cuvier) for not going beyond an empirical distribution of differences and resemblances. These purely anatomical and atomic elements, such as small bones, are linked by ideal relations of reciprocal determination: they thereby constitute an 'essence' which is the Animal in itself. It is these differential relations between pure anatomical elements which are incarnated in diverse animal configurations, with their diverse organs and functions. Such is the threefold character of anatomy: atomic, comparative and transcendent. In his *Notions synthétiques et historiques de philosophie naturelle* (1837), Geoffroy spells out his dream which, he says, was also that of the young Napoleon: to be the Newton of the infinitely small, to discover 'the world of details' or 'very short distance' ideal connections beneath the cruder play of sensible and conceptual differences and resemblances. An organism is a set of real terms and relations (dimension, position, number) which actualises on its own account, to this or that degree, relations between differential elements: for example, the hyoid of a cat has nine small bones, whereas in man it has only five; the other four are found towards the skull, outside the organ reduced in this way by the upright position. The genesis of development in organisms must therefore be understood as the actualisation of an essence, in accordance with reasons and at speeds determined by the environment, with accelerations and interruptions, but independently of any transformist passage from one actual term to another.

Such is the genius of Geoffroy. Here too, however, the question of a structuralism in biology (in accordance with the word 'structure', which Geoffroy often employed) depends upon the ultimate determination of the differential elements and of the type of relations between them. Are anatomical elements, principally bones, capable of fulfilling this role, as though the necessity for muscles did not set limits to their relations; and as though these elements did not themselves still enjoy an actual, or too actual, existence? It may be, then, that structure reappears on a quite different level, with a completely new determination of differential elements and ideal connections. This occurs with genetics. There are perhaps as many differences between genetics and Geoffroy as there are between modern atomism and Epicurus. Nevertheless, chromosomes appear as *loci*; in other words, not simply as places in space but as complexes of relations of proximity; genes express differential elements which also characterise an organism in a global manner, and play the role of distinctive points in a double process of reciprocal and complete determination; the double aspect of genes involves commanding several characteristics at once, and acting only in relation to other genes; the whole constitutes a virtuality, a potentiality; and this structure is incarnated in actual organisms, as much from the point of view of the determination of their species as from that of the differenciation of their parts, according to rhythms that are precisely called 'differential', according to comparative speeds or slownesses which measure the movement of actualisation.

Third example: are there social Ideas, in a Marxist sense? In what Marx calls 'abstract labour', abstraction is made from the particular qualities of the products of labour and the qualities of the labourers, but not from the conditions of productivity, the labour-power and the means of labour in a society. The social Idea is the element of quantitability, qualitability and potentiality of societies. It expresses a system of multiple ideal connections, or differential relations between differential elements: these include relations of production and property relations which are established not between concrete individuals but between atomic bearers of labour-power or representatives of property. The economic instance is constituted by such a social multiplicity – in other words, by the varieties of these differential relations. Such a variety of relations, with its corresponding distinctive points, is then incarnated in the concrete differenciated labours which characterise a determinate society, in the real relations of that society (juridical, political, ideological) and in the actual terms of those relations (for example, capitalist–wage-labourer). Althusser and his collaborators are, therefore, profoundly correct in showing the presence of a genuine structure in *Capital*, and in rejecting historicist interpretations of Marxism, since this structure never acts transitively, following the order of succession in time; rather, it acts by incarnating its varieties in diverse societies and by accounting for the simultaneity of all the relations and terms which, each time and in each case, constitute the present: that is why 'the economic' is never given properly speaking, but rather designates a differential virtuality to be interpreted, always covered over by its forms of actualisation; a theme or 'problematic' always covered over by its cases of solution.[11] In short, the economic is the social dialectic itself – in other words, the totality of the problems posed to a given society, or the synthetic and problematising field of that society. In all rigour, there are only economic social problems, even though the solutions may be juridical, political or ideological, and the problems may be expressed in these fields of resolvability. The famous phrase of the *Contribution to the Critique of Political Economy*, 'mankind always sets itself only such tasks as it can solve', does not mean that the problems are only apparent or that they are already solved, but, on the contrary, that the economic conditions of a problem determine or give rise to the manner in which it finds a solution within the framework of the real relations of the society. Not that the observer can draw the least optimism from this, for these 'solutions' may involve stupidity or cruelty, the horror of war or 'the solution of the Jewish problem'. More precisely, the solution is always that which a society deserves or gives rise to as a consequence of the manner in which, given its real relations, it is able to pose the problems set within it and to it by the differential relations it incarnates.

Ideas are complexes of coexistence. In a certain sense all Ideas coexist, but they do so at points, on the edges, and under glimmerings which never have the uniformity of a natural light. On each occasion, obscurities and zones of shadow correspond to their distinction. Ideas are distinguished from one another, but not at all in the same manner as forms and the terms in which these are incarnated. They are objectively made and unmade according to the conditions which determine their fluent synthesis. This is because they combine the greatest power of being differen*t*iated with an inability to be differen*c*iated. Ideas are varieties which include in themselves sub-varieties. We can distinguish three dimensions of variety. In the first, vertical dimension we can distinguish *ordinal varieties* according to the nature of the elements and the differential relations: for example, mathematical, mathematico-physical, chemical, biological, physical, sociological and linguistic Ideas. ... Each level implies differentials of a different dialectical 'order', but the elements of one order can pass over into those of another under new relations, either by being dissolved in the larger superior order or by being reflected in the inferior order. In the second, horizontal dimension we can distinguish characteristic varieties corresponding to the degrees of a differential relation within a given order, and to the distribution of singular points for each degree (such as the equation for conic sections which gives according to the case an ellipse, a hyperbola, a parabola or a straight line; or the varieties of animal ordered from the point of view of unity of composition; or the varieties of language ordered from the point of view of their phonological system). Finally, in depth we can distinguish axiomatic varieties which determine a common axiom for differential relations of a different order, on condition that this axiom itself coincides with a third-order differential relation (for example, the addition of real numbers and the composition of displacements; or, in an altogether different domain, the weaving-speech practised by the Griaule Dogons). Ideas and the distinctions between Ideas are inseparable from their types of varieties, and from the manner in which each type enters into the others. We propose the term 'perplication' to designate this distinctive and coexistent state of Ideas. Not that the corresponding connotation of 'perplexity' signifies a coefficient of doubt, hesitation or astonishment, or anything whatsoever incomplete about Ideas themselves. On the contrary, it is a question of the identity of Ideas and problems, of the exhaustively problematic character of Ideas – in other words, of the manner in which problems are objectively determined by their conditions to participate in one another according to the circumstantial requirements of the synthesis of Ideas.

Ideas are by no means essences. In so far as they are the objects of Ideas, problems belong on the side of events, affections, or accidents rather than on that of theorematic essences. Ideas are developed in the auxiliaries and the adjunct fields by which their synthetic power is measured. Consequently, the domain of Ideas is that of the inessential. They proclaim their affinity with the inessential in a manner as deliberate and as fiercely obstinate as that in which rationalism proclaimed its possession and comprehension of essences. Rationalism wanted to tie the fate of Ideas to abstract and dead essences; and to the extent that the problematic form of Ideas was recognised, it even wanted that form tied to the question of essences – in other words, to the 'What is X?'. How many misunderstandings are contained in this will! It is true that Plato employs *this* question in order to refute those who content themselves with offering empirical responses, and to oppose essence and appearance. His aim, however, is to silence the empirical responses in order to open up the indeterminate horizon of a transcendental problem which is the object of an Idea. Once it is a question of determining the problem or the Idea as such, once it is a question of setting the dialectic in motion, the question 'What is X?' gives way to other questions, otherwise powerful and efficacious, otherwise imperative: 'How much, how and in what cases?' The question 'What is X?' animates only the so-called aporetic dialogues – in other words, those in which the very form of the question gives rise to contradiction and leads to nihilism, no doubt because they have only propaedeutic aims – the aim of opening up the region of the problem in general, leaving to other procedures the task of determining it as a problem or as an Idea. When Socratic irony was taken seriously and the dialectic as a whole was confused with its propaedeutic, extremely troublesome consequences followed: for the dialectic ceased to be the science of problems and ultimately became confused with the simple movement of the negative, and of contradiction. Philosophers began to talk like young men from the farmyard. From this point of view, Hegel is the culmination of a long tradition which took the question 'What is X?' seriously and used it to determine Ideas as essences, but in so doing substituted the negative for the nature of the problematic. This was the outcome of a distortion of the dialectic. Moreover, how many theological prejudices were involved in that tradition, since the answer to 'What is X?' is always God as the locus of the combinatory of abstract predicates. It should be noticed how few philosophers have placed their trust in the question 'What is X?' in order to have Ideas. Certainly not Aristotle. ... Once the dialectic brews up its matter instead of being applied in a vacuum for propaedeutic ends, the questions 'How much?', 'How?', 'In what cases?' and 'Who?' abound – questions the function and sense of which we shall see below.[12] These questions are those of the accident, the event, the multiplicity – of difference – as opposed to that of the essence, or that of the One, or those of the contrary and the contradictory. Hippias triumphs everywhere, even already in Plato: Hippias who refused essences, but nevertheless did not content himself with examples.

Problems are of the order of events – not only because cases of solution emerge like real events, but because the conditions of a problem themselves imply events such as sections, ablations, adjunctions. In this sense, it is correct to represent a double series of events which develop on two planes, echoing without resembling each other: real events on the level of the engendered solutions, and ideal events embedded in the conditions of the problem, like the acts – or, rather, the dreams – of the gods who double our history. The ideal series enjoys the double property of transcendence and immanence in relation to the real. In effect, we have seen how the existence and distribution of singular points belongs entirely to the Idea, even though their specification was immanent in the solution-curves of their neighbouring regions – or, in other words, in the real relations in which the Idea is incarnated. In his wonderful description of the event, Péguy deployed two lines, one horizontal and another vertical, which repeated in depth the distinctive points corresponding to the first, and even anticipated and eternally engendered these distinctive points and their incarnation in the first. At the intersection of these lines – where a powder fuse forms the link between the Idea and the actual – the 'temporally eternal' is formed, and our greatest mastery or greatest power is decided, that which concerns problems themselves:

> Suddenly, we felt that we were no longer the same convicts. Nothing had happened. Yet a problem in which a whole world collided, a problem without issue, in which no end could be seen, suddenly ceased to exist and we asked ourselves what we had been talking about. Instead of an ordinary solution, a found solution, this problem, this difficulty, this impossibility had just passed what seemed like a physical point of resolution. A crisis point. At the same time, the whole world had passed what seemed like a physical crisis point. There are critical points of the event just as there are critical points of temperature: points of fusion, freezing and boiling points; points of coagulation and crystallization. There are even in the case of events states of superfusion which are precipitated, crystallized or determined only by the introduction of a fragment of some future event.[13]

For this reason, the procedure capable of following and describing multiplicities and themes, the procedure of *vice-diction*, is more important than that of contradiction, which purports to determine essences and preserve their simplicity. It will be said that the essence is by nature the most 'important' thing. This, however, is precisely what is at issue: whether the notions of importance and non-importance are not precisely notions which concern events or accidents, and are much more 'important' within accidents than the crude opposition between essence and accident itself. The problem of thought is tied not to essences but to the evaluation of what is important and what is not, to the distribution of singular and regular, distinctive and ordinary points, which takes place entirely within the inessential or within the description of a multiplicity, in relation to the ideal events which constitute the conditions of a 'problem'. To have an Idea means no more than this, and erroneousness or stupidity is defined above all by its perpetual confusion with regard to the important and the unimportant, the ordinary and the singular. It is vice-diction which engenders cases, on the basis of auxiliaries and adjunctions. It presides over the distribution of distinctive points within the Idea; it decides the manner in which a series must be continued, from one singular point among regular points up to which other; it determines whether the series obtained within the Idea are convergent or divergent (there are therefore singularities which are themselves ordinary because of the convergence of the series, and singularities which are distinctive because of their divergence). Vice-diction has two procedures which intervene both in the determination of the conditions of the problem and in the correlative genesis of cases of solution: these are, in the first case, the *specification of adjunct fields* and, in the second, the *condensation of singularities*. On the one hand, in the progressive determination of the conditions, we must in effect discover the adjunctions which complete the initial field of the problem as such – in other words, the varieties of the multiplicity in all its dimensions, the fragments of ideal future or past events which, by the same token, render the problem solvable; and we must establish the modality in which these enclose or are connected with the initial field. On the other hand, we must condense all the singularities, precipitate all the circumstances, points of fusion, congelation or condensation in a sublime occasion, *Kairos*, which makes the solution explode like something abrupt, brutal and revolutionary. Having an Idea is this as well. It is as though every Idea has two faces, which are like love and anger: love in the search for fragments, the progressive determination and linking of the ideal adjoint fields; anger in the condensation of singularities which, by dint of ideal events, defines the concentration of a 'revolutionary situation' and causes the Idea to explode into the actual. It is in this sense that Lenin had Ideas. (There is an objectivity on the part of adjunction and condensation, and an objectivity of conditions, which implies that Ideas no more than Problems do not exist only in our heads but occur here and there in the production of an actual historical world.) Furthermore we must not see mathematical metaphors in all these expressions such as 'singular and distinctive points', 'adjunct fields', and 'condensation of singularities', nor physical metaphors in 'points of fusion or congelation ...', nor lyrical or mystical metaphors in 'love and anger'. These are categories of the dialectical Idea, the extensions of the differential calculus (*mathesis universalis* but also universal physics, universal psychology and universal sociology) corresponding to the Idea in all its domains of multiplicity. They are what is amorous or revolutionary in every Idea, that by virtue of which Ideas are always unequal glimmers of love and wrath which have nothing in common with any natural light.

(The most important aspect of Schelling's philosophy is his consideration of powers. How unjust, in this respect, is Hegel's critical remark about the black cows! Of these two philosophers, it is Schelling who brings difference out of the night of the Identical, and with finer, more varied and more terrifying flashes of lightning than those of contradiction: with *progressivity*. Anger and love are powers of the Idea which develop on the basis of a *mē on* – in other words, not from a negative or a non-being [*ouk on*] but from a problematic being or non-existent, a being implicit in those existences beyond the ground. The God of love and the God of anger are required in order to have an Idea. A, A^2, A^3 form the play of pure depotentialisation and potentiality, testifying to the presence in Schelling's philosophy of a differential calculus adequate to the dialectic. Schelling was Leibnizian, but also Neo-Platonic. The great Neo-Platonic fantasy which offered a response to the problem of the *Phaedrus*, stacking or embedding types of Zeus by a method of exhaustion and evolution of powers: Zeus, $Zeus^2$, $Zeus^3$. ... It is here that division finds its scope, which is not in breadth in the differen*c*iation of species within the same genus, but in depth in derivation and potentialisation, already a kind of differen*t*iation. Thus, in a serial dialectic, the powers of a Difference which draws together and assembles [*ho synochikos*] are awakened and become Titanic with anger, demiurgic with love, and even Apolloniac, Aretic and Athenaic.[14])

There is no more opposition between event and structure or sense and structure than there is between structure and genesis. Structures include as many ideal events as they do varieties of relations and singular points, which intersect with the real events they determine. Those systems of differential elements and relations which we call structures are also *senses* from a genetic point of view, with regard to the actual terms and relations in which they are incarnated. The true opposition lies elsewhere: between Idea (structure–event–sense) and representation. With representation, concepts are like possibilities, but the subject of representation still determines the object as really conforming to the concept, as an essence. That is why representation as a whole is the element of knowledge which is realised by the recollection of the thought object and its recognition by a thinking subject. The Idea makes a virtue of quite different characteristics. The virtuality of the Idea has nothing to do with possibility. Multiplicity tolerates no dependence on the identical in the subject or in the object. The events and singularities of the Idea do not allow any positing of an essence as 'what the thing is'. No doubt, if one insists, the word 'essence' might be preserved, but only on condition of saying that the essence is precisely the accident, the event, the sense; not simply the contrary of what is ordinarily called the essence but the contrary of the contrary: multiplicity is no more appearance than essence, no more multiple than one. The procedures of vice-diction cannot, therefore, be expressed in terms of representation, even infinite: as we saw with Leibniz, they thereby lose their principal power, that of affirming divergence or decentring. In fact, the Idea is not the element of knowledge but that of an infinite 'learning', which is of a different nature to knowledge. For learning evolves entirely in the comprehension of problems as such, in the apprehension and condensation of singularities and in the composition of ideal events and bodies. Learning to swim or learning a foreign language means composing the singular points of one's own body or one's own language with those of another shape or element, which tears us apart but also propels us into a hitherto unknown and unheard-of world of problems. To what are we dedicated if not to those problems which demand the very transformation of our body and our language? In short, representation and knowledge are modelled entirely upon propositions of consciousness which designate cases of solution, but those propositions by themselves give a completely inaccurate notion of the instance which engenders them as cases, and which they resolve or conclude. By contrast, the Idea and 'learning' express that extra-propositional or sub-representative problematic instance: the presentation of the unconscious, not the representation of consciousness. It is not surprising that, among many of the authors who promote it, *structuralism* is so often accompanied by calls for a new theatre or a new (non-Aristotelian) interpretation of the theatre: a theatre of multiplicities opposed in every respect to the theatre of representation, which leaves intact neither the identity of the thing represented, nor author, nor spectator, nor character, nor representation which, through the vicissitudes of the play, can become the object of a production of knowledge or final recognition. Instead, a theatre of problems and always open questions which draws spectator, setting and characters into the real movement of an apprenticeship of the entire unconscious, the final elements of which remain the problems themselves.

How should the necessarily unconscious nature of Ideas be understood? Must it be supposed that Ideas are the objects of a particular exclusive faculty, and that to the extent that they cannot be grasped by its empirical exercise they expose the transcendent or limit element of that faculty? This hypothesis would already have the advantage of eliminating Reason or even the understanding as the faculty of Ideas, and more generally of eliminating every faculty constitutive of a common sense under which is subsumed the empirical exercise of the other faculties with regard to a supposed same object. It is incomprehensible only from the point of view of a common sense or that of an exercise traced from the empirical that, for example, thought should find within itself something which it *cannot* think, something which is both unthinkable and that which must be thought. According to an objection often made against Maïmon, Ideas, understood as the differentials of thought, themselves introduce a minimum of 'given' which cannot be thought; they restore the duality of infinite and finite understanding, which function respectively as the conditions of existence and the conditions of knowledge, and which the entire Kantian Critique nevertheless proposed to eliminate. This objection, however, applies only to the extent that the faculty of Ideas according to Maïmon is the understanding, just as it was reason according to Kant; that is, in either case, a faculty which constitutes a common sense and cannot tolerate the presence within itself of a kernel on which the empirical exercise of the conjoint faculties would break. It is only under these conditions that the unthought in thought, the unconscious of a pure thought, must be realised in an infinite understanding which serves as the ideal of *knowledge*, and that the differentials are condemned to the status of mere *fictions* unless they acquire the status of a fully *actual* reality in that infinite understanding. Once again, however, the alternative is false. We might as well say that the specificity of the problematic and the presence of the unconscious in finite thought remain misunderstood. This is no longer so when Ideas are related to the transcendent exercise of a particular faculty liberated from any common sense.

However, we do not believe this first response to be sufficient, nor that Ideas and structures refer to a particular faculty. Ideas occur throughout the faculties and concern them all. According to the place and the existence of a faculty determined as such, they render possible both the differential object and the transcendent exercise of that faculty. Take, for example, the linguistic multiplicity, regarded as a virtual system of reciprocal connections between 'phonemes' which is incarnated in the actual terms and relations of diverse languages: such a multiplicity renders possible speech as a faculty as well as the transcendent object of that speech, that 'metalanguage' which cannot be spoken in the empirical usage of a given language, but must be spoken and can be spoken only in the poetic usage of speech coextensive with virtuality. Take the social multiplicity: it determines sociability as a faculty, but also the transcendent object of sociability which cannot be lived within actual societies in which the multiplicity is incarnated, but must be and can be lived only in the element of social upheaval (in other words, freedom, which is always hidden among the remains of an old order and the first fruits of a new). The same could be said for other Ideas or multiplicities: the psychic multiplicities of imagination and phantasy, the biological multiplicities of vitality and 'monstrosity', the physical multiplicities of sensibility and sign. ... In this manner, Ideas correspond in turn to each of the faculties and are not the exclusive object of any one in particular, not even of thought. The essential point is that in this way we do not reintroduce any form of common sense – quite the contrary. We saw how the discord between the faculties, which followed from the exclusive character of the transcendent object apprehended by each, nevertheless implied a harmony such that each transmits its violence to the other by powder fuse, but precisely a 'discordant harmony' which excludes the forms of identity, convergence and collaboration which define a common sense. This harmonious Discord seemed to us to correspond to that Difference which by itself articulates or draws together. There is thus a point at which thinking, speaking, imagining, feeling, etc., are one and the same thing, but that *thing* affirms only the divergence of the faculties in their transcendent exercise. It is a question, therefore, not of a common sense but, on the contrary, of a 'para-sense' (in the sense that paradox is also the contrary of good sense). The elements of this para-sense are Ideas, precisely because Ideas are pure multiplicities which do not presuppose any form of identity in a common sense but, on the contrary, animate and describe the disjoint exercise of the faculties from a transcendental point of view. Ideas are thus multiplicities with differential glimmers, like will-o'-the-wisps, 'virtual trails of fire', from one faculty to another, without ever having the homogeneity of that natural light which characterises common sense. That is why learning may be defined in two complementary ways, both of which are opposed to representation in knowledge: learning is either a matter of penetrating the Idea, its varieties and distinctive points, or a matter of raising a faculty to its disjoint transcendent exercise, raising it to that encounter and that violence which are communicated to the others. That is also why the unconscious has two complementary determinations which necessarily exclude it from representation but render it worthy and capable of a pure presentation: the unconscious may be defined either by the extra-propositional and non-actual character of Ideas in the *para-sense*, or by the non-empirical character of the *paradoxical* exercise of the faculties.

It is nevertheless true that Ideas have a very special relationship to pure thought. Thought here must undoubtedly be regarded not as the form of identity of all the faculties but as a particular faculty defined in the same manner as the others by its differential object and its separate exercise. The para-sense or violence which is communicated from one faculty to another according to an order then assigns a particular place to thought: thought is determined in such a manner that it grasps its own *cogitandum* only at the extremity of the fuse of violence which, from one Idea to another, first sets in motion sensibility and its *sentiendum*, and so on. This extremity might just as well be regarded as the ultimate origin of Ideas. In what sense, however, should we understand 'ultimate origin'? In this same sense, while the opposition between thought and all forms of common sense remains stronger than ever, Ideas must be called 'differentials' of thought, or the 'Unconscious' of pure thought. Ideas, therefore, are related not to a Cogito which functions as ground or as a proposition of consciousness, but to the fractured I of a dissolved Cogito; in other words, to the universal *ungrounding* which characterises thought as a faculty in its transcendental exercise. Ideas are not the object of a particular faculty, but nevertheless particularly concern a special faculty to the point that one can say: they come from it (in order to consititute the para-sense of all the faculties). Once again, what does 'come from' or 'find its origin' mean here? Where do Ideas come from, where do problems, their elements and ideal relations come from?

The time has come to determine the difference between the two instances of the problem and the question that we have until now left vague. It must be remembered to what extent modern thought and the renaissance of ontology is based upon the question–problem complex. This complex has ceased to be considered the expression of a provisional and subjective state in the representation of knowledge in order to become the intentionality of Being *par excellence*, the only instance to which, properly speaking, Being answers without the question thereby becoming lost or overtaken. On the contrary, it alone has an opening coextensive with that which must respond to it and can respond to it only by retaining, repeating and continually going over it. This conception of the ontological scope of the question animates works of art as much as philosophical thought. Works are developed around or on the basis of a fracture that they never succeed in filling. The fact that the novel, particularly since Joyce, has found a new language in the mode of an 'Enquiry' or 'Questionnaire' and presents essentially problematic events and characters obviously does not mean that nothing is certain; it is obviously not the application of a generalised method of doubt nor the sign of a modern scepticism but, on the contrary, the discovery of the question and the problematic as a transcendental horizon, as the transcendental element which belongs 'essentially' to beings, things and events. It is the novelistic or theatrical or musical or philosophical, etc., discovery of the Idea, and at the same time the discovery of a transcendent exercise of sensibility, of image-memory, language and thought, by means of which each of these faculties communicates in full discordance with the others and opens on to the difference of Being by taking its own difference as object – in other words, by posing the question of its own difference. Hence that form of writing which is nothing but the question 'what is writing?', or that sensibility which is nothing but the question 'what is it to sense?', or that thought which asks 'what does it mean to think?'. These give rise to the greatest monotonies and the greatest weaknesses of a new-found common sense in the absence of the genius of the Idea, but also to the most powerful 'repetitions', the most prodigious inventions in the para-sense when the Idea emerges in all its violence. Let us recall the mere principles of this ontology of the question: (1) far from being an empirical state of knowledge destined to disappear in the response once a response is given, the question silences all empirical responses which purport to suppress it, in order to force the one response which always continues and maintains it: like Job, in his insistence upon a first-hand response which becomes confused with the question itself (first power of the absurd); (2) whence the power of the question to put in play the questioner as much as that which is questioned, and to put itself in question: Oedipus and his manner of never being finished with the Sphinx (second power of the enigma); (3) whence the revelation of Being as corresponding to the question, reducible neither to the questioned nor to the questioner but that which unites both in the articulation of its own Difference: a *mē on* which is neither non-being [*non-être*] nor the being of the negative, but non-being [*non-étant*] or the being of the question: Ulysses and the response 'No one' (third power, which is that of the philosophical Odyssey).

This modern ontology nevertheless remains inadequate. It sometimes plays upon the indeterminate as an objective power of the question, only to introduce a subjective emptiness which is then attributed to Being, thereby substituting for the force of repetition the impoverishment of the already said or the stereotypes of a new common sense. Sometimes it even manages to dissociate the complex, thereby entrusting questions to the religiosity of a beautiful soul while relegating problems to the status of external obstacles. However, what would a question be if it were not developed under the auspices of those problematising fields alone capable of determining it within a characteristic 'science'? The beautiful soul never ceases to pose its own question, that of betrothal, but how many fiancées were abandoned or disappeared once the question found its right problem which then reacts upon it, corrects it and displaces it with all the difference of a thought (thus Proust's hero asking 'Will I marry Albertine?', but developing the question in the *problem of the work of art to be undertaken*, where the very question undergoes a radical metamorphosis). We must investigate the manner in which questions develop into problems within Ideas, how problems are enveloped by questions within thought. Here too, the classical image of thought must be confronted with another image, this one suggested by the contemporary renaissance of ontology.

From Plato to the post-Kantians, philosophy has defined the movement of thought as a certain type of passage from the hypothetical to the apodictic. Even the Cartesian movement from doubt to certainty is a variant of the passage. Another is the passage from hypothetical necessity to metaphysical necessity in the *On the Ultimate Origination of Things*. Already with Plato the dialectic was defined in this manner: depart from hypotheses, use hypotheses as springboards or 'problems' in order to attain the an-hypothetical principle which determines the solution to the problems as well as the truth of the hypotheses. The whole structure of the *Parmenides* follows from this, under conditions such that it is no longer possible to see therein a propaedeutics, a gymnastics, a game or a formal exercise, as has nevertheless been done ever so delicately. Kant himself is more Platonic than he thinks when he passes from the *Critique of Pure Reason*, entirely subordinated to the hypothetical form of possible experience, to the *Critique of Practical Reason* in which, with the aid of problems, he discovers the pure necessity of a categorical principle. Even more so the post-Kantians when they wish to transform hypothetical judgement into thetic judgement immediately, without changing 'critiques'.[15] It is not illegitimate, therefore, to summarise in this way the movement of philosophy from Plato to Fichte or Hegel by way of Descartes, whatever the diversity of the initial hypotheses or the final apodicticities. There is at least something in common: namely, the point of departure found in a 'hypothesis' or proposition of consciousness affected by a coefficient of uncertainty (as with Cartesian doubt) and the point of arrival found in an eminently moral apodicticity or imperative (Plato's One-Good, the non-deceiving God of the Cartesian Cogito, Leibniz's principle of the best of all possible worlds, Kant's categorical imperative, Fichte's Self, Hegel's 'Science'). However, while this procedure maximally approximates the real movement of thought, it also maximally betrays and distorts this movement: this conjoint hypotheticism and moralism, this scientistic hypotheticism and this rationalist moralism, render unrecognisable what they approximate.

Suppose we say instead that the movement goes not from the hypothetical to the apodictic but from the problematical to the question: at first the difference seems very slight – all the slighter to the extent that while the apodictic is inseparable from a moral imperative, the question, for its part, is also inseparable from an imperative, albeit of another kind. A chasm nevertheless separates these two formulae. The assimilation of the problem and the hypothesis is already a betrayal of the problem or Idea, involving the illegitimate reduction of the latter to propositions of consciousness and to representations of knowledge: the problematical is different in kind from the hypothetical; the *thematic* is not to be confused with the *thetic.* At issue in this difference is the whole distribution, the whole determination, destination and exercise of the faculties within a general doctrine. Moreover, to speak of the apodictic instance and the question-instance is to speak of very different things, since these involve two kinds of imperative, incomparable in every respect. Questions are imperatives – or rather, *questions express the relation between problems and the imperatives from which they proceed.* Is it necessary to take the example of the police in order to demonstrate the imperative character of questions? 'I'm asking the questions.' In fact, however, it is already the dissolved self of the one being questioned which speaks through his torturer. Problems or Ideas emanate from imperatives of adventure or from events which appear in the form of questions. This is why problems are inseparable from a power of decision, a *fiat* which, when we are infused by it, makes us semi-divine beings. Did not mathematicians declare themselves to be descended from the gods? This power of decision is exercised to the highest degree in the two fundamental procedures of adjunction and condensation. It is grounded in the nature of the problems to be resolved, since it is always in relation to an ideal field added by the mathematician that an equation turns out to be reducible or not. The infinite power to add an arbitrary quantity: it is no longer a question of a game after the manner of Leibniz, where the moral imperative of predetermined rules combines with the condition of a given space which must be filled *ex hypothesi.* It is rather a question of a throw of the dice, of the whole sky as open space and of throwing as the only rule. The singular points are on the die; the questions are the dice themselves; the imperative is to throw. Ideas are the problematic combinations which result from throws. The throw of the dice is in no way suggested as an abolition of chance (the sky-chance). To abolish chance is to fragment it according to the laws of probability over several throws, in such a way that the problem is already dismembered into hypotheses of win and loss, while the imperative is moralised into the principle of choosing the best hypothesis which determines a win. By contrast, the throw of the dice affirms chance every time; each throw of the dice affirms the whole of chance each time. The repetition of throws is not subject to the persistence of the same hypothesis, nor to the identity of a constant rule. The most difficult thing is to make chance an object of *affirmation*, but it is the sense of the imperative and the questions that it launches. Ideas emanate from it just as singularities emanate from that aleatory point which every time condenses the whole of chance into one time. It will be said that by assigning the imperative origin of Ideas to this point we invoke only the arbitrary, the simple arbitrariness of a child's game, the child-god. This, however, would be to misunderstand what it means to 'affirm'. Chance is arbitrary only in so far as it is not affirmed or not sufficiently affirmed, in so far as it is distributed within a space, a number and under rules destined to avert it. When chance is sufficiently affirmed the player can no longer lose, since every combination and every throw which produces it is by nature adequate to the place and the mobile command of the aleatory point. What does it mean, therefore, to affirm the whole of chance, every time, in a single time? This affirmation takes place to the degree that the disparates which emanate from a throw begin to resonate, thereby forming a problem. The whole of chance is then indeed in each throw, even though this be partial, and it is there in a single time even though the combination produced is the object of a progressive determination. The throw of the dice carries out the calculation of problems, the determination of differential elements or the distribution of singular points which constitute a structure. The circular relation between imperatives and the problems which follow from them is formed in this manner. Resonance constitutes the truth of a problem as such, in which the imperative is tested, even though the problem itself is born of the imperative. Once chance is affirmed, all arbitrariness is abolished every time. Once chance is affirmed, divergence itself is the object of affirmation within a problem. The ideal fields of adjunction which determine a problem remain in the grip of the arbitrary so long as the basic field does not resonate by incorporating all the values expressible by the adjunct. In general a work is always in itself an ideal field, an ideal field of adjunction. The work is a problem born of the imperative; it is all the more perfect and total in a single throw as the problem is all the more progessively determined as a problem. The author of the work is therefore justly called the operator of the Idea. When Raymond Roussel poses his 'equations of facts' as problems to be solved, as ideal facts or events which begin to resonate as an effect of an imperative of language, or as facts which are themselves *fiats*; when many modern novelists install themselves in this aleatory point, this imperative and questioning 'blind spot' from which the work develops like a problem by making divergent series resonate – they are not doing applied mathematics, or employing a mathematical or physical metaphor. Rather, by establishing that 'science' or universal *mathesis* immediately in each domain, they make the work a process of learning or experimentation, but also something total every time, where the whole of chance is affirmed in each case, renewable every time, perhaps without any subsistent arbitrariness.[16]

This power of decision at the heart of problems, this creation or throw which makes us descendant from the gods, is nevertheless not our own. The gods themselves are subject to the *Anankē* or sky-chance. The imperatives and questions with which we are infused do not emanate from the I: it is not even there to hear them. The imperatives are those of being, while every question is ontological and distributes 'that which is' among problems. Ontology is the dice throw, the chaosmos from which the cosmos emerges. If the imperatives of Being have a relation with the I, it is with the fractured I in which, every time, they displace and reconstitute the fracture according to the order of time. Imperatives do indeed form the *cogitanda* of pure thought, the differentials of thought, at once that which cannot be thought and that which must be thought and can be thought only from the point of view of the transcendent exercise. Questions are these pure thoughts of the *cogitanda.* Imperatives in the form of questions thus signify our greatest powerlessness, but also that point of which Maurice Blanchot speaks endlessly: that blind, acephalic, aphasic and aleatory original point which designates 'the impossibility of thinking that is thought', that point at which 'powerlesness' is transmuted into power, that point which develops in the work in the form of a problem. Far from referring back to the Cogito as a proposition of consciousness, imperatives are addressed to the fractured I as though to the unconscious of thought. For the I has the rights of an unconscious without which it would not think, and in particular would not think the pure *cogitanda.* Contrary to what is stated by the banal propositions of consciousness, thought thinks only on the basis of an unconscious, and thinks that unconscious in the transcendent exercise. Consequently, far from being the properties or attributes of a thinking substance, the Ideas which derive from imperatives enter and leave only by that fracture in the I, which means that another always thinks in me, another who must also be thought. Theft is primary in thought. Of course powerlessness can remain powerlessness, but it alone can also be raised to the highest power. This is precisely what Nietzsche meant by will to power: that imperative transmutation which takes powerlessness itself as an object (be cowardly, lazy or obedient if you wish! on condition that ...) – that dice throw capable of affirming the whole of chance, those questions with which we are infused during torrid or glacial hours, those imperatives which dedicate us to the problems they launch. For 'There is something irreducible in the depths of the spirit: a monolithic bloc of Fatum, of decision already taken on all problems in their measure and their relation to us; and also a right that we have to accede to certain problems, like a hot-iron brand imprinted on our names.'[17]

How disappointing this answer seems to be! We asked what was the origin of Ideas and where problems come from: in reply we invoke throws of the dice, imperatives and questions of chance instead of an apodictic principle; an aleatory point at which everything becomes *ungrounded* instead of a solid ground. We contrast this chance with arbitrariness to the extent that it is affirmed, imperatively affirmed, affirmed in the particular manner of the question; but we measure this affirmation itself by the resonance established between the problematic elements which result from a throw of the dice. In what circle do we turn such that we cannot speak of the origin in any other way? We distinguished four instances: imperative or ontological questions; dialectical problems or the themes which emerge from them; symbolic fields of solvability in which these problems are 'scientifically' expressed in accordance with their conditions; the solutions given in these fields when the problems are incarnated in the actuality of cases. From the outset, however, what are these fiery imperatives, these questions which are the beginning of the world? The fact is that every thing has its beginning in a question, but one cannot say that the question itself begins. Might the question, along with the imperative which it expresses, have no other origin than *repetition*? Great authors of our time (Heidegger, Blanchot) have exploited this most profound relation between the question and repetition. Not that it is sufficient, however, to repeat a single question which would remain intact at the end, even if this question is 'What is being?' [*Qu'en est-il de l'être?*]. It is the bad throws of the dice which are inscribed in the same hypotheses (representing propositions of consciousness or the opinions of a common sense) and approach what is more or less the same apodictic principle (representing the determination of the winning throw). It is the bad players who repeat only by fragmenting chance and dividing it among several throws. By contrast, the good throw of the dice affirms all of chance in one throw, and it is here that we find the essence of what is called a question. There are nevertheless several throws of the dice: the throw of the dice is repeated. Each, however, takes the chance all at once, and instead of having the different, or different combinations, result from the Same, has the same, or the repetition, result from the Different. In this sense, the repetition which is consubstantial with the question is at the source of the 'perplication' of Ideas. The differential of the Idea is itself inseparable from the process of repetition which defined the throw of the dice. There is an iteration in calculus just as there is a repetition in problems which reproduces that of the questions or the imperatives from which it proceeds. Here again, however, it is not an ordinary repetition. Ordinary repetition is prolongation, continuation or that length of time which is stretched into duration: bare repetition (it can be discontinued, but remains fundamentally the repetition of the same). However, *who* is prolonged in this manner? A singularity, as far as the vicinity of another singularity? On the contrary, what defines the extraordinary power of that clothed repetition more profound than bare repetition is the reprise of singularities by one another, the condensation of singularities one into another, as much in the same problem or Idea as between one problem and another or from one Idea to another. Repetition is this emission of singularities, always with an echo or resonance which makes each the double of the other, or each constellation the redistribution of another. Moreover, it amounts to the same thing to say that clothed repetition is more profound at the level of problems, and that repetition results from the different at the level of the questions from which these proceed.

Heidegger shows clearly how the repetition of the question itself develops in the relation between the problem and repetition:

> By a repetition of a fundamental problem we understand the disclosure of the primordial possibilities concealed in it. The development of these possibilities has the effect of transforming the problem and thus preserving it in its import as a problem. To preserve a problem means to free and to safeguard its *intrinsic powers, which are the source of its essence and which make it possible as a problem.* The repetition of the possibilities of a problem, therefore, is not a simple taking up of that which is 'in vogue' with regard to this problem. ... The possible, thus understood, in fact hinders all genuine repetition and thereby all relation to history. ... [A good interpretation must, on the contrary, decide] how far the understanding of the possible which governs all repetition extends and whether it is equal to that which is repeatable.[18]

What is this possible at the heart of a problem which stands opposed to the possibilities or propositions of consciousness, to the currently accepted opinions which make up hypotheses? Nothing but the potentiality of an Idea, its determinable virtuality. On this point, Heidegger is Nietzschean. Of what is repetition said in the eternal return if not the will to power, the world of the will to power with its imperatives, its throws of the dice and its problems resulting from such throws? Repetition in the eternal return never means continuation, perpetuation or prolongation, nor even the discontinuous return of something which would at least be able to be prolonged in a partial cycle (an identity, an I, a Self) but, on the contrary, the reprise of pre-individual singularities which, in order that it can be grasped as repetition, presupposes the dissolution of all prior identities. Every origin is a singularity and every singularity a commencement on the horizontal line, the line of ordinary points on which it is prolonged like so many reproductions or copies which form the moments of a bare repetition. It is also, however, a recommencement on the vertical line which condenses singularities and on which is woven the other repetition, the line of the affirmation of chance. If 'being' is above all difference and commencement, Being is itself repetition, the recommencement of being. Repetition is the 'provided' of the condition which authenticates the imperatives of Being. This is the constant ambiguity of the notion of origin and the reason for our earlier deception: origins are assigned only in a world which challenges the original as much as the copy, and an origin assigns a ground only in a world already precipitated into universal *ungrounding*.

One final consequence remains, concerning the status of negation. There is a non-being, yet there is neither negative nor negation. There is a non-being which is by no means the being of the negative, but rather the being of the problematic. The symbol for this (non)-being or ?-being is 0/0. The zero here refers only to difference and its repetition. This (non)-being which corresponds to the form of a problematic field, even though the modalities of proposition tend to assimilate it to negative non-being, reappears with the so-called expletive 'Ne' which grammarians have so much difficulty in interpreting: like the witness of an extra-propositional grammatical instance, an expletive 'Ne' always appears in propositions where there is a question developed into a problem. The negative is an illusion, no more than a shadow of problems. We have seen how problems were necessarily hidden by possible propositions corresponding to cases of solution: instead of being grasped as problems, they can then appear as no more than hypotheses or series of hypotheses. As a proposition of consciousness, each of these hypotheses is flanked by a double negative: whether the One is, whether the One is not ... whether it is fine, whether it is not fine. ... The negative is an illusion because the form of negation appears with propositions which express the problem on which they depend only by distorting it and obscuring its real structure. Once the problem is translated into hypotheses, each hypothetical affirmation is doubled by a negation, which amounts to the state of a problem betrayed by its shadow. There is no Idea of the negative any more than there are hypotheses in nature, even though nature does proceed by means of problems. That is why it matters little whether the negative is understood as logical limitation or real opposition. Consider the great negative notions such as the many in relation to the One, disorder in relation to order, nothingness in relation to being: it makes no difference whether they are interpreted as the limit of a process of degeneration or as the antithesis of a thesis. At best, the process will be grounded, either in the analytic substance of God or in the synthetic form of the Self. God or the self, it is the same thing. In both cases we remain in the hypothetical element of a simple concept, under which are subsumed either all the infinite degrees of an identical representation or the infinite opposition of two contrary representations. Critiques of the negative are never decisive as long as they invoke the rights of a first concept (the One, order, being); they are no more so as long as they are content to translate opposition into limitation. The critique of the negative is effective only when it denounces the interchangeability of opposition and limitation, thereby denouncing the hypothetical conceptual element which necessarily sustains one or the other, or even one by means of the other. In short, the critique of the negative must be conducted on the basis of the ideal, differential and problematic element, on the basis of the Idea. It is the notion of multiplicity which denounces simultaneously the One and the many, the limitation of the One by the many and the opposition of the many to the One. It is variety which denounces simultaneously order and disorder, and (non)-being or ?-being which denounces simultaneously both being and non-being. The complicity of the negative and the hypothetical must everywhere be dissolved in favour of a more profound link between difference and the problematic. In effect, the Idea is made up of reciprocal relations between differential elements, completely determined by those relations which never include any negative term or relation of negativity. The oppositions, conflicts and contradictions in the concept appear such crude and rough measures by contrast with the fine and differential mechanisms which characterise the Idea – weight in contrast to lightness. We should reserve the name 'positivity' for this state of the multiple Idea or this consistency of the problematic. Moreover, we must guard every time against the manner in which this perfectly positive (non)-being leans towards a negative non-being and tends to collapse into its own shadow, finding there its most profound distortion, to the further advantage of the illusion of consciousness.

Take the example of the linguistic Idea, so frequently invoked today. As defined by phonology, the linguistic Idea certainly has all the characteristics of a structure: the presence of differential elements, called phonemes, extracted from the continuous sonorous flux; the existence of differential relations (distinctive features) which reciprocally and completely determine these elements; the value of singular points assumed by the phonemes in that determination (pertinent particularities); the manner in which the system of language so constituted assumes the character of a multiplicity, the problematic nature of which objectively represents the set of problems which the language poses for itself, and solves in the constitution of significations; the unconscious, non-actual and virtual character of the elements and relations, along with their double status of transcendence and immanence with regard to the sounds actually articulated; the double actualisation of the differential elements, the double incarnation of the differential relations at once both in different languages and in the different significant parts of the same language (differen*c*iation), each language incarnating certain varieties of relation and certain singular points; the complementarity of sense and structure, genesis and structure, where this takes the form of a passive genesis which is revealed in this actualisation. Now, despite all these aspects which define a fully positive multiplicity, linguists constantly speak in negative terms and assimilate the differential relations between phonemes to relations of opposition. Perhaps it might be said that this is only a matter of conventional terminology, and that 'opposition' here means simply correlation. It is true that the notion of opposition employed by linguists seems particularly pluralised and relativised, since each phoneme enters into several distinct oppositions with other phonemes from different points of view. For example, in Trubetzkoy's classification, opposition is so dismembered and distributed among the coexisting varieties of relation that it no longer exists as opposition but rather as a complex or perplexed differential mechanism. A Hegelian would not be at home there, in the absence of the uniformity of a large contradiction. Nevertheless, we touch here upon an essential point: here as elsewhere, in phonology as well as in other domains and with regard to other Ideas, it is a question of knowing whether it is enough to pluralise opposition or to overdetermine contradiction and to distribute them among different figures which, despite everything, still preserve the form of the negative. It seems to us that pluralism is a more enticing and dangerous thought: fragmentation implies overturning. The discovery in any domain of a plurality of coexisting oppositions is inseparable from a more profound discovery, that of difference, which denounces the negative and opposition itself as no more than appearances in relation to the problematic field of a positive multiplicity.[19] One cannot pluralise opposition without leaving its domain and entering the caves of difference which resonate with a pure positivity and reject opposition as no more than a shadow cavern seen from without.

To return to the linguistic Idea: why does Saussure, at the very moment when he discovers that 'in language there are only differences', add that these differences are 'without positive terms' and 'eternally negative'? Why does Trubetzkoy maintain as sacred the principle that 'the idea of difference' which is constitutive of language 'presupposes the idea of opposition'? Everything points to the contrary. Is this not a way of introducing the point of view of consciousness and actual representations into what should be the transcendent exploration of the Idea of the linguistic unconscious – in other words, the highest exercise of speech in relation to the point zero of language? When we interpret differences under the category of opposition and as negatives, are we not already on the side of the listener, even that of the bad listener who hesitates between several possible versions of what was actually said and tries to find himself by establishing oppositions? In other words, are we not on the lesser side of language rather than the side of the one who speaks and assigns meaning? Have we not already betrayed the nature of the play of language – in other words, the sense of that combinatory, of those imperatives or linguistic throws of the dice which, like Artaud's cries, can be understood only by the one who speaks in the transcendent exercise of language? In short, the translation of difference into opposition seems to us to concern not a simple question of terminology or convention, but rather the essence of language and the linguistic Idea. When difference is read as opposition, it is deprived of the peculiar thickness in which its positivity is affirmed. Modern phonology lacks a dimension which would prevent it from playing with shadows on a single plane. In a sense, this is Gustave Guillaume's message throughout his work, the importance of which is today beginning to be understood. For opposition teaches us nothing about the nature of that which is thought to be opposed. The selection of phonemes possessing pertinent value in this or that language is inseparable from that of morphemes as elements of grammatical constructions. Moreover, the morphemes, which on their own account bring into play the virtual whole of the language, are the object of a progressive determination which proceeds by 'differential thresholds' and implies a purely logical time capable of measuring the genesis or actualisation. The formal reciprocal determination of the phonemes refers to that progressive determination which expresses the action of the virtual system on the phonic matter; and it is only when the phonemes are considered abstractly – in other words, when the virtual is reduced to a simple possible – that their relations take the negative form of an empty opposition, rather than that of filling differential positions around a threshold. The fundamental lesson of Guillaume's work is the substitution of a principle of *differential position* for that of distinctive opposition.[20] This substitution takes place to the extent that morphology is no longer simply a continuation of phonology, but rather introduces properly problematic values which determine the significant selection of phonemes. For us, it is from this linguistic point of view that non-being finds the confirmation of its necessary dissociation: on the one hand, in a NE that we have called 'discordant', *disparate* or differential rather than negative, a problematic NE which should be written as (non)-being or ?-being; on the other hand, in a so-called 'foreclusive' PAS which should be written as *non*-being, but which indicates in the engendered proposition only the result of the preceding process. In fact, it is not the expletive NE which presents a little-understood special case of negation: rather, the expletive NE is the original sense from which emerges the negation PAS, both as a necessary consequence and as an inevitable illusion. 'Ne ... pas' divides into a problematic NE and a negative PAS which are like two instances differing in kind, the second of which attracts the first only in order to betray it.

The genesis of the negative is as follows: the affirmations of being are genetic elements in the form of imperative questions; these develop in the positivity of problems; the propositions of consciousness are engendered affirmations which designate cases of solution. Each proposition, however, has a double negative which expresses the shadow of the problem in the domain of solutions – in other words, it expresses the manner in which the problem subsists in the distorted image of it given in representation. The formula 'That is not the case' means that a hypothesis passes over into the negative in so far as it does not represent the currently fulfilled conditions of a problem, to which, on the contrary, another proposition corresponds. The negative is indeed, therefore, the turning shadow of the problematic upon the set of propositions that it subsumes as cases. As a general rule, the critique of the negative remains ineffective so long as it assumes as given the form of affirmation ready made in the proposition. The critique of the negative is radical and well grounded only when it carries out a genesis of affirmation and, *simultaneously*, the genesis of the appearance of negation. For the question is to know how affirmation itself can be multiple, or how difference as such can be the object of pure affirmation. This is possible only to the extent that affirmation as a mode of the proposition is produced from extra-propositional genetic elements (the imperative questions or original ontological affirmations), then 'carried through' or determined by way of problems (multiplicities or problematic Ideas, ideal positivities). Under these conditions, it must be said in effect that the negative in the proposition sits alongside affirmation, but only as the shadow of the problem to which the proposition is thought to respond – in other words, like the shadow of the genetic instance which produces the affirmation itself.

Ideas contain all the varieties of differential relations and all the distributions of singular points coexisting in diverse orders 'perplicated' in one another. When the virtual content of an Idea is actualised, the varieties of relation are incarnated in distinct species while the singular points which correspond to the values of one variety are incarnated in the distinct parts characteristic of this or that species. The Idea of colour, for example, is like white light which perplicates in itself the genetic elements and relations of all the colours, but is actualised in the diverse colours with their respective spaces; or the Idea of sound, which is also like white noise. There is even a white society and a white language, the latter being that which contains in its virtuality all the phonemes and relations destined to be actualised in diverse languages and in the distinctive parts of a given language. Thus, with actualisation, a new type of specific and partitive distinction takes the place of the fluent ideal distinctions. We call the determination of the virtual content of an Idea differen*t*iation; we call the actualisation of that virtuality into species and distinguished parts differen*c*iation. It is always in relation to a differen*t*iated problem or to the differen*t*iated conditions of a problem that a differen*c*iation of species and parts is carried out, as though it corresponded to the cases of solution of the problem. It is always a problematic field which conditions a differen*c*iation within the milieu in which it is incarnated. Consequently – and this is all we wish to say – the negative appears neither in the process of differen*t*iation nor in the process of differen*c*iation. The Idea knows nothing of negation. The first process is identical with the description of a pure positivity, in the form of a problem to which are assigned relations and points, places and functions, positions and differential thresholds which exclude all negative determination and find their source in the genetic or productive elements of affirmation. The other process is identical with the production of finite engendered affirmations which bear upon the actual terms which occupy these places and positions, and upon the real relations which incarnate these relations and these functions. Forms of the negative do indeed appear in actual terms and real relations, but only in so far as these are cut off from the virtuality which they actualise, and from the movement of their actualisation. Then, and only then, do the finite affirmations appear limited in themselves, opposed to one another, and suffering from lack or privation. In short, the negative is always derived and represented, never original or present: the process of difference and of differenciation is primary in relation to that of the negative and opposition. Those commentators on Marx who insist upon the fundamental difference between Marx and Hegel rightly point out that in *Capital* the category of differenciation (the differenciation at the heart of a social multiplicity: the division of labour) is substituted for the Hegelian concepts of opposition, contradiction and alienation, the latter forming only an apparent movement and standing only for abstract effects separated from the principle and from the real movement of their production.[21] Clearly, at this point the philosophy of difference must be wary of turning into the discourse of beautiful souls: differences, nothing but differences, in a peaceful coexistence in the Idea of social places and functions ... but the name of Marx is sufficient to save it from this danger.

The problems of a society, as they are determined in the infrastructure in the form of so-called 'abstract' labour, receive their solution from the process of actualisation or differenciation (the concrete division of labour). However, as long as the problem throws its shadow over the ensemble of differenciated cases forming the solution, these will present a falsified image of the problem itself. It cannot even be said that the falsification comes afterwards: it accompanies or doubles the actualisation. A problem is always reflected in *false problems* while it is being solved, so that the solution is generally perverted by an inseparable falsity. For example, according to Marx, fetishism is indeed an absurdity, an illusion of social consciousness, so long as we understand by this not a subjective illusion born of individual consciousness but an objective or transcendental illusion born out of the conditions of social consciousness in the course of its actualisation. There are those for whom the whole of differenciated social existence is tied to the false problems which enable them to live, and others for whom social existence is entirely contained in the false problems of which they occupy the fraudulent positions, and from which they suffer. All the figures of non-sense appear in the objective field of the false problem: that is, all the counterfeit forms of affirmation, distortions of elements and relations, and confusions of the distinctive with the ordinary. This is why history is no less the locus of non-sense and stupidity than it is the process of sense or meaning. While it is the nature of consciousness to be false, problems by their nature escape consciousness. The natural object of social consciousness or common sense with regard to the recognition of value is the fetish. Social problems can be grasped only by means of a 'rectification' which occurs when the faculty of sociability is raised to its transcendent exercise and breaks the unity of fetishistic common sense. The transcendent object of the faculty of sociability is revolution. In this sense, revolution is the social power of difference, the paradox of society, the particular wrath of the social Idea. Revolution never proceeds by way of the negative. We could not have established the first determination of the negative, as *shadow of the problem as such*, without already being embarked upon a second determination: the negative is *the objective field of the false problem*, the fetish in person. The negative is both shadow of the problem and false problem *par excellence*. Practical struggle never proceeds by way of the negative but by way of difference and its power of affirmation, and the war of the righteous is for the conquest of the highest power, that of deciding problems by restoring them to their truth, by evaluating that truth beyond the representations of consciousness and the forms of the negative, and by acceding at last to the imperatives on which they depend.

We have ceaselessly invoked the virtual. In so doing, have we not fallen into the vagueness of a notion closer to the undetermined than to the determinations of difference? It is precisely this, however, that we wished to avoid in speaking of the virtual. We opposed the virtual and the real: although it could not have been more precise before now, this terminology must be corrected. The virtual is opposed not to the real but to the actual. *The virtual is fully real in so far as it is virtual.* Exactly what Proust said of states of resonance must be said of the virtual: 'Real without being actual, ideal without being abstract'; and symbolic without being fictional. Indeed, the virtual must be defined as strictly a part of the real object – as though the object had one part of itself in the virtual into which it plunged as though into an objective dimension. Accounts of the differential calculus often liken the differential to a 'portion of the difference'. Or, following Lagrange's method, the question is asked which part of the mathematical object presents the relations in question and must be considered derived. The reality of the virtual consists of the differential elements and relations along with the singular points which correspond to them. The reality of the virtual is structure. We must avoid giving the elements and relations which form a structure an actuality which they do not have, and withdrawing from them a reality which they have. We have seen that a double process of reciprocal determination and complete determination defined that reality: far from being undetermined, the virtual is completely determined. When it is claimed that works of art are immersed in a virtuality, what is being invoked is not some confused determination but the completely determined structure formed by its genetic differential elements, its 'virtual' or 'embryonic' elements. The elements, varieties of relations and singular points coexist in the work or the object, in the virtual part of the work or object, without it being possible to designate a point of view privileged over others, a centre which would unify the other centres. How, then, can we speak simultaneously of both complete determination and only a part of the object? The determination must be a complete determination of the object, yet form only a part of it. Following suggestions made by Descartes in his *Replies to Arnaud*, we must carefully distinguish the object in so far as it is complete and the object in so far as it is whole. What is complete is only the ideal part of the object, which participates with other parts of objects in the Idea (other relations, other singular points), but never constitutes an integral whole as such. What the complete determination lacks is the whole set of relations belonging to actual existence. An object may be *ens*, or rather *(non)-ens omni modo determinatum*, without being entirely determined or actually existing.

There is thus another part of the object which is determined by actualisation. Mathematicians ask: What is this other part represented by the so-called primitive function? In this sense, integration is by no means the inverse of differen*t*iation but, rather, forms an original process of differen*c*iation. Whereas differentiation determines the virtual content of the Idea as problem, differenciation expresses the actualisation of this virtual and the constitution of solutions (by local integrations). Differenciation is like the second part of difference, and in order to designate the integrity or the integrality of the object we require the complex notion of differen*t*/*c*iation. The *t* and the *c* here are the distinctive feature or the phonological relation of difference in person. Every object is double without it being the case that the two halves resemble one another, one being a virtual image and the other an actual image. They are unequal odd halves. Differentiation itself already has two aspects of its own, corresponding to the varieties of relations and to the singular points dependent upon the values of each variety. However, differenciation in turn has two aspects, one concerning the qualities or diverse species which actualise the varieties, the other concerning number or the distinct parts actualising the singular points. For example, genes as a system of differential relations are incarnated at once both in a species and in the organic parts of which it is composed. There is in general no quality which does not refer to a space defined by the singularities corresponding to the differential relations incarnated in that quality. The work of Lavelle and of Nogué, for example, has shown the existence of spaces belonging to qualities and the manner in which these spaces are constructed alongside singularities, so that a difference in quality is always subtended by a spatial difference (*diaphora*). Furthermore, the reflections of painters teach us everything about the space of each colour and the alignment of such spaces within a work. Species are differenciated only in so far as each has parts which are themselves differenciated. Differenciation is always simultaneously differenciation of species and parts, of qualities and extensities: determination of qualities or determination of species, but also partition or organisation. How, then, do these two aspects of differen*c*iation connect with the two preceding aspects of differen*t*iation? How do the two dissimilar halves of an object fit together? Qualities and species incarnate the varieties of actual relation; organic parts incarnate the corresponding singularities. However, the precision with which they fit together is better seen from two complementary points of view.

On the one hand, complete determination carries out the differentiation of singularities, but it bears only upon their existence and their distribution. The nature of these singular points is specified only by the form of the neighbouring integral curves – in other words, by virtue of the actual or differenciated species and spaces. On the other hand, the essential aspects of sufficient reason – determinability, reciprocal determination, complete determination – find their systematic unity in progressive determination. In effect, the reciprocity of determination does not signify a regression, nor a marking time, but a veritable progression in which the reciprocal terms must be secured step by step, and the relations themselves established between them. The completeness of the determination also implies the progressivity of adjunct fields. In going from A to B and then B to A, we do not arrive back at the point of departure as in a bare repetition; rather, the repetition between A and B and B and A is the progressive tour or description of the whole of a problematic field. It is like Vitrac's poem, where the different steps which each form a poem (Writing, Dreaming, Forgetting, Looking for the opposite, Humourising and finally *Rediscovering by analysing*) progressively determine the whole poem as a problem or a multiplicity. In this sense, by virtue of this progressivity, every structure has a purely logical, ideal or dialectical time. However, this virtual time itself determines a time of differenciation, or rather rhythms or different times of actualisation which correspond to the relations and singularities of the structure and, for their part, measure the passage from virtual to actual. In this regard, four terms are synonymous: actualise, differenciate, integrate and solve. For the nature of the virtual is such that, for it, to be actualised is to be differenciated. Each differenciation is a local integration or a local solution which then connects with others in the overall solution or the global integration. This is how, in the case of the organic, the process of actualisation appears simultaneously as the local differenciation of parts, the global formation of an internal milieu, and the solution of a problem posed within the field of constitution of an organism.[22] An organism is nothing if not the solution to a problem, as are each of its differenciated organs, such as the eye which solves a light 'problem'; but nothing within the organism, no organ, would be differenciated without the internal milieu endowed with a general effectivity or integrating power of regulation. (Here again, in the case of living matter, the negative forms of opposition and contradiction, obstacle and need, are secondary and derivative in relation to the imperatives of an organism to be constructed or a problem to be solved.)

The only danger in all this is that the virtual could be confused with the possible. The possible is opposed to the real; the process undergone by the possible is therefore a 'realisation'. By contrast, the virtual is not opposed to the real; it possesses a full reality by itself. The process it undergoes is that of actualisation. It would be wrong to see only a verbal dispute here: it is a question of existence itself. Every time we pose the question in terms of possible and real, we are forced to conceive of existence as a brute eruption, a pure act or leap which always occurs behind our backs and is subject to a law of all or nothing. What difference can there be between the existent and the non-existent if the non-existent is already possible, already included in the concept and having all the characteristics that the concept confers upon it as a possibility? Existence is *the same* as but outside the concept. Existence is therefore supposed to occur in space and time, but these are understood as indifferent milieux instead of the production of existence occurring in a characteristic space and time. Difference can no longer be anything but the negative determined by the concept: either the limitation imposed by possibles upon each other in order to be realised, or the opposition of the possible to the reality of the real. The virtual, by contrast, is the characteristic state of Ideas: it is on the basis of its reality that existence is produced, in accordance with a time and a space immanent in the Idea.

Secondly, the possible and the virtual are further distinguished by the fact that one refers to the form of identity in the concept, whereas the other designates a pure multiplicity in the Idea which radically excludes the identical as a prior condition. Finally, to the extent that the possible is open to 'realisation', it is understood as an image of the real, while the real is supposed to resemble the possible. That is why it is difficult to understand what existence adds to the concept when all it does is double like with like. Such is the defect of the possible: a defect which serves to condemn it as produced after the fact, as retroactively fabricated in the image of what resembles it. The actualisation of the virtual, on the contrary, always takes place by difference, divergence or differenciation. Actualisation breaks with resemblance as a process no less than it does with identity as a principle. Actual terms never resemble the singularities they incarnate. In this sense, actualisation or differenciation is always a genuine creation. It does not result from any limitation of a pre-existing possibility. It is contradictory to speak of 'potential', as certain biologists do, and to define differenciation by the simple limitation of a global power, as though this potential were indistinguishable from a logical possibility. For a potential or virtual object, to be actualised is to create divergent lines which correspond to – without resembling – a virtual multiplicity. The virtual possesses the reality of a task to be performed or a problem to be solved: it is the problem which orientates, conditions and engenders solutions, but these do not resemble the conditions of the problem. Bergson was right, therefore, to say that from the point of view of differenciation, even the resemblances which appear along divergent lines of evolution (for example, the eye as an 'analogous' organ) must be related first of all to the heterogeneity in the production mechanism. Moreover, the subordination of difference to identity and that of difference to similitude must be overturned in the same movement. What is this correspondence, however, without resemblance or creative differenciation? The Bergsonian schema which unites *Creative Evolution* and *Matter and Memory* begins with the account of a gigantic memory, a multiplicity formed by the virtual coexistence of all the sections of the 'cone', each section being the repetition of all the others and being distinguished from them only by the order of the relations and the distribution of singular points. Then, the actualisation of this mnemonic virtual appears to take the form of the creation of divergent lines, each of which corresponds to a virtual section and represents a manner of solving a problem, but also the incarnation of the order of relations and distribution of singularities peculiar to the given section in differenciated species and parts.[23] Difference and repetition in the virtual ground the movement of actualisation, of differenciation as creation. They are thereby substituted for the identity and the resemblance of the possible, which inspires only a pseudo-movement, the false movement of realisation understood as abstract limitation.

Any hesitation between the virtual and the possible, the order of the Idea and the order of the concept, is disastrous, since it abolishes the reality of the virtual. There are traces of such an oscillation in the philosophy of

Leibniz. Every time Leibniz speaks of Ideas, he presents them as virtual multiplicities made of differential relations and singular points, which thought apprehends in a state close to sleep, stupor, swooning, death, amnesia, murmuring or intoxication. ...[24] However, that in which Ideas are actualised is rather conceived as a possible, a realised possible. This hesitation between the possible and the virtual explains why no one has gone further than Leibniz in the exploration of sufficient reason, and why, nevertheless, no one has better maintained the illusion of a subordination of that sufficient reason to the identical. No one has come closer to a movement of vice-diction in the Idea, but no one has better maintained the supposed right of representation, albeit at the price of rendering it infinite. No one has been better able to immerse thought in the element of difference and provide it with a differential unconscious, surround it with little glimmerings and singularities, all in order to save and reconstitute the homogeneity of a natural light *à la* Descartes. It is in effect with Descartes that the principle of representation as good sense or common sense appears in its highest form. We can call this the principle of the 'clear *and* distinct', or the principle of the proportionality of the clear and the distinct: an idea is all the more distinct the clearer it is, and clarity-distinctness constitutes the light which renders thought possible in the common exercise of all the faculties. Given this principle, we cannot overemphasize the importance of a remark that Leibniz constantly makes in his logic of ideas: a clear idea is in itself confused; it is confused *in so far as it is clear*. Without doubt, this remark may be accommodated within the Cartesian logic, and taken to mean simply that a clear idea is confused because it is not yet clear enough in all its parts. Moreover, is this not how Leibniz himself finally tends to interpret it? However, is it not also susceptible to another more radical interpretation, according to which there would be a difference between the clear and the distinct, not just of degree but in kind, such that the clear would be in itelf confused and the distinct in itself obscure? What is this distinct–obscure which corresponds to the clear–confused? Consider Leibniz's famous passages on the murmuring of the sea. Here too, two interpretations are possible. Either we say that the apperception of the whole noise is clear but confused (not distinct) because the component little perceptions are themselves not clear but obscure; or we say that the little perceptions are themselves distinct and obscure (not clear): distinct because they grasp differential relations and singularities; obscure because they are not yet 'distinguished', not yet differenciated. These singularities then condense to determine a threshold of consciousness in relation to our bodies, a threshold of differenciation on the basis of which the little perceptions are actualised, but actualised in an apperception which in turn is only clear and confused; clear because it is distinguished or differenciated, and confused because it is clear. The problem is then no longer posed in terms of whole–parts (from the point of view of logical possibility) but in terms of virtual–actual (actualisation of differential relations, incarnation of singular points). At this point, the value of representation in the common sense divides into two irreducible values in the para-sense: a distinctness which can only be obscure, the more obscure the more it is distinct; and a confusion–clarity which can only be confused. The nature of the Idea is to be distinct and obscure. In other words, the Idea is precisely *real without being actual, differentiated without being differenciated, and complete without being entire.* Distinctness–obscurity is intoxication, the properly philosophical stupor or the Dionysian Idea. Leibniz very nearly encountered Dionysus at the sea shore or near the water mill. Perhaps Apollo, the clear–confused thinker, is needed in order to think the Ideas of Dionysus. However, the two never unite in order to reconstitute a natural light. Rather, they compose two languages which are encoded in the language of philosophy and directed at the divergent exercise of the faculties: the disparity of style.

How does actualisation occur in things themselves? Why is differenciation at once both composition and determination of qualities, organisation and determination of species? Why is differenciation differenciated along these two complementary paths? Beneath the actual qualities and extensities, species and parts, there are spatio–temporal dynamisms. These are the actualising, differenciating agencies. They must be surveyed in every domain, even though they are ordinarily hidden by the constituted qualities and extensities. Embryology shows that the division of an egg into parts is secondary in relation to more significant morphogenetic movements: the augmentation of free surfaces, stretching of cellular layers, invagination by folding, regional displacement of groups. A whole kinematics of the egg appears, which implies a dynamic. Moreover, this dynamic expresses something ideal. Transport is Dionysian, divine and delirious, before it is local transfer. Types of egg are therefore distinguished by the orientations, the axes of development, the differential speeds and rhythms which are the primary factors in the actualisation of a structure and create a space and a time peculiar to that which is actualised. Baër concluded, on the one hand, that differenciation went from the more general to the less general because the dynamic structural characteristics of the major types or branches appeared before the merely formal characteristics of the species, the genus or even the class; and, on the other hand, that the irreducibility of these dynamisms, the fault lines between these types, imposed actual distinctions between Ideas and singular limitations upon the possibilities of evolution. However, these two points raise many problems. In the first place, the highest generalities put forward by Baër are generalities only for an adult observer who contemplates them from without. In themselves, they are lived by the individual-embryo in its field of individuation. Furthermore –

as Vialleton, a disciple of Baër, points out – they can only be lived, and lived only by the individual-embryo: there are 'things' that only an embryo can do, movements that it alone can undertake or even withstand (for example, the anterior member of the tortoise undergoes a relative displacement of 180 degrees, while the neck involves the forward slippage of a variable number of proto-vertebrae).[25] The destiny and achievement of the embryo is to live the unlivable, to sustain forced movements of a scope which would break any skeleton or tear ligaments. It is indeed true that differenciation is progressive and serial: the characteristics of the major types appear before those of genus and species in the order of the determination of species; and in the order of organisation, this shoot is the beginning of a paw before it becomes a right or left paw. Rather than a difference in generality, however, this movement implies a difference in kind: rather than discovering the more general beneath the less general, we discover pure spatio–temporal dynamisms (the lived experience of the embryo) with regard to the constituted parts and qualities, beneath the morphological, histological, anatomical, physiological and other characteristics. Rather than going from more to less general, determination progresses from virtual to actual in accordance with the primary factors of actualisation. The notion of 'generality' here suffers the disadvantage of suggesting a confusion between the virtual, in so far as it is actualised by a process of creation, and the possible, in so far as it is realised by limitation. Before the embryo as general support of qualities and parts there is the embryo as individual and patient subject of spatio–temporal dynamisms, the larval subject.

As for the other aspect, that of the possibility of evolution, we must approach it in terms of pre-evolutionist polemics. The great controversy between Cuvier and Geoffroy Saint-Hilaire concerns the unity of composition: is there an Animal in itself or an Idea of the universal animal – or do the sub-kingdoms introduce impassable gulfs between the types of animal? The discussion finds its poetic method and test in *folding*: is it possible to pass by folding from Vertebrate to Cephalopod? Can a Vertebrate be folded in such a manner that the two ends of the spine approach one another, the head moving towards the feet, the pelvis towards the neck, and the viscera arranged in the manner of Cephalopods? Cuvier denies that folding can produce such an arrangement. What animal could pass the test, even reduced to its dry skeleton? Geoffroy, it is true, does not claim that the passage is carried out by folding; his argument is more profound: that there are developmental times which stop a given animal at a particular degree of composition ('organ A would be in an unusual relation to organ C if B were not produced, or if development had stopped too soon and prevented its production').[26] The introduction of the temporal factor is essential, even though Geoffroy conceives of it only in the form of stoppages – in other words, progressive stages ordered according to the realisation of a *possible* common to all animals. It is enough to endow time with its true meaning of creative actualisation for evolution to find a principle which conditions it. For if, from the point of view of actualisation, the dynamism of spatial directions determines a differenciation of types, then the more or less rapid times immanent to these dynamisms ground the passage from one to the other, from one differenciated type to another, either by deceleration or by acceleration. With contracted or extended times and according to the reasons for acceleration or delay, other spaces are created. Even the stoppage assumes the aspect of a creative actualisation in the case of neoteny. In principle, the temporal factor allows the transformation of dynamisms, even though these may be asymmetrical, spatially irreducible and completely differenciated – or rather, differenciating. In this sense, Perrier saw phenomena of 'accelerated repetition' (tachygenesis) at the origin of the branchings of the animal kingdom, and found in the precocity of the appearance of types a superior proof of evolution itself.[27]

The entire world is an egg. The double differenciation of species and parts always presupposes spatio–temporal dynamisms. Take a division into 24 cellular elements endowed with similar characteristics: nothing yet tells us the dynamic process by which it was obtained – 2 x 12, (2 x 2) + (2 x 10), or (2 x 4) + (2 x 8) ...? Even Platonic division would lack a rule with which to distinguish the two sides, if movements and orientations or spatial lines did not provide one. Thus, in the case of fishing: entrap the prey or strike it, strike it from top to bottom or from bottom to top. It is the dynamic processes which determine the actualisation of Ideas. But what is their relation to this actualisation? They are precisely *dramas*, they dramatise the Idea. On the one hand, they create or trace a space corresponding to the differential relations and to the singularities to be actualised. When a cellular migration takes place, as Raymond Ruyer shows, it is the requirements of a 'role' in so far as this follows from a structural 'theme' to be actualised which determines the situation, not the other way round.[28] The world is an egg, but the egg itself is a theatre: a staged theatre in which the roles dominate the actors, the spaces dominate the roles and the Ideas dominate the spaces. Furthermore, by virtue of the complexity of Ideas and their relations with other Ideas, the spatial dramatisation is played out on several levels: in the constitution of an internal space, but also in the manner in which that space extends into the external extensity, occupying a region of it. For example, the internal space of a colour is not to be confused with the manner in which it occupies an extensity where it enters into relations with other colours, whatever the affinity between these two processes. A living being is not only defined genetically, by the dynamisms which determine its internal milieu, but also ecologically, by the external movements which preside over its distribution within an extensity. A kinetics of population adjoins, without resembling, the kinetics of the egg; a geographic process of isolation may be no less formative of species than internal genetic variations, and sometimes precedes the latter.[29] Everything is even more complicated when we consider that the internal space is itself made up of multiple spaces which must be locally integrated and connected, and that this connection, which may be achieved in many ways, pushes the object or living being to its own limits, all in contact with the exterior; and that this relation with the exterior, and with other things and living beings, implies in turn connections and global integrations which differ in kind from the preceding. Everywhere a staging at several levels.

On the other hand, the dynamisms are no less temporal than spatial. They constitute a time of actualisation or differenciation no less than they outline spaces of actualisation. Not only do these spaces begin to incarnate differential relations between elements of the reciprocally and completely determined structure, but the times of differenciation incarnate the time of the structure, the time of progressive determination. Such times may be called differential rhythms in view of their role in the actualisation of the Idea. Finally, beneath species and parts, we find only these times, these rates of growth, these paces of development, these decelerations or accelerations, these durations of gestation. It is not wrong to say that time alone provides the response to a question, and space alone provides the solution to a problem. Consider the following example, concerning sterility and fecundity (in the case of the female sea-urchin and the male annelid): *problem* – will certain paternal chromosomes be incorporated into new nuclei, or will they be dispersed into the protoplasm? *question* – will they arrive soon enough? However, the distinction is obviously relative, for it is clear that the dynamism is simultaneously temporal and spatial – in other words, spatio–temporal (in this case, the formation of cones of division, the splitting of chromosomes and the movement which takes them to the poles of the cones). The duality does not exist in the process of actualisation itself, but only in its outcome, in the actual terms, species and parts. Nor is it a question of a real distinction but rather a strict complementarity, since the species designates the quality of the parts just as the parts designate the number of the species. More precisely, the species gathers the time of the dynamism into a quality (lion-ness, frog-ness) while the parts outline its space. A quality always flashes within a space and endures the whole time of that space. In short, dramatisation is the differenciation of differenciation, at once both qualitative and quantitative. However, in saying 'at once' we mean that differenciation differenciates itself into these two correlative paths, species and parts, determination of species and determination of parts. Just as there is a difference of difference which gathers up the different, so there is a differenciation of differenciation which integrates and welds together the differenciated. This is a necessary outcome to the extent that dramatisation inseparably incarnates the two traits of the Idea, differential relations and corresponding singular points, the latter being actualised in the parts while the former are actualised in the species.

Are not these spatio–temporal determinations what Kant called schemata? There is, nevertheless, an important difference. A schema is indeed a rule of determination for time and of construction for space, but it is conceived and put to work in relation to concepts understood in terms of logical possibility: this is so much part of its nature that it does no more than convert logical possibility into transcendental possibility. It brings spatio–temporal relations into correspondence with the logical relations of the concept. However, since it remains external to the concept, it is not clear how it can ensure the harmony of the understanding and sensibility, since it does not even have the means to ensure its own harmony with the understanding without appeal to a miracle. Schematism possesses an immense power: it can divide a concept and specify it according to a typology. A concept alone is completely incapable of specifying or dividing itself; the agents of differenciation are the spatio–temporal dynamisms which act within or beneath it, like a hidden art. Without these, we would still confront the questions which Aristotle raised with regard to Platonic division: where do the halves come from? However, the schema does not account for the power *with which* it acts. Everything changes when the dynamisms are posited no longer as schemata of concepts but as dramas of Ideas. For if the dynamism is external to concepts – and, as such, a schema – it is internal to Ideas – and, as such, a drama or dream. Species are divided into lineages, Linnaeons into Jordanons, concepts into types, but these divisions do not have the same criteria as the divided, they are not homogeneous with the divided, and they are established in a domain external to that of concepts but internal to that of the Ideas which preside over division itself. Dynamism thus comprises its own power of determining space and time, since it immediately incarnates the differential relations, the singularities and the progressivities immanent in the Idea.[30] *The shortest* is not simply the schema of the concept of straight, but the dream, the drama or the dramatisation of the Idea of a line in so far as it expresses the differenciation of the straight from the curved. We distinguish Ideas, concepts and dramas: the role of dramas is to specify concepts by incarnating the differential relations and singularities of an Idea.

Dramatisation takes place under the critical eye of the savant as much as it does in the head of the dreamer. It acts below the sphere of concepts and the representations subsumed by them. There is nothing which does not lose its identity as this is constituted by concepts, and its similarity as this is constituted in representation, when the dynamic space and time of its actual constitution is discovered. The 'type hill' is no more than a stream along parallel lines, the 'type slope' an outcrop of hard layers along which the rocks are buried in a direction perpendicular to that of the hills; but on the scale of millions of years which constitutes the time of their actualisation, the hardest rocks in turn are fluid matters which flow under the weak constraints exercised on their singularities. Every typology is dramatic, every dynamism a catastrophe. There is necessarily something cruel in this birth of a world which is a chaosmos, in these worlds of movements without subjects, roles without actors. When Artaud spoke of the theatre of cruelty, he defined it only in terms of an extreme 'determinism', that of spatio–temporal determination in so far as it incarnates an Idea of mind or nature, like a 'restless space' or movement of turning and wounding gravitation capable of directly affecting the organism, a pure staging without author, without actors and without subjects. Spaces are hollowed out, time is accelerated or decelerated, only at the cost of strains and displacements which mobilise and compromise the whole body. Shining points pierce us, singularities turn us back upon ourselves: everywhere the tortoise's neck with its vertiginous sliding of proto-vertebrae. Even the sky suffers from its cardinal points and its constellations which, like 'actor-suns', inscribe Ideas in its flesh. There are indeed actors and subjects, but these are larvae, since they alone are capable of sustaining the lines, the slippages and the rotations. Afterwards it is too late. It is true that every Idea turns us into larvae, having put aside the identity of the I along with the resemblance of the self. This is badly described as a matter of regression, fixation or arrestation of development, for we are never fixed at a moment or in a given state but always fixed by an Idea as though in the glimmer of a look, always fixed in a movement that is under way. What would Ideas be if not the fixed and cruel Ideas of which Villiers de l'Isle-Adam speaks? We are always patients where Ideas are concerned. This, however, is not an ordinary fixation or patience. What is fixed is not ready-made or already complete. When we remain or again become embryos, it is rather because of this pure movement of repetition which is fundamentally distinguished from all regression. The larvae bear Ideas in their flesh, while we do not go beyond the representations of the concepts. They know nothing of the domain of the possible, being close to the virtual, the first actualisations of which they bear as though they had chosen them. Such is the intimacy of the Leech and the Higher Man: they are at once dream and science, object of dreams and object of science, bite and knowledge, mouth and brain (Perrier spoke of the conflict between mouth and brain played out between the Vertebrates and the annulate Worms).

Ideas are dramatised at several levels, but so too dramatisations of different orders echo one another across these levels. Take the Idea of an Island: geographical dramatisation differenciates it or divides the concept into two types, the original oceanic type which signals an eruption or raising above the sea, and the continental drift type which results from a disarticulation or fracture. The Island dreamer, however, rediscovers this double dynamism because he dreams of becoming infinitely cut off, at the end of a long drift, but also of an absolute beginning by means of a radical foundation. It has often been remarked that the global sexual behaviour of men and women tends to reproduce the movement of their organs, and that the latter in turn tend to reproduce the dynamism of the cellular elements: psychic, organic and chemical – three dramatisations of different orders echo one another. While it is thought which must explore the virtual down to the ground of its repetitions, it is imagination which must grasp the process of actualisation from the point of view of these echoes or reprises. It is imagination which crosses domains, orders and levels, knocking down the partitions coextensive with the world, guiding our bodies and inspiring our souls, grasping the unity of mind and nature; a larval consciousness which moves endlessly from science to dream and back again.

Actualisation takes place in three series: space, time and also consciousness. Every spatio–temporal dynamism is accompanied by the emergence of an elementary consciousness which itself traces directions, doubles movements and migrations, and is born on the threshold of the condensed singularities of the body or object whose consciousness it is. It is not enough to say that consciousness is consciousness of something: it is the double of this something, and everything is consciousness because it possesses a double, even if it is far off and very foreign. Repetition is everywhere, as much in what is actualised as in its actualisation. It is in the Idea to begin with, and it runs through the varieties of relations and the distribution of singular points. It also determines the reproductions of space and time, as it does the reprises of consciousness. In every case, repetition is the power of difference and differenciation: because it condenses the singularities, or because it accelerates or decelerates time, or because it alters spaces. Repetition is never explained by the form of identity in the concept, nor by the similar in representation. No doubt conceptual blockage gives rise to a bare repetition that we can effectively represent as the repetition of the same. However, *who* blocks the concept, if not the Idea? Moreover, as we have seen, the blockage takes place along the three lines of space, time and consciousness. It is the excess in the Idea which explains the lack in the concept. Similarly, it is the clothed, singular or extraordinary repetition, dependent upon the Idea, which explains that ordinary, bare repetition which is dependent upon the concept and plays only the role of the outer garment. In the Idea and its actualisation, we find at once both the natural reason for conceptual blockage and the supernatural reason for a repetition superior to that subsumed within the blocked concept. What remains outside the concept refers more profoundly to what is inside the Idea. The entire Idea is caught up in the mathematico–biological system of differen*t*/*c*iation. However, mathematics and biology appear here only in the guise of technical models which allow the exposition of the virtual and the process of actualisation, along with the exploration of the two halves of difference, the dialectical half and the aesthetic half. The dialectical Idea is doubly determined by the variety of differential relations and the distribution of correlative singularities (differen*t*iation). Aesthetic actualisation is doubly determined by the determination of species and by composition (differen*c*iation). The determination of species incarnates the relations, just as composition does the singularities. The actual qualities and parts, species and numbers, correspond to the element of qualitability and the element of quantitability in the Idea. However, what carries out the third aspect of sufficient reason – namely, the element of potentiality in the Idea? No doubt the pre-quantitative and pre-qualitative dramatisation. It is this, in effect, which determines or unleashes, which differenciates the differen*c*iation of the actual in its correspondence with the differen*t*iation of the Idea. Where, however, does this power of dramatisation come from? Is it not, beneath the species and parts, the qualities and numbers, the most intense or most individual act? We have not yet shown what grounds dramatisation, both for the actual and the Idea, as the development of the third element of sufficient reason.

Chapter V
Asymmetrical Synthesis of the Sensible

Difference is not diversity. Diversity is given, but difference is that by which the given is given, that by which the given is given as diverse. Difference is not phenomenon but the noumenon closest to the phenomenon. It is therefore true that God makes the world by calculating, but his calculations never work out exactly [*juste*], and this inexactitude or injustice in the result, this irreducible inequality, forms the condition of the world. The world 'happens' while God calculates; if the calculation were exact, there would be no world. The world can be regarded as a 'remainder', and the real in the world understood in terms of fractional or even incommensurable numbers. Every phenomenon refers to an inequality by which it is conditioned. Every diversity and every change refers to a difference which is its sufficient reason. Everything which happens and everything which appears is correlated with orders of differences: differences of level, temperature, pressure, tension, potential, *difference of intensity*. Carnot's principle says this in one fashion, Curie's principle in another.[1] There are locks everywhere. Every phenomenon flashes in a signal–sign system. In so far as a system is constituted or bounded by at least two heterogeneous series, two disparate orders capable of entering into communication, we call it a signal. The phenomenon that flashes across this system, bringing about the communication between disparate series, is a sign. 'The emerald hides in its facets a bright-eyed water-sprite ...': every phenomenon is of the 'bright-eyed water-sprite' type, made possible by an emerald. Every phenomenon is composite because not only are the two series which bound it heterogeneous but each is itself composed of heterogeneous terms, subtended by heterogeneous series which form so many sub-phenomena. The expression 'difference of intensity' is a tautology. Intensity is the form of difference in so far as this is the reason of the sensible. Every intensity is differential, by itself a difference. Every intensity is E – E', where E itself refers to an *e* – *e*', and *e* to ε – ε' etc. : each intensity is already a coupling (in which each element of the couple refers in turn to couples of elements of another order), thereby revealing the properly qualitative content of quantity.[2] We call this state of infinitely doubled difference which resonates to infinity *disparity*. Disparity – in other words, difference or intensity (difference of intensity) – is the sufficient reason of all phenomena, the condition of that which appears. Novalis, with his tourmaline, is closer to the conditions of the sensible than Kant, with space and time. The reason of the sensible, the condition of that which appears, is not space and time but the Unequal in itself, *disparateness* as it is determined and comprised in difference of intensity, in intensity as difference.

Nevertheless, we encounter severe difficulties when we attempt to consider Carnot's or Curie's principles as local manifestations of a transcendental principle. We know only forms of energy which are already localised and distributed in extensity, or extensities already qualified by forms of energy. Energetics defined a particular energy by the combination of two factors, one *intensive* and one *extensive* (for example, force and distance for linear energy, surface tension and surface area for surface energy, pressure and volume for volume energy, height and weight for gravitational energy, temperature and entropy for thermal energy ...). It turns out that, in experience, *intensio* (intension) is inseparable from an *extensio* (extension) which relates it to the *extensum* (extensity).[3] In these conditions, intensity itself is subordinated to the qualities which fill extensity (primary physical qualities or *qualitas*, and secondary perceptible qualities or *quale*). In short, we know intensity only as already developed within an extensity, and as covered over by qualities. Whence our tendency to consider intensive quantity as a badly grounded empirical concept, an impure mixture of a sensible quality and extensity, or even of a physical quality and an extensive quantity.

It is true that this tendency would lead nowhere if intensity, for its own part, did not present a corresponding tendency within the extensity in which it develops and under the quality which covers it. Intensity is difference, but this difference tends to deny or to cancel itself out in extensity and underneath quality. It is true that qualities are signs which flash across the interval of a difference. In so doing, however, they measure the time of an equalisation – in other words, the time taken by the difference to cancel itself out in the extensity in which it is distributed. This is the most general content of the principles of Carnot, Curie, Le Chatelier, *et al.* : difference is the sufficient reason of change only to the extent that the change tends to negate difference. It is indeed in this manner that the principle of causality finds in the signalling process its categorical physical determination: intensity defines an objective sense for a series of irreversible states which pass, like an 'arrow of time', from more to less differenciated, from a productive to a reduced difference, and ultimately to a cancelled difference. We know how these themes of a reduction of difference, a uniformisation of diversity, and an equalisation of inequality stitched together for the last time a strange alliance at the end of the nineteenth century between science, good sense and philosophy. Thermodynamics was the powerful furnace of that alloy. A system of basic definitions was established which satisfied everybody, including a certain Kantianism: the given as diverse; reason as a process of identification and equalisation tending towards identity; the absurd or irrational as the resistance of the diverse to that identificatory reason. The words 'the real is rational' found there a new sense, for diversity tended to be reduced in Nature no less than in reason. As a result, difference was neither a law of nature nor a category of the mind but only the origin = x of the diverse: a given, but not a 'value' (except a regulative or compensatory value).[4] In truth, our epistemological tendency to be suspicious of the notion of intensive quantity would prove nothing were it not linked to this other tendency on the part of differences of intensity to cancel themselves out in qualified extended systems. Intensity is suspect only because it seems to rush headlong into suicide.

Science and philosophy here gave a final satisfaction to good sense. For it is not science that is in question – it remains indifferent to the extension of Carnot's principle – nor philosophy, which also, after a fashion, remains indifferent to Carnot's principle. Every time science, philosophy and good sense come together it is inevitable that good sense should take itself for a science and a philosophy (that is why such encounters must be avoided at all costs). It is therefore a question of the essence of good sense. This essence is clearly and concisely outlined by Hegel in *The Difference between the Systems of Fichte and Schelling*: good sense is partial truth in so far as this is joined to the feeling of the absolute. The truth in the form of reason is present in a partial state, and the absolute is there in the form of a feeling. But how is the feeling of the absolute attached to the partial truth? Good sense essentially distributes or repartitions: 'on the one hand' and 'on the other hand' are the characteristic formulae of its false profundity or platitude. It distributes things. It is obvious, however, that not every distribution flows from good sense: there are distributions inspired by madness, mad repartitions. Perhaps good sense even presupposes madness in order to come after and correct what madness there is in any prior distribution. A distribution is in conformity with good sense when it tends to banish difference from the distributed. Only when the inequality of the portions is supposed to disappear from the milieu over time does the repartition effectively conform to good sense, or follow a sense which is called good. Good sense is by nature eschatological, the prophet of a final compensation and homogenization. If it comes second, this is because it presupposes mad distribution – instantaneous, nomadic distribution, crowned anarchy or difference. However, this sedentary, patient figure which has time on its side corrects difference, introduces it into a milieu which leads to the cancellation of differences or the compensation of portions. It is itself this 'milieu'. Thinking itself to be in between the extremes, it holds them off and fills in the interval. It does not negate differences – on the contrary: it arranges things in the order of time and under the conditions of extensity such that they negate themselves. It multiplies the intermediates and, like Plato's demiurge, ceaselessly and patiently transforms the unequal into the divisible. Good sense is the ideology of the middle classes who recognise themselves in equality as an abstract product. It dreams less of acting than of constituting a natural milieu, the element of an action which passes from more to less differenciated: for example, the good sense of eighteenth-century political economy which saw in the commercial classes the natural compensation for the extremes, and in the prosperity of commerce the mechanical process of the equalisation of portions. It therefore dreams less of acting than of foreseeing, and of allowing free rein to action which goes from the unpredictable to the predictable (from the production of differences to their reduction). Neither contemplative nor active, it is prescient. In short, it goes from the side of things to the side of fire: from differences produced to differences reduced. It is thermodynamic. In this sense it attaches the feeling of the absolute to the partial truth. It is neither optimistic nor pessimistic, but assumes a pessimistic or optimistic tint depending upon whether the side of fire, which consumes everything and renders all portions uniform, bears the sign of an inevitable death and nothingness (we are all equal before death) or, on the contrary, bears the happy plenitude of existence (we all have an equal chance in life). Good sense does not negate difference: on the contrary, it recognises difference just enough to affirm that it negates itself, given sufficient extensity and time. Between mad difference and difference cancelled, between the unequal in the divisible and the divisible equalised, between the distribution of the unequal and equality distributed, good sense necessarily lives itself as a universal rule of distribution, and therefore as universally distributed.

Good sense is based upon a synthesis of time, in particular the one which we have determined as the first synthesis, that of habit. Good sense is good only because it is wedded to the sense of time associated with that synthesis. Testifying to a living present (and to the fatigue of that present), it goes from past to future as though from particular to general. However, it defines this past as the improbable or the less probable. In effect, since every partial system has its origin in a difference which individualises its domain, how would an observer situated within the system grasp this difference except as past and highly 'improbable', given that it is behind him? On the other hand, at the heart of the same system, the future, the probable and the cancellation of difference are identified in the direction indicated by the arrow of time – in other words, the right direction. This condition grounds prediction itself (it has often been noticed that if initially indistinguishable temperatures are allowed to differenciate, it cannot be predicted which will increase or decrease; and if viscosity is accelerated, it will tear moving bodies from their state of rest, but in an unpredictable direction). Well-known pages by Boltzmann comment upon this scientific and thermodynamic guarantee of good sense: they show how within a partial system difference, the improbable and the past are identified on the one hand, while uniformity, the probable and the future are identified on the other.[5] In the dream of a truly universal good sense, one which attaches the feeling of the absolute to partial truths, along with the moon to the earth, this equalisation and homogenisation do not occur only in each partial system, but continue from one system to another. However, as Boltzmann shows, this attachment is not legitimate, any more than this synthesis of time is sufficient.

We are at least in a position to clarify the relation between good sense and common sense. Common sense was defined subjectively by the supposed identity of a Self which provided the unity and ground of all the faculties, and objectively by the identity of whatever object served as a focus for all the faculties. This double identity, however, remains static. We no more find ourselves before a universal indeterminate object than we are a universal Self. Objects are divided up in and by fields of individuation, as are Selves. Common sense must therefore point beyond itself towards another, dynamic instance, capable of determining the indeterminate object as this or that, and of individualising the self situated in this ensemble of objects. This other instance is good sense, which takes its point of departure from a difference at the origin of individuation. However, precisely because it ensures the distribution of that difference in such a manner that it tends to be cancelled in the object, and because it provides a rule according to which the different objects tend to equalise themselves and the different Selves tend to become uniform, good sense in turn points towards the instance of a common sense which provides it with both the form of a universal Self and that of an indeterminate object. Good sense, therefore, has two definitions, one objective and one subjective, which correspond to those of common sense: a rule of universal distribution and a rule universally distributed. Good sense and common sense each refer to the other, each reflect the other and constitute one half of the orthodoxy. In view of this reciprocity and double reflection, we can define common sense by the process of recognition and good sense by the process of prediction. The one involves the qualitative synthesis of diversity, the static synthesis of qualitative diversity related to an object supposed the same for all the faculties of a single subject; the other involves the quantitative synthesis of difference, the dynamic synthesis of difference in quantity related to a system in which it is objectively and subjectively cancelled.

Nevertheless, difference remains not the given itself but that by which the given is given. How could thought avoid going that far, how could it avoid thinking that which is most opposed to thought? With the identical, we think with all our force, but without producing the least thought: with the different, by contrast, do we not have the highest thought, but also that which cannot be thought? This protestation of the Different is full of sense. Even if difference tends to be distributed thoughout diversity in such a manner as to disappear, and to render uniform the diversity it creates, it must first be sensed as that which gives diversity to be sensed. Moreover, it must be thought as that which creates diversity. (Not because we would then return to the common exercise of the faculties, but precisely because the dissociated faculties enter into the violent relation in which each transmits its constraint to the other.) Delirium lies at the base of good sense, which is why good sense is always secondary. Thought must think difference, that absolutely different from thought which nevertheless gives it thought, gives to be thought. In some fine pages, Lalande says that reality is difference, whereas the law of reality, or principle of thought, is identification: 'Reality is therefore in opposition to the law of reality, the present state with what it will become. How could such a state of affairs come to be? How could it be that the physical world is constituted by a fundamental property which its own laws endlessly attenuate?'[6] In other words, reality is not the result of the laws which govern it, and a saturnine God devours at one end what he has made at the other, legislating against his creation because he has created against his legislation. Thus we are forced to sense and to think difference. We sense something which is contrary to the laws of nature; we think something which is contrary to the principles of thought. Moreover, even if the production of difference is by definition 'inexplicable', how can we avoid *implicating* the inexplicable at the heart of thought itself? How can the unthinkable not lie at the heart of thought? Or delirium at the heart of good sense? How can we be content to relegate the improbable to the beginning of a partial evolution, without also grasping it as the highest power of the past, or as the immemorial in memory? (In this sense the partial synthesis of the present already led us into another synthesis of time, that of the immemorial memory, at the risk of leading us further still ...)

Philosophy is revealed not by good sense but by paradox. Paradox is the pathos or the passion of philosophy. There are several kinds of paradox, all of which are opposed to the complementary forms of orthodoxy – namely, good sense and common sense. Subjectively, paradox breaks up the common exercise of the faculties and places each before its own limit, before its incomparable: thought before the unthinkable which it alone is nevertheless capable of thinking; memory before the forgotten which is also its immemorial; sensibility before the imperceptible which is indistinguishable from its intensive. ... At the same time, however, paradox communicates to the broken faculties that relation which is far from good sense, aligning them along a volcanic line which allows one to ignite the other, leaping from one limit to the next. Objectively, paradox displays the element which cannot be totalised within a common element, along with the difference which cannot be equalised or cancelled at the direction of a good sense. It is correct to say that the only refutation of paradoxes lies in good sense and common sense themselves, but on condition that they are already allowed everything: the role of judge as well as that of party to the case, the absolute along with the partial truth.

It is not surprising that, strictly speaking, difference should be 'inexplicable'. Difference is explicated, but in systems in which it tends to be cancelled; this means only that difference is essentially implicated, that its being is implication. For difference, to be explicated is to be cancelled or to dispel the inequality which constitutes it. The formula according to which 'to explicate is to identify' is a tautology. We cannot conclude from this that difference is cancelled out, or at least that it is cancelled in itself. It is cancelled in so far as it is drawn outside itself, *in* extensity and *in* the quality which fills that extensity. However, difference creates both this extensity and this quality. Intensity is developed and explicated by means of an extension [*extensio*] which relates it to the extensity [*extensum*] in which it appears outside itself and hidden beneath quality. Difference of intensity is cancelled or tends to be cancelled in this system, but it creates this system by explicating itself. Whence the double aspect of the quality as a sign: it refers to an implicated order of constitutive differences, and tends to cancel out those differences in the extended order in which they are explicated. This is also why causality finds in signalling at once both an origin and an orientation or destination, where the destination in a sense denies the origin. The peculiarity of 'effects', in the causal sense, is to have a perceptual 'effect' and to be able to be called by a proper name (Seebeck effect, Kelvin effect ...), because they emerge in a properly differential field of individuation which the name symbolises. The vanishing of difference is precisely inseparable from an 'effect' of which we are victims. Difference in the form of intensity remains implicated in itself, while it is cancelled by being explicated in extensity. It is therefore unnecessary, in order to save the universe from heat death or to safeguard the chances of eternal return, to imagine highly 'improbable' extensive mechanisms supposedly capable of restoring difference. For difference has never ceased to be in itself, to be implicated in itself even while it is explicated outside itself. Therefore, not only are there sensory illusions but there is also a transcendental physical illusion. In this regard, we believe that Léon Selme made a profound discovery.[7] In opposing Carnot and Clausius, he wanted to show that the increase of entropy was illusory. Moreover, he pointed out certain empirical or contingent factors of this illusion: the relative smallness of the differences in temperature produced in thermal machines, the enormity of the dampening which seems to preclude the construction of a 'thermal ram'. Above all, however, he discovered a transcendental form of illusion: of all extensions, entropy is the only one which is not measurable either directly or indirectly by any procedure independent of energetics. If it were the same for volume or for quantity of electricity, we would necessarily have the impression that these increase through irreversible transformations. The paradox of entropy is the following: entropy is an extensive factor but, unlike all other extensive factors, it is an extension or 'explication' which is implicated as such in intensity, which does not exist outside the implication or except as implicated, and this is because it has the function of *making possible* the general movement by which that which is implicated explicates itself or is extended. There is thus a transcendental illusion essentially tied to the *qualitas*, Heat, and to the extension, Entropy.

It is notable that extensity does not account for the individuations which occur within it. No doubt the high and the low, the right and the left, the figure and the ground are individuating factors which trace rises and falls, currents and descents in extensity. However, since they take place within an already developed extensity, their value is only relative. They therefore flow from a 'deeper' instance – depth itself, which is not an extension but a pure *implex*. No doubt every depth is also a possible length and size, but this possibility is realised only in so far as an observer changes place and gathers into an abstract concept that which is length for itself and that which is length for others: in fact, it is always on the basis of a new depth that the old one becomes length or is explicated in length. It obviously amounts to the same thing whether we consider a simple plane, or an extensity in three dimensions where the third is homogeneous with the other two. Once depth is grasped as an extensive quantity, it belongs to engendered extensity and ceases to include in itself its own heterogeneity in relation to the other two. We see then that it is the ultimate dimension of extensity, but we see this only as a fact without understanding the reason, since we no longer know that it is original. We also then note the presence in extensity of individuating factors, but without understanding where their power comes from, since we no longer know that they express the original depth. It is depth which explicates itself as right and left in the first dimension, as high and low in the second, and as figure and ground in the homogenised third. Extensity does not develop or appear without presenting a left and a right, a high and a low, an above and a below, which are like the dissymmetrical marks of its own origin. The relativity of these determinations, moreover, is further testimony to the absolute from which they come. Extensity as a whole comes from the depths. Depth as the (ultimate and original) heterogeneous dimension is the matrix of all extensity, including its third dimension considered to be homogeneous with the other two.

The ground [*fond*] as it appears in a homogeneous extensity is notably a projection of something 'deeper' [*profond*]: only the latter may be called *Ungrund* or groundless. The law of figure and ground would never hold for objects distinguished from a neutral background or a background of other objects unless the object itself entertained a relation to its own depth. The relation between figure and ground is only an extrinsic plane relation which presupposes an internal, voluminous relation between surfaces and the depth which they envelop. This synthesis of depth which endows the object with its shadow, but makes it emerge from that shadow, bears witness to the furthest past and to the coexistence of the past with the present. We should not be surprised that the pure spatial syntheses here repeat the temporal syntheses previously specified: the explication of extensity rests upon the first synthesis, that of habit or the present; but the implication of depth rests upon the second synthesis, that of Memory and the past. Furthermore, in depth the proximity and simmering of the third synthesis make themselves felt, announcing the universal 'ungrounding'. Depth is like the famous geological line from NE to SW, the line which comes diagonally from the heart of things and distributes volcanoes: it unites a bubbling sensibility and a thought which 'rumbles in its crater'. Schelling said that depth is not added from without to length and breadth, but remains buried, like the sublime principle of the *differend* which creates them.

Extensity can emerge from the depths only if depth is definable independently of extensity. The extensity whose genesis we are attempting to establish is extensive magnitude, the *extensum* or term of reference of all the *extensio*. The original depth, by contrast, is indeed space as a whole, but space as an intensive quantity: the pure *spatium*. We know that sensation or perception has an ontological aspect: precisely in the syntheses which are peculiar to it, confronted by that which can only be sensed or that which can only be perceived. Now, it appears that depth is essentially *implicated* in the perception of extensity: neither depth nor distances are judged by the apparent magnitude of objects, but, on the contrary, depth envelops in itself distances which develop in extensity and explicate in turn the apparent magnitudes. It also appears that depth and distances, in this state of implication, are fundamentally linked to the intensity of the sensation: it is the power of diminution of the intensity experienced that provides a perception of depth (or rather, provides depth to perception). The perceived quality presupposes intensity, because it expresses only a resemblance to a 'band of isolatable intensities', within the limits of which a permanent object is constituted – the qualified object which affirms its identity across variable distances.[8] Intensity, which envelops distances, is explicated in extensity, while extensity develops, exteriorises and homogenises these very distances. At the same time, a quality occupies this extensity, either in the form of a *qualitas* which defines the milieu of a direction, or in the form of a *quale* which characterises a given object in relation to that direction. Intensity is simultaneously the imperceptible and that which can only be sensed. How could it be sensed for itself, independently of the qualities which cover it and the extensity in which it is distributed? But how could it be other than 'sensed', since it is what gives to be sensed, and defines the proper limits of sensibility? Depth is simultaneously the imperceptible and that which can only be perceived (in this sense, Paliard called it simultaneously both conditioning and conditioned, and showed the existence of an inverse complementary relation between distance as ideal existence and distance as visual existence). The strangest alliance is formed between intensity and depth, which carries each faculty to its own limit and allows it to communicate only at the peak of its particular solitude: an alliance between Being and itself in difference. Depth and intensity are the same at the level of being, but the same in so far as this is said of difference. Depth is the intensity of being, or vice versa. Out of this intensive depth emerge at once the *extensio* and the *extensum*, the *qualitas* and the *quale*. The vectors or vectorial magnitudes which occur throughout extensity, but also the scalar magnitudes or particular cases of vector-potentials, are the eternal witness to the intensive origin: for example, altitudes. The fact that they cannot be added in any order whatsoever, or that they have an essential relation to an order of succession, refers us back to the synthesis of time which acts in depth.

Kant defined all intuitions as extensive quantities – in other words, quantities such that the representation of the parts necessarily preceded and made possible the representation of the whole. However, space and time are not presented as they are represented. On the contrary, the presentation of the whole grounds the possibility of the parts, the latter being only virtual and actualised only by the determinate values of empirical intuition. It is empirical intuition which is extensive. While he refuses a logical extension to space and time, Kant's mistake is to maintain a geometrical extension for it, and to reserve intensive quantity for the matter which fills a given extensity to some degree or other. In the case of enantiomorphic bodies, Kant recognised precisely an *internal difference*. However, since it was not a conceptual difference, on his view it could refer only to an *external relation* with extensity as a whole in the form of extensive magnitude. In fact, the paradox of symmetrical objects, like everything concerning right and left, high and low, figure and ground, has an intensive source. Space as pure intuition or *spatium* is an intensive quantity, and intensity as a transcendental principle is not merely the anticipation of perception but the source of a quadruple genesis: that of the *extensio* in the form of schema, that of extensity in the form of extensive magnitude, that of *qualitas* in the form of matter occupying extensity, and that of the *quale* in the form of designation of an object. Hermann Cohen was right, therefore, to attach full value to the principle of intensive quantities in his reinterpretation of Kantianism.[9] While space may be irreducible to concepts, its affinity with Ideas cannot nevertheless be denied – in other words, its capacity (as intensive *spatium*) to determine in extensity the actualisation of ideal connections (as differential relations contained in the Idea). Finally, while the conditions of possible experience may be related to extension, there are also subjacent conditions of real experience which are indistinguishable from intensity as such.

Intensity has three characteristics. According to the first, intensive quantity includes the unequal in itself. It represents difference in quantity, that which cannot be cancelled in difference in quantity or that which is unequalisable in quantity itself: it is therefore the quality which belongs to quantity. It appears less as a species of the genus quantity than as the figure of a fundamental or original moment present in every quantity. On the other hand, this means that extensive quantity is the figure of another moment which indicates, rather, quantitative destination or finality (in a partial numerical system). In the history of number, we see that every systematic type is constructed on the basis of an essential inequality, and retains that inequality in relation to the next-lowest type: thus, fractions involve the impossibility of reducing the relation between two quantities to a whole number; irrational numbers in turn express the impossibility of determining a common aliquot part for two quantities, and thus the impossibility of reducing their relation to even a fractional number, and so on.

It is true that a given type of number does not retain an inequality in its essence without banishing or cancelling it within the new order that it installs. Thus, fractional numbers compensate for their characteristic inequality by the equality of an aliquot part; irrational numbers subordinate their inequality to an equality of purely geometric relations – or, better still, arithmetically speaking, to a limit-equality indicated by a convergent series of rational numbers. Here, however, we rediscover only the duality between explication and the implicit, between extensity and the intensive: for if a type of number cancels its difference, it does so only by explicating it within the extension that it installs. Nevertheless, it maintains this difference in itself in the implicated order by which it is grounded. Every number is originally intensive and vectorial in so far as it implies a difference of quantity which cannot properly be cancelled, but extensive and scalar in so far as it cancels this difference on another plane that it creates and on which it is explicated. Even the simplest type of number confirms this duality: natural numbers are first ordinal – in other words, originally intensive. Cardinal numbers result from these and are presented as the explication of the ordinal. It is often objected that ordination cannot lie at the origin of number because it already implies cardinal operations of colligation. This, however, is because the formula 'the cardinal results from the ordinal' has been poorly understood. Ordination in no way presupposes the repetition of the same unit which must be 'cardinalised' every time the following ordinal number is reached. Ordinal construction does not imply a supposed same unit but only, as we shall see, an irreducible notion of distance – the distances implicated in the depth of an intensive *spatium* (ordered differences). Identical unity is not presupposed by ordination; on the contrary, this belongs to cardinal number and presupposes an extensive equality among cardinal numbers, a relative equivalence of exteriorised terms. We should not, therefore, believe that cardinal number results analytically from ordinal, or from the final terms of finite ordinal series (the preceding objection would then be justified). In fact, ordinal number becomes cardinal only by extension, to the extent that the distances enveloped in the *spatium* are explicated, or developed and equalised in an extensity established by natural number. We should therefore say that, from the outset, the concept of number is synthetic.

Intensity is the uncancellable in difference of quantity, but this difference of quantity is cancelled by extension, extension being precisely the process by which intensive difference is turned inside out and distributed in such a way as to be dispelled, compensated, equalised and suppressed in the extensity which it creates. Nevertheless, how many necessary operations must intervene in this process! Admirable pages in the *Timaeus* bring together the divisible and the indivisible.[10] The important point is that the divisible is defined as that which bears in itself the unequal, whereas the indivisible (the Same or the One) seeks to impose an equality upon it, and thereby render it docile. God begins by making a mixture of the two elements. However, precisely because the divisible, B, escapes the mixture and shows its inequality and oddness, God obtains only $A + B/2 = C$. As a result, he must make a second mixture: $A + B/2 + C$ – in other words, $A + B/2 + (A + B/2)$. This mixture, however, also rebels, and he must avert the rebellion: he distributes it into parts according to two arithmetic progressions, one whose principle is 2, which refers to the element A (1, 2, 4, 8); and the other whose principle is 3, which refers to C and recognises the oddness of B (1, 3, 9, 27). Now God is faced with intervals, with *distances* to fill: he does this with two intermediates, one of which is arithmetic (corresponding to A), while the other is harmonic (corresponding to C). From this may be derived the relations, and the relations between these relations, which pursue the task of tracking the unequal in the divisible throughout the entire mixture. Furthermore, God must cut the whole in two, cross over the two halves and then bend them into two circles, such that the outer circle contains the equal in the form of the movement of the Same, while the other, inner circle, orientated along a diagonal, retains what subsists of inequality in the divisible by distributing it among secondary circles. Finally, God has not defeated the unequal in itself but only separated it from the divisible and enclosed it within an outer circle, *kuklos exothen*. He has equalised the divisible in this extension which is the extension of the Soul of the world, but underneath, at the deepest layer of the divisible, the unequal still rumbles in intensity. This is of little consequence to God, for he fills the entire expanse of the soul with the extensity of bodies and their qualities. He covers everything.

Nevertheless, he dances upon a volcano. Never have so many, so diverse and such demented operations been multiplied in order to draw from the depths of an intensive *spatium* a serene and docile extensity, and to dispel a Difference which subsists in itself even when it is cancelled outside itself. The labour of God is always threatened by the third hypothesis of the *Parmenides*, that of the differential or intensive instant.

A second characteristic flows from the first: since it is already difference in itself and comprises inequality as such, intensity *affirms* difference. It makes difference an object of affirmation. Curie commented that it was useful but misleading to speak of dissymmetry in negative terms, as though it were the absence of symmetry, without inventing positive terms capable of designating the infinite number of operations with unmatched outcomes. The same goes for inequality: it is through inequalities that we discover the affirmative formula for irrational numbers (for p and q whole, each number $(p-q\sqrt{2})^2$ will always exceed a certain value). It is also through inequalities that we can positively establish the convergence of a series (rounding up to the highest integer). The important enterprise of a mathematics without negation is obviously not based upon identity, which, on the contrary, determines the negative by the excluded middle and non-contradiction. It rests axiomatically upon an affirmative definition of inequality ($\neq$) for two natural numbers, and in other cases, upon a positive definition of *distance* ($\neq \neq$) which brings into play three terms in an infinite series of affirmative relations. In order to appreciate the logical power of an affirmation of distances in the pure element of positive difference, we need only consider the formal difference between the following two propositions: 'if $a \neq b$ is *impossible*, then $a = b$'; 'if a is *distant* from every number c which is distant from b, then $a = b$'.[11] We shall see, however, that the distance referred to here is by no means an extensive magnitude, but must be related to its intensive origin. Since intensity is already difference, it refers to a series of other differences that it affirms by affirming itself. It is said that in general there are no reports of null frequencies, no effectively null potentials, no absolutely null pressure, as though on a line with logarithmic graduations where zero lies at the end of an infinite series of smaller and smaller fractions. We must advance further, at the risk of falling into an 'ethics' of intensive quantities. Constructed on at least two series, one superior and one inferior, with each series referring in turn to other implicated series, intensity affirms even the *lowest*; it makes the lowest an object of affirmation. The power of a Waterfall or a very deep descent is required to go that far and make an affirmation even of descent. Everything is like the flight of an eagle: overflight, suspension and descent. Everything goes from high to low, and by that movement affirms the lowest: asymmetrical synthesis. High and low, moreover, are only a manner of speaking. It is a question of depth, and of the lower depth which essentially belongs to it. There is no depth which is not a 'seeker' of a lower depth: it is there that distance develops, but distance understood as the affirmation of that which it distances, or difference as the sublimation of the lower.

When does the negative emerge? Negation is the inverted image of difference – in other words, the image of intensity seen from below. In effect, everything is overturned. What, from on high, is affirmation of difference becomes from below the negation of that which differs. Here again, therefore, the negative appears only with extensity and quality. We have seen that the first dimension of extensity was a power of limitation, while the second was a power of opposition. These two figures of the negative are grounded upon the 'conservative' character of extensions (an extension within a system cannot be increased without decreasing the extension of the same kind in a related system). Quality in turn seems inseparable from opposition: the opposition of contradiction, as Plato showed, to the extent that each quality presupposes the identity of 'more' and 'less' in the intensities it isolates; the opposition of contrariety in the paired distribution of qualities themselves. Moreover, when contrariety fails, as in the case of odours, this is in order to make room for a play of limitations in a series of increasing or decreasing resemblances. There is no doubt that resemblance is the law of quality, just as equality is that of extensity (or invariance that of extension): as a result, extensity and quality are the two forms of generality. However, precisely this is sufficient to make them the elements of representation, without which representation itself would not be able to fulfil its dearest task, which is to relate difference to the identical. We can therefore add a third reason to the two which we we have already given in order to explain the illusion of the negative.

Difference is not negation. On the contrary, the negative is difference inverted, seen from below. Always the candle in the bovine eye. Difference is inverted, first, by the requirements of representation which subordinate it to identity. Then, by the shadow of 'problems' which give rise to the illusion of the negative. Finally, by extensity and quality which cover or explicate intensity. *It is underneath quality and within extensity that Intensity appears upside down*, and that its characteristic difference takes the form of the negative (either of limitation or of opposition). The fate of difference is tied to the negative only within extensity and quality, which precisely tend to cancel difference. Every time we find ourselves confronted with qualified oppositions and in an extensity in which these are distributed, we must not count upon an extensive synthesis which would overcome and resolve them. On the contrary, the constituent disparities or enveloped distances inhabit intensive depth. These are the source of the illusion of the negative, but also the principle of the denunciation of this illusion. Only depth resolves, because only difference gives rise to problems. It is not the synthesis of the different which leads to reconciliation in extensity (pseudo-affirmation) but, on the contrary, the *differenciation* of their difference which affirms them in intensity. Oppositions are always planar; they express on a given plane only the distorted effect of an original depth. This has often been commented upon for stereoscopic images. More generally, every field of forces refers back to a potential energy, every opposition refers to a deeper 'disparateness', and oppositions are resolved in time and extensity only to the extent that the disparates have first invented their order of communication in depth and rediscovered that dimension in which they envelop one another, tracing hardly recognisable intensive paths through the ulterior world of qualified extensity.[12]

What is the being *of* the sensible? Given the conditions of this question, the answer must designate the paradoxical existence of a 'something' which simultaneously cannot be sensed (from the point of view of the empirical exercise) and can only be sensed (from the point of view of the transcendent exercise). In a passage from Book VII of the *Republic*, Plato showed how such a being transmits a shock to the other faculties, shaking them from their torpor, stirring the memory and constraining thought. However, Plato characterises this being as the contrary–sensible, that which gives rise to contrary sensations at the same time. As the *Philebus* expressly shows, Plato means that sensible qualities or relations are not in themselves separable from a contrariety, or even a contradiction, in the subject to which they are attributed. Since every quality is a becoming, one does not become 'harder' (or taller) than one was without at the same time becoming 'softer' (or smaller) than one is in the process of becoming. We cannot avoid this by distinguishing times, since the distinction between times is subsequent to the becoming which interposes the one in the other and, at the same time, posits both the movement by which the new present is constituted and the movement by which the former present is constituted as past. It seems impossible to escape a mad-becoming or an unlimited becoming which implies the identity of opposites in the form of the coexistence of *more* and *less* with a given quality. However, this Platonic response will not do: in fact, it rests upon intensive quantities, but recognises these only in qualities in the course of development – and for this reason, it assigns both the being of the sensible and contrariety to qualities. However, while the contrary–sensible or contrariety in the quality may constitute sensible being *par excellence*, they by no means constitute the being *of* the sensible. It is difference in intensity, not contrariety in quality, which constitutes the being 'of' the sensible. Qualitative contrariety is only the reflection of the intense, a reflection which betrays it by explicating it in extensity. It is intensity or difference in intensity which constitutes the peculiar limit of sensibility. As such, it has the paradoxical character of that limit: it is the imperceptible, that which cannot be sensed because it is always covered by a quality which alienates or contradicts it, always distributed within an extensity which inverts and cancels it. In another sense, it is that which can only be sensed or that which defines the transcendent exercise of sensibility, because it gives to be sensed, thereby awakening memory and forcing thought. The point of sensory distortion is often to grasp intensity independently of extensity or prior to the qualities in which it is developed. A pedagogy of the senses, which forms an integral part of 'transcendentalism', is directed towards this aim. Pharmacodynamic experiences or physical experiences such as vertigo approach the same result: they reveal to us that difference in itself, that depth in itself or that intensity in itself at the original moment at which it is neither qualified nor extended. At this point, the harrowing character of intensity, however weak, restores its true meaning: not the anticipation of perception but the proper limit of sensibility from the point of view of a transcendent exercise.

In terms of a third characteristic which includes the other two, intensity is an implicated, enveloped or 'embryonised' quantity. Not implicated in quality, for it is only secondarily so. Intensity is primarily implicated in itself: implicating and implicated. We must conceive of implication as a perfectly determined form of being. Within intensity, we call that which is really implicated and enveloping *difference*; and we call that which is really implicated or enveloped *distance*. For this reason, intensity is neither divisible, like extensive quantity, nor indivisible, like quality. The divisibility of extensive quantities is defined in the following manner: by the relative determination of a unit (this unit itself never being indivisible but only marking the level at which division ceases); by the equivalence of the parts determined by the unit; by the consubstantiality of the parts with the whole which is divided. Division can therefore take place and be continued without any change in the nature of what is being divided. By contrast, when it is pointed out that a temperature is not composed of other temperatures, or a speed of other speeds, what is meant is that each temperature is already a difference, and that differences are not composed of differences of the same order but imply series of heterogeneous terms. As Rosny showed, the fiction of a homogeneous quantity vanishes with intensity. An intensive quantity may be divided, but not without changing its nature. In a sense, it is therefore indivisible, but only because no part exists prior to the division and no part retains the same nature after division. We should nevertheless speak of 'smaller' and 'greater', according to whether the nature of a given part presupposes a given change of nature or is presupposed by it. Thus, the acceleration or deceleration of a movement defines within it intensive parts that must be called greater or smaller, even while these undergo a change of nature and following the order of these changes (ordered differences). In this sense, difference in depth is composed of distances, 'distance' being not an extensive quantity but an indivisible asymmetrical relation, ordinal and intensive in character, which is established between series of heterogeneous terms and expresses at each moment the nature of that which does not divide without changing its nature.[13] By contrast with extensive quantities, intensive quantities are therefore defined by the enveloping difference, the enveloped distances, and the unequal in itself which testifies to the existence of a natural 'remainder' which provides the material for a change of nature. We must henceforth distinguish between two types of multiplicities, such as those represented by distances and lengths respectively: implicit as opposed to explicit multiplicities; those whose metric varies with division and those which carry the invariable principle of their metric. Difference, distance and inequality are the positive characteristics of depth as intensive *spatium*. Furthermore, the movement of explication is the movement by which difference tends to be cancelled, but also by which distances tend to be extended and developed into lengths, and the divisible tends to be equalised. (Once again, Plato's greatness lies in having seen that the divisible formed a nature in itself only by including the unequal.)

We could be criticized for having included all differences in kind within intensity, thereby inflating it with everything that normally belongs to quality. Equally, we could be criticized for having included within distances what normally belongs to extensive quantities. To us, these criticisms do not appear well founded. It is true that in being developed in extension, difference becomes simple difference of degree and no longer has its reason in itself. It is true that quality benefits from that alienated reason and takes over differences in kind. However, the distinction between the two, like that between mechanism and 'qualitativism', rests upon a sleight of hand: the one profits from what has disappeared in the other, but the true difference belongs to neither. Difference becomes qualitative only in the process by which it is cancelled in extension. In its own nature, difference is no more qualitative than extensive. We should note, first, that qualities have much more stability, immobility and generality than is often admitted. They are orders of resemblance. Certainly they differ, and differ in kind, but always within a supposed order of resemblance. Moreover, their variations in resemblance refer to variations of a quite different sort. Certainly, a qualitative difference does not reproduce or express a difference of intensity. However, in the passage from one quality to another, even where there is a maximum of resemblance or continuity, there are phenomena of delay and plateau, shocks of difference, distances, a whole play of conjunctions and disjunctions, a whole depth which forms a graduated scale rather than a properly qualitative duration. Finally, if intensity were not there to attend to, support and relay quality, what would the duration attributed to quality be but a race to the grave, what time would it have other than the time necessary for the annihilation of difference in the corresponding extensity, or the time necessary for the uniformisation of qualities themselves? In short, there would no more be qualitative differences or differences in kind than there would be quantitative differences or differences of degree, if intensity were not capable of constituting the former in qualities and the latter in extensity, even at the risk of appearing to extinguish itself in both.

This is why the Bergsonian critique of intensity seems unconvincing. It assumes qualities ready-made and extensities already constituted. It distributes difference into differences in kind in the case of qualities and differences in degree in the case of extensity. From this point of view, intensity necessarily appears as no more than an impure mixture, no longer sensible or perceptible. However, Bergson has thereby already attributed to quality everything that belongs to intensive quantities. He wanted to free quality from the superficial movement which ties it to contrariety or contradiction (that is why he opposed duration to becoming); but he could do so only by attributing to quality a depth which is precisely that of intensive quantity. One cannot be against both the negative and intensity at once. It is striking that Bergson should define qualitative duration not as indivisible but as that which changes its nature in dividing, that which does not cease to divide and change its nature: virtual multiplicity, he says, in opposition to the actual multiplicities of number and extensity which retain only differences of degree. There comes a moment, however, in this philosophy of Difference which the whole of Bergsonism represents, when Bergson raises the question of the double genesis of quality and extensity. This fundamental differenciation (quality–extensity) can find its reason only in the great synthesis of Memory which allows all the degrees of difference to coexist as degrees of relaxation and contraction, and rediscovers at the heart of duration the implicated order of that intensity which had been denounced only provisionally and from without.[14] For the differences of degree and the extensity which represents them mechanically do not carry their reason within themselves; but neither do the differences in kind and the duration which represents them qualitatively. The soul of mechanism says that everything is difference of degree. The soul of quality replies that there are differences in kind everywhere. However, these are false souls, minor and auxiliary souls. Let us take seriously the famous question: is there a difference in kind, or of degree, between differences of degree and differences in kind? Neither. Difference is a matter of degree only within the extensity in which it is explicated; it is a matter of kind only with regard to the quality which covers it within that extensity. Between the two are all the degrees of difference – beneath the two lies the entire nature of difference – in other words, the intensive. Differences of degree are only the lowest degree of difference, and differences in kind are the highest form of difference. What differences in kind or of degree separate or differenciate, the degrees or nature of difference make the Same, but the same which is said of the different. Bergson, as we have seen, went as far as this extreme conclusion: perhaps this 'same', the identity of nature and degrees of difference, is Repetition (ontological repetition) ...

There is an illusion tied to intensive quantities. This illusion, however, is not intensity itself, but rather the movement by which difference in intensity is cancelled. Nor is it only apparently cancelled. It is really cancelled, but outside itself, in extensity and underneath quality. We must therefore distinguish two orders of implication or degradation: a secondary implication which designates the state in which intensities are enveloped by the qualities and extensity which explicate them; and a primary implication designating the state in which intensity is implicated in itself, at once both enveloping and enveloped. In other words, a secondary degradation in which difference in intensity is cancelled, the highest rejoining the lowest; and a primary power of degradation in which the highest affirms the lowest. The illusion is precisely the confusion of these two instances or extrinsic and intrinsic states. How could it be avoided from the point of view of the empirical exercise of sensibility, since the latter can grasp intensity only in the order of quality and extensity? Only transcendental enquiry can discover that intensity remains implicated in itself and continues to envelop difference at the very moment when it is reflected in the extensity and the quality that it creates, which implicate it only secondarily, just enough to 'explicate it'. Extensity, quality, limitation, opposition indeed designate realities, but the form which difference assumes here is illusory. Difference pursues its subterranean life while its image reflected by the surface is scattered. Moreover, it is in the nature of that image, but only that image, to be scattered, just as it is in the nature of the surface to cancel difference, but only on the surface.

We asked how a transcendental principle might be extracted from the empirical principles of Carnot or Curie. When we seek to define *energy* in general, either we take account of the extensive and qualified factors of extensity – in which case we are reduced to saying 'there is something which remains constant', thereby formulating the great but flat tautology of the Identical – or, on the contrary, we consider pure intensity in so far as it is implicated in that deep region where no quality is developed, or any extensity deployed. In this case, we define energy in terms of the difference buried in this pure intensity and it is the formula 'difference of intensity' which bears the tautology, but this time the beautiful and profound tautology of the Different. Energy in general will not then be confused with a uniform energy at rest, which would render any transformation impossible. Only a particular form of empirical energy, qualified in extensity, can be at rest; one in which the difference in intensity is already cancelled because it is drawn outside itself and distributed among the elements of the system. However, energy in general or intensive quantity is the *spatium*, the theatre of all metamorphosis or difference in itself which envelops all its degrees in the production of each. In this sense, energy or intensive quantity is a transcendental principle, not a scientific concept. In terms of the distinction between empirical and transcendental principles, an empirical principle is the instance which governs a particular domain. Every domain is a qualified and extended partial system, governed in such a manner that the difference of intensity which creates it tends to be cancelled within it (*law of nature*). But the domains are distributive and cannot be added: there is no more an extensity in general than there is an energy in general within extensity. On the other hand, there is an intensive space with no other qualification, and within this space a pure energy. The transcendental principle does not govern any domain but gives the domain to be governed to a given empirical principle; it accounts for the subjection of a domain to a principle. The domain is created by difference of intensity, and given by this difference to an empirical principle according to which and in which the difference itself is cancelled. It is the transcendental principle which maintains itself in itself, beyond the reach of the empirical principle. Moreover, while the laws of nature govern the surface of the world, the eternal return ceaselessly rumbles in this other dimension of the transcendental or the volcanic *spatium*.

When we say that the eternal return is not the return of the Same, or of the Similar or the Equal, we mean that it does not presuppose any identity. On the contrary, it is said of a world *without identity*, without resemblance or equality. It is said of a world the very ground of which is difference, in which everything rests upon disparities, upon differences of differences which reverberate to infinity (the world of intensity). The eternal return is itself the Identical, the similar and the equal, but it presupposes nothing of itself in that of which it is said. It is said of that which has no identity, no resemblance and no equality. It is the identical which is said of the different, the resemblance which is said of the pure *disparate*, the equal which is said only of the unequal and the proximity which is said of all distances. Things must be dispersed within difference, and their identity must be dissolved before they become subject to eternal return and to identity in the eternal return. We can therefore measure the chasm which separates eternal return as a 'modern' belief, or even a belief of the future, from eternal return as an ancient or supposedly ancient belief. In fact, it is a meagre achievement on the part of our philosophy of history to oppose what is taken to be our historical time with the cyclical time supposed to be that of the Ancients. It is supposed that for the Ancients *things revolve*, whereas for we Moderns they progress in a straight line. However, this opposition between cyclical and linear time is a weak idea. Every time such a schema is tested it fails for several reasons. In the first place, the eternal return that is attributed to the Ancients presupposes the identity in general of that which it is supposed to make return. This return of the identical, however, is subject to certain conditions which contradict it in fact. For it is grounded either upon the cyclical transformation of qualitative elements into one another (physical eternal return) or upon the circular movement of incorruptible celestial bodies (astronomical eternal return). In both cases, return is presented as a 'law of nature'. In the one case, it is interpreted in terms of quality, in the other case, in terms of extensity. However, whether astronomical or physical, extensive or qualitative, this interpretation of eternal return has already reduced the identity that it presupposes to a simple and very general resemblance: for the 'same' qualitative process, or the 'same' respective position of the stars determine only very crude resemblances among the phenomena they govern. Moreover, eternal return is here so badly understood that it is opposed to what is intimately connected with it: on the one hand, with the ideal of an exit from the 'wheel of births', it finds a first qualitative limit in the form of metamorphoses and transmigrations; on the other hand, with the irreducible inequality of the celestial periods, it finds a second quantitative limit in the form of irrational numbers. Thus the two themes most profoundly linked to eternal return, that of qualitative metamorphosis and that of quantitative inequality, are turned back against it, having lost all intelligible relation to it. We are not saying that eternal return 'as it was believed by the Ancients' is erroneous or unfounded. We are saying that the Ancients only approximately and partially believed in it. It was not so much an eternal return as a system of partial cycles and cycles of resemblance. It was a generality – in short, a law of nature. (Even the great year of Heraclitus was only the time necessary for that part of fire which constituted a living being to transform itself into earth and back into fire.)[15] Alternatively, if there is, in Greece or elsewhere, a genuine knowledge of eternal return, it is a cruel and esoteric knowledge which must be sought in another dimension, more mysterious and more uncommon than that of astronomical or qualitative cycles and their generalities.

Why did Nietzsche, who knew the Greeks, know that the eternal return was *his* own invention, an untimely belief or belief of the future? Because 'his' eternal return is in no way the return of a same, a similar or an equal. Nietzsche says clearly that if there were identity, if there were an undifferentiated qualitative state of the world or a position of equilibrium for the stars, then this would be a reason never to leave it, not a reason for entering into a cycle. Nietzsche thereby links eternal return to what appeared to oppose it or limit it from without – namely, complete metamorphosis, the irreducibly unequal. Depth, distance, caves, the lower depths, the tortuous, and the unequal in itself form the only landscape of the eternal return. Zarathustra reminds the buffoon as well as the eagle and the serpent that it is not an astronomical 'refrain', nor a physical circle. ... It is not a law of nature. The eternal return is elaborated within a ground, or within a groundlessness in which original Nature resides in its chaos, beyond the jurisdictions and laws which constitute only second nature. Nietzsche opposes 'his' hypothesis to the cyclical hypothesis, 'his' depth to the absence of depth in the sphere of the immutable. The eternal return is neither qualitative nor extensive but intensive, purely intensive. In other words, it is said of difference. This is the fundamental connection between the eternal return and the will to power. The one does not hold without the other. The will to power is the flashing world of metamorphoses, of communicating intensities, differences of differences, of *breaths*, insinuations and exhalations: a world of intensive intentionalities, a world of simulacra or 'mysteries'.[16] Eternal return is the being of this world, the only Same which is said of this world and excludes any prior identity therein. It is true that Nietzsche was interested in the energetics of his time, but this was not the scientific nostalgia of a philosopher. We must discover what it was that he sought to find in the science of intensive quantities – namely, the means to realise what he called Pascal's prophecy: to make chaos an object of affirmation. Difference in the will to power is the highest object of sensibility, the *hohe Stimmung*, sensed against the laws of nature (remember that the will to power was first presented as a feeling, a feeling of distance). A thought contrary to the laws of nature, repetition in the eternal return is the highest thought, the *gross Gedanke*. Difference is the first affirmation; eternal return is the second, the 'eternal affirmation of being' or the 'nth' power which is said of the first. It is always on the basis of a signal – or, in other words, a primary intensity – that thought occurs. Along the broken chain or the tortuous ring we are violently led from the limit of sense to the limit of thought, from what can only be sensed to what can only be thought.

It is because nothing is equal, because everything bathes in its difference, its dissimilarity and its inequality, even with itself, that everything returns – or rather, everything does not return. What does not return is that which denies eternal return, that which does not pass the test. It is quality and extensity which do not return, in so far as within them difference, the condition of eternal return, is cancelled. So too the negative, in so far as difference is thereby inverted and cancelled. So too the identical, the similar and the equal, in so far as these constitute the forms of indifference. So too God, along with the self as the form and guarantee of identity: everything which appears only under the law of 'once and for all', including repetition when it is subject to the condition of the identity of a same quality, a same extended body, a same self (as in the 'resurrection'). ... Does this truly mean that neither quality nor extensity returns? Or were we not, rather, led to distinguish two states of quality along with two states of extension? One in which quality flashes like a sign in the distance or interval created by a difference of intensity; the other in which, as an effect, it reacts upon its cause and tends to cancel difference. One in which extension remains implicated in the enveloping order of differences; the other in which extensity explicates difference and cancels it within a qualified system. This distinction, which cannot be drawn within experience, becomes possible from the point of view of the thought of eternal return. The hard law of explication is that what is explicated is *explicated once and for all.* The ethics of intensive quantities has only two principles: affirm even the lowest, do not explicate oneself (too much). We must be like the father who criticised the child for having uttered all the dirty words he knew – not only because it was wrong but because he had said everything at once, because he kept nothing in reserve, no remainder for the subtle, implicated matter of the eternal return. Moreover, if the eternal return reduces qualities to the status of pure signs, and retains of extensities only what combines with the original depth, even at the cost of our coherence and in favour of a superior coherence, then the most beautiful qualities will appear, the most brilliant colours, the most precious stones and the most vibrant extensions. For once reduced to their seminal reasons, and having broken all relation with the negative, these will remain for ever affixed in the intensive space of positive differences. Then, in turn, the final prediction of the *Phaedo* will be realised, in which Plato promised to the sensibility disconnected from its empirical exercise temples, stars and gods such as had never before been seen, unheard-of affirmations. The prediction is realised, it is true, only by the very overturning of Platonism.

The affinity between intensive quantities and differentials has often been denied. Such criticism, however, bears only upon a misconception of this affinity. This should be grounded not upon the consideration of a series, the terms of a series and the differences between consecutive terms, but upon the confrontation between two types of relation: differential relations in the reciprocal synthesis of the Idea and relations of intensity in the asymmetrical synthesis of the sensible. The reciprocal synthesis dy/dx is continued in the asymmetrical synthesis which connects y to x. The intensive factor is a partial derivative or the differential of a composite function. A whole flow of exchange occurs between intensity and Ideas, as though between two corresponding figures of difference. Ideas are problematic or 'perplexed' virtual multiplicities, made up of relations between differential elements. Intensities are implicated multiplicities, 'implexes', made up of relations between asymmetrical elements which direct the course of the actualisation of Ideas and determine the cases of solution for problems. The aesthetic of intensities thus develops each of its moments in correspondence with the dialectic of Ideas: the power of intensity (depth) is grounded in the potentiality of the Idea. Already the illusion we encountered on the level of the aesthetic repeats that of the dialectic, and the form of the negative is the shadow projected by problems and their elements before it is the inverted image of intensive differences. Just as intensive quantities seem to be cancelled, so problematic Ideas seem to disappear. The unconscious of little perceptions or intensive quantities refers to the unconscious of Ideas, and the art of the aesthetic echoes that of the dialectic. The latter is irony, understood as the art of problems and questions which is expressed in the handling of differential relations and in the distribution of the ordinary and the singular. By contrast, the art of the aesthetic is humour, a physical art of signals and signs determining the partial solutions or cases of solution – in short, an implicated art of intensive quantities.

These very general correspondences do not, nevertheless, indicate precisely how the affinity works, nor how the connection between intensive quantities and differentials operates. Let us reconsider the movement of Ideas, which is inseparable from a process of actualisation. For example, an Idea or multiplicity such as that of colour is constituted by the virtual coexistence of relations between genetic or differential elements of a particular order. These relations are actualised in qualitatively distinct colours, while their distinctive points are incarnated in distinct extensities which correspond to these qualities. The qualities are therefore differenciated, along with the extensities, in so far as these represent divergent lines along which the differential relations which coexist only in the Idea are actualised. We have seen that every process of actualisation was in this sense a double differenciation, qualitative and extensive. The categories of differenciation no doubt change according to the order of the differentials constitutive of the Idea: qualification and partition are the two aspects of physical actualisation, just as organisation and the determination of species are of biological actualisation. However, the qualities differenciated by virtue of the relations they actualise impose their own requirements, as do the extensities differenciated by virtue of the distinctive points they incarnate. That is why we proposed the concept of differen*t*/*c*iation to indicate at once both the state of differential relations in the Idea or virtual multiplicity, and the state of the qualitative and extensive series in which these are actualised by being differenciated. Thereby, however, the condition of such actualisation remains completely indeterminate. How is the Idea determined to incarnate itself in differenciated qualities and differenciated extensities? What determines the relations coexisting within the Idea to differenciate themselves in qualities and extensities? The answer lies precisely in the intensive quantities. Intensity is the determinant in the process of actualisation. It is intensity which *dramatises*. It is intensity which is immediately expressed in the basic spatio–temporal dynamisms and determines an 'indistinct' differential relation in the Idea to incarnate itself in a distinct quality and a distinguished extensity. In this way, after a fashion (but, as we shall see, only after a fashion), the movement and the categories of differenciation reproduce those of explication. We speak of differenciation in relation to the Idea which is actualised. We speak of explication in relation to the intensity which 'develops' and which, precisely, determines the movement of actualisation. However, it remains literally true that intensity creates the qualities and extensities in which it explicates itself, because these qualities and extensities do not in any way resemble the ideal relations which are actualised within them: differenciation implies the creation of the lines along which it operates.

How does intensity fulfil this determinant role? In itself, it must be no less independent of the differenciation than of the explication which proceeds from it. It is independent of the explication by virtue of the order of implication which defines it. It is independent of the differenciation by virtue of its own essential process. The essential process of intensive quantities is individuation. Intensity is individuating, and intensive quantities are individuating factors. Individuals are signal–sign systems. All individuality is intensive, and therefore serial, stepped and communicating, comprising and affirming in itself the difference in intensities by which it is constituted. Gilbert Simondon has shown recently that individuation presupposes a prior metastable state – in other words, the existence of a 'disparateness' such as at least two orders of magnitude or two scales of heterogeneous reality between which potentials are distributed. Such a pre-individual state nevertheless does not lack singularities: the distinctive or singular points are defined by the existence and distribution of potentials. An 'objective' problematic field thus appears, determined by the distance between two heterogeneous orders. Individuation emerges like the act of solving such a problem, or – what amounts to the same thing – like the actualisation of a potential and the establishing of communication between disparates. The act of individuation consists not in suppressing the problem, but in integrating the elements of the disparateness into a state of coupling which ensures its internal resonance. The individual thus finds itself attached to a pre-individual half which is not the impersonal within it so much as the reservoir of its singularities.[17] In all these respects, we believe that individuation is essentially intensive, and that the pre-individual field is a virtual–ideal field, made up of differential relations. Individuation is what responds to the question 'Who?', just as the Idea responds to the questions 'How much?' and 'How?'. 'Who?' is always an intensity. ... Individuation is the act by which intensity determines differential relations to become actualised, along the lines of differenciation and within the qualities and extensities it creates. The total notion is therefore that of: indi-differen*t*/*c*iation (indi-drama-differen*t*/*c*iation). Irony, as the art of differential Ideas, is by no means unaware of singularity: on the contrary, it plays upon the entire distribution of ordinary and distinctive points. However, it is always a question of pre-individual singularities distributed within the Idea. It is unaware of the individual. Humour, the art of intensive quantities, plays upon the individual and individuating factors. Humour bears witness to the play of individuals as cases of solution, in relation to the differenciations it determines, whereas irony, for its part, proceeds to the differentiations necessary within the calculation of problems or the determination of their conditions.

The individual is neither a quality nor an extension. The individual is neither a qualification nor a partition, neither an organisation nor a determination of species. The individual is no more an *infima species* than it is composed of parts. Qualitative or extensive interpretations of individuation remain incapable of providing reasons why a quality ceases to be general, or why a synthesis of extensity begins here and finishes there. The determination of qualities and species presupposes individuals to be qualified, while extensive parts are relative to an individual rather than the reverse. It is not sufficient, however, to mark a difference in kind between individuation and differenciation in general. This difference in kind remains unintelligible so long as we do not accept the necessary consequence: that individuation precedes differenciation in principle, that every differenciation presupposes a prior intense field of individuation. It is because of the action of the field of individuation that such and such differential relations and such and such distinctive points (pre-individual fields) are actualised – in other words, organised within intuition along lines differenciated in relation to other lines. As a result, they then form the quality, number, species and parts of an individual in short, its generality. Because there are individuals of different species and individuals of the same species, there is a tendency to believe that individuation is a continuation of the determination of species, albeit of a different kind and proceeding by different means. In fact any confusion between the two processes, any reduction of individuation to a limit or complication of differenciation, compromises the whole of the philosophy of difference. This would be to commit an error, this time in the actual, analogous to that made in confusing the virtual with the possible. Individuation does not presuppose any differenciation; it gives rise to it. Qualities and extensities, forms and matters, species and parts are not primary; they are imprisoned in individuals as though in a crystal. Moreover, the entire world may be read, as though in a crystal ball, in the moving depth of individuating differences or differences in intensity.

All differences are borne by individuals, but they are not all individual differences. Under what conditions does a difference become regarded as individual? The problem of classification was clearly always a problem of ordering differences. However, plant and animal classifications show that we can order differences only so long as we are provided with a multiple network of continuity of resemblance. The idea of a continuity among living beings was never distinct from that of classification, much less opposed to it. It was not even an idea supposed to limit or nuance the demands of classification. On the contrary, it is the prerequisite of any possible classification. For example, one asks which among several differences is the one which truly forms a 'characteristic' – in other words, the one which allows to be grouped under a reflected identity those beings which resemble one another on a maximum number of points. It is in this sense that a genus may be simultaneously both a concept of reflection and also a natural concept (to the extent that the identity it 'carves out' is related to that of neighbouring species). If we consider three plants, A, B and C, of which A and B are ligneous while C is non-ligneous, B and C are blue while A is red, then 'ligneous' will be the characteristic, since it ensures the greatest subordination of differences to the order of increasing and decreasing resemblances. No doubt the order of resemblances may be denounced as belonging to crude perception. This, however is so only on condition that one substitutes for units of reflection the great constitutive units (either Cuvier's great functional units or Geoffroy's great units of composition), in relation to which difference is still understood in terms of judgements of analogy or in terms of variation within a universal concept. In any case, so long as it is subordinated to the criteria of resemblance within perception, identity within reflection, analogy within judgement and opposition within the concept, difference is not regarded as individual difference. It remains only general difference, even though it is borne by the individual.

Darwin's great novelty, perhaps, was that of inaugurating the thought of individual difference. The leitmotiv of *The Origin of Species* is: we do not know what individual difference is capable of! We do not know how far it can go, assuming that we add to it natural selection. Darwin's problem is posed in terms rather similar to those employed by Freud on another occasion: it is a question of knowing under what conditions small, unconnected or free-floating differences become appreciable, connected and fixed differences. Natural selection indeed plays the role of a principle of reality, even of success, and shows how differences become connected to one another and accumulate in a given direction, but also how they tend to diverge further and further in different or even opposed directions. Natural selection plays an essential role: the differenciation of difference (survival of the most divergent). Where selection does not occur or no longer occurs, differences remain or once more become free-floating; where it occurs, it does so to fix the differences and make them diverge. The great taxonomic units – genera, families, orders and classes – no longer provide a means of understanding difference by relating it to such apparent conditions as resemblances, identities, analogies and determined oppositions. *On the contrary*, these taxonomic units are understood on the basis of such fundamental mechanisms of natural selection as difference and the differenciation of difference. For Darwin, no doubt, individual difference does not yet have a clear status, to the extent that it is considered for itself and as primary matter of selection or differenciation: understood as free-floating or unconnected difference, it is not distinguished from an indeterminate variability. That is why Weissmann makes an essential contribution to Darwinism when he shows how individual difference finds a natural cause in sexed reproduction: sexed reproduction as the principle of the 'incessant production of varied individual differences'. To the extent that sexual differenciation itself results from sexed reproduction, we see that the three great biological differenciations – that of species, that of organic parts and that of the sexes – turn around individual difference, not vice versa. These are the three figures of the Copernican Revolution of Darwinism. The first concerns the differenciation of individual differences in the form of the divergence of characteristics and the determination of groups. The second concerns the connection of differences in the form of the co-ordination of characteristics within the same group. The third concerns the production of differences as the continuous matter of differenciation and connection.

In appearance – well-founded appearance, certainly – sexed reproduction is subordinated to the criteria of the species and the demands of the organic parts. It is true that the egg must reproduce all the parts of the organism to which it belongs. It is also more or less true that sexed reproduction operates within the limits of the species. However, it has often been noticed that all modes of reproduction imply phenomena of organic 'de-differenciation'. The egg reconstitutes the parts only on condition that it develops within a field which does not depend upon them. It develops within the limits of the species only on condition that it also presents phenomena of specific de-differenciation. Only beings of the same species can effectively overcome the limits of the species and produce beings which function as sketches, provisionally reduced to supra-specific characteristics. This is what von Baër discovered when he showed that an embryo does not reproduce ancestral adult forms belonging to other species, but rather experiences or undergoes states and undertakes movements which are not viable for the species but go beyond the limits of the species, genus, order or class, and can be sustained only by the embryo itself, under the conditions of embryonic life. Baër concludes that epigenesis proceeds from more to less general – in other words, from the most general types to generic and specific determinations. However, this high level of generality has nothing to do with an abstract taxonomic concept since it is, as such, *lived* by the embryo. It refers, on the one hand, to the differential relations which constitute the virtuality which exists prior to the actualisation of the species; on the other hand, it refers to the first movements of that actualisation, and particularly to its condition – namely, individuation as it finds its field of constitution in the egg. The highest generalities of life, therefore, point beyond species and genus, but point beyond them in the direction of the individual and pre-individual singularities rather than towards an impersonal abstraction. If we notice, with Baër, that not only the type but also the specific form of the embryo appears very early, we should not necessarily take this to indicate the irreducibility of types and branchings, but rather the speed and relative acceleration of the influence exercised by individuation upon actualisation or the determination of species.[18] It is not the individual which is an illusion in relation to the genius of the species, but the species which is an illusion – inevitable and well founded, it is true – in relation to the play of the individual and individuation. The question is not whether in fact the individual can be separated from its species and its parts. It cannot. However, does not this very 'inseparability', along with the speed of appearance of the species and its parts, testify to the primacy in principle of individuation over differenciation? It is the individual which is above the species, and precedes the species in principle. Moreover, the embryo is the individual as such directly caught up in the field of its individuation. Sexed reproduction defines this very field: if it is accompanied in the product by an all the more precocious apparition of the specific form, this is because the very notion of the species depends first upon sexed reproduction, which accelerates the movement of the unfolding of actualisation by individuation (the egg itself is already the site of the first developments). The embryo is a sort of phantasm of its parents; every embryo is a chimera, capable of functioning as a sketch and of living that which is unlivable for the adult of every species. It undertakes forced movements, constitutes internal resonances and dramatises the primordial relations of life. The problem of comparison between animal and human sexuality consists of finding out how sexuality ceases to be a function and breaks its attachments to reproduction, for human sexuality interiorises the conditions of the production of phantasms. Dreams are our eggs, our larvae and our properly psychic individuals. The vital egg is nevertheless already a field of individuation, and the embryo is a pure individual, and the one in the other testifies to the primacy of individuation over actualisation – in other words, over both organisation and the determination of species.

Individuating difference must be understood first within its field of individuation – not as belated, but as in some sense in the egg. Since the work of Child and Weiss, we recognise the axes or planes of symmetry within an egg. Here too, however, the positive element lies less in the elements of the given symmetry than in those which are missing. An intensity forming a wave of variation throughout the protoplasm distributes its difference along the axes and from one pole to another. The region of maximal activity is the first to come into play, exercising a dominant influence on the development of the corresponding parts at a lower rate: the individual in the egg is a genuine descent, going from the highest to the lowest and affirming the differences which comprise it and in which it falls. In a young amphibian *gastrula* the intensity seems to be maximal in a mid '*sub-blastoporal*' region and to decrease in all directions, but less rapidly towards the animal pole. In the middle layer of a young vertebrate *neurula* the intensity decreases, for each transverse section, from the mid-dorsal to the mid-ventral line. In order to plumb the intensive depths or the *spatium* of an egg, the directions and distances, the dynamisms and dramas, the potentials and potentialities must be multiplied. The world is an egg. Moreover, the egg, in effect, provides us with a model for the order of reasons: (organic and species related) differentiation–individuation–dramatisation–differenciation. We think that difference of intensity, as this is implicated in the egg, expresses first the differential relations or virtual matter to be organised. This intensive field of individuation determines the relations that it expresses to be incarnated in spatio–temporal dynamisms (dramatisation), in species which correspond to these relations (specific differenciation), and in organic parts which correspond to the distinctive points in these relations (organic differenciation). Individuation always governs actualisation: the organic parts are induced only on the basis of the gradients of their intensive environment; the types determined in their species only by virtue of the individuating intensity. Throughout, intensity is primary in relation to organic extensions and to species qualities. Notions such as 'morphogenetic potential', 'field–gradient–threshold' put forward by Dalcq, which essentially concern the relations of intensity as such, account for this complex ensemble. This is why the question of the comparative role of the nucleus and the cytoplasm, in the egg as in the world, is not easily solved. The nucleus and the genes designate only the differentiated matter – in other words, the differential relations which constitute the pre-individual field to be actualised; but their actualisation is determined only by the cytoplasm, with its gradients and its fields of individuation.

Species do not resemble the differential relations which are actualised in them; organic parts do not resemble the distinctive points which correspond to these relations. Species and parts do not resemble the intensities which determine them. As Dalcq says, when a caudal appendix is induced by its intensive environment, that appendix corresponds to a certain level of morphogenetic potential and depends upon a system in which 'nothing is *a priori* caudal'.[19] The egg destroys the model of similitude. To the extent that the requirements of resemblance disappear, two quarrels seem to lose much of their meaning. On the one hand, pre-formism and epigenesis cease to be opposed once we admit that the enveloped pre-formations are intensive while the developed formations are qualitative and extensive, and that they do not resemble one another. On the other hand, fixism and evolutionism tend to be reconciled to the extent that movement does not go from one actual term to another, nor from general to particular, but – by the intermediary of a determinant individuation – from the virtual to its actualisation.

Nevertheless, we have not advanced with regard to the principal difficulty. We invoke a field of individuation or individuating difference as the condition of the organisation and determination of species. However, this field of individuation is posited only formally and in general: it seems to be 'the same' for a given species, and to vary in intensity from one species to another. It seems, therefore, to depend upon the species and the determination of species, and to refer us once more to differences borne by the individual, not to individual differences. In order for this difficulty to disappear, the individuating difference must not only be conceived within a field of individuation in general, but must itself be conceived as an individual difference. The form of the field must be necessarily and in itself filled with individual differences. This plenitude must be immediate, thoroughly precocious and not delayed in the egg, to such a degree that the principle of indiscernibles would indeed have the formula given it by Lucretius: no two eggs or grains of wheat are identical. These conditions, we believe, are fully satisfied in the order of implication of intensities. Intensities presuppose and express only differential relations; individuals presuppose only Ideas. Furthermore, the differential relations within Ideas are not more species (or genera, or families, etc.) than their distinctive points form parts. They by no means constitute either qualities or extensions. On the contrary, all the Ideas, all the relations with their variations and points, coexist, even though there are changes of order according to the elements considered: they are fully determined and differen*t*iated even though they are completely undifferen*c*iated. Such a mode of 'distinction' seemed to us to correspond to the *perplication* of Ideas – in other words, to their problematic character and to the reality of the virtual which they represent. This is why Ideas have the logical character of being simultaneously both distinct and obscure. They are obscure (undifferenciated and coexisting with other Ideas, 'perplicated' with them) in so far as they are distinct [*omni modo determinata*]. The question then is what happens when Ideas are expressed by intensities or individuals in this new dimension of implication.

Intensity or difference in itself thus expresses differential relations and their corresponding distinctive points. It introduces a new type of distinction into these relations and between Ideas a new type of distinction. Henceforward, the Ideas, relations, variations in those relations and distinctive points are in a sense separated: instead of coexisting, they enter states of simultaneity or succession. Nevertheless, all the intensities are implicated in one another, each in turn both enveloped and enveloping, such that each continues to express the changing totality of Ideas, the variable ensemble of differential relations. However, each intensity *clearly* expresses only certain relations or certain degrees of variation. Those that it expresses clearly are precisely those on which it is focused when it has the *enveloping* role. In its role as the *enveloped*, it still expresses all relations and all degrees, but *confusedly*. As the two roles are reciprocal, and as intensity is in the first instance enveloped by itself, it must be said that the clear and the confused, as logical characteristics in the intensity which expresses the Idea – in other words, in the individual which thinks it – are no more separable than the distinct and the obscure are separable in the Idea itself. The clear–confused as individuating intensive unit corresponds to the distinct–obscure as ideal unit. Clear–confused does not qualify the Idea, but the thinker who thinks or expresses it. The thinker is the individual. The distinct was precisely the obscure: it was the obscure in so far as it was distinct. In the present case, however, the clear is precisely the confused; it is confused in so far as it is clear. We saw that the weakness of the theory of representation, from the point of view of the logic of knowledge, was to have established a direct proportion between the clear and the distinct, at the expense of the inverse proportion which relates these two logical values: the entire image of thought was compromised as a result. Only Leibniz approached the conditions of a logic of thought, inspired by his theory of individuation and expression. For despite the complexity and ambiguity of the texts, it does indeed seem at times that the expressed (the continuum of differential relations or the unconscious virtual Idea) should be in itself distinct and obscure: for example, all the drops of water in the sea like so many genetic elements with the differential relations, the variations in these relations and the distinctive points they comprise. In addition, it seems that the expressor (the perceiving, imagining or thinking individual) should be by nature clear and confused: for example, our perception of the noise of the sea, which confusedly includes the whole and clearly expresses only certain relations or certain points by virtue of our bodies and a threshold of consciousness which they determine.

The order of implication includes the enveloping no less than the enveloped, depth as well as distance. When an enveloping intensity clearly expresses certain differential relations and certain distinctive points, it still expresses confusedly all the other relations, all their variations and points. It expresses these in the intensities it envelops. These latter enveloped intensities are then within the former. The enveloping intensities (depth) constitute the field of individuation, the individuating differences. The enveloped intensities (distances) constitute the individual differences. The latter necessarily fill the former. Why is the enveloping intensity already a field of individuation? Because the differential relation on which it is focused is not yet a species, nor are its distinctive points yet parts. They will become so, but only in being actualised by the action of this field which it constitutes. Must we say at least that all the individuals of a given species have the same field of individuation, since they point originally to the same relation? Certainly not, for while two individuating intensities may be abstractly the same by virtue of their clear expression, they are never the same by virtue of the order of intensities which they envelop or the relations which they confusedly express. There is a variable order according to which the ensemble of relations is diversely implicated in these secondary intensities. We should nevertheless avoid saying that an individual has individual difference only by virtue of its confused sphere. This would be again to neglect the indissolubility of the clear and the confused. It would be to forget that the clear is confused by itself, in so far as it is clear. In effect, the secondary intensities represent the fundamental property of the primary intensities – namely, the power to divide in changing their nature. Two intensities are never identical except abstractly. Rather, they differ in kind, if only by the manner in which they divide within the intensities they include. Finally, we should not say that the individuals of a given species are distinguished by their participation in other species: as if, for example, there was ass or lion, wolf or sheep, in every human being. There is indeed all that, and metempsychosis retains all its symbolic truth. However, the ass and the wolf can be considered species only in relation to the fields of individuation which clearly express them. In the confused and in the enveloped, they play only the role of variables, of individual differences or composing souls. That is why Leibniz was right to substitute the notion of 'metaschematism' for that of metempsychosis, meaning by this that a soul never changed bodies, but its body could be re-enveloped or reimplicated in order to enter, if need be, other fields of individuation, thereby returning to a 'more subtle theatre'.[20] Every body, every thing, thinks and is a thought to the extent that, reduced to its intensive reasons, it expresses an Idea the actualisation of which it determines. However, the thinker himself makes his individual differences from all manner of things: it is in this sense that he is laden with stones and diamonds, plants 'and even animals'. The thinker, undoubtedly the thinker of eternal return, is the individual, the universal individual. It is he who makes use of all the power of the clear and the confused, of the clear–confused, in order to think Ideas in all their power as the distinct–obscure. The multiple, mobile and communicating character of individuality, its implicated character, must therefore be constantly recalled. The indivisibility of the individual pertains solely to the property of intensive quantities not to divide without changing nature. We are made of all these depths and distances, of these intensive souls which develop and are re-enveloped. We call individuating factors the ensemble of these enveloping and enveloped intensities, of these individuating and individual differences which ceaselessly interpenetrate one another throughout the fields of individuation. Individuality is not a characteristic of the Self but, on the contrary, forms and sustains the system of the dissolved Self.

We must give a more precise account of the relations between explication and differenciation. Intensity creates the extensities and the qualities in which it is explicated; these extensities and qualities are differenciated. Extensities are formally distinct from one another, and comprise within themselves the distinctions between parts corresponding to the distinctive points. Qualities are materially distinct, and comprise the distinctions corresponding to the variations of relations. Creation is always the production of lines and figures of differenciation. It is nevertheless true that intensity is explicated only in being cancelled in this differenciated system that it creates. Equally, we notice that the differenciation of a system occurs by linkage with a more general system which is 'de-differenciated'. In this sense, even living beings do not contradict the empirical principle of degradation, and the local differenciations are compensated by an overall tendency towards uniformity, in exactly the same way as a final cancellation compensates the originary creations. We nevertheless see that very important variations occur from one domain to the next. Physical and biological systems are distinguished first by the order of the Ideas they incarnate or actualise: differentials of this or that order. Secondly, they are distinguished by the process of individualisation which determines that actualisation: in a physical system, this happens all at once, and affects only the boundaries, whereas a biological system receives successive waves of singularities and involves its whole internal milieu in the operations which take place at the outer limits. Finally, they are distinguished by the figures of differenciation which represent actualisation itself: organisation and the determination of biological species as opposed to simple physical qualification and distribution. Nevertheless, whatever the domain under consideration, the law of explication remains the cancellation of productive difference and the erasure of the differenciation produced which is manifest in physical equilibrium as well as in biological death. Once again, the principle of degradation is never negated or contradicted. Yet if it 'explicates' everything, it accounts for nothing. As has been said: if everything goes into this principle, nothing comes out. If nothing contradicts it, if there is no counter-order or exception, then there are, on the contrary, many things of another order. While local increases in entropy may be compensated by a more general degradation, they are in no way comprised in or produced by the latter. Empirical principles tend to leave out the elements of their own foundation. The principle of degradation obviously does not account either for the creation of the most simple system or for the evolution of systems (the threefold difference between biological systems and physical ones). The living therefore testifies to the existence of another order, a heterogeneous order of another dimension – as though the individuating factors or the atoms taken individually with their power of mutual communication and fluent instability there enjoyed a higher degree of expression.[21]

What is the formula for this 'evolution'? The more complex a system, the more the *values peculiar to implication* appear within it. The presence of these values is what allows a judgement of the complexity or the complication of a system, and determines the preceding characteristics of biological systems. The values of implication are centres of envelopment.

These centres are not the intensive individuating factors themselves, but they are their representatives within a complex whole in the process of explication. It is these which constitute the little islands and the local increases of entropy at the heart of systems which nevertheless conform overall to the principle of degradation: atoms taken individually, for example, even though they none the less confirm the law of increasing entropy when considered *en masse* in the order of explication of the system in which they are implicated. In so far as it testifies to individual actions between directed molecules, an organism such as a mammal may be assimilated to a microscopic being. The function of these centres may be defined in several ways. First, to the extent that the individuating factors form a kind of noumenon of the phenomenon, we claim that the noumenon tends to appear as such in complex systems, that it finds its own phenomenon in the centres of envelopment. Second, to the extent that sense is tied to the Ideas which are incarnated and to the individuations which determine that incarnation, we claim that these centres are expressive, or that they reveal sense. Finally, to the extent that every phenomenon finds its reason in a difference of intensity which frames it, as though this constituted the boundaries between which it flashes, we claim that complex systems increasingly tend to interiorise their constitutive differences: the centres of envelopment carry out this interiorisation of the individuating factors. The more the difference on which the system depends is interiorised in the phenomenon, the more repetition finds itself interior, the less it depends upon external conditions which are supposed to ensure the reproduction of the 'same' differences.

As the movement of life shows, difference and repetition tend to become interiorised in signal–sign systems both at once. Biologists are right when, in posing the problem of heredity, they avoid allocating distinct functions, such as variation and reproduction, to these systems, but rather seek to show the underlying unity or reciprocal conditioning of these functions. At this point, the theories of heredity necessarily open on to a philosophy of nature. It is as if repetition were never the repetition of the 'same' but always of the Different as such, and the object of difference in itself were repetition. At the moment when they are explicated in a system (once and for all) the differential, intensive or individuating factors testify to their persistence in implication, and to eternal return as the truth of that implication. Mute witnesses to degradation and death, the centres of envelopment are also the dark precursors of the eternal return. Here again, it is the mute witnesses or dark precusors which do everything – or, at least, it is in these that everything happens.

Speaking of evolution necessarily leads us to psychic systems. For each type of system, we must ask what pertains to Ideas and what pertains to implication–individuation and explication–differenciation respectively. With psychic systems the problem assumes a particular urgency, since it is by no means certain that either the I or the Self falls within the domain of individuation. They are, rather, figures of differenciation. The I forms the properly psychic determination of species, while the Self forms the psychic organisation. The I is the quality of human being as a species. The determination of psychic species is not of the same type as the determination of biological species, since here the determination must equal, or be of the same power as, the determinable. That is why Descartes refused any definition of human being which would proceed by genus and difference as in the case of animal species: for example, 'rational animal'. On the contrary, he presents the *I think* as another procedure of *definition*, one capable of demonstrating the specificity of humanity or the quality of its substance. In correlation with the I, the Self must understand itself in extension: the Self designates the properly psychic organism, with its distinctive points represented by the diverse faculties which enter into the comprehension of the I. As a result, the fundamental psychic correlation is expressed in the formula '*I* think *Myself*', just as the biological correlation is expressed in the complementarity of species and their parts, of quality and extension. That is why both the I and the Self each begin with differences, but these differences are distributed in such a way as to be cancelled, in accordance with the requirements of good sense and common sense. The I therefore appears at the end as the universal form of psychic life, just as the Self is the universal matter of that form. The I and the Self explicate one another, and do so endlessly throughout the entire history of the Cogito.

The individuating factors or the implicated factors of individuation therefore have neither the form of the I nor the matter of the Self. This is because the I is inseparable from a form of identity, while the Self is indistinguishable from a matter constituted by a continuity of resemblances. The differences included within the I and the Self are, without doubt, borne by individuals: nevertheless, they are not individual or individuating to the extent that they are understood in relation to this identity in the I and this resemblance in the Self. By contrast, every individuating factor is already difference and difference of difference. It is constructed upon a fundamental disparity, and functions on the edges of that disparity as such. That is why these factors endlessly communicate with one another across fields of individuation, becoming enveloped in one another in a demesne which disrupts the matter of the Self as well as the form of the I. Individuation is mobile, strangely supple, fortuitous and endowed with fringes and margins; all because the intensities which contribute to it communicate with each other, envelop other intensities and are in turn enveloped. The individual is far from indivisible, never ceasing to divide and change its nature. It is not a Self with regard to what it expresses, for it expresses Ideas in the form of internal multiplicities, made up of differential relations and distinctive points or pre-individual singularities. Nor is it an I with regard to its expressive character, for here again it forms a multiplicity of actualisation, as though it were a condensation of distinctive points or an open collection of intensities. The fringe of indetermination which surrounds individuals and the relative, floating and fluid character of individuality itself has often been commented upon (for example, the case of two physical particles whose individuality can no longer be observed when their fields of individuation or domains of presence encroach upon one another; or the case of the biological distinction between an organ and an organism which depends on the situation of the corresponding intensities according to whether or not these are enveloped within a larger field of individuation). The error, however, is to believe that this indetermination or this relativity indicates something incomplete in individuality or something interrupted in individuation. On the contrary, they express the full, positive power of the individual as such, and the manner in which it is distinguished in nature from both an I and a self. The individual is distinguished from the I and the self just as the intense order of implications is distinguished from the extensive and qualitative order of explication. Indeterminate, floating, fluid, communicative and enveloping–enveloped are so many positive characteristics affirmed by the individual. It is therefore insufficient to multiply selves or to 'attenuate' the I in order to discover the true status of individuation. We have seen to what extent selves must be presupposed as a condition of passive organic syntheses, already playing the role of mute witnesses. However, the synthesis of time which is carried out in them refers precisely to other syntheses as though to other witnesses, thereby leading us into the domain of another nature in which there is no longer either self or I, and in which, by contrast, we encounter the chaotic realm of individuation. For each self still retains some resemblance in its matter, while each I retains an identity, however attenuated. However, that which has its ground in dissemblance, or its lack of ground in a difference of difference, does not fit the categories of the I and the Self.

The great discovery of Nietzsche's philosophy, which marks his break with Schopenhauer and goes under the name of the will to power or the Dionysian world, is the following: no doubt the I and the Self must be replaced by an undifferenciated abyss, but this abyss is neither an impersonal nor an abstract Universal beyond individuation. On the contrary, it is the I and the self which are the abstract universals. They must be replaced, but in and by individuation, in the direction of the individuating factors which consume them and which constitute the fluid world of Dionysus. What cannot be replaced is individuation itself. Beyond the self and the I we find not the impersonal but the individual and its factors, individuation and its fields, individuality and its pre-individual singularities. For the pre-individual is still singular, just as the ante-self and the ante-I are still individual – or, rather than simply 'still', we should say 'finally'. That is why the individual in intensity finds its psychic image neither in the organisation of the self nor in the determination of species of the I, but rather in the fractured I and the dissolved self, and in the correlation of the fractured I with the dissolved self. This correlation seems clear, like that of the thinker and the thought, or that of the clear–confused thinker with distinct–obscure Ideas (the Dionysian thinker). It is Ideas which lead us from the fractured I to the dissolved Self. As we have seen, what swarms around the edges of the fracture are Ideas in the form of problems – in other words, in the form of multiplicities made up of differential relations and variations of relations, distinctive points and transformations of points. These Ideas, however, are expressed in individuating factors, in the implicated world of intensive quantities which constitute the universal concrete individuality of the thinker or the system of the dissolved Self.

Death is inscribed in the I and the self, like the cancellation of difference in a system of explication, or the degradation which compensates for the processes of differenciation. From this point of view, death may well be inevitable, but every death is none the less accidental and violent, and always comes from without. Simultaneously, however, death has quite another face hidden among the individuating factors which dissolve the self: here it is like a 'death instinct', an internal power which frees the individuating elements from the form of the I or the matter of the self in which they are imprisoned. It would be wrong to confuse the two faces of death, as though the death instinct were reduced to a tendency towards increasing entropy or a return to inanimate matter. Every death is double, and represents the cancellation of large differences in extension as well as the liberation and swarming of little differences in intensity. Freud suggested the following hypothesis: the organism wants to die, but to die in its own way, so that real death always presents itself as a foreshortening, as possessing an accidental, violent and external character which is anathema to the internal will-to-die. There is a necessary non-correspondence between death as an empirical event and death as an 'instinct' or transcendental instance. Freud and Spinoza are both right: one with regard to the instinct, the other with regard to the event. Desired from within, death always comes from without in a passive and accidental form. Suicide is an attempt to make the two incommensurable faces coincide or correspond. However, the two sides do not meet, and every death remains double. On the one hand, it is a 'de-differenciation' which compensates for the differenciations of the I and the Self in an overall system which renders these uniform; on the other hand, it is a matter of individuation, a protest by the individual which has never recognised itself within the limits of the Self and the I, even where these are universal.

There must none the less be values of implication in psychic systems in the process of being explicated; in other words, there must be centres of envelopment which testify to the presence of individuating factors. These centres are clearly constituted neither by the I nor by the Self, but by a completely different structure belonging to the I–Self system. This structure should be designated by the name 'other'. It refers only to the self for the other I and the other I for the self. Theories tend to oscillate mistakenly and ceaselessly from a pole at which the other is reduced to the status of object to a pole at which it assumes the status of subject. Even Sartre was content to inscribe this oscillation in the other as such, in showing that the other became object when I became subject, and did not become subject unless I in turn became object. As a result, the structure of the other, as well as its role in psychic systems, remained misunderstood. The other who is nobody, but who is self for the other and the other for the self in two systems, the *a priori Other* is defined in each system by its expressive value – in other words, its implicit and enveloping value. Consider a terrified face (under conditions such that I do not see and do not experience the causes of this terror). This face expresses a possible world: the terrifying world. By 'expression' we mean, as always, that relation which involves a torsion between an expressor and an expressed such that the expressed does not exist apart from the expressor, even though the expressor relates to it as though to something completely different. By 'possible', therefore, we do not mean any resemblance but that state of the implicated or enveloped in its very heterogeneity with what envelops it: the terrified face does not resemble what terrifies it, it envelops a state of the terrifying world. In every psychic system there is a swarm of possibilities around reality, but our possibles are always Others. The Other cannot be separated from the expressivity which constitutes it. Even when we consider the body of another as an object, its ears and eyes as anatomical pieces, we do not remove all expressivity from them even though we simplify in the extreme the world they express: the eye is an implicated light or the expression of a possible light, while the ear is that of a possible sound.[22] Concretely, however, it is the so-called tertiary qualities whose mode of existence is in the first instance enveloped by the other. The I and the Self, by contrast, are immediately characterised by functions of development or explication: not only do they experience qualities in general as already developed in the extensity of their system, but they tend to explicate or develop the world expressed by the other, either in order to participate in it or to deny it (I unravel the frightened face of the other, I either develop it into a frightening world the reality of which seizes me, or I denounce its unreality). However, these relations of development, which form our commonalities as well as our disagreements with the other, also dissolve its structure and reduce it either to the status of an object or to the status of a subject. That is why, in order to grasp the other as such, we were right to insist upon special conditions of experience, however artificial – namely, the moment at which the expressed has (for us) no existence apart from that which expresses it: the Other as *the expression of a possible world.*

In the psychic system of the I–Self, the Other thus functions as a centre of enwinding, envelopment or implication. It is the representative of the individuating factors. Moreover, if an organism may be regarded as a microscopic being, how much more is this true of the Other in psychic systems. It gives rise there to local increases in entropy, whereas the explication of the other by the self represents a degradation in accordance with law. The rule invoked earlier – not to be explicated too much – meant, above all, not to explicate oneself too much with the other, not to explicate the other too much, but to maintain one's implicit values and multiply one's own world by populating it with all those expresseds that do not exist apart from their expressions. For it is not the other which is another I, but the I which is an other, a fractured I. There is no love which does not begin with the revelation of a possible world as such, enwound in the other which expresses it. Albertine's face expressed the blending of beach and waves: 'From what unknown world does she distinguish me?' The entire history of that exemplary love is the long explication of the possible worlds expressed by Albertine, which transform her now into a fascinating subject, now into a deceptive object. It is true that the other disposes of a means to endow the possibles that it expresses with reality, independently of the development we cause them to undergo. This means is language. Words offered by the other confer reality on the possible as such; whence the foundation of the lie inscribed within language itself. It is this role of language as a result of the values of implication or the centres of envelopment which endows it with its powers within internal resonance systems. The structure of the other and the corresponding function of language effectively represent the manifestation of the noumenon, the appearance of expressive values – in short, the tendency towards the interiorisation of difference.

Conclusion

Difference is not and cannot be thought in itself, so long as it is subject to the requirements of representation. The question whether it was 'always' subject to these requirements, and for what reasons, must be closely examined. But it appears that pure *disparates* formed either the celestial beyond of a divine understanding inaccessible to our representative thought, or the infernal and unfathomable for us below of an Ocean of dissemblance. In any case, difference in itself appears to exclude any relation between different and different which would allow it to be thought. It seems that it can become thinkable only when tamed – in other words, when subject to the four iron collars of representation: identity in the concept, opposition in the predicate, analogy in judgement and resemblance in perception. As Foucault has shown, the classical world of representation is defined by these four dimensions which co-ordinate and measure it. These are the four roots of the principle of reason: the identity of the concept which is reflected in a *ratio cognoscendi*; the opposition of the predicate which is developed in a *ratio fiendi*; the analogy of judgement which is distributed in a *ratio essendi*; and the resemblance of perception which determines a *ratio agendi*. Every other difference, every difference which is not rooted in this way, is an unbounded, uncoordinated and inorganic difference: too large or too small, not only to be thought but to exist. Ceasing to be thought, difference is dissipated in non-being. From this, it is concluded that difference in itself remains condemned and must atone or be redeemed under the auspices of a reason which renders it livable and thinkable, and makes it the object of an organic representation.

The greatest effort of philosophy was perhaps directed at rendering representation infinite (orgiastic). It is a question of extending representation as far as the too large and the too small of difference; of adding a hitherto unsuspected perspective to representation – in other words, inventing theological, scientific and aesthetic techniques which allow it to integrate the depth of difference in itself; of allowing representation to conquer the obscure; of allowing it to include the vanishing of difference which is too small and the dismemberment of difference which is too large; of allowing it to capture the power of giddiness, intoxication and cruelty, and even of death. In short, it is a question of causing a little of Dionysus's blood to flow in the organic veins of Apollo. This effort has always permeated the world of representation. The ultimate wish of the organic is to become orgiastic and to conquer the in-itself, but this effort found two culminating moments in Leibniz and Hegel. With the former, representation conquers the infinite because a technique for dealing with the infinitely small captures the smallest difference and its disappearance. With the latter, representation conquers the infinite because a technique for dealing with the infinitely large captures the largest difference and its dismembering. The two are in agreement, since the Hegelian problem is *also* that of disappearance, while the Leibnizian problem is also that of dismembering. Hegel's technique lies in the movement of contradiction (difference must attain that point, it must be extended that far). It consists of inscribing the inessential in the essence, and in conquering the infinite with the weapons of a synthetic finite identity. Leibniz's technique lies in the movement we call vice-diction: it consists in constructing the essence from the inessential, and conquering the finite by means of an infinite analytic identity (difference must be developed to that point). But what is the point of making representation infinite? It retains all its requirements. All that is discovered is a *ground* which relates the excess and default of difference to the identical, the similar, the analogous and the opposed: reason, – that is, sufficient reason – has become the ground which no longer allows anything to escape. Nothing, however, has changed: difference remains subject to malediction, and all that has happened is the discovery of more subtle and more sublime means to make it atone, or to redeem it and subject it to the categories of representation.

Thus, Hegelian contradiction appears to push difference to the limit, but this path is a dead end which brings it back to identity, making identity the sufficient condition for difference to exist and be thought. It is only in relation to the identical, as a function of the identical, that contradiction is the *greatest* difference. The intoxications and giddinesses are feigned, the obscure is already clarified from the outset. Nothing shows this more clearly than the insipid monocentricity of the circles in the Hegelian dialectic. Moreover, in another manner perhaps the same should be said of the condition of convergence in the Leibnizian world. Take a notion such as that of Leibnizian incompossibility. Everyone recognises that incompossibility is not reducible to contradiction, and compossibility is not reducible to the identical. It is indeed in this sense that the compossible and the incompossible testify to a specific sufficient reason and to a presence of the infinite – not only in the totality of possible worlds, but in each chosen world. It is more difficult to say in what these new notions consist. It seems to us that compossibility consists uniquely in the following: the condition of a maximum of continuity for a maximum of difference – in other words, a condition of convergence of established series around the singularities of the continuum. Conversely, the incompossibility of worlds is decided in the vicinity of those singularities which give rise to divergent series between themselves. In short, representation may well become infinite; *it nevertheless does not acquire the power to affirm either divergence or decentring.* It requires a convergent and monocentric world: a world in which one is only apparently intoxicated, in which reason acts the drunkard and sings a Dionysian tune while none the less remaining 'pure' reason. The ground or sufficient reason is nothing but a means of allowing the identical to rule over infinity itself, and allowing the continuity of resemblance, the relation of analogy and the opposition of predicates to invade infinity. This is the originality of sufficient reason: better to ensure the subjection of difference to the quadripartite yoke. The damage is done not only by the requirement of finite representation, which consists of fixing a propitious moment for difference, neither too large nor too small, in between excess and default; but also by the apparently contrary requirement of infinite representation, which purports to integrate the infinitely large and the infinitely small of difference, excess and default themselves. *The entire alternative between finite and infinite applies very badly to difference*, because it constitutes only an antinomy of representation. We saw this, moreover, in the case of calculus: modern finitist interpretations betray the nature of the differential no less than the former infinitist interpretations, because both fail to capture the extra-propositional or sub-representative source – in other words, the 'problem' from which the calculus draws its power. In addition, the alternative of the Small and the Large, whether in finite representation which excludes both, or in infinite representation which wants to include both, and each within the other, does not, in general, fit difference. The reason is that this alternative expresses only the oscillations of representation with regard to an always dominant identity, or rather the oscillations of the Identical with regard to an always rebellious matter, the excess and default of which it sometimes rejects and sometimes tries to integrate. Finally, returning to Leibniz and Hegel and their common attempt to extend representation to infinity: we are not sure that Leibniz does not go 'farthest' (nor that, of the two, he is not the least theological). His conception of the Idea as an ensemble of differential relations and singular points, the manner in which he begins with the inessential and constructs essences in the form of centres of envelopment around singularities, his presentiment of divergences, his procedure of vice-diction, his approximation to an inverse ratio between the distinct and the clear, all show why the ground rumbles with greater power in the case of Leibniz, why the intoxication and giddiness are less feigned in his case, why obscurity is better understood and the Dionysian shores are closer.

What motivated the subordination of difference to the requirements of finite or infinite representation? It is correct to define metaphysics by reference to Platonism, but insufficient to define Platonism by reference to the distinction between essence and appearance. The primary distinction which Plato rigorously establishes is the one between the model and the copy. The copy, however, is far from a simple appearance, since it stands in an internal, spiritual, noological and ontological relation with the Idea or model. The second and more profound distinction is the one between the copy itself and the phantasm. It is clear that Plato distinguishes, and even opposes, models and copies only in order to obtain a selective criterion with which to separate copies and simulacra, the former founded upon their relation to the model while the latter are disqualified because they fail both the test of the copy and the requirements of the model. While there is indeed appearance, it is rather a matter of distinguishing the splendid and well-grounded Apollonian appearances from the other, insinuative, malign and maleficent appearances which respect the ground no more than the grounded. This Platonic wish to exorcize simulacra is what entails the subjection of difference. For the model can be defined only by a positing of identity as the essence of the Same [*auto kath' hauto*], and the copy by an affection of internal resemblance, the quality of the Similar. Moreover, because the resemblance is internal, the copy must itself have an internal relation to being and the true which is analogous to that of the model. Finally, the copy must be constructed by means of a method which, given two opposed predicates, attributes to it the one which agrees with the model. In all these ways, copies are distinguished from simulacra only by subordinating difference to instances of the Same, the Similar, the Analogous and the Opposed. No doubt with Plato these instances are not yet distributed as they will be in the deployed world of representation (from Aristotle onwards). Plato inaugurates and initiates because he evolves within a theory of Ideas which *will* allow the deployment of representation. In his case, however, a moral motivation in all its purity is avowed: the will to eliminate simulacra or phantasms has no motivation apart from the moral. What is condemned in the figure of simulacra is the state of free, oceanic differences, of nomadic distributions and crowned anarchy, along with all that malice which challenges both the notion of the model and that of the copy. Later, the world of representation will more or less forget its moral origin and presuppositions. These will nevertheless continue to act in the distinction between the originary and the derived, the original and the sequel, the ground and the grounded, which animates the hierarchies of a representative theology by extending the complementarity between model and copy.

Representation is a site of transcendental illusion. This illusion comes in several forms, four interrelated forms which correspond particularly to thought, sensibility, the Idea and being. In effect, thought is covered over by an 'image' made up of postulates which distort both its operation and its genesis. These postulates culminate in the position of an identical thinking subject, which functions as a principle of identity for concepts in general. A slippage occurs in the transition from the Platonic world to the world of representation (which again is why we can present Plato as the origin or at the crossroads of a decision). The 'sameness' of the Platonic Idea which serves as model and is guaranteed by the Good gives way to the identity of an originary concept grounded in a thinking subject. The thinking subject brings to the concept its subjective concomitants: memory, recognition and self-consciousness. Nevertheless, it is the moral vision of the world which is thereby extended and represented in this subjective identity affirmed as a *common sense* [*Cogitatio natura universalis*]. When difference is subordinated by the thinking subject to the identity of the concept (even where this identity is synthetic), difference in thought disappears. In other words, what disappears is that difference that thinking makes in thought, that *genitality* of thinking, that profound fracture of the I which leads it to think only in thinking its own passion, and even its own death, in the pure and empty form of time. To restore difference in thought is to untie this first knot which consists of representing difference through the identity of the concept and the thinking subject.

The second illusion concerns the subordination of difference to resemblance. Given the manner in which it is distributed in representation, resemblance need no longer be just that between copy and model. It can be determined as the resemblance of the (diverse) sensible to itself, in such a way that the identity of the concept should be applicable to it, and receive from it in turn the possibility of specification. The illusion takes the following form: difference necessarily tends to be cancelled in the quality which covers it, while at the same time inequality tends to be equalised within the extension in which it is distributed. The theme of quantitative equality or equalisation doubles that of qualitative resemblance and assimilation. As we saw, this was the illusion of 'good sense', complementary to the preceding illusion and its 'common sense'. It is a transcendental illusion because it is entirely true that difference is cancelled qualitatively and in extension. It is nevertheless an illusion, since the nature of difference lies neither in the quality by which it is covered nor in the extensity by which it is explicated. Difference is intensive, indistinguishable from depth in the form of an non-extensive and non-qualified *spatium*, the matrix of the unequal and the different. Intensity is not the sensible but the being *of* the sensible, where different relates to different. To restore difference within intensity as the being of the sensible is to untie the second knot, one which subordinates difference to the similar within perception, allowing it to be experienced only on condition that there is an assimilation of diversity taken as raw material for the identical concept.

The third illusion concerns the negative and the manner in which it subordinates difference to itself, in the form of both limitation and opposition. The second illusion already prepared us for this discovery of a mystification on the part of the negative: it is in quality and extensity that intensity is inverted and appears upside down, and its power of affirming difference is betrayed by the figures of quantitative and qualitative limitation, qualitative and quantitative opposition. Limitation and opposition are first- and second-dimension surface effects, whereas the living depths, the diagonal, is populated by differences without negation. Beneath the platitude of the negative lies the world of 'disparateness'. The origin of the illusion which subjects difference to the false power of the negative must therefore be sought, not in the sensible world itself, but in that which acts in depth and is incarnated in the sensible world. We have seen that Ideas are genuine objectivities, made up of differential elements and relations and provided with a specific mode – namely, the 'problematic'. Problems thus defined do not designate any ignorance on the part of a thinking subject, any more than they express a conflict, but rather objectively characterise the nature of Ideas as such. There is indeed, therefore, a *mē on*, which must not be confused with the *ouk on*, and which means the being of the problematic and not the being of the negative: an expletive NE rather than a negative 'not'. This *mē on* is so called because it precedes all affirmation, but is none the less completely positive. Problems–Ideas are positive multiplicities, full and differentiated positivities described by the process of complete and reciprocal determination which relates problems to their conditions. The positivity of problems is constituted by the fact of being 'posited' (thereby being related to their conditions and fully determined). It is true that, from this point of view, problems give rise to propositions which give effect to them in the form of answers or cases of solution. These propositions in turn represent affirmations, the objects of which are those differences which correspond to the relations and the singularities of the differential field. In this sense, we can establish a distinction between the positive and the affirmative – in other words, between the positivity of Ideas understood as differential positings and the affirmations to which they give rise, which incarnate and solve them. With regard to the latter, we should say not only that they are different affirmations but that they are *affirmations of differences*, as a consequence of the multiplicity which belongs to each Idea. Affirmation, understood as the affirmation of difference, is produced by the positivity of problems understood as differential positings; multiple affirmation is produced by problematic multiplicity. It is of the essence of affirmation to be in itself multiple and to affirm difference. As for the negative, this is only the shadow cast upon the affirmations produced by a problem: negation appears alongside affirmation like a powerless double, albeit one which testifies to the existence of another power, that of the effective and persistent problem.

Everything, however, is reversed if we begin with the propositions which represent these affirmations in consciousness. For Problems–Ideas are by nature unconscious: they are extra-propositional and sub-representative, and do not resemble the propositions which represent the affirmations to which they give rise. If we attempt to reconstitute problems in the image of or as resembling conscious propositions, then the illusion takes shape, the shadow awakens and appears to acquire a life of its own: it is as though each affirmation referred to its negative, or has 'sense' only by virtue of its negation, while at the same time a generalised negation, an *ouk on*, takes the place of the problem and its *mē on*. Thus begins the long history of the distortion of the dialectic, which culminates with Hegel and consists in substituting the labour of the negative for the play of difference and the differential. Instead of being defined by a (non)-being which is the being of problems and questions, the dialectical instance is now defined by a *non*-being which is the being of the negative. The false genesis of affirmation, which takes the form of the negation of the negation and is produced by the negative, is substituted for the complementarity of the positive and the affirmative, of differential positing and the affirmation of difference. Furthermore, if the truth be told, none of this would amount to much were it not for the moral presuppositions and practical implications of such a distortion. We have seen all that this valorisation of the negative signified, including the conservative spirit of such an enterprise, the platitude of the affirmations supposed to be engendered thereby, and the manner in which we are led away from the most important task, that of determining problems and realising in them our power of creation and decision. That is why conflicts, oppositions and contradictions seemed to us to be surface effects and conscious epiphenomena, while the unconscious lived on problems and differences. History progresses not by negation and the negation of negation, but by deciding problems and affirming differences. It is no less bloody and cruel as a result. Only the shadows of history live by negation: the good enter into it with all the power of a posited differential or a difference affirmed; they repel shadows into the shadows and deny only as the consequence of a primary positivity and affirmation. For them, as Nietzsche says, affirmation is primary; it affirms difference, while the negative is only a consequence or a reflection in which affirmation is doubled.[1] That is why real revolutions have the atmosphere of fétes. Contradiction is not the weapon of the proletariat but, rather, the manner in which the bourgeoisie defends and preserves itself, the shadow behind which it maintains its claim to decide what the problems are. Contradictions are not 'resolved', they are dissipated by capturing the problem of which they reflect only the shadow. The negative is always a conscious reaction, a distortion of the true agent or actor. As a result, as long as it remains within the limits of representation, philosophy is prey to the theoretical antinomies of consciousness. The choice whether difference must be understood as quantitative limitation or qualitative opposition is no less devoid of sense than that between the Small and the Large. For whether it is limitation or opposition, difference is unjustly assimilated to a negative non-being. Whence another illusory choice: either being is full positivity, pure affirmation, but undifferenciated being, without difference; or being includes differences, it is Difference and there is non-being, a being of the negative. All these antinomies are connected, and depend upon the same illusion. We must say both that being is full positivity and pure affirmation, and that there is (non)-being which is the being of the problematic, the being of problems and questions, not the being of the negative. In truth, the origin of the antinomies is as follows: once the nature of the problematic and the multiplicity which defines the Idea is misrecognised, once the Idea is reduced to the Same or even to the identity of a concept, the negative takes wing. Instead of the positive process of determination in the Idea, what emerges is a process of opposition of contrary predicates or limitation of primary predicates. To restore the differential in the Idea, and difference to the affirmation which flows from it, is to break this unholy bond which subordinates difference to the negative.

Finally, the fourth illusion concerns the subordination of difference to the analogy of judgement. In effect, the identity of the concept does not yet give us a concrete rule of determination, since it appears only as the identity of an indeterminate concept; Being or I am (that 'I am' which Kant said was the perception or the feeling of an existence independently of any determination). The ultimate concepts or primary and originary predicates must therefore be posited as determinable. They are recognised by the fact that each maintains an internal relation to being. In this sense, these concepts are analogues, or Being is analogous in relation to them and acquires simultaneously the identity of a distributive common sense and that of an ordinal good sense (we have seen how analogy took two forms, which rested not upon equality but upon the interiority of the relation of judgement). It is not sufficient, therefore, that representation be grounded upon the identity of an indeterminate concept. Identity must itself be represented every time in a certain number of determinable concepts. These originary concepts, in relation to which Being is distributive and ordinal, are called categories or genera of being. On the basis of such categories, specific derived concepts can in turn be determined by a method of division – in other words, by the play of contrary predicates within each genus. In this manner, difference is assigned two limits, in the form of two irreducible but complementary figures which indicate precisely its belonging to representation (the Large and the Small): the categories as *a priori* concepts and the empirical concepts; the originary determinable concepts and the derived determined concepts; the analogous and the opposed; *the large genera and the species*. This distribution of difference in a manner entirely dependent upon the requirements of representation essentially belongs within the analogical vision of the world. However, this form of distribution commanded by the categories seemed to us to betray the nature of Being (as a cardinal and collective concept) and the nature of the distributions themselves (as nomadic rather than sedentary and fixed distributions), as well as the nature of difference (as individuating difference). In terms of this distribution, the individual is only, and only understood as, that which bears differences in general, while Being distributes itself among the fixed forms of these differences and is said analogically of that which is.

Nevertheless, it should be noted that the four illusions of representation distort repetition no less than they distort difference, and for reasons which are in certain respects comparable. In the first place, representation provides no direct and positive criteria for distinguishing between repetition and the order of generality, resemblance or equivalence. That is why repetition is represented as a perfect resemblance or an extreme equality. Second, representation in effect invokes the identity of the concept in order to explain repetition no less than to understand difference. Difference is represented *in* the identical concept, and thereby reduced to a merely conceptual difference. Repetition, by contrast, is represented *outside* the concept, as though it were a difference without concept, *but always with the presupposition of an identical concept.* Thus, repetition occurs when things are distinguished *in numero*, in space and time, while their concept remains the same. In the same movement, therefore, the identity of the concept in representation includes difference and is extended to repetition. A third aspect follows from this: it is apparent that repetition can no longer receive anything but a negative explanation. In effect, it is a matter of explaining the possibility of differences without concept. Or one invokes a logical limitation of the concept at each of its moments – in other words, a relative 'blockage' such that, however far the comprehension of the concept is pushed, there is always an infinite number of things which can correspond to it, since in fact one can never encompass the infinity of that comprehension which would make every difference a conceptual difference. Repetition is then explained only in terms of a relative limitation in our representation of the concept and, from precisely this point of view, we deprive ourselves of any means of distinguishing repetition from simple resemblance. Alternatively, a real opposition is invoked, one that is capable of imposing an absolute natural blockage on the concept: by assigning to it a comprehension that is in principle necessarily finite, by defining an order external to the comprehension of even an indefinite concept, or by bringing in forces opposed to the subjective concomitants of the infinite concept (memory, recognition, self-consciousness). We have seen how these three cases seemed to be illustrated respectively by nominal concepts, concepts of nature and concepts of freedom: words, Nature and the unconscious. In all these cases, thanks to the distinction between absolute natural blockage and artificial or logical blockage, there is no doubt that we have the means to distinguish between repetition and simple resemblance, since things are said to repeat when they differ even though their concept is *absolutely* the same. However, not only this distinction but repetition itself is explained here in an entirely negative fashion. *It* (language) repeats because *it* (the words) is not real, because there is no definition other than nominal. *It* (nature) repeats because *it* (matter) has no interiority, because it is *partes extra partes*. *It* (the unconscious) repeats because *it* (the Ego) represses, because *it* (the Id) has no memory, no recognition and no consciousness of itself – ultimately because it has no instinct, instinct being the subjective concomitant of the species as concept. In short, things repeat always by virtue of what they are not and do not have. We repeat because we do not hear. As Kierkegaard said, it is the repetition of the deaf, or rather for the deaf: deafness of words, deafness of nature, deafness of the unconscious. Within representation, the forces which ensure repetition – in other words, a multiplicity of things for a concept absolutely the same – can only be negatively determined.

Fourth, repetition is not only defined in relation to the absolute identity of the concept; it must, in a certain manner, itself represent this identical concept. A phenomenon corresponding to the analogy of judgement emerges here. Repetition is not content with multiplying instances of the same concept; it puts the concept outside itself and causes it to exist in so many instances *hic et nunc*. It fragments identity itself, just as Democritus fragmented the One-Being of Parmenides and multiplied it into atoms. Or rather, the multiplication of things under an absolutely identical concept has as its consequence the division of the concept into absolutely identical things. Matter realises this state of the concept outside itself or the infinitely repeated element. That is why the model of repetition is indistinguishable from pure matter understood as the fragmentation of the identical or the repetition of a minimum. Repetition, therefore, has a *primary sense* from the point of view of representation – namely, that of a material and bare repetition, a repetition *of* the same (and not only *under* the same concept). All the other senses will be derived from this extrinsic model. In other words, every time we encounter a variant, a difference, a disguise or a displacement, we will say that it is a matter of repetition, but only in a derivative and 'analogical' manner. (Even in the case of Freud, the prodigious conception of repetition in psychic life is dominated not only by a schema of opposition in the case of the theory of repression, but by a material model in that of the death instinct.) This extrinsic material model, however, takes repetition as already accomplished and presents it to a spectator who contemplates it from without. It suppresses the thickness in which repetition occurs and unfolds, even in the case of matter and death. Whence the attempt, by contrast, to represent disguise and displacement as the constituent elements of repetition, but on condition that repetition is confounded with analogy itself. Identity is no longer that of an element but, in accordance with the traditional signification, that of a relation between distinct elements or a relation between relations. Earlier, physical matter provided repetition with its *primary sense*, and the other senses (biological, psychic, metaphysical...) were said by analogy. Now, analogy by itself is the logical matter of repetition, providing it with a *distributive sense.*[2] However, it is still a sense understood in relation to a thought identity or to a represented equality, with the result that repetition remains a concept of reflection which ensures the distribution and the displacement of terms, the transportation of the element, but only within representation and for a spectator who remains extrinsic.

To ground is to determine. But what is determination, and upon what is it exercised? Grounding is the operation of the logos, or of sufficient reason. As such, it has three senses. In its first sense, the ground is the Same or the Identical. It enjoys supreme identity, that which is supposed to belong to Ideas or to the *auto kath' hauto*. What it is, and what it possesses, it is and it possesses primarily, in the utmost. What, apart from Courage, would be courageous, or virtuous apart from Virtue? What the ground has to ground, therefore, is only the claim of those who come after, all those who at best possess secondarily. It is always a claim or an 'image' that requires a ground or appeals to a ground: for example, the claim of men to be courageous, to be virtuous – in short, to have part or to participate in (*metexein* means to have after). As such, we may distinguish between the ground or ideal Essence, the grounded in the form of Claimant or claim, and that upon which the claim bears – in other words, the Quality that the ground possesses primarily and the claimant will possess secondarily, assuming that its claim is well grounded. This quality, the object of the claim, is difference – the fiancée, Ariadne. The essence or ground is the identical in so far as it originarily includes the difference of its object. The operation of grounding renders the claimant *similar* to the ground, endowing it with resemblance from within and thereby allowing it to participate in the quality or the object which it claims. As similar to the same, the claimant is said to *resemble* – this, however, is not an external resemblance to the object but an internal resemblance to the ground itself. In order to have the daughter, one must resemble the father. Difference is thought here in terms of the principle of Sameness and the condition of resemblance. Moreover, there will be claimants in third place, fourth place and fifth place, as many as there are images grounded in the hierarchy of this internal resemblance. That is why the ground selects and establishes the difference between the claimants themselves. Each well-grounded image or claim is called a representation [*icône*], since the first in the order of claims is still second in itself in relation to the foundation. It is in this sense that Ideas inaugurate or ground the world of representation. As for the rebellious images which lack resemblance [*simulacra*], these are eliminated, rejected and denounced as ungrounded, false claimants.

In a second sense, once the world of representation is established, the ground is no longer defined by the identical. The identical has become the internal character of representation itself, while resemblance has become its external relation with the thing. The identical now expresses a claim which must in turn be grounded. For the object of the claim is no longer difference understood as the quality, but that which is too large or too small in the difference, the excess and the default – in other words, the infinite. What must be grounded is the claim of representation to conquer the infinite, in order that it be indebted to no one for the daughter and capture the heart of difference. It is no longer the image which seeks to conquer difference as this seemed to be originarily included in the identical, but, on the contrary, identity which seeks to conquer that which it does not include of difference. *To ground no longer means to inaugurate and render possible representation, but to render representation infinite.* The ground must now operate in the heart of representation, in order to extend its limits to both the infinitely small and the infinitely large. This operation is carried out by a method which ensures a monocentricity of all the possible centres of finite representation, a convergence of all the finite points of view of representation. This operation expresses sufficient reason. The latter is not identity but, rather, the means of subordinating to the identical and the other requirements of representation that part of difference which escaped them in the first sense.

The two senses of the ground are nevertheless united in a third. In effect, to ground is always to bend, to curve and recurve – to organise the order of the seasons, the days and years. The object of the claim (the quality, difference) finds itself placed in a circle; the arcs of the circle are distinguished to the extent that the ground establishes moments of stasis within qualitative becoming, stoppages in between the two extremes of more and less. The claimants are distributed around the mobile circle, each receiving the lot which corresponds to the worth of its life: a life is here assimilated to a strict *present* which stakes its claim upon a portion of the circle, which 'contracts' that portion and draws from it a loss or a gain in the order of more and less according to its own progression or regression in the hierarchy of images (another present or another life contracts another portion). In Platonism we see clearly how the rotation of the circle and the distribution of lots, cycle and metempsychosis, form a grounding test or lottery. With Hegel again, however, all the possible *beginnings* and all the presents are distributed within the unique incessant principle of a grounding circle, which includes these in its centre while it distributes them along its circumference. With Leibniz, too, compossibility itself is a circle of convergence on which are distributed all the *points of view*, all the presents of which the world is composed. To ground, in this third sense, is to represent the present – in other words, to make the present arrive and pass within representation (finite or infinite). The ground then appears as an immemorial Memory or pure past, a past which itself was never present but which causes the present to pass, and in relation to which all the presents coexist in a circle.

To ground is always to ground representation. How, then, are we to explain the ambiguity that is essential to the ground? It is as though it were attracted by the representation that it grounds (in these three senses), while at the same time it is drawn towards a beyond; as though it vacillated between a fall into the grounded and an engulfment in a groundlessness [*sans fond*]. We saw this in the case of the Memory-ground: it tended to represent itself as a former present and to enter into the circle which it organised in principle. Is this not the most general characteristic of the ground – namely, that the circle which it organises is also the vicious circle of philosophical 'proof', in which representation must prove what proves it, just as for Kant the possibility of experience serves as the proof of its own proof? On the other hand, when transcendental memory overcomes its vertigo and maintains the irreducibility of the pure past to any present which passes in representation, it is only to see this pure past dissolve in another manner, and to see unravelled the circle on which it too simply distributes difference and repetition. In this manner, the second synthesis of time which united Eros and Mnemosyne (Eros as the seeker after memories, Mnemosyne as the treasure of the pure past) is overcome or overturned in a third synthesis, one which brings together a desexualised death instinct and an essentially amnesiac narcissistic ego *within the form of empty time*. Moreover, how can the ground in its other senses be protected from challenge at the hands of the simulacra and all the forces of divergence and decentring which overturn the false distributions and the false repartitions as they do the false circle and the false lottery? The world of the ground is undermined by what it tries to exclude, by the simulacrum which draws it in only to fragment it. When the ground in the first sense appeals to the Idea, it is on condition that the latter be attributed an identity that it does not have by itself, but which it derives solely from the requirements of that which it claims to prove. The Idea no more implies an identity than its process of actualisation is explicated by resemblance. An entire multiplicity rumbles underneath the 'sameness' of the Idea. There is no doubt that describing Ideas as substantive multiplicities, irreducible to any same or One, showed us how sufficient reason was capable of engendering itself independently of the requirements of representation, along the pathways of the multiple as such, by determining the elements, relations and singularities corresponding to a given Idea in terms of the threefold principle of determinability, reciprocal determination and complete determination. Upon precisely what ground, however, is this multiple reason engendered and played out; in what unreason is it submerged, and from what new type of game or lottery does it draw its singularities and its distributions which remain irreducible to all that we have just seen? In short, *sufficient reason or the ground is strangely bent*:

on the one hand, it leans towards what it grounds, towards the forms of representation; on the other hand, it turns and plunges into a groundlessness beyond the ground which resists all forms and cannot be represented. If difference is the fiancée, Ariadne, then it passes from Theseus to Dionysus, from the grounding principle to the universal 'ungrounding'.

The fact is that to ground is to determine the indeterminate, but this is not a simple operation. When determination as such occurs, it does not simply provide a form or impart form to a given matter on the basis of the categories. Something of the ground rises to the surface, without assuming any form but, rather, insinuating itself between the forms; a formless base, an autonomous and faceless existence. This ground which is now on the surface is called depth or groundlessness. Conversely, when they are reflected in it, forms decompose, every model breaks down and all faces perish, leaving only the abstract line as the determination absolutely adequate to the indeterminate, just as the flash of lightning is equal to the night, acid equal to the base, and distinction adequate to obscurity as a whole: monstrosity. (A determination which is not opposed to the indeterminate and does not limit it.) That is why the matter–form couple is not sufficient to describe the mechanism of determination: matter is already informed, form is not separable from the model of the *species* or that of the *morphē*, and the whole is under the protection of the categories. In fact, this couple is completely internal to representation, serving to define its first state as this was established by Aristotle. It is already progress to invoke the complementarity of force and the ground as the sufficient reason of form, matter and their union. More profound and threatening still is the couple formed by the abstract line and the groundlessness which dissolves matters and breaks down models. Thought understood as pure determination or abstract line must confront this indeterminate, this groundlessness. This indeterminate or groundlessness is also the animality peculiar to thought, the genitality of thought: not this or that animal form, but stupidity [*bétise*]. For if thought thinks only when constrained or forced to do so, if it remains stupid so long as nothing forces it to think, is it not also the existence of stupidity which forces it to think, precisely the fact that it does not think so long as nothing forces it to do so? Recall Heidegger's statement: 'What gives us most cause for thought is the fact that we do not yet think.' Thought is the highest determination, confronting stupidity as though face to face with the indeterminate which is adequate to it. Stupidity (not error) constitutes the greatest weakness of thought, but also the source of its highest power in that which forces it to think. Such is the prodigious adventure of Bouvard and Pécuchet or the play of sense and non-sense.[3] As a result, determination and the indeterminate remain equal and do not progress, the one always adequate to the other – a strange repetition which ties them to the wheel, or rather to the same double pulpit. Shestov saw in Dostoyevsky the outcome of the *Critique of Pure Reason* in the sense of both culmination and exit. Let us for a moment be allowed to see Bouvard and Pécuchet as the outcome of the *Discourse on Method*. Is the Cogito a stupidity? It is necessarily a non-sense to the extent that this proposition purports to state both itself and its sense. However, it is also a confusion (as Kant showed) to the extent that the determination 'I think' purports to bear immediately on the indeterminate existence 'I am', without specifying the form under which the indeterminate is determinable. The subject of the Cartesian Cogito does not think: it only has the possibility of thinking, and remains stupid at the heart of that possibility. It lacks the form of the determinable: not a specificity, not a specific form informing a matter, not a memory informing a present, but the pure and empty form of time. It is the empty form of time which introduces and constitutes Difference in thought, on the basis of which it thinks, in the form of the difference between the indeterminate and the determination. It is this form of time which distributes throughout itself an I fractured by the abstract line, a passive self produced by a groundlessness that it contemplates. It is this which engenders thought within thought, for thought thinks only by means of difference, around this point of ungrounding. It is difference or the form of the determinable which causes thought to function – in other words, the entire machine of determination and the indeterminate. The theory of thought is like painting: it needs that revolution which took art from representation to abstraction. This is the aim of a theory of thought without image.

Representation, especially when it becomes infinite, is imbued with a presentiment of groundlessness. Because it has become infinite in order to include difference within itself, however, it represents groundlessness as a completely undifferenciated abyss, a universal lack of difference, an indifferent black nothingness. For representation began by connecting individuation to the form of the I and the matter of the self. In effect, for representation the I is not only the superior form of individuation but the principle of recognition and identification for all judgements of individuality bearing upon things: 'It is the same wax ...'. *For representation, every individuality must be personal* (I) *and every singularity individual* (Self). Where one no longer says I, individuation also ceases, and where individuation ceases, so too does all possible singularity. Since groundlessness lacks both individuality and singularity, it is therefore necessarily represented as devoid of any difference. We see this with Schelling, with Schopenhauer, and even with the first Dionysus, that of the *Birth of Tragedy*: their groundlessness cannot sustain difference. However, the self in the form of passive self is only an event which takes place in pre-existing fields of individuation: it contemplates and contracts the individuating factors of such fields, and constitutes itself at the points of resonance of their series. Similarly, the I in the form of a fractured I allows to pass all the Ideas defined by their singularities, themselves prior to fields of individuation.

Just as singularity as differential determination is pre-individual, so is individuation as individuating difference an ante-I or ante-self. The world of 'one' or 'they' is a world of *impersonal individuations* and *pre-individual singularities*; a world which cannot be assimilated to everyday banality but one in which, on the contrary, we encounter the final face of Dionysus, and in which resonates the true nature of that profound and that groundlessness which surrounds representation, and from which simulacra emerge. (Hegel criticized Schelling for having surrounded himself with an indifferent night in which all cows are black. What a presentiment of the differences swarming behind us, however, when in the weariness and despair of our thought without image we murmur 'the cows', 'they exaggerate', etc.; how differenciated and differenciating is this blackness, even though these differences remain unidentified and barely or non-individuated; how many differences and singularities are distributed like so many aggressions, how many simulacra emerge in this night which has become white in order to compose the world of 'one' and 'they'.)[4] The ultimate, external illusion of representation is this illusion that results from all its internal illusions – namely, that groundlessness should lack differences, when in fact it swarms with them. What, after all, are Ideas, with their constitutive multiplicity, if not these ants which enter and leave through the fracture in the I?

Systems in which different relates to different through difference itself are systems of simulacra. Such systems are intensive; they rest ultimately upon the nature of intensive quantities, which precisely communicate through their differences. The fact that conditions are necessary for such communication to take place (small difference, proximity, etc.) should lead us to believe not in a condition of prior resemblance, but only in the particular properties of intensive quantities which may divide, but do so only in changing their nature according to their own particular order. As for resemblance, it seems to us to result from the functioning of the system, like an 'effect' which it would be wrong to take for a cause or condition. In short, systems of simulacra must be described with the help of notions which, from the outset, appear very different from the categories of representation:

(1) the depth or *spatium* in which intensities are organised;

(2) the disparate series these form, and the fields of individuation that they outline (individuating factors);

(3) the 'dark precursor' which causes them to communicate;

(4) the linkages, internal resonances and forced movements which result;

(5) the constitution of passive selves and larval subjects in the system, and the formation of pure spatio–temporal dynamisms;
(6) the qualities and extensions, species and parts which form the double differenciation of the system and cover over the preceding factors;
(7) the centres of envelopment which nevertheless testify to the persistence of these factors in the developed world of qualities and extensities. Systems of simulacra affirm divergence and decentring: the only unity, the only convergence of all the series, is an informal chaos in which they are all included. No series enjoys a privilege over others, none possesses the identity of a model, none the resemblance of a copy. None is either opposed or analogous to another. Each is constituted by differences, and communicates with the others through differences of differences. Crowned anarchies are substituted for the hierarchies of representation; nomadic distributions for the sedentary distributions of representation.

We saw how these systems were sites for the actualisation of Ideas. An Idea, in this sense, is neither one nor multiple, but a multiplicity constituted of differential elements, differential relations between those elements, and singularities corresponding to those relations. These three dimensions, elements, relations and singularities, constitute the three aspects of multiple reason: determinability or the principle of quantitability, reciprocal determination or the principle of qualitability, and complete determination or the principle of potentiality. All three are projected in an ideal temporal dimension which is that of progressive determination. There is therefore an empiricism of the Idea. In the most diverse cases, we must ask whether we are indeed confronted by ideal elements – in other words, elements without figure or function, but reciprocally determined within a network of differential relations (ideal non-localisable connections). For example, we must ask whether any physical particles are elements of this kind and, if so, which ones? Are biological genes such elements? Are phonemes? We must also ask what distribution of singularities, what repartitioning of singular and regular, distinctive and ordinary points, corresponds to the values of the given relations. A singularity is the point of departure for a series which extends over all the ordinary points of the system, as far as the region of another singularity which itself gives rise to another series which may either converge with or diverge from the first. Ideas have the power to affirm divergence; they establish a kind of resonance between divergent series. It is probable that the notions of singular and regular, distinctive and ordinary, have for philosophy an ontological and epistemological importance much greater than those of truth and falsity in relation to representation: for what is called *sense* depends upon the distinction and distribution of these shining points in the structure of a given Idea. It is therefore the play of reciprocal determination from the point of view of its relations, and of complete determination from the point of view of its singularities, which makes an Idea in itself progressively determinable. This play in the Idea is that of the differential: it runs throughout the Idea understood as multiplicity and constitutes the method of *vice-diction* (which Leibniz employed with such genius, even though he subordinated it to illegitimate conditions of convergence, thereby indicating the presence of a continuing pressure on the part of the requirements of representation).

Ideas thus defined possess no actuality. They are pure virtuality. All the differential relations brought about by reciprocal determination, and all the repartitions of singularities brought about by complete determination, coexist according to their own particular order in the virtual multiplicities which form Ideas. In the first place, Ideas are incarnated in fields of individuation: the intensive series of individuating factors envelop ideal singularities which are in themselves pre-individual; the resonances between series put the ideal relations in play. Here too, Leibniz showed profoundly that the individual essences were constituted on the ground of these relations and these singularities. Second, Ideas are actualised in species and parts, qualities and extensities which cover and develop these fields of individuation. A species is made up of differential relations between genes, just as the organic parts and the extensity of a body are made up of actualised pre-individual singularities. However, the absolute condition of non-resemblance must be emphasized: neither species nor qualities resemble the differential relations that they actualise, any more than the organic parts resemble the singularities. The possible and the real resemble one another, but not the virtual and the actual. The incarnation and the actualisation of Ideas no more rely upon similarity or proceed by resemblance than Ideas themselves possess a given identity or may be assimilated to the Identical.

If it is true that the two aspects of *differenciation* are constituted by species and parts, qualities and extensities – or rather, division and the determination of species, qualification and extension – then we should say that Ideas are actualised by differen*c*iation. For Ideas, to be actualised is to be differen*c*iated. In themselves and in their virtuality they are thus completely undifferen*c*iated. However, they are by no means indeterminate: on the contrary, they are completely differen*t*iated. (In this sense the virtual is by no means a vague notion, but one which possesses full objective reality; it cannot be confused with the possible which lacks reality. As a result, whereas the possible is the mode of identity of concepts within representation, the virtual is the modality of the differential at the heart of Ideas.) The greatest importance must be attached to the 'distinctive feature' *t/c* as the symbol of Difference: differen*t*iate and differen*c*iate. The totality of the system which brings into play the Idea, its incarnation and its actualisation must be expressed in the complex notion of '(indi)-differen*t/c*iation'. It is as though everything has two odd, dissymmetrical and dissimilar 'halves', the two halves of the Symbol, each dividing itself in two: an ideal half submerged in the virtual and constituted on the one hand by differential relations and on the other by corresponding singularities; an actual half constituted on the one hand by the qualities actualising those relations and on the other by the parts actualising those singularities. Individuation ensures the embedding of the two dissimilar halves. The question of the *ens omni modo determinatum* must be posed as follows: something which exists only in the Idea may be completely determined (differentiated) and yet lack those determinations which constitute actual existence (it is undifferenciated, not yet even individuated). If we call the state of a completely differentiated Idea 'distinct', and the forms of quantitative and qualitative differenciation 'clear', then we must reject the rule of proportionality between the clear and the distinct: Ideas as they exist in themselves are distinct–obscure. Opposed to the clear-and-distinct of Apollonian representation, Ideas are Dionysian, existing in an obscure zone which they themselves preserve and maintain, in an indifferenciation which is nevertheless perfectly differentiated, in a pre-individuality which is nevertheless singular: the obscure zone of an intoxication which will never be calmed; the distinct–obscure as the double colour with which philosophy paints the world, with all the forces of a differential unconscious.

It is an error to see *problems* as indicative of a provisional and subjective state, through which our knowledge must pass by virtue of its empirical limitations. This error liberates negation and leads to the distortion of the dialectic by substituting the non-being of the negative for the (non)-being of problems. The 'problematic' is a state of the world, a dimension of the system, and even its horizon or its home: it designates precisely the objectivity of Ideas, the reality of the virtual. The problem as problem is completely determined: to the extent that it is related to its perfectly positive conditions, it is necessarily differentiated, even though it may not yet be 'solved', and thereby remains undifferenciated. Or rather, it is solved once it is posited and determined, but still objectively persists in the solutions to which it gives rise and from which it differs in kind. That is why the metaphysics of differential calculus finds its true signification when it escapes the antinomy of the finite and the infinite in representation in order to appear in the Idea as the first principle of the theory of problems. '*Perplication*' is what we called this state of Problems–Ideas, with their multiplicities and coexistent varieties, their determination of elements, their distribution of mobile singularities and their formation of ideal series around these singularities. The word 'perplication' here designates something other than a conscious state. '*Complication*' is what we called the state of chaos which retains and comprises all the actual intensive series which correspond to these ideal series, incarnating them and affirming their divergence. This chaos thus gathers in itself the being of the problems and distributes it to all the systems and fields which form within it the persistent value of the problematic. '*Implication*' is what we called the state of intensive series in so far as these communicate through their differences and resonate in forming fields of individuation. Each is 'implicated' by the others, which it implicates in turn; they constitute the 'enveloping' and the 'enveloped', the 'solving' and the 'solved' of the system. Finally, '*explication*' is what we called the state of qualities and extensities which cover and develop the system, between the basic series: it is here that the differenciations and integrations which define the totality of the final solution are traced out. The *centres of envelopment* still testify to the persistence of the problems or the persistence of the values of implication in the movement which explicates and solves them [*replication*].

We saw this in the case of the Other in psychic systems. The Other is not reducible to the individuating factors implicated in the system, but it 'represents' or stands for them in a certain sense. In effect, among the developed qualities and extensities of the perceptual world, it envelops and expresses possible worlds which do not exist outside their expression. In this manner, it testifies to the persistent values of implication which confer upon it an essential function in the represented world of perception. For if the Other presupposes the organisation of fields of individuation, it is, on the other hand, the condition under which we *perceive* distinct objects and subjects in these fields, and perceive them as forming diverse kinds of identifiable and recognisable individuals. That the Other should not, properly speaking, be anyone, neither you nor I, signifies that it is a structure which is implemented only by variable terms in different perceptual worlds – me for you in yours, you for me in mine. It is not even enough to see in the Other a specific or particular structure of the perceptual world in general: in fact, it is a structure which grounds and ensures the overall functioning of this world as a whole.

Notions necessary for the description of this world – such as those of form–ground, profile–unity of the object, depth–length, horizon–focus – would remain empty and inapplicable if the Other were not there to give expression to those possible worlds in which that which is (for us) in the background is pre-perceived or sub-perceived as a possible form; that which is in depth as a possible length, etc. The delineation of objects, the transitions as well as the ruptures, the passage from one object to another, and even the fact that one world disappears in favour of another, the fact that there is always something else implicated which remains to be explicated or developed – all this is made possible only by the Other-structure and its expressive power in perception. In short, it is the Other-structure that ensures individuation within the perceptual world. It is not the I, nor the self: on the contrary, these need this structure in order to be perceived as individualities. Everything happens as though *the Other integrated the individuating factors and pre-individual singularities within the limits of objects and subjects*, which are then offered to representation as perceivers or perceived. As a result, in order to rediscover the individuating factors as they are in the intensive series along with the pre-individual singularities as they are in the Idea, this path must be followed in reverse so that, departing from the subjects which give effect to the Other-structure, we return as far as this structure in itself, thus apprehending the Other as No-one, then continue further, following the bend in sufficient reason until we reach those regions where the Other-structure no longer functions, far from the objects and subjects that it conditions, where singularities are free to be deployed or distributed within pure Ideas, and individuating factors to be distributed in pure intensity. In this sense, it is indeed true that the thinker is necessarily solitary and solipsistic.

For where do Ideas come from, with their variations of relations and their distributions of singularities? Here, too, we follow the path to the bend at which 'reason' plunges into the beyond. The ultimate origin was always assimilated to a solitary and divine game. There are several ways to play, however, and collective and human games do not resemble this solitary divine game. Several characteristics allow us to oppose the human and the ideal as two species of game. First, human games presuppose pre-existing categorical rules. Second, these rules serve to determine the probabilities – in other words, the winning and losing 'hypotheses'. Third, these games never affirm the whole of chance: on the contrary, they fragment it and, for each case, subtract or remove the consequences of the throw from chance, since they assign this or that loss or gain as though it were necessarily tied to a given hypothesis. Finally, this is why human games proceed by sedentary distributions: in effect, the prior categorical rule here plays the invariant role of the Same and enjoys a metaphysical or moral necessity; as such, it subsumes opposing hypotheses by establishing a corresponding series of numerically distinct turns or throws which are supposed to effect a distribution among them; the outcomes or results of these throws are distributed according to their consequences following a hypothetical necessity – in other words, according to the hypothesis carried out. This is sedentary distribution, in which the fixed sharing out of a distributed occurs in accordance with a proportion fixed by rules. This false and human manner of playing does not hide its presuppositions, which are moral presuppositions, the hypothesis here being that of Good and Evil, and the game an apprenticeship in morality. Pascal's wager is the model for this bad game, with its manner of fragmenting chance and distributing the morsels in order to separate out the modes of human existence, under the constant rule of the existence of a God who is never put in question. This conception of a game completely inscribed in the grid of necessity, of the hypothetical and hypothetical necessity (categorical or apodictic principle, hypothesis, consequence), reappears from the Platonic lottery to the Leibnizian game of chess in *On the Ultimate Origination of*

Things. This game is indistinguishable from the practice of representation, of which it presents all the elements: the superior identity of the principle, the opposition of hypotheses, the resemblance of numerically distinct throws, and proportion in the relation between the hypothesis and the consequence.

The divine game is quite different – that of which Heraclitus, perhaps, speaks; that which Mallarmé evokes with such religious fear and repentance, and Nietzsche with such decisiveness – for us it is the most difficult game to understand, impossible to deal with in the world of representation.[5] First, there is no pre-existent rule, since the game includes its own rules. As a result, every time, the whole of chance is affirmed in a necessarily winning throw. Nothing is exempt from the game: consequences are not subtracted from chance by connecting them with a hypothetical necessity which would tie them to a determinate fragment; on the contrary, they are adequate to the whole of chance, which retains and subdivides all possible consequences. The different throws can then no longer be said to be numerically distinct: each necessarily winning throw entails the reproduction of the act of throwing under another rule which still draws all its consequences from among the consequences of the preceding throw. Every time, the different throws are distinguished not numerically but *formally*, the different rules being the forms of a single ontologically unique throw, the same across all occasions. The different outcomes are no longer separated according to the distribution of the hypotheses which they carry out, but distribute themselves in the open space of the unique and non-shared throw: nomadic rather than sedentary distribution. A pure Idea of play – in other words, of a game which would be nothing else but play instead of being fragmented, limited and intercut with the work of men. (What is the human game closest to this solitary divine game? As Rimbaud said: look for H, the work of art.) The variations of relations and the distributions of singularities as these occur in the Idea have no origin except these rules which are formally distinct for this ontologically unique throw. This is the point at which the ultimate origin is overturned into an absence of origin (in the always displaced circle of the eternal return). An aleatory point is displaced through all the points on the dice, as though one time for all times. These different throws which invent their own rules and compose the unique throw with multiple forms and within the eternal return are so many imperative questions subtended by a single response which leaves them open and never closes them. They animate ideal problems, determining their relations and singularities. Moreover, by the intermediary of these problems they inspire the outcomes – in other words, the differenciated solutions which incarnate these relations and singularities. The world of the 'will', in which the entire positivity of Ideas is developed between the affirmations of chance (imperative and decisive questions) and the resultant affirmations to which these give rise (decisive resolutions or cases of solution). The game of the problematic and the imperative has replaced that of the hypothetical and the categorical; the game of difference and repetition has replaced that of the Same and representation. The dice are thrown against the sky, with all the force of displacement of the aleatory point, with their imperative points like lightning, forming ideal problem-constellations in the sky. They fall back to Earth with all the force of the victorious solutions which bring back the throw. It is a game on two tables. How could there not be a fracture at the limit or along the hinge between the two tables? And how can we recognise on the first a substantial I identical to itself, on the second a continuous self similar to itself? The identity of the player has disappeared, as has the resemblance of the one who pays the price or profits from the consequences. The fracture or hinge is the form of empty time, the *Aion* through which pass the throws of the dice. On one side, nothing but an I fractured by that empty form. On the other, nothing but a passive self always dissolved in that empty form. A broken Earth corresponds to a fractured sky. 'O sky above me, you pure, lofty sky! This is now your purity to me ... that you are to me a dance floor for divine chances, that you are to me a gods' table for divine dice and dicers!' To which the reply on the other table: 'If ever I have played dice with gods at their table, the earth, so that the earth trembled and broke open and streams of fire snorted forth: for the earth is a table of the gods, and trembling with creative new words and the dice throws of the gods ...'. Both together, however, the fractured sky and the broken earth, do not support the negative but vomit it out through that which fractures or breaks them; they expel all the forms of negation, including precisely those which represent the false game: 'A *throw* you made had failed. But what of that, you dice-throwers! You have not learned to play and mock as a man ought to play and mock!'.[6]

We have continually proposed descriptive notions. These describe actual series, or virtual Ideas, or indeed the groundlessness from which everything comes: intensity–linkage–resonance–forced movement; differential and singularity; complication–implication–explication; differentiation–individuation–differenciation; question–problem–solution, etc. None of this, however, amounts to a list of categories. It is pointless to claim that a list of categories can be open in principle: it can be in fact, but not in principle. For categories belong to the world of representation, where they constitute forms of distribution according to which Being is repartitioned among beings following the rules of sedentary proportionality. That is why philosophy has often been tempted to oppose notions of a quite different kind to categories, notions which are really open and which betray an empirical and pluralist sense of Ideas: 'existential' as against essential, percepts as against concepts, or indeed the list of empirico–ideal notions that we find in Whitehead, which makes *Process and Reality* one of the greatest books of modern philosophy. Such notions, which must be called 'phantastical' in so far as they apply to phantasms and simulacra, are distinguished from the categories of representation in several respects. First, they are conditions of real experience, and not only of possible experience. In this sense, because they are no larger than the conditioned, they reunite the two parts of Aesthetics so unfortunately dissociated: the theory of the forms of experience and that of the work of art as experimentation. This aspect, however, does not yet allow us to determine the difference in kind between these two types of notions. Second, these types preside over completely distinct, irreducible and incompatible distributions: the nomadic distributions carried out by the phantastical notions as opposed to the sedentary distributions of the categories. The former, in effect, are not universals like the categories, nor are they the *hic et nunc* or *now here*, the diversity to which categories apply in representation. They are complexes of space and time, no doubt transportable but on condition that they impose their own scenery, that they set up camp there where they rest momentarily: they are therefore the objects of an essential encounter rather than of recognition. The best word to designate these is undoubtedly that forged by Samuel Butler: *erewhon*.[7] They are *erewhons*. Kant had the liveliest presentiment of such notions participating in a phantasmagoria of the imagination, irreducible both to the universality of the concept and to the particularity of the now here. For while synthesis is exercised upon the diverse here and now, and the synthetic units or categories are continuous universals which condition all possible experience, the schemata are *a priori* determinations of space and time which transport real complexes of place and time to all places and times, but in a discontinuous manner. The Kantian schemata would take flight and point beyond themselves in the direction of a conception of differential Ideas, if they were not unduly subordinated to the categories which reduce them to the status of simple mediations in the world of representation. Further still, beyond the world of representation, we suppose that a whole problem of Being is brought into play by these differences between the categories and the nomadic or phantastical notions, the problem of the manner in which being is distributed among beings: is it, in the last instance, by analogy or univocality?

When we consider repetition as an object of representation, we understand it in terms of identity, but we also then explain it in a negative manner. In effect, the identity of a concept does not qualify a repetition unless, at the same time, a negative force (whether of limitation or of opposition) prevents the concept from being further specified or differenciated in relation to the multiplicity that it subsumes. As we saw, matter unites the following two characteristics: it allows a concept which is absolutely identical in as many exemplars as there are 'times' or 'cases'; and it prevents this concept from being further specified by virtue of its natural poverty, or its natural state of unconsciousness or alienation. Matter, therefore, is the identity of spirit – in other words, of the concept, but in the form of an alienated concept, without self-consciousness and outside itself. An essential feature of representation is that it takes a bare and material repetition as its model, a repetition understood in terms of the Same and explained in terms of the negative. Is this not, however, another antinomy of representation: namely, that it can represent repetition only in this manner, and that it nevertheless cannot represent it in this manner without contradiction? For this bare and material model is, properly speaking, unthinkable. (How can consciousness, which has only a single presence, represent to itself the unconscious?) Identical elements repeat only on condition that there is an independence of 'cases' or a discontinuity of 'times' such that one appears only when the other has disappeared: within representation, repetition is indeed forced to undo itself even as it occurs. Or rather, it does not occur at all. Repetition in itself cannot occur under these conditions. That is why, in order to represent repetition, contemplative souls must be installed here and there; passive selves, sub-representative syntheses and habituses capable of *contracting* the cases or the elements into one another, in order that they can subsequently be reconstituted within a space or time of conservation which belongs to representation itself. The consequences of this are very important: since this contraction is a difference or a modification of the contemplative soul – indeed, *the* modification of this soul, the only modification which truly belongs to it and after which it dies – it appears that the most material repetition occurs only by means of and within a difference which is drawn off by contraction, by means of and within a soul which draws a difference from repetition. Repetition is therefore represented, but on the condition of a soul of a quite different nature: contemplative and contracting, but non-representing and non-represented. Matter is, in effect, populated or covered by such souls, which provide it with a depth without which it would present no bare repetition on the surface. Nor should we believe that the contraction is external to what it contracts, or that this difference is external to the repetition: it is an integral part of it, the constituent part, the depth without which nothing would repeat on the surface.

Everything then changes. If a difference is necessarily (in depth) part of the superficial repetition from which *it* is drawn, the question is: Of what does this difference consist? This difference is a contraction, but in what does this contraction consist? Is it not itself the most contracted degree or the most concentrated level of a past which coexists with itself at all levels of relaxation and in all degrees? This was Bergson's splendid hypothesis: the entire past at every moment but at diverse degrees and levels, of which the present is only the most contracted, the most concentrated. The present difference is then no longer, as it was above, a difference drawn from a superficial repetition of moments in such a way as to sketch a depth without which the latter would not exist. Now, it is this depth itself which develops itself for itself. Repetition is no longer a repetition of successive elements or external parts, but of totalities which coexist on different levels or degrees. Difference is no longer drawn *from* an elementary repetition but is *between* the levels or degrees of a repetition which is total and totalising every time; it is displaced and disguised from one level to another, each level including its own singularities or privileged points. What, then, is to be said of the elementary repetition which proceeds by moments, except that it is itself the most relaxed level of this total repetition? And what is to be said of the difference drawn from the elementary repetition, except that it is, on the contrary, the most contracted degree of this total repetition? Difference itself is therefore between two repetitions: between the superficial repetition of the identical and instantaneous external elements that it contracts, and the profound repetition of the internal totalities of an always variable past, of which it is the most contracted level. This is how difference has two faces, or the synthesis of time has two aspects: one, Habitus, turned towards the first repetition which it renders possible; the other, Mnemosyne, offered up to the second repetition from which it results.

It therefore amounts to the same thing to say that material repetition has a secret and passive subject, which does nothing but in which everything takes place, and that there are two repetitions, of which the material is the most superficial. Perhaps it is incorrect to attribute all the characteristics of the other to Memory, even if by memory is meant the transcendental faculty of a pure past which invents no less than it remembers. Memory is, nevertheless, the first form in which the opposing characteristics of the two repetitions appear. One of these repetitions is of the same, having no difference but that which is subtracted or drawn off; the other is of the Different, and includes difference. One has fixed terms and places; the other essentially includes displacement and disguise. One is negative and by default; the other is positive and by excess. One is of elements, extrinsic parts, cases and times; the other is of variable internal totalities, degrees and levels. One involves succession in fact, the other coexistence in principle. One is static; the other dynamic. One is extensive, the other intensive. One is ordinary; the other distinctive and involving singularities. One is horizontal; the other vertical. One is developed and must be explicated; the other is enveloped and must be interpreted. One is a repetition of equality and symmetry *in the effect*; the other is a repetition of inequality as though it were a repetition of asymmetry *in the cause*. One is repetition of mechanism and precision; the other repetition of selection and freedom. One is bare repetition which can be masked only afterwards and in addition; the other is a clothed repetition of which the masks, the displacements and the disguises are the first, last and only elements.

We must draw two consequences from these opposing characteristics.

First, it is at the same time and from the same point of view that we claim to understand repetition in terms of the Same and explain it in negative fashion. Here, there is a confusion in the philosophy of repetition which corresponds exactly to that which compromised the philosophy of difference. In effect, the concept of difference was defined by the moment or the manner in which it was inscribed within the concept in general. The concept of difference was thereby confused with a simply conceptual difference, and difference was thereby understood *within* identity, since the concept in general was only the manner in which the principle of identity was deployed within representation. Repetition, for its part, could no longer be defined as other than a difference *without* concept. This definition obviously continued to presuppose the identity of the concept for that which was repeated, but instead of inscribing the difference within the concept, it placed it outside the concept in the form of a numerical difference, and placed the concept itself outside itself, as existing in as many exemplars as there were numerically distinct cases or times. It thereby invoked an external force, a form of exteriority capable of putting difference outside the identical concept, and the identical concept outside itself, by blocking its specification, in the same way as an internal force or form of interiority capable of putting difference into the concept and the concept into itself by means of a continued specification was invoked earlier. It was therefore at the same time and from the same point of view that the supposed identity of the concept integrated and internalised difference in the form of conceptual difference, while, on the contrary, projecting repetition as a correlative difference, but without concept and explained negatively or by default. However, if everything is related in this chain of confusions, so must everything be related in the rectification of difference and repetition. Ideas are not concepts; they are a form of eternally positive differential multiplicity, distinguished from the identity of concepts. Instead of representing difference by subordinating it to the identity of concepts, and thereby to the resemblance of perception, the opposition of predicates and the analogy of judgement, they liberate it and cause it to evolve in positive systems in which different is related to different, making divergence, disparity and decentring so many objects of affirmation which rupture the framework of conceptual representation. The powers of repetition include displacement and disguise, just as difference includes power of divergence and decentring. The one no less than the other belongs to Ideas, for Ideas no more have an inside than they do an outside (they are *erewhons*). The Idea makes *one and the same problem* of difference and repetition. There is an excess and an exaggeration peculiar to Ideas which makes difference and repetition the combined object, the 'simultaneous' of the Idea. It is from this excess peculiar to Ideas that concepts unjustly profit, but in so doing betray and distort the nature of Ideas: in effect, concepts repartition this ideal excess into two parts, that of conceptual difference and that of difference without concept; that of the becoming-equal or the becoming-similar to its own proper identity on the part of the concept, and that of the condition by default which continues to presuppose this same identity, but as though blocked. Nevertheless, if we ask what blocks the concept, we see clearly that it is never some lack, default or opposing thing. It is not a nominal limitation of the concept, nor a natural indifference of space and time, nor a spiritual opposition on the part of the unconscious. It is always the excess of the Idea which constitutes the superior positivity that arrests the concept or overturns the requirements of representation. Moreover, it is at the same time and from the same point of view that difference ceases to be reduced to a simply conceptual difference, and repetition establishes its most profound link with difference and finds a positive principle both for itself and for this link. (Beyond memory, the evident paradox of the *death instinct* lay in the fact that, despite its name, it seemed to us from the outset to be endowed with a double role: to include all the force of the different in repetition, and at the same time to provide the most positive and most excessive account of repetition.)

The second consequence is that it is not enough to oppose two repetitions, one bare and material in accordance with the identity and default of the concept, the other clothed, psychical and metaphysical in accordance with the difference and excess of the always positive Idea. This second repetition should be seen as the 'reason' of the first. The clothed and living, vertical repetition which includes difference should be regarded as the cause, of which the bare, material and horizontal repetition (from which a difference is merely drawn off) is only an effect. We saw this repeatedly in the three cases of concepts of freedom, concepts of nature and nominal concepts: every time, the material repetition results from the more profound repetition which unfolds in depth and produces it as an effect, like an external envelope or a detachable shell which loses all meaning and all capacity to reproduce itself once it is no longer animated by the other repetition which is its *cause*. In this manner, the clothed lies underneath the bare, and produces or excretes it as though it were the effect of its own secretion. The secret repetition surrounds itself with a mechanical and bare repetition as though this were the final barrier which indicates here and there the outer limits of the differences that it communicates within a mobile system. It is always *in one and the same movement that repetition includes difference* (not as an accidental and extrinsic variant but at its heart, as the essential variant of which it is composed, the displacement and disguise which constitute it as a difference that is itself divergent and displaced) *and that it must receive a positive principle which gives rise to material and indifferent repetition* (the abandoned snake skin, the envelope emptied of what it implicates, the epidermis which lives and dies only from its own soul or latent content).

This is the case with concepts of nature. Nature would never repeat, its repetitions would always be hypothetical, dependent upon the good will of the experimenter and the savant, if it were reducible to the superficiality of matter, if that matter itself did not involve a depth or side of Nature in which living and mortal repetition unfolds and becomes positive and imperative, on condition that it displaces and disguises an ever-present difference which makes repetition an evolution as such. One savant does not make a spring, nor a series of savants the return of the seasons. The Same would never leave itself to be distributed across several 'equivalents' in cyclical alternation if difference were not displacing itself in these cycles and disguising itself in this same, rendering repetition imperative but offering only the bare to the eyes of the external observer who believes that the variants are not the essential and have little effect upon that which they nevertheless constitute from within.

This is even more true of concepts of freedom and nominal concepts. The words and actions of men give rise to bare, material repetitions, but as effects of more profound repetitions of a different kind ('effects' in a causal, optical and vestiary sense). Repetition is pathos and the philosophy of repetition is pathology. However, there are so many pathologies, so many repetitions entwined in one another. When an obsessive repeats a ceremony once, twice; or when he repeats an enumeration, 1, 2, 3, ... he carries out a repetition of elements in extension which both translate and ward off another, vertical and intensive repetition, that of a past which is displaced each time or with each number, and is disguised in the overall set of numbers and times. It is the equivalent of a cosmological proof in pathology: the horizontal linkage of causes and effects in the world requires a totalising, extra-worldly first Cause as the vertical cause of the causes and effects. We repeat twice simultaneously, but not the same repetition: once mechanically and materially in breadth, and once symbolically and by means of simulacra in depth; first we repeat the parts, then we repeat the whole on which the parts depend. These two repetitions do not take place in the same dimension, they coexist: one is a repetition of instants, the other of the past; one is a repetition of elements, the other is totalising; and the most profound and 'productive' is obviously not the most visible or the one which produces the most 'effect'. In general, the two repetitions enter into so many different relations that it would require an extremely systematic clinical study, of a kind yet to be undertaken, in order to distinguish the cases which correspond to their possible combinations. Consider the gestural or linguistic repetitions and iterations or stereotypical behaviours associated with dementia and schizophrenia. These no longer seem to manifest a will capable of investing an object within the context of a ceremony; rather, they function like reflexes which indicate a general breakdown of investment (whence the impossibility for patients to repeat at will in the tests to which they are subjected). It is nevertheless the case that 'involuntary' repetition depends not upon aphasic or amnesiac difficulties, as a negative explanation would suggest, but on subcortical lesions and 'thymic' disorders. Is this another way of explaining repetition negatively, as though the patient reverted through degeneration to primitive, non-integrated circuits? In fact, in cases of iterations and even of stereotypes, we should note the constant presence of *contractions*, which show up at least in parasitic vowels or consonants. Contraction continues to have two aspects: one by which it bears upon a physical element of repetition which it modifies, the other by which it concerns a psychic totality which is repeatable in different degrees. In this sense, we can recognise a persistent intentionality in every stereotype, even in a schizophrenic grinding of the jaws. This intentionality amounts to investing the entire psychic life in a fragment, gesture or word, in the absence of any other object of investment, these in turn becoming the elements of the other repetition: for example, the patient who turns ever more rapidly on one foot, the other leg extended in such a way as to repel any person approaching from behind, thereby miming his horror of women and his fear of being surprised by them.[8] The properly pathological aspect lies in the fact that, on the one hand, the contraction no longer ensures a resonance between two or more levels, simultaneously 'playable' in differenciated manners, but rather crushes them all and compresses them into the stereotypical fragment. On the other hand, contraction no longer draws from the element a difference or modification which would permit repetition within a space and time organised by the will. On the contrary, it makes the modification itself the element to be repeated, taking itself as object in an acceleration which precisely renders impossible any bare repetition of elements. Thus, in these cases of iteration and stereotype we see not an independence of purely mechanical repetition, but rather a specific difficulty in the relation between the two repetitions, and in the process by which one is and remains the cause of the other.

Repetition is the power of language, and far from being explicable in negative fashion by some default on the part of nominal concepts, it implies an always excessive Idea of poetry. The coexistent levels of a psychic totality may be considered to be actualised in differenciated series, according to the singularities which characterise them. These series are liable to resonate under the influence of a fragment or 'dark precursor' which stands for this totality in which all the levels coexist: each series is therefore repeated in the other, at the same time as the precursor is displaced from one level to another and disguised in all the series. It therefore does not belong to any level or degree. In the case of verbal series, we call a word which designates the *sense* of a preceding word a 'word of higher degree'. However, the linguistic precursor, the esoteric or poetic word *par excellence* (object = x) transcends all degrees to the extent that it purports to say both itself and its sense, while appearing as always displaced and disguised nonsense (the secret word which has no sense: Snark or Blituri ...). All the verbal series themselves therefore form so many 'synonyms' in relation to this word, while it plays the role of a 'homonym' for all the series. It is therefore by virtue of its entirely positive and ideal power that language organises its entire system in the form of a clothed repetition. Of course, it goes without saying that real poems are not supposed to be adequate to this Idea of poetry. In order for a real poem to emerge, we must 'identify' the dark precursor and confer upon it at least a nominal identity – in short, we must provide the resonance with a body; then, as in a song, the differenciated series are organised into couplets or verses, while the precursor is incarnated in an antiphon or chorus. The couplets turn around the chorus. What combines nominal concepts and concepts of freedom better than a song? A bare repetition is produced under these conditions: at once in the return of the chorus which represents the object = *x*, and in certain aspects of the differenciated couplets which represent in turn the interpenetration of the series (measure, rhyme, or even verses rhyming with the chorus). In some cases almost bare repetitions take the place of synonymy and homonymy, as they do with Péguy and Raymond Roussel. Here, the genius of poetry identifies itself with these brute repetitions. Nevertheless, this genius belongs in the first place to the Idea, and to the manner in which it produces brute repetitions on the basis of a more secret repetition.

The distinction between the two repetitions, however, is still not enough. The second repetition still participates in all the ambiguities of memory and ground. It includes difference, but includes it only *between* the degrees or levels. As we saw, it appears first in the form of the circles of the past coexistent in themselves; then in the form of a circle of coexistence of the past and the present; and finally in the form of a circle of all the presents which pass and which coexist in relation to the object = *x*. In short, metaphysics makes a circle of the physical or *physis*. How, then, are we to avoid this profound repetition being hidden by the bare repetitions that it inspires, and succumbing to the illusion of a primacy of brute repetition? In the same movement, the ground falls back into the representation of what it grounds, while the circles begin to turn in the manner of the Same. For this reason, it always seemed to us that the circles were unravelled in a third synthesis, where the ground was abolished in a groundlessness, the Ideas were separated from the forms of memory, and the displacement and disguise of repetition engaged divergence and decentring, the powers of difference. Beyond the cycles, the at first straight line of the empty form of time; beyond memory, the death instinct; beyond resonance, forced movement. Beyond bare repetition and clothed repetition, beyond that from which difference is drawn and that which includes it, a repetition which 'makes' the difference. Beyond the grounded and grounding repetitions, a repetition of *ungrounding* on which depend both that which enchains and that which liberates, that which dies and that which lives within repetition. Beyond physical repetition and psychic or metaphysical repetition, an *ontological* repetition? The role of the latter would not be to suppress the other two but, on the one hand, to distribute difference to them (in the form of difference drawn off or included); and, on the other hand, to produce the illusion by which they are affected while nevertheless preventing them from developing the related error into which they fall. In a certain sense, the ultimate repetition, the ultimate theatre, therefore encompasses everything; while in another sense it destroys everything; and in yet another sense selects among everything.

Perhaps the highest object of art is to bring into play simultaneously all these repetitions, with their differences in kind and rhythm, their respective displacements and disguises, their divergences and decentrings; to embed them in one another and to envelop one or the other in illusions the 'effect' of which varies in each case. Art does not imitate, above all because it repeats; it repeats all the repetitions, by virtue of an internal power (an imitation is a copy, but art is simulation, it reverses copies into simulacra). Even the most mechanical, the most banal, the most habitual and the most stereotyped repetition finds a place in works of art, it is always displaced in relation to other repetitions, and it is subject to the condition that a difference may be extracted from it for these other repetitions. For there is no other aesthetic problem than that of the insertion of art into everyday life. The more our daily life appears standardised, stereotyped and subject to an accelerated reproduction of objects of consumption, the more art must be injected into it in order to extract from it that little difference which plays simultaneously between other levels of repetition, and even in order to make the two extremes resonate – namely, the habitual series of consumption and the instinctual series of destruction and death. Art thereby connects the tableau of cruelty with that of stupidity, and discovers underneath consumption a schizophrenic clattering of the jaws, and underneath the most ignoble destructions of war, still more processes of consumption. It aesthetically reproduces the illusions and mystifications which make up the real essence of this civilisation, in order that Difference may at last be expressed with a force of anger which is itself repetitive and capable of introducing the strangest selection, even if this is only a contraction here and there – in other words, a freedom for the end of a world. Each art has its interrelated techniques or repetitions, the critical and revolutionary power of which may attain the highest degree and lead us from the sad repetitions of habit to the profound repetitions of memory, and then to the ultimate repetitions of death in which our freedom is played out. We simply wish to offer three examples, however diverse and disparate these may be: first, the manner in which all the repetitions coexist in modern music (such as the development of the *leitmotiv* in Berg's *Wozzeck*); second, the manner in which, within painting, Pop Art pushed the copy, copy of the copy, etc., to that extreme point at which it reverses and becomes a simulacrum (such as Warhol's remarkable 'serial' series, in which all the repetitions of habit, memory and death are conjugated); and finally the novelistic manner in which little modifications are torn from the brute and mechanical repetitions of habit, which in turn nourish repetitions of memory and ultimately lead to repetitions in which life and death are in play, and risk reacting upon the whole and introducing into it a new selection, all these repetitions coexisting and yet being displaced in relation to one another (Butor's *La modification*; or indeed *Last Year at Marienbad*, which shows the particular techniques of repetition which cinema can deploy or invent).

Are not all the repetitions ordered in the pure form of time? In effect, this pure form or straight line is defined by an order which distributes a *before*, a *during* and an *after*; by a totality which incorporates all three in the simultaneity of its *a priori* synthesis; and by a series which makes a type of repetition correspond to each. From this point of view, we must essentially distinguish between the pure form and the empirical contents. The empirical contents are mobile and succeed one another, while the *a priori* determinations of time, on the contrary, are fixed or held, as though in a photo or a freeze-frame, coexisting within the static synthesis which distinguishes a redoubtable action in relation to the image. This action may be anything from an empirical point of view, or at least its occasion may be found in any empirical circumstances (action = x); all that is required is that the circumstances allow its 'isolation' and that it is sufficiently embedded in the moment such that its image extends over time as a whole and becomes, as it were, the *a priori* symbol of the form. On the other hand, with regard to the empirical contents of time, we distinguish the *first, second, third* ... in their indefinite succession: it may be that this succession can be defined as a cycle, and that repetition is therefore impossible, either in an intracyclic form in which 2, repeats 1, 3 repeats 2 and so on; or in an intercyclic form in which 1' repeats 1, 2' repeats 2, 3' repeats 3. (Even if an indefinite succession of cycles is supposed, the first time will be defined as the Same or the undifferenciated, either at the origin of all cycles or in between two cycles.) In any case, the repetition remains external to something which is repeated and must be supposed primary; a frontier is established between a first time and repetition itself. The question whether the first time escapes repetition (in which case it is referred to as 'once and for all'), or, on the contrary, is repeated within a cycle or from one cycle to another, depends entirely upon the reflection of an observer. The first time being regarded as the Same, the question is asked whether the second displays sufficient resemblance with the first to be identified as the Same again: a question which can be answered only by the establishment of relations of analogy within judgement, taking into account the variations in empirical circumstances (is Luther the analogue of Paul, the French Revolution the analogue of the Roman republic?). Things are very different, however, from the point of view of the pure form or straight line of time. Now, each determination (the first, second and third; the before, during and after) is already repetition in itself, in the pure form of time and in relation to the image of the action. The before or the first time is no less repetition than the second or the third time. Each time being in itself repetition, the problem is no longer susceptible to the analogies of reflection on the part of a supposed observer; rather, it must be lived as a problem of the internal conditions of the action in relation to the redoubtable image. Repetition no longer bears (hypothetically) upon a first time which escapes it, and in any case remains external to it: repetition bears upon repetitions, upon modes and types of repetition, in an imperative manner. The frontier or 'difference' is therefore singularly displaced: it is no longer between the first time and the others, between the repeated and the repetition, but between these types of repetition. It is repetition itself that is repeated. Furthermore, 'once and for all' no longer qualifies a first time which would escape repetition, but on the contrary a type of repetition which opposes another type operating an infinity of times (in this manner Christian repetition is opposed to atheist repetition, and Kierkegaardian to Nietzschean, for in the case of Kierkegaard it is repetition itself which takes place once and for all, whereas according to Nietzsche it operates for all times. Nor is this simply a numerical difference; it is, rather, a fundamental difference between these two kinds of repetition).

How are we to explain the fact that once repetition bears upon repetitions, once it assembles them all and introduces difference between them, it thereby acquires a formidable power of selection? Everything depends on the distribution of repetitions in the form, the order, the totality and the series of time. This distribution is extremely complex. At a first level, the repetition of the Before is defined by default or in a negative manner: *one* repeats because one does not know, because one does not remember, etc: or because one is not capable of performing the action (whether this action remains to be performed or is already performed). 'One' therefore signifies here the unconscious of the Id as the first power of repetition. The repetition of the During is defined by a becoming-similar or a becoming-equal: *one* becomes capable of performing the action, one becomes equal to the image of the action, the 'one' now signifying the unconscious of the Ego, its metamorphosis, its projection in an I or ego ideal in the form of the second power of repetition. However, since to become similar or equal is always to become similar or equal to something that is supposed to be identical in itself, or supposed to enjoy the privilege of an originary identity, it appears that the image of the action to which one becomes similar or equal stands here only for the identity of the concept in general, or that of the I. At this level, the first two repetitions gather together and distribute amongst themselves the characteristics of the negative and the identical, which, as we have seen, constitute the limits of representation. At another level, the hero repeats the first, that of the Before, as though in a dream and in a bare, mechanical and stereotypical manner which constitutes the comic; yet this repetition would be nothing if it did not refer to something hidden or disguised in its own series, capable of introducing contractions therein as though it were a hesitant Habitus in which the other repetition ripened. This second repetition of the During is one in which the hero himself embraces disguise and assumes the metamorphosis which re-places him on a tragic plane, with his own identity, the inner depths of his memory and that of the whole world, in order that, having become capable of action, he purports to be equal to the whole of time. At this second level, the two repetitions rework and redistribute in their own way the two syntheses of time, and the two forms, bare and clothed, which characterize them.

Certainly, we could imagine that the two repetitions enter into a cycle of which they form two analogous parts; and also that they begin again at the end of a cycle, embarking upon a new path itself analogous to the first; and finally, that these two intracyclic and extracyclic hypotheses are not mutually exclusive but reinforce one another and repeat the repetitions on different levels. *In all this, however, everything depends upon the nature of the third time*: analogy requires that a third time be given, just as the circle of the *Phaedo* requires that its two arcs be completed by a third on which everything is decided with regard to their own return. For example, we distinguished between the Old Testament with its repetition by default and the New Testament with its repetition by metamorphosis (Joachim of Flora); or indeed, in another manner, we distinguished between the age of the gods, by default in the human unconscious, and the age of heroes by metamorphosis in the human Self (Vico). The answer to the double question – (1) Do the two times repeat one another in an analogical manner within the same cycle? (2) Are these two times themselves repeated in a new analogous cycle? – depends solely and above all upon the nature of the third time (Flora's 'Testament' to come, Vico's 'The Age of Men', Ballanche's 'Man without Name'). For if this third time, the future, is the proper place of decision, it is entirely likely that, by virtue of its nature, it eliminates the two intracyclic and extracyclic hypotheses; that it *undoes* them both and puts time into a straight line, straightening it out and extracting the pure form; in other words, it takes time out of 'joint' and, being itself the third repetition, renders the repetition of the other two impossible. Far from ensuring the occurrence of the cycle and analogy, the third time excludes them. In accordance with the new frontier, the difference between the two repetitions becomes the following: the Before and the During are and remain repetitions, but operate only once and for all. The third repetition distributes them in accordance with the straight line of time, but also eliminates them, determining them to operate only once and for all, keeping the 'all times' for the third time alone. In this sense, Joachim of Flora saw the essential: there are two significations for a single signifier. The essential is the third Testament. There are two repetitions for a single repeated, but only the signified or the repeated repeats itself, abolishing its significations along with its conditions. The frontier is no longer between a first time and a repetition that it renders hypothetically possible, but between the conditional repetitions and the third repetition or *repetition within the eternal return* which renders impossible the return of the other two. Only the third Testament turns on itself. There is eternal return only in the third time: it is here that the freeze-frame begins to move once more, or that the straight line of time, as though drawn by its own length, re-forms a strange loop which in no way resembles the earlier cycle, but leads into the formless, and operates only for the third time and for that which belongs to it. As we have seen, the condition of the action by default does not return; the condition of the agent by metamorphosis does not return; all that returns, the eternal return, is the *unconditioned* in the product. The expulsive and selective force of the eternal return, its centrifugal force, consists of distributing repetition among the three times of the pseudo-cycle, but also of ensuring that the first two repetitions do not return, that they occur only once and for all, and that only the third repetition which turns upon itself returns for all times, for eternity. The negative, the similar and the analogous are repetitions, but they do not return, forever driven away by the wheel of eternal return.

We know that Nietzsche gave no exposition of the eternal return, for reasons which pertain both to the simplest 'objective criticism' of the texts and to their most modest dramatic or poetic comprehension. In *Thus Spoke Zarathustra*, the question of the eternal return arises twice, but each time it appears as a truth not yet reached and not expressed: once when the dwarf speaks (III, 'Of the Vision and the Riddle'); and a second time when the animals speak (III, 'The Convalescent'). The first time is enough to make Zarathustra ill, producing his terrible nightmare and leading him to undertake a sea voyage. The second time, after a further crisis, the convalescent Zarathustra smiles indulgently at his animals, knowing that his destiny will be decided only in an unsaid third time (that announced at the end: 'The sign has come'). We cannot make use of the posthumous notes, except in directions confirmed by Nietzsche's published works, since these notes are reserved material, as it were, put aside for future elaboration. We know only that *Thus Spoke Zarathustra* is unfinished, and that it was supposed to have a further section concerning the death of Zarathustra: as though a third time and a third occasion. Nevertheless, the existing dramatic progression of *Thus Spoke Zarathustra* allows a series of questions and answers.

1. Why, on the first occasion, does Zarathustra become angry and suffer such a terrible nightmare when the dwarf says: 'All truth is crooked, time itself is a circle'? As he explains later in interpreting his nightmare: he fears that eternal return means the return of Everything, of the Same and the Similar, including the dwarf and including the smallest of men (see III, 'The Convalescent'). He particularly fears that repetition will only be negative and will occur only by default: that one repeats only because one is deaf, lame and a dwarf, perched on the shoulders of others; or because one is incapable of an act (the death of God), even though the act has already occurred. He knows that a circular repetition would necessarily be of this type. That is why Zarathustra denies that time is a circle, and replies to the dwarf: 'Spirit of Gravity, do not simplify matters too much!'. By contrast, he holds that time is a straight line in two opposing directions. If a strangely decentred circle should form, this will be only 'at the end' of the straight line ...
2. Why does Zarathustra undergo a further crisis and become convalescent? Zarathustra is like Hamlet; the sea voyage has made him *capable*, he has reached the becoming-similar or the becoming-equal of the heroic metamorphosis; yet he feels that the hour has not yet come (see III, 'Of Involuntary Bliss'). He has already banished the shadow of the negative: he knows that repetition is not that of the dwarf. Nevertheless, the becoming-equal or becoming-capable of the metamorphosis has only brought him to a supposed originary identity: he has not yet banished the apparent positivity of the identical. That requires the new crisis and convalescence. The animals can then say that it is the Same and the Similar that return; they can expound the eternal return in the form of a positive natural certitude: Zarathustra, feigning sleep, no longer listens to them, for he knows that the eternal return is something different again, and that it does not cause the same and the similar to return.
3. Why does Zarathustra still say nothing; why is he not yet 'ripe', and why will he become so only in a third unsaid time? The revelation that not everything returns, nor does the Same, implies as much distress as the belief in the return of the Same and of everything, even though it is a different distress. The highest test is to understand the eternal return as a selective thought, and repetition in the eternal return as selective being. Time must be understood and lived as out of joint, and seen as a straight line which mercilessly eliminates those who embark upon it, who come upon the scene but repeat only once and for all. The selection occurs between two repetitions: those who repeat negatively and those who repeat identically will be eliminated. They repeat only once. The eternal return is only for the third time: the time of the drama, after the comic and

after the tragic (the drama is defined when the tragic becomes joyful and the comic becomes the comedy of the Overman). The eternal return is only for the third repetition, only in the third repetition. The circle is at the end of the line. Neither the dwarf nor the hero, neither Zarathustra ill nor Zarathustra convalescent, will return. Not only does the eternal return not make everything return, it causes those who fail the test to perish. (Nietzsche carefully indicates the two distinct types who do not survive the test: the passive small man or last man, and the great heroic active man, the one who has become a man 'who wants to perish').[9] The Negative does not return. The Identical does not return. The Same and the Similar, the Analogous and the Opposed, do not return. Only affirmation returns – in other words, the Different, the Dissimilar. Nothing which denies the eternal return returns, neither the default nor the equal, only the excessive returns: how much distress before one extracts joy from such a selective affirmation? Only the third repetition returns. At the cost of the resemblance and identity of Zarathustra himself: Zarathustra must lose these, the resemblance of the Self and the identity of the I must perish, and Zarathustra must die. Zarathustra-hero became equal, but what he became equal to was the unequal, at the cost of losing the sham identity of the hero. For 'one' repeats eternally, but 'one' now refers to the world of impersonal individualities and pre-individual singularities. The eternal return is not the effect of the Identical upon a world become similar, it is not an external order imposed upon the chaos of the world; on the contrary, the eternal return is the internal identity of the world and of chaos, the Chaosmos. How could the reader believe that Nietzsche, who was the greatest critic of these categories, implicated Everything, the Same, the Identical, the Similar, the Equal, the I and the Self in the eternal return? How could it be believed that he understood the eternal return as a cycle, when he opposed 'his' hypothesis to every cyclical hypothesis?[10] How could it be believed that he lapsed into the false and insipid idea of an *opposition* between a circular time and a linear time, an ancient and a modern time?

What, however, is the content of this third time, this formlessness at the end of the form of time, this decentred circle which displaces itself at the end of the straight line? What is this content which is affected or 'modified' by the eternal return? We have tried to show that it is a question of simulacra, and simulacra alone. The power of simulacra is such that they essentially implicate at once the object = x in the unconscious, the word = x in language, and the action = x in history. Simulacra are those systems in which different relates to different *by means of* difference itself. What is essential is that we find in these systems no *prior identity*, no *internal resemblance*. It is all a matter of difference in the series, and of differences of difference in the communication between series. What is displaced and disguised in the series cannot and must not be identified, but exists and acts as the differenciator of difference. Moreover, repetition necessarily flows from this play of difference in two ways. On the one hand, because each series is explicated and unfolded only in implicating the others, it therefore repeats the others and is repeated in the others, which in turn implicate it. However, it is *implicated* by the others only in so far as it simultaneously *implicates* those others, with the result that it returns to itself as many times as it returns to another. Returning to itself is the ground of the bare repetitions, just as returning to another is the ground of the clothed repetitions. On the other hand, the play which presides over the distribution of simulacra ensures the repetition of each numerically distinct combination, since the different 'throws' are not, for their own part, numerically but only 'formally' distinct. As a result, all the outcomes are included in the number of each according to the relations between implicated and implicator just referred to, each returning in the others in accordance with the formal distinction of throws, but also always returning to itself in accordance with the unity of the play of difference. Repetition in the eternal return appears under all these aspects as the peculiar power of difference, and the displacement and disguise of that which repeats only reproduce the divergence and the decentring of the different in a single movement of *diaphora* or transport. The eternal return affirms difference, it affirms dissemblance and disparateness, chance, multiplicity and becoming. Zarathustra is the dark precursor of eternal return. The eternal return eliminates precisely all those instances which strangle difference and prevent its transport by subjecting it to the quadruple yoke of representation. Difference is recovered, liberated, only at the limit of its power – in other words, by repetition in the eternal return. The eternal return eliminates that which renders it impossible by rendering impossible the transport of difference. It eliminates the presuppositions of representation, namely the Same and the Similar, the Analogue and the Negative. For representation and its presuppositions return, but only once; they return no more than one time, once and for all, thereafter eliminated for all times.

Nevertheless, we speak of the unity of the play of difference; we speak of the 'the same series' when it returns to itself, and of 'similar series' when one returns to another. However, very small linguistic shifts express upheavals and reversals in the concept. We saw that the two formulae 'similars differ' and 'differents resemble one another', belong to entirely foreign worlds. It is the same here: *the eternal return is indeed the Similar, repetition in the eternal return is indeed the Identical – but precisely the resemblance and the identity do not pre-exist the return of that which returns.* They do not in the first instance qualify what returns, they are indistinguishable from its return. *It is not the same which returns, it is not the similar which returns*; rather, the Same is the returning of that which returns, – *in other words, of the Different*; the similar is the returning of that which returns, – *in other words, of the Dissimilar*. The repetition in the eternal return is the same, but the same in so far as it is said uniquely of difference and the different. This is a complete reversal of the world of representation, and of the sense that 'identical' and 'similar' had in that world. This reversal is not merely speculative but eminently practical, since it defines the conditions of legitimate use of the words 'identical' and 'similar' by linking them exclusively to simulacra, while denouncing the ordinary usage made from the point of view of representation. For this reason, the philosophy of Difference seems to us badly established as long as it is content with the terminological opposition between the platitude of the Identical as equal to itself and the profundity of the Same which is supposed to incorporate the different.[11] For while the Same which includes difference and the identical which excludes it may be opposed in many ways, they remain no less principles of representation. At most, they inspire the dispute between infinite representation and finite representation. The true distinction is not between the identical *and* the same, but between the identical, the same or the similar – it matters little which, once these are posited as primary on various grounds – and the identical, the same or the similar understood as secondary powers, but all the more powerful as such, turning around difference, being said of difference itself. At this point, everything effectively changes. The Same, for ever decentred, effectively turns around difference only once difference, having assumed the whole of Being, applies only to simulacra which have assumed the whole of 'being'.

The history of the long error is the history of representation, the history of the icons. For the Same, or the Identical, has an ontological sense: the repetition in the eternal return of that which differs (the repetition of each implicating series). The Similar has an ontological sense: the eternal return of that which makes dissimilar (the repetition of implicated series). However, the eternal return itself, in turning, gives rise to a certain illusion in which it delights and admires itself, and which it employs in order to double its affirmation of that which differs: it produces an image of identity as though this were the *end* of the different. It produces an image of resemblance as the external *effect* of 'the disparate'. It produces an image of the negative as the *consequence* of what it affirms, the consequence of its own affirmation. It surrounds the simulacra and surrounds itself with this identity, this resemblance and this negative. However, these are precisely a simulated identity, resemblance and negative. It plays upon these as though upon a never attained end, an always distorted effect and an always perverted consequence: they are the products of the functioning of simulacra. It employs them each time in order to decentre the identical, distort the similar and pervert the consequence. For it is true that there are only perverted consequences, only distorted similarities, only decentred identities and only unattained ends. Revelling in what it produces, the eternal return denounces every other use of ends, identities, resemblances and negations: even – and especially – negation, which it employs in the service of simulacra in the most radical manner – namely, to deny everything which denies multiple and different affirmation, in order to double what it affirms. It is essential to the function of simulacra to simulate the identical, the similar and the negative.

There is a necessary linkage between the ontological sense and the simulated sense. The second derives [*dérive*] from the first – in other words, it remains adrift [*à la dérive*] without autonomy or spontaneity, a simple effect of the ontological cause which plays upon it like a tempest. How could representation not profit from this? How could representation not be born once, in the trough of a wave, to the advantage of the illusion? How could it not make of the illusion an 'error'? By this means, the identity of the simulacra, simulated identity, finds itself projected or retrojected on to the internal difference. The simulated external resemblance finds itself interiorised in the system. The negative becomes principal and agent. Each product of the functioning assumes an autonomy. It is then supposed that difference is valid, exists and is thinkable only within a pre-existing Same which understands it as conceptual difference and determines it by means of opposition between predicates. It is supposed that repetition is valid, exists and is thinkable only under an Identical which in turn posits it as a difference without concept and explains it negatively. Instead of understanding bare repetition as the product of clothed repetition, and the latter as the power of difference, difference itself is made into a by-product of the same in the concept, clothed repetition into a derivative of bare repetition, and bare repetition a by-product of the identical outside the concept. It is in the same milieu, that of representation, that difference is posited on the one hand as conceptual difference, and repetition on the other hand as difference without a concept. Moreover, since there is no longer any conceptual difference between the ultimate determinable concepts among which the same is distributed, the world of representation finds itself in the grip of a network of analogies which makes difference and repetition simple concepts of reflection. The Same and the Identical may be interpreted in many ways: in the sense of a perseveration (A is A), in the sense of an equality (A = A) or a resemblance (A # B), in the sense of an opposition (A = non-A), or in the sense of an analogy (as is suggested by the excluded third term, which determines the conditions under which the third term is determinable only in a relation identical to the relation between two others: A = non-A(B) = C/non-C(D). But all these ways belong to representation, to which analogy brings a final touch, a specific closure or the last element. They are the development of the *erroneous sense* which betrays both the nature of difference and that of repetition. The long error begins here – all the longer since it occurs only once.

We have seen how analogy essentially belonged to the world of representation. Once the limits of the inscription of difference in the concept in general are fixed, the upper limit is represented by the ultimate determinable concepts (the genera of being or categories), while the lower limit is represented by the smallest determined concepts (species). In the case of finite representation, generic and specific difference have different procedures and differ in kind, but they are strictly complementary: the equivocity of the one has its correlate in the univocity of the other. In effect, the genus *in relation to its species* is univocal, while Being *in relation to the genera or categories themselves* is equivocal. The analogy of being implies both these two aspects at once: one by which being is distributed in determinable forms which necessarily distinguish and vary the sense; the other by which being so distributed is necessarily repartitioned among well-determined beings, each endowed with a unique sense. What is missed at the two extremities is the collective sense of being [*étre*] and the play of individuating difference in being [*étant*]. Everything takes place between generic difference and specific difference. The genuine universal is missed no less than the true singular: the only common sense of being is distributive, and the only individual difference is general. The list of categories may well be 'opened up' or representation may be made infinite; nevertheless, being continues to be said in several senses according to the categories, and that of which it is said is determined only by differences 'in general'. The world of representation presupposes a certain type of sedentary distribution, which divides or shares out that which is distributed in order to give 'each' their fixed share (as in the bad game or the bad way to play, the pre-existing rules define distributive hypotheses according to which the results of the throws are repartitioned). Representation essentially implies an analogy of being. However, the only realised Ontology – in other words, the univocity of being – is repetition. From Duns Scotus to Spinoza, the univocal position has always rested upon two fundamental theses. According to one, there are indeed forms of being, but contrary to what is suggested by the categories, these forms involve no division within being or plurality of ontological senses. According to the other, that of which being is said is repartitioned according to essentially mobile individuating differences which necessarily endow 'each one' with a plurality of modal significations. This programme is expounded and demonstrated with genius from the beginning of the *Ethics*: we are told that the *attributes* are irreducible to genera or categories because while they are *formally* distinct they all remain equal and *ontologically* one, and introduce no division into the substance which is said or expressed through them in a single and same sense (in other words, the real distinction between attributes is a formal, not a numerical distinction). We are told, on the other hand, that the *modes* are irreducible to species because they are repartitioned within attributes according to individuating differences which are degrees of power operating in intensity, and immediately relate them to univocal being (in other words, the numerical distinction between 'beings' is a modal, not a real distinction). Is it not the same with the true throw of the dice? The throws are formally distinct, but with regard to an ontologically unique throw, while the outcomes implicate, displace and recover their combinations in one another throughout the unique and open space of the univocal? All that Spinozism needed to do for the univocal to become an object of pure affirmation was to make substance turn around the modes – *in other words, to realise univocity in the form of repetition in the eternal return.* For while it is true that analogy has two aspects – one according to which being is said in several senses, and the other according to which it is said of something fixed and well determined – univocity, for its part, has two completely opposing aspects according to which being is said 'in all manners' in a single same sense, but is said thereby of that which differs, is said of a difference which is itself always mobile and displaced within being. The univocity of being and individuating difference are connected outside representation as profoundly as generic difference and specific difference are connected within representation from the point of view of analogy. Univocity signifies that being itself is univocal, while that of which it is said is equivocal: precisely the opposite of analogy. Being is said according to forms which do not break the unity of its sense; it is said in a single same sense throughout all its forms – that is why we opposed to categories notions of a different kind. That of which it is said, however, differs; it is said of difference itself. It is not analogous being which is distributed among the categories and allocates a fixed part to beings, but the beings which are distributed across the space of univocal being, opened by all the forms. Opening is an essential feature of univocity. The nomadic distributions or crowned anarchies in the univocal stand opposed to the sedentary distributions of analogy. Only there does the cry resound: 'Everything is equal!' and 'Everything returns!'. However, this 'Everything is equal' and this 'Everything returns' can be said only at the point at which the extremity of difference is reached. A single and same voice for the whole thousand-voiced multiple, a single and same Ocean for all the drops, a single clamour of Being for all beings: on condition that each being, each drop and each voice has reached the state of excess – in other words, the difference which displaces and disguises them and, in turning upon its mobile cusp, causes them to return.

Notes

Translator's Preface

1 Deleuze and Guattari, *A Thousand Plateaus*, transl. Brian Massumi, London: Athlone, 1988, p. 22.

Preface

1 *Nietzsche, 'On the uses and disadvantages of history for life', in *Untimely Meditations*, transl. R.J. Hollingdale, Cambridge: Cambridge University Press, 1983, p. 60.
2 *Jorge Luis Borges, *Ficciones*, New York: Grove Press, 1962, p. 52.

Introduction

1 Charles Péguy, *Clio*, Paris: NRF, 1917, 33rd edn, pp. 45, 114.
2 Pius Servien, *Principes d'Esthétique*, Paris: Boivin, 1935, pp. 3–5; *Science et Poésie*, Paris: Flammarion, 1947, pp. 44–7.
3 *Georg Büchner, *Danton's Death*, transl. Howard Brenton, London: Methuen, 1982, p. 25. Translation modified in the light of the French version.
4 In the preceding comparison, we are referring to some of the best-known texts of Nietzsche and Kierkegaard. In the case of Kierkegaard, these include *Fear and Trembling* and *Repetition*, ed. and transl. H.V. and E.H. Hong, published as two volumes in one by Princeton University Press, 1983; the very important note in *The Concept of Anxiety*, transl. R. Thomte, ed. H.V. and E.H. Hong, Princeton, NJ: Princeton University Press, 1980; passages from the *Journals and Papers*, ed. H.V. and E.H. Hong, Bloomington: Indiana University Press, 1967–78. On the critique of memory, see *Philosophical Fragments*; or *A Fragment of Philosophy*, revised transl. H.V. Hong, Princeton, NJ: Princeton University Press, 1962; and *Stages on Life's Way: Studies by Various Persons*, ed. and transl. H.V. and E.H. Hong, Princeton, NJ: Princeton University Press, 1988.

In the case of Nietzsche, see *Thus Spoke Zarathustra* (especially Part II, 'Of Redemption'; and the two main passages in Part III, 'Of the Vision and the Riddle' and 'The Convalescent', one concerning Zarathustra ill, talking to his demon; the other Zarathustra convalescent, conversing with his animals), transl. R.J. Hollingdale, Harmondsworth: Penguin, 1961; but also the Notes of 1881–2 (in which Nietzsche explicitly opposes 'his' hypothesis to the cyclical hypothesis and criticises all notions of resemblance, equilibrium and identity. cf. *La Volonté de Puissance*, transl. Bianquis, Paris: NRF, pp. 295–301). Finally, for Péguy, see essentially *Clio* and *Le mystère de la charité de Jeanne d'Arc*, Paris: Gallimard, 1955 (transl. Julien Green as *The Mystery of the Charity of Joan of Arc*, London: Hollis & Carter, 1950).

5 Compare Kierkegaard, *Fear and Trembling* (*Crainte et Tremblement*, transl. Tisseau, Paris: Aubier, pp. 52–67) on the nature of the real movement which is not mediation but 'repetition' and which stands opposed to the abstract, logical, false movement described by Hegel. See also the remarks from the *Journal* published as an appendix to *La Répétition*, transl. and ed. Tisseau. One also finds in Péguy a profound critique of 'logical movement': Péguy denounces this as a conservative, accumulative and capitalistic pseudo-movement: *Clio*, pp. 45 ff. This is close to the Kierkegaardian critique.

6 Nietzsche, *Thus Spoke Zarathustra*, Part III, 'Of Old and New Law-Tables', section 4: 'But only a buffoon thinks: "Man can also be jumped over".'

7 The formula and the phenomenon of discrete extension are clearly identified by Michel Tournier in *Les Météores*, Paris: Gallimard, 1975. English version entitled *Gemini*, transl. Anne Carter, New York: Doubleday, 1981.

8 With Kant, there is indeed an infinite specification of concepts; but because this infinite is only virtual (indefinite), no argument favourable to posing a principle of indiscernibles can be drawn from it. On the contrary, according to Leibniz it is very important that the comprehension of the concept of a (possible or real) existent be actually infinite: Leibniz clearly affirms this in *On Freedom* ('Only God being able to see, not the end of the analysis indeed, since there is no end ...'). When Leibniz employs the word 'virtually' to characterize the inherence of predicates in the case of truths of fact (for example, in the *Discourse on Metaphysics*, section 8), 'virtual' should be understood not as the contrary of actual but as signifying 'enveloped', 'implicated' or 'impressed', which is by no means exclusive of actuality. In the strict sense, the notion of virtuality is indeed invoked by Leibniz, but only apropos of a species of necessary truths (non-reciprocal propositions); see Leibniz, *On Freedom*, in *Philosophical Papers and Letters*, transl. and ed. Leroy E. Loemker, 2nd edn, Dordrecht, Holland: D. Reidel, 1969, pp. 262–6.

9 Freud, 'Remembering, Repeating and Working-Through (Further Recommendations on the Technique of Psycho-Analysis, II)', 1914, in James Strachey (transl. and ed.), *The Standard Edition of the Complete Psychological Works of Sigmund Freud*, 24 vols, London: Hogarth, 1953–73 (1958) vol. 12, pp. 147–56. This negative interpretation of psychical repetition (one repeats because one is mistaken, because one has not worked through the memory, because one lacks consciousness,

because one has no instincts) has nowhere been developed further or with greater rigour than in Ferdinand Alquié, *Le désir d'éternité*, Paris: Presses Universitaires de France, 1943, chs 2–4.

10 Freud invokes transference in particular to call into question his global law of the inverse relation. See *Beyond the Pleasure Principle*, 1920, *Standard Edition*, vol. 18, p. 19: memory and reproduction, remembrance and repetition, are opposed in principle, but in practice one must accept that the patient will relive certain repressed elements during the cure: 'the ratio between what is remembered and what is reproduced varies from case to case'. Those who insisted most profoundly upon the therapeutic and liberatory aspect of repetition as it appears in transference were Ferenczi and Rank in *Entwicklungziele der Psychoanalyse*, Vienna: *Neue Arbeiten zur ärtzlichen Psychoanalyse*, 1924.

11 *Henry Miller, *The Time of the Assassins*, London: Neville Spearman Ltd, 1956, p. 3.

12 Claude Lévi-Strauss, *Tristes Tropiques*, transl. John and Doreen Weightman, London: Jonathan Cape, 1973, p. 191.

13 Matila Ghyka, *Le Nombre d'Or: Rites et Rhythmes Pythagoriciens Dans le Développement de la Civilisation Occidentale*, Paris: Gallimard, 1931, vol. I, p. 65.

14 On the relation between repetition and language, but also between repetition and masks and death in the work of Raymond Roussel, see Michel Foucault's fine book *Death and the Labyrinth: The World of Raymond Roussel*, transl. Charles Ruas, London: Athlone, 1987: 'Both the repetition and the difference are so intricately linked, and adjusted with such exactitude, that it is not possible to distinguish which came first ...' (p. 24); 'Far from being a language that seeks to begin, it is the second form of words already spoken: it is everyday language ravaged by destruction and death .... By nature it is repetitive .... there is a profound repetition. It is not the lateral one of things said again, but the radical one which has gone beyond nonbeing and, because it has come through this void, is poetry ...' (pp. 45–6). See also Michel Butor's article on Roussel which analyses the double aspect of the repetition that enchains and saves, in *Répertoire, I*, Paris: Editions de Minuit, 1960.

15 In his *Lois de l'imitation*, Paris: Alcan, 1890 (transl. Elsie Clews Parsons, as *The Laws of Imitation*, New York: Henry Holt, 1903; republished Gloucester, MA.: Peter Smith Publishing, 1962) Gabriel Tarde shows how resemblance between, for example, different species refers back to the identity of the physical milieu; that is, to a repetitive process affecting elements inferior to the forms in question. All of Tarde's philosophy, as we shall see more clearly later, is founded upon the two categories of difference and repetition: difference is simultaneously both the origin and the destination of repetition, in a more and more

'forceful and ingenious' movement which takes 'greater and greater account of degrees of freedom'. Tarde proposes to substitute this differential and differenciating repetition for opposition in every domain. Roussel or Péguy could adopt his formula: 'Repetition is a more powerful and less tiring stylistic procedure than antithesis, and moreover better suited to renew a subject' (*L'opposition universelle*, Paris: Alcan, 1897, p. 119). Tarde regarded repetition as a thoroughly French idea; Kierkegaard, it is true, saw it as a thoroughly Danish concept. They meant that it gives rise to a dialectic quite different to that of Hegel.

16 On internal difference which is nevertheless neither intrinsic nor conceptual, see Kant, *Prolegomena to Any Future Metaphysics*, transl. Norman Kemp Smith, London: Macmillan, 1933, section 13 (note the opposition between *innere Verschiedenheit* and *innerlich Verschiedenheit*).

Chapter I Difference in Itself

1 Odilon Redon, *A soi-même: Journal, 1867–1915*, Paris: Fleury, 1922, p. 63: 'No plastic form will be found in my works, I mean any form perceived objectively, for itself, according to the laws of light and shadow, through the conventional means of relief. ... All of my art is confined solely to the resources of *chiaroscuro*, and also owes much to the effects of the abstract line, that agent from a profound source, acting directly on the spirit.'

2 Aristotle, *Metaphysics*, Book X, 4, 8, 9; transl. W.D. Ross, Oxford: The Clarendon Press, 1924; reprinted in *The Complete Works of Aristotle*, ed. Jonathan Barnes, vol. 2, Princeton, NJ: Princeton University Press, 1984. On the three kinds of difference, common, proper and strict, see Porphyry the Phoenician, *Isagoge*, transl. Edward W. Warren, Toronto: The Pontifical Institute of Mediaeval Studies, 1975, paras 8–9. See also The Thomist manuals: for example the chapter '*De differentia*' in the *Elementa philosophia aristotelico-thomisticae* by Joseph Gredt, Fribourg: Herder, 1909–12, vol. I, pp. 122–5.

3 Porphyry, *Isagoge*, para. 9, pp. 42–3: 'The difference 'rational' added to animal makes another essence [*allo*], but the difference 'moving' only makes something qualitatively different from resting, so that the one makes a difference-in-essence, the other only a difference-in-quality.'

4 Aristotle, *Metaphysics*, Book III, 3, 998b, 20–27; *Topics*, VI, 6, 144a, 35–40.

5 We know that Aristotle himself did not speak of analogy with regard to being. He determined the categories as *pros hen* and no doubt also as *ephexēs* (these are are the two cases, apart from pure equivocity, where there is 'difference' without a common genus). The *pros hen* are said in relation to a unique term. This is like a *common sense*, but this common sense is not a genus, for it forms only a distributive unity (im-

plicit and confused), not a collective, explicit and distinct unity such as we find with genera. The scholastics are therefore right to translate the *pros hen* as 'analogy of proportionality'. In effect, this analogy must not be understood in the strict mathematical sense and does not presuppose any *equality* of relation. It is defined by something completely different – by an *interiority* of relation: the relation of each category with being is interior to each category, it is on its own account that each has unity and being, by virtue of its own nature. This distributive character is clearly noted by Aristotle when he identifies categories with *diaireseis*. Moreover, despite certain recent interpretations there is indeed a division of being corresponding to the ways in which it is distributed to 'beings'. However, in the *pros hen* the unique term is not only being as common sense but already substance as *first sense* – whence the slide towards the idea that *ephexēs* imply a hierarchy. The scholastics speak here of 'analogy of proportion': there is no longer a distributive concept which is formally related to different terms but a serial concept which is formally–eminently related to a principal term and to others in a lesser degree. Being is first, in act, analogy of proportionality; but does it not also 'virtually' present an analogy of proportion?

6 See E. Laroche, *Histoire de la racine nem – en grec ancien*, Paris: Klincksieck, 1949. Laroche shows that the idea of distribution in *nomos–nemō* does not stand in a simple relation to that of allocation [*temnō*, *diaō*, *diaireō*]. The pastoral sense of *nemo* (to pasture) only belatedly implied an allocation of the land. Homeric society had neither enclosures nor property in pastures: it was not a question of distributing the land among the beasts but, on the contrary, of distributing the beasts themselves and dividing them up here and there across an unlimited space, forest or mountainside. The *nomos* designated first of all an occupied space, but one without precise limits (for example, the expanse around a town) – whence, too, the theme of the 'nomad'.

7 Etienne Gilson raises all these questions in his book *Jean Duns Scot: Introduction à ses positions fondamentales*, Paris: Vrin, 1952, pp. 87–88, 114, 236–7, 629. He insists on the relation between analogy and judgement, especially the judgement of existence (p. 101).

8 Nietzsche: 'That dangerous word hubris is indeed the touchstone for every Heraclitan': *Philosophy in the Tragic Age of the Greeks*, transl. by M. Cowan, Chicago: Henry Regnery, 1962, S. 7, p. 61. And on the problem of order and rank, 'of which we may say it is *our* problem, we free spirits', see *Human, All Too Human*, transl. R.J. Hollingdale, Cambridge: Cambridge University Press, 1986, Preface, S. 6–7, pp. 9–10. For the Overman as 'the superior form of everything that is', see *Ecce Homo*, 'Thus Spake Zarathustra', S. 6. (*In Kaufmann's translation this phrase is rendered as 'the supreme type of all beings'.)

9 On this indifference towards the small or the large, see Leibniz, '*Tentamen Anagogicum*', in *Philosophical Papers and Letters*, transl. and ed. Leroy E. Loemker, 2nd edn, Dordrecht, Holland: D. Reidel, 1969. Note that for Leibniz no less than for Hegel, infinite representation cannot be reduced to a mathematical structure: there is a non-mathematical or supra-mathematical architectonic element in continuity and in the differential calculus. Conversely, Hegel seems to recognise the presence of a genuine infinite in the differential calculus, the infinity of 'relation'. He criticizes calculus only for expressing this genuine infinite in the mathematical form of the 'series', which is a bad infinity: *Hegel's Science of Logic*, transl. A.V. Miller, London: George Allen & Unwin, 1969, pp. 240ff. We know that modern interpretations give an account of the differential calculus entirely in terms of finite representation: this point of view will be analysed in Chapter IV.

10 *Hegel's Science of Logic*, pp. 431, 442. See also *Hegel's Logic*, Part One of the Encyclopaedia of the Philosophical Sciences (1830), transl. William Wallace, Oxford: Clarendon Press, 1975, S. 116–22. On the passage from difference to opposition and to contradiction, see the comments by Jean Hyppolite, *Logique et Existence: Essai sur la Logique de Hegel*, Paris: Presses Universitaires de France, 1953, pp. 146–57.

11 *Hegel's Science of Logic*, p. 432.

12 On the infinite, genus and species, see Hegel's *Phenomenology of Spirit*, transl. A.V. Miller, Oxford: Clarendon Press, 1977, pp. 98–101, 107–9, 175–8.

13 See Leibniz, '*Nova calculi differentialis applicatio ...*' (1694). On the principle of reciprocal determination which Salomon Maïmon draws from Leibniz, see M. Guéroult, *La philosophie transcendentale de Salomon Maïmon*, Paris: Alcan, 1929, p. 75 ff. (Neither Maïmon nor Leibniz distinguishes between the reciprocal determination of relations and the complete determination of the object.)

14 Leibniz, Correspondence with Arnauld, 9 October 1687: 'I have said that the soul, which naturally expresses the entire universe in a certain sense and according to the relationship which other bodies have to its own, and which as a consequence expresses more immediately the properties of the parts of its body, must therefore, by virtue of the laws of relationship which are essential to it, particularly express certain unusual motions of the parts of its body': *Philosophical Papers and Letters*, p. 339. see also the 'degrees of accidental unity' among things as a result of the degrees of relation between their component elements, in the Letter of 30 April 1687 (in Leibniz, *Discourse on Metaphysics. Correspondence with Arnauld. Monadology*, transl. George Montgomery, La Salle, IL: Open Court Publishing Company, 1979, pp. 180–99).

15 Louis Althusser denounces the all-powerful character of identity in

Hegel's philosophy, in the form of the *simplicity of its internal principle*: 'The simplicity of the Hegelian contradiction is made possible *only* by the simplicity of the *internal principle* that constitutes the essence of any historical period. It is because it is possible in principle to reduce the totality, the infinite diversity of a given historical society ... to a simple internal principle, that this very simplicity thereby accrues by right to contradiction and may be reflected in it.' This is why he criticizes the Hegelian circle for having only a single centre in which all the figures are reflected and retained. In opposition to Hegel, Althusser proposes a principle of multiple or overdetermined contradiction which he finds in the young Marx: 'This means that if the "differences" that constitute each of the instances in play ... *"merge"* into a real unity, they are not "*dissipated*" as pure *phenomena* in the internal unity of a *simple* contradiction.' (It is still the case that for Althusser it is contradiction which is overdetermined and differential, and the totality of these differences remains legitimately grounded in a principal contradiction). See Louis Althusser, *For Marx*, transl. Ben Brewster, London: New Left Review Editions, 1977, pp. 100, 103 (*translation modified).

16 Nietzsche never ceases to denounce the assimilation of 'affirm' with 'bear'. See *Beyond Good and Evil*, S. 213, where he says of most thinkers and scholars: ' "Thinking" and "taking something seriously", taking on its weight – to them these things go together, they have no other experience of it.' **Beyond Good and Evil*, transl. R.J. Hollingdale, Harmondsworth: Penguin, 1973, p. 126, has ' "taking something seriously", giving it "weighty consideration".' The point is that *to bear* implies a false activity, a false affirmation which concerns itself only with the products of nihilism. Thus Nietzsche defines Kant and Hegel as 'philosophical labourers' who amass and conserve an enormous pile of established value judgements, even if for them it is a matter of overcoming the past. In this sense, they are still enslaved to the negative (S. 211).

17 *Beyond Good and Evil*, S. 211. On the 'no' of the master which is a consequence, by contrast with the 'no' of the slave which is a principle, see *On the Genealogy of Morals*, I, S. 10.

18 Cited by Jean Wahl, *Les philosophies pluralistes d'Angleterre et d'Amérique*, Paris: Alcan, 1920, p. 37. All Jean Wahl's work is a profound meditation on difference: on the possibilities within empiricism for expressing its poetic, free and wild nature; on the irreducibility of difference to the simple negative; on the *non-Hegelian* relations between affirmation and negation.

*Citation modified. These lines are quoted from *The Anaesthetic Revelation* (1874), by the American poet and philosopher Benjamin Paul Blood (1822–1919). Wahl cites them from the essay on Blood's pamphlet by William James, entitled 'A Pluralistic Mystic' and first published in the *Hibbert Journal*, July 1910. This essay is republished in

James's *Memories and Studies*, London: Longmans Green, 1911, (see pp. 394, 409); and in vol. 15 of *The Works of William James*, Cambridge, MA: Harvard University Press, 1987.

19 In two articles which renew the interpretation of Nietzsche, Pierre Klossowski uncovers this element: '*God is dead* does not mean that the divinity ceases to provide a clarification of existence, but rather that the absolute guarantee of the identity of the responsible self disappears from the horizon of Nietzsche's consciousness, which in turn becomes indistinguishable from that disappearance. ... All that is left (to consciousness) is to declare that its very identity is a chance case arbitrarily maintained as necessary, even if this means taking itself for that universal wheel of chance, even if this means embracing if possible the totality of cases, chance itself in its necessary totality. What subsists is thus being, and the verb "to be", which is never applied to being itself but to the fortuitous': 'Nietzsche, le polythéisme et la parodie', in *Un si funeste désir*, Paris: NRF, 1963, pp. 220–21. 'Does this mean that the thinking subject loses its identity on the basis of a coherent thought which excludes it? ... What is my role in this circular movement in relation to which I am incoherent, in relation to that thought so perfectly coherent that it excludes me at the very moment I think it? ... How does it threaten the reality of the self, of this self which it nevertheless exalts? By liberating the fluctuations which signify it as a self in such a fashion that it is only ever the completed which resound in its present. ... *Circulus vitiosus deus* is only a denomination of this sign which here takes on a divine physiognomy after the manner of Dionysus': 'Oubli et anamnèse dans l'expérience vécue de l'éternel retour du Même', in *Nietzsche: Cahiers de Royaumont*, Philosophie No. vi, Paris: Editions de Minuit, 1967, pp. 233–5.

20 On Aristotle's critique of Platonic division, cf. *Prior Analytics*, I, 31; *Posterior Analytics*, II, 5 and 13 (In the latter text Aristotle maintains a certain role for division in the determination of species, even though the insufficiencies that he finds in Plato's conception are corrected by a principle of continuity). But we can see clearly how far the determination of species is merely an ironic appearance and not the aim of Platonic division, for example, in *The Statesman*, 266 b–d.

21 It is with regard to this aspect that the myth must be completed by another kind of model, the paradigm, which enables Plato to distinguish parents, servants, auxiliaries and counterfeits by means of analogy. In the same manner, assaying gold involves several selections: the removal of impurities, the elimination of other metals 'from the same family' (cf. *The Statesman*, 303 d–e).

22 See Note 19 above. On this notion of simulacra as it appears in Klossowski in connection with eternal return, see Michel Foucault, 'La

Prose d'Actéon', *Nouvelle Revue Française*, March 1964; Maurice Blanchot, 'Le rire des dieux', *Nouvelle Revue Française*, July 1965.

23 See Umberto Eco, *The Open Work*, transl. Anna Cancogni, with an Introduction by David Robey, Cambridge, MA: Harvard University Press, 1989. Eco shows clearly that the 'classical' work of art may be seen from several perspectives and is susceptible to several interpretations, but that there is no autonomous work corresponding to each point of view or interpretation, all included in the the chaos of the work as a whole. The characteristic of the 'modern' work of art appears to be precisely the absence of any such centre or convergence (see Chapters 1 and 6).

Chapter II Repetition for Itself

1 The Bergson text is in *Time and Free-Will: An Essay on the Immediate Data of Consciousness*, transl. F.L. Pogson, New York: Harper & Row, 1960, ch. 2. There Bergson clearly distinguishes the two aspects: fusion or contraction in the mind, and deployment in space. Contraction as the essence of duration, and as operating on elementary material agitations in order to constitute the perceived quality, is even more precisely dealt with in *Matter and Memory*, transl. Nancy Margaret Paul and W. Scott Palmer, New York: Zone Books, 1988.

The Hume texts are in *A Treatise of Human Nature*, especially Part III section 16 of Book I. Hume forcefully distinguishes the union or fusion of cases in the imagination – a union which takes place independently of memory or understanding – and the separation of these same cases in the memory and the understanding.

2 Samuel Butler, *Life and Habit*, London: Jonathan Cape, 1910, p. 82.

3 The philosophy of Gabriel Tarde is one of the last great philosophies of nature, in the tradition of Leibniz. It unfolds on two levels. On the first level it deploys three fundamental categories which govern all phenomena: repetition, opposition and adaptation (see *Les lois sociales*, Paris: Alcan, 1898; transl. Howard C. Warren, as *Social Laws: An Outline of Sociology*, New York: Arno Press, 1899). Opposition, however, is only the figure by means of which a difference is distributed throughout repetition in order to limit it and to open up a new order or a new infinity: for example, when the parts of life are opposed in pairs, it renounces any indefinite growth or multiplication in order to form limited wholes. Nevertheless, life thereby attains an infinity of another kind, a different sort of repetition: that of generation (*L'opposition universelle*, Paris: Alcan, 1897). Adaptation itself is the figure by means of which the repetitive currents meet and become integrated into superior repetitions. As a result, *difference appears between two kinds of repetition*, and each repetition presupposes a difference of the same degree as itself (imitation as the repetition of an invention, reproduction as the repeti-

tion of a variation, diffusion as the repetition of a perturbation, summation as the repetition of a differential ... See Tarde, *Les lois d'imitation*, Paris: Alcan, 1890 (transl. Elsie Clews Parsons as *The Laws of Imitation*, New York: Henry Holt, 1903; republished Gloucester, MA: Peter Smith Publishing, 1962).

On a deeper level, however, it is rather repetition which serves difference. For neither opposition nor even adaptation presents the free figure of difference: that difference 'which opposes nothing and which serves no purpose', which is 'the final end of all things' (*L'opposition universelle*, p. 445). From this point of view, *repetition is between two differences*; it is what enables us to pass from one order of difference to another: from external to internal difference, from elementary difference to transcendent difference, from infinitesimal difference to personal and monadological difference. Repetition, therefore, is not the process by which difference is augmented or diminished, but the process by which it 'goes on differing' and 'takes itself as its end' (see Tarde, 'Monadologie et sociologie' et 'La variation universelle', in *Essais et mélanges sociologiques*, Paris: Editions Maloine, 1895).

It is completely wrong to reduce Tarde's sociology to a psychologism or even an interpsychology. Tarde criticizes Durkheim for assuming what must be explained – namely, 'the similarity of thousands of men'. For the alternative – impersonal givens or the Ideas of great men – he substitutes the little ideas of little men, the little inventions and interferences between imitative currents. *What Tarde inaugurates is a microsociology*, which is not necessarily concerned with what happens between individuals but with what happens within a single individual: for example, hesitation understood as 'infinitesimal social opposition', or invention as 'infinitesimal social adaptation': *Social Laws: An Outline of Sociology*. It is by following this method, through a series of monographs, that it will be possible to show how repetition adds and integrates the small variations, always with a view to discovering the 'differently different' (*La logique sociale*, Paris: Alcan, 1893). All of Tarde's philosophy may be presented in this light: as a dialectic of difference and repetition which founds the possibility of a microsociology upon a whole cosmology.

4 Michel Souriau, *Le Temps*, Paris: Alcan, 1937, p. 55.

5 These three paradoxes are discussed in Chapter III of *Matter and Memory*. Under these three aspects, Bergson opposes the pure past or pure memory, which is without psychological *existence*, to representation – that is, to the psychological reality of the image-memory.

6 Bergson, *Matter and Memory*, p. 105: 'The same psychical life, therefore, must be supposed to be repeated an endless number of times on the different stories of memory, and the same act of the mind may be performed at varying heights'; p. 162: 'there is room, as we indicated in

the previous chapter, for a thousand repetitions of our psychical life, figured by as many sections A'B', A'' B'', etc., of the same cone.' Notice that repetition here concerns psychological life but is not itself psychological: in effect, psychology begins only with the memory-image, whereas the sections or levels of the cones are drawn in the pure past. It is therefore a question of a metapsychological repetition *of* psychological life. Moreover, when Bergson speaks of 'successive stages', *successive* must be understood figuratively as a function of the eye which scans his proposed drawing; for, in their own terms, all the levels are supposed to coexist with one another.

7 Leibniz, *New Essays on Human Understanding*, transl. and ed. Peter Remnant and Jonathan Bennett, Cambridge: Cambridge University Press, 1981, Book I, ch. I, p. 71.

8 Immanuel Kant, *Critique of Pure Reason*, transl. Norman Kemp Smith, London: Macmillan, 1933: 'General Note on the Transition from Rational Psychology to Cosmology', p. 382.

9 Kant, *Critique of Pure Reason*, 'Analytic of Concepts', note to section 25, p. 169.

10 On the pure form of time and the fracture or 'caesura' that it introduces into the I, see Hölderlin, *Remarques sur Oedipe, Remarques sur Antigone*, and Jean Beaufret's commentary 'Hölderlin et Sophocle', in ibid., Paris: Union Générale d'Editions (10/18), 1965. Beaufret's commentary strongly underlines Kant's influence upon Hölderlin: see especially pp. 16–26. (On the theme of a 'fracture' within the I which is essentially related to the form of time understood as a death instinct, recall three great but very different literary works: Zola, *La bête humaine*; F. Scott Fitzgerald, *The Crack-Up*; and Malcolm Lowry, *Under the Volcano*.)

11 On the explicit opposition between reminiscence and innateness, see *Phaedo* 76 a–d.

12 On the manner in which Kierkegaardian repetition is opposed to the customary cycle and also to the cycle of reminiscences, see Mircea Eliade's comments regarding Abraham's sacrifice, in *The Myth of the Eternal Return*, transl. William R. Trask, New York: Pantheon, 1984, pp.108 ff. The author concludes from this that the categories of history and faith are new.

The very important text by Kierkegaard on the true repetition from which no difference may be 'drawn' can be found in *The Concept of Anxiety*, Princeton, NJ: Princeton University Press, 1980, pp. 17–19. The Kierkegaardian theory of the condition, the unconditioned and the absolutely different is put forward in *Philosophical Fragments*.

13 Daniel Lagache has examined the possibility of applying the psychological concept of habit to the unconscious and to repetition in the unconscious (but it seems that that repetition is here considered only from the

perspective of a mastery of tensions): 'Le problème du transfert', *Revue française de psychanalyse*, January 1952, pp. 84–97.

14 Henri Maldiney, *Le Moi*, course summary, Bulletin Faculté de Lyon, 1967.

15 Jacques Lacan, 'Seminar on *The Purloined Letter*', transl. Jeffrey Mehlmann, *Yale French Studies*, no. 48, 1972, p. 55. This text is undoubtedly the one in which Lacan most profoundly develops his conception of repetition.

Certain disciples of Lacan have strongly insisted upon this theme of the 'non-identical' and on the relation between difference and repetition which follows from it: J.-A. Miller, 'La Suture' (transl. 'Suture (elements of the logic of the signifier)', *Screen*, vol. xviii, no. 4, 1977/8, pp. 24–34); J.-C. Milner, 'Le point du signifiant'; S. Leclaire, 'Les éléments en jeu dans une psychanalyse', *Cahiers pour l'analyse*, nos 1, 3 and 5 respectively, 1966.

16 Lacan discloses the existence of series in two very important texts: 'The Seminar on *The Purloined Letter*', cited above (first series: 'king–queen–minister', second series: 'police–minister–Dupin'); and in a commentary on 'the rat man', 'Le mythe individuel du névrose', C.D.U. ('The Neurotic's Individual Myth', transl. Martha Noel Evans, *The Psychoanalytic Quarterly*, 48, 1979, pp. 405–25) (here the two series, one paternal and one filial, put into play in different situations the debt, the friend, the poor woman and the rich woman). The elements and relations in each series are determined by their position in relation to the always displaced virtual object – the letter in the first example; the debt in the second: 'it is not only the subject, but the subjects, grasped in their intersubjectivity, who line up ... the displacement of the signifier determines the subjects in their acts, in their destiny, in their refusals, in their blindnesses, in their end and in their fate, their innate gifts and social acquisitions notwithstanding, without regard for character or sex ...' *Yale French Studies*, no. 48, 1972, p. 60. In this manner, an intersubjective unconscious is defined which reduces neither to an individual unconscious nor to a collective unconscious, and in relation to which one can no longer describe one series as original and the other as derived (even though Lacan continues to use these terms – for ease of expression, it seems).

17 Serge Leclaire has outlined a theory of neuroses and psychoses in terms of the notion of the question as the fundamental category of the unconscious. In this connection he distinguishes between the hysteric's mode of questioning ('Am I a man or a woman?') and that of the obsessive ('Am I dead or alive?'); he also distinguishes the respective positions of the neurotic and the psychotic in relation to this instance of the question: 'La mort dans la vie de l'obsédé', *La psychanalyse*, no. 2, 1956 ('Jerome, or Death in the Life of the Obsessional', *Returning to Freud:*

Clinical Psychoanalysis in the School of Lacan, ed. and transl. Stuart Schneiderman, New Haven and London: Yale University Press, 1980, pp. 94–113); 'A la recherche des principes d'une psychothérapie des psychoses', *Evolution psychiatrique*, II, 1958. This research on the form and content of the questions lived by patients seems to us of enormous importance, implying a revision of the role of the negative and of conflict in the unconscious in general. Here again, they have their origin in some remarks by Lacan: on the kinds of question in hysteria and obsession, see *Ecrits, A Selection*, transl. Alan Sheridan, London: Tavistock/Routledge, 1989: 'The function and field of speech and language in psychoanalysis', pp. 89–90; on desire, its difference from need and its relation with 'enquiry' and with the 'question', see ibid: 'The direction of the treatment and the principles of its power', pp. 263–5; 'The signification of the phallus', pp. 285–8.

Was not one of the most important points of Jung's theory already to be found here: the force of 'questioning' in the unconscious, the conception of the unconscious as an unconscious of 'problems' and 'tasks'? Drawing out the consequences of this led Jung to the discovery of a process of differenciation more profound than the resulting oppositions (see *The Ego and the Unconscious*). Freud, it is true, violently criticised this point of view, notably in 'The Wolf Man', s. 5, where he maintains that the child does not question but desires, and that rather than being confronted with tasks it is confronted with emotions governed by opposition; and also in 'Dora', s. 2, where he shows that the kernel of the dream can only be a desire engaged in a corresponding conflict. Nevertheless, the discussion between Jung and Freud is perhaps not well situated, since it is a question of knowing whether or not the unconscious can do anything other than desire. In truth, should it not be asked whether desire is only an oppositional force rather than a force completely founded in the power [*puissance*] of the question? Even Dora's dream, which Freud invokes, can be interpreted only from the perspective of a problem (with the two series father–mother, Herr K.–Frau K.) which develops an hysterical question (with the jewel box playing the role of the object = x).

18 Even though Eros implies the union of two cellular bodies, thereby introducing new 'vital differences', 'we still feel our line of thought appreciably hampered by the fact that we cannot ascribe to the sexual instinct the characteristic of a compulsion to repeat which first put us on the track of the death instincts'. Freud, *Beyond the Pleasure Principle*, 1920, *Standard Edition*, vol. 18, p. 56.

19 See Paul Ricoeur, *De l'interprétation*, Paris: Editions du Seuil, 1965, pp. 413–14, transl. Denis Savage as *Freud and Philosophy: An Essay on Interpretation*, New Haven, CT and London: Yale University Press, 1970.

20 Freud, *The Ego and the Id*, 1923, *Standard Edition*, vol. 19, pp. 43–7.

21 Freud, *Inhibitions, Symptoms and Anxiety*, 1926 [1925], *Standard Edition*, vol. 20, pp. 138 ff. It is all the more strange that Freud reproaches Rank for having a too objective conception of birth.

22 Maurice Blanchot, *The Space of Literature*, transl. Ann Smock, Lincoln and London: University of Nebraska Press, 1982, pp. 106, 154–5.

23 Jorge Luis Borges, *Ficciones*, New York: Grove Press, 1962, 'The Babylon Lottery', pp. 69–70; 'The Garden of Forking Paths' p. 98.

24 See Claude Lévi-Strauss, *Totemism*, transl. Rodney Needham, Boston, MA: Beacon Press, 1963, p. 77: 'If we may be allowed the expression, it is not the resemblances, but the differences, which resemble each other.' Lévi-Strauss shows how this principle develops in the constitution of at least two series, the terms of each series being different amongst themselves (for example, in the case of totemism, the series of distinct species of animals and that of the differential social positions): the resemblance is 'between these two series of differences'.

25 Léon Selme showed that the illusion of an annulment of difference must be all the greater the smaller the differences realised within a system (and therefore in thermal machines), in his *Principe de carnot contre formule empirique de Clausius*, Paris: H. Dunod & E. Pinat, 1917.

On the importance of disparate series and their internal resonance in the constitution of systems, see Gilbert Simondon, *L'individu et sa genèse physico-biologique*, Paris: Presses Universitaires de France, 1964, p. 20. (However, Simondon maintains as a condition the requirement of resemblance between series, or the smallness of the differences in play: pp. 254–7.)

26 Witold Gombrowicz, *Cosmos*, transl. into French by Georges Sedir, Paris: Denoël, 1966. The preface to this edition of *Cosmos* outlines a theory of disparate series, their resonance and of chaos. *The English edition of *Cosmos*, transl. by Eric Mosbacher, New York: Grove Press, 1967, has no preface.

See also the theme of repetition in *Ferdydurke*, transl. Eric Mosbacher, London: Marion Boyars, 1979, pp. 70–87.

27 On this problem, see J. Laplanche and J.-B. Pontalis, 'Fantasme originaire, fantasmes des origines, origine du fantasme', *Les Temps modernes*, no. 215, April 1964. Transl. as 'Fantasy and the Origins of Sexuality', *International Journal of Psycho-Analysis*, 49, 1968; reprinted, with an afterword, in V. Burgin, J. Donald, C. Kaplan eds., *Formations of Fantasy*, London: Methuen, 1968.

28 In lines which apply particularly to Freudian phantasy, Jacques Derrida writes: 'It is thus the delay which is in the beginning. Without which, *différance* would be the lapse which a consciousness, a self-presence of the present, accords itself. ... To say that *différance* is originary is simultaneously to erase the myth of a present origin. Which is why

'originary' must be understood as having been *crossed out*, without which *différance* would be derived from an original plenitude. It is a non-origin which is originary': *Writing and Difference*, transl. Alan Bass, London: Routledge & Kegan Paul, 1978, p. 203; see also Maurice Blanchot, 'Le rire des dieux', *Nouvelle Revue Française*, July 1965: 'The image must cease to be second in relation to a supposedly prior object and must demand a certain primacy, just as the original and then the origin will lose their initial privileges. ... There is no longer any original but an eternal twinkling in which the absence of any origin is dispersed in the flash of detour and return.'

29 Plato's arguments are marked by stylistic reprises and repetitions which testify to a meticulous attention to detail, as though there were an effort to 'correct' a theme in order to defend it against a neighbouring but dissimilar theme that is likely to 'insinuate itself'. The repetition of the Platonic theme serves to neutralise and ward off the return of pre-Socratic themes: parricide is therefore consummated several times, and never more than when Plato imitates those he denounces. See P.-M. Schuhl, 'Remarques sur la technique de la répétition dans le *Phédon*', in *Etudes platoniciennes*, Paris: Presses Universitaires de France, 1960, pp. 118–25 (what P.-M. Schuhl calls the 'litanies of the idea').

30 On this 'other' model, which amounts to a kind of equivalent in Platonism of the evil demon or the God who misleads us, see *Theaetetus*, 176e, and especially *Timaeus*, 28b ff. On phantasms and the distinction between *icônes* and *phantasms*, the principal texts are in the *Sophist*, 235e–236d (also the *Republic*, X, 601 ff.).

*The Greek term *phantasma*, for which Deleuze often uses the French equivalent *phantasme*, is frequently rendered in English translations of Plato as 'appearance'. I have preferred to use 'phantasm' in order to retain the connection with 'phantasy' in the preceding section of the text, where Deleuze uses the same French word as equivalent to the Freudian term *Phantasie*.

Chapter III The Image of Thought

1 See Descartes, 'The Search for Truth by Means of the Natural Light', in *The Philosophical Writings of Descartes*, transl. John Cottingham, Robert Stoothoff and Dugald Murdoch, Cambridge: Cambridge University Press, 1984, vol. II.

2 Feuerbach is among those who have pursued farthest the problem of where to begin. He denounces the implicit presuppositions of philosophy in general, and those of Hegel in particular. He shows that philosophy must not begin with its accord with a *pre-philosophical* image, but with its 'difference' from *non-philosophy*. (However, he supposes that this exigency of the true beginning is sufficiently met by beginning with empirical, perceptible and concrete being.) See *Contribution à la Cri-*

tique de la Philosophie de Hegel, transl. Louis Althusser, in *Manifestes philosophiques*, Paris: Presses Universitaires de France, 1960, especially p. 33.

3 *The sentence 'Good sense is of all things in the world the most equally distributed', opens Part 1 of the *Discourse on the Method*, which appears in *The Philosophical Writings of Descartes*, vol. I.

4 *Descartes, 'Second Meditation', in *The Philosophical Writings of Descartes*, vol. II, p. 21.

5 Nietzsche, 'Schopenhauer as Educator', in *Untimely Meditations*, transl. by R.J. Hollingdale, Cambridge: Cambridge University Press, 1983, p. 137.

6 On this common sense and the persistence of the model of recognition, see Maurice Merleau-Ponty, *Phenomenology of Perception*, transl. Colin Smith, London: Routledge & Kegan Paul, 1962, pp. 239 ff, 313 ff. On the Kantian theory of common senses, see especially the *Critique of Judgment*, transl. Werner S. Pluhar, Indianapolis, IN: Hackett, 1987, sections 18–22 and 40, and the declarations of principle in the *Critique of Pure Reason*: 'The ideas of pure reason can never be dialectical in themselves; any deceptive illusion to which they give occasion must be due solely to their misemployment. For they arise from the very nature of our reason; and it is impossible that this highest tribunal of all the rights and claims of speculation should itself be the source of deceptions and illusions' (Kant, *Critique of Pure Reason*, transl. Norman Kemp Smith, London: Macmillan, 1973, Appendix to the Transcendental Dialectic, p. 533); 'in regard to the essential ends of human nature the highest philosophy cannot advance further than is possible under the guidance which nature has bestowed even upon the most ordinary understanding.' (from 'The Transcendental Doctrine of Method', ch. 2, *Critique of Pure Reason*, p. 652).

7 On the double subordination of difference to conceived identity and perceived resemblance in the 'classical' world of representation, see Michel Foucault, *The Order of Things*, transl. Alan Sheridan, London: Tavistock, 1977, pp. 54 ff, 67 ff.

8 Plato, *The Republic*, Book VII, 523b, transl. Paul Shorey, in *Plato: The Collected Dialogues*, ed. E. Hamilton and H. Cairns, Princeton, NJ: Princeton University Press, 1963.

9 Ibid., 524a, b. Note that Gaston Bachelard opposes the problem or the object-bearer of problem to Cartesian doubt, and denounces the recognition model in philosophy: *Le rationalisme appliqué*, Paris: Presses Universitaires de France, 1949, pp. 51–6.

10 The case of the imagination: this is the only case in which Kant considers a faculty liberated from the form of a common sense, and discovers for it a truly legitimate 'transcendent' exercise. In effect, the schematic imagination in the *Critique of Pure Reason* is still under the logical

common sense; the reflective imagination of judgements of beauty is still under the aesthetic common sense. Yet with the sublime, according to Kant, the imagination is forced or constrained to confront its own limit, its *phantasteon*, its maximum which is equally the unimaginable, the unformed or the deformed in nature (*Critique of Judgment*, s. 26). Moreover, it transmits this constraint to thought itself, which in turn is forced the think the supra-sensible as foundation of both nature and the faculty of thought: thought and imagination here enter into an essential discordance, a reciprocal violence which conditions a new type of accord (s. 27). As a result, in the case of the sublime, the recognition model and the form of common sense are found wanting in favour of a quite different conception of thought (s. 29).

11 Martin Heidegger, *What is Called Thinking?* transl. J. Glenn Gray, New York: Harper & Row, 1968, p. 3. It is true that Heidegger retains the theme of a desire or a *philia*, of an analogy – or rather, a homology – between thought and that which is to be thought. The point is that he retains the primacy of the Same, even if this is supposed to include and comprehend difference as such – whence the metaphors of gift which are substituted for those of violence. In all these senses, Heidegger does not abandon what we called above the subjective presuppositions. As can be seen in *Being and Time* (transl. John Macquarie and Edward Robinson, Oxford: Basil Blackwell, 1987), there is in effect a pre-ontological and implicit understanding of being, *even though*, Heidegger specifies, *the explicit conception must not follow from it.*

12 The notion of a 'discordant – harmony' is well specified by Kostas Axelos, who applies it to the world and employs a particular sign ('and/or') to designate ontological difference in this sense: see *Vers la pensée planétaire*, Paris: Editions de Minuit, 1964.

13 Artaud, 'Correspondence with Jacques Rivière', *Collected Works*, vol. 1, transl. Victor Corti, London: John Calder, 1968, p.19 (*translation modified).

14 See Hegel, *Phenomenology of Spirit*, transl. A.V. Miller, Oxford: Oxford University Press, 1977, p. 23: 'Dogmatism as a way of thinking, whether in ordinary knowing or in the study of philosophy, is nothing else but the opinion that the true consists in a proposition which is a fixed result, or which is immediately known. To such questions as, when was Caesar born? or how many feet were there in a stadium?, etc., a clear-cut answer ought to be given ... but the nature of a so-called truth of that kind is different from the nature of philosophical truth.'

15 Flaubert, *Bouvard et Pécuchet*. Schelling wrote some splendid pages on evil (stupidity and malevolence), its source which is like the Ground become autonomous (essentially related to individuation), and on the entire history which follows from this, in 'Recherches philosophiques sur

la nature de la liberté humaine', in *Essais*, transl. S. Jankélévitch, Paris: Aubier, 1949, pp. 265–7: 'God allowed this ground to act quite independently ...'

16 *Bertrand Russell, *An Inquiry into Meaning and Truth*, Harmondsworth: Penguin, 1962, p. 201.

17 Whence Russell's attitude, which privileges singular propositions: see his polemic with Carnap in *An Inquiry into Meaning and Truth*, pp. 244 ff.

18 See Hubert Elie's excellent book *Le complexe significabile*, Paris: Vrin, 1936, which shows the importance and the paradoxes of this theory of sense as it was developed in the course of the fourteenth century among Ockham's school (Gregory of Rimini, Nicholas d'Autrecourt), and also as it was rediscovered by Meinong. The sterility and ineffectiveness of sense conceived in this manner appears again in Husserl when he writes: 'The stratum of expression – and this constitutes its peculiarity – apart from the fact that it lends expression to all other intentionalities, is not productive. Or if one prefers: its productivity, its noematic service, exhausts itself in *expressing* and in the form of the conceptual introduced by that function': *Ideas: General Introduction to Pure Phenomenology*, transl. W.R. Boyce Gibson, London: George Allen & Unwin, 1931, Section 124.

19 *These paradoxes of sense are discussed further, with reference to Lewis Carroll, in *The Logic of Sense*, transl. Mark Lester, New York: Columbia University Press, 1990, pp. 28–35.

20 Aristotle, *Topics*, I, 4, 101b, 30–35, in *The Complete Works of Aristotle*, ed. Jonathan Barnes, Princeton, NJ: Princeton University Press, 1984, vol. I, p. 169. The same illusion continues within modern logic: the calculus of problems as it is defined – notably by Kolgomoroff – still remains traced from a calculus of propositions, in 'isomorphism' with it. See Paulette Destouches-Février, 'Rapports entre le calcul des problèmes et le calcul des propositions', *Comptes rendus des séances de l'Académie des Sciences*, April 1945. As we shall see, an attempt at 'mathematics without negation' such as that of G.F.C. Griss is limited only by this false conception of the category of problems.

Leibniz, on the other hand, was aware of the variable but always profound gap between problems or themes and propositions: 'There are indeed "themes" which can be said to be midway between an idea and a proposition, namely *questions*. Some of these ask only for a Yes or a No, and these are the closest to propositions; but there are others which ask how, and ask for details, and so on, and more must be added to these if they are to become propositions: *New Essays on Human Understanding*, transl. and ed. Peter Remnant and Jonathan Bennett, Cambridge: Cambridge University Press, 1981, Book 4, ch. 1, p. 356.

21 In his *Rules for the Direction of the Mind*, Descartes distinguishes the precepts relating to 'simple propositions' from the precepts relating to 'questions' (Rule XII). The latter begin only with Rule XIII, and are the first to be concluded. Descartes himself underlines the point of resemblance between his method and the Aristotelian dialectic: 'This is the sole respect in which we imitate the dialecticians: when they *exposed* the forms of the syllogisms, they presupposed that the terms or the subject-matter of the syllogisms are known; similarly, we are making it a prerequisite here that the problem under investigation is perfectly understood': *The Philosophical Writings of Descartes*, vol. I, p. 51. Similarly, 'questions' have a subordinate role in Malebranche – see *The Search After Truth*, transl. T.M. Lennon and P.J. Olscamp, Columbus: Ohio State University Press, 1980, VI, 2, ch. 7 – and in Spinoza, where the use of the geometric method involves no 'problems' at all.

In the *Geometry*, however, Descartes underlines the importance of the analytic procedure from the point of view of the constitution of problems, and not only with regard to their solution (Auguste Comte, in some fine pages, insists on this point, and shows how the distribution of 'singularities' determines the 'conditions of the problem': *Traité élémentaire de géométrie analytique*, 1843). In this sense we can say that Descartes the geometer goes further than Descartes the philosopher.

22 One of the most original characteristics of modern epistemology is the recognition of this double irreducibility of 'problems' (in this sense the use of the word 'problematic' as a substantive seems to us an indispensable neologism). See Georges Bouligand and his distinction between the 'problem-element' and the 'global synthesis-element' (notably in *Le déclin des absolus mathématico-logiques*, Editions d'Enseignement supérieur, 1949); Georges Canguilhem and his problem–theory distinction (notably in *On the Normal and the Pathological*, transl. Carolyn R. Fawcett, Dordrecht, Holland: D. Reidel, 1978.

23 Proclus, *A Commentary on the First Book of Euclid's Elements*, transl. Glenn R. Morrow, Princeton, NJ: Princeton University Press, 1970, pp. 63–7.

24 Albert Lautman, *Essai sur les notions de structure et d'existence en mathématiques*, Paris: Hermann, 1938, vol. I, p. 13; vol. II, p.149 ('the only *a priori* element we allow is that given in the experience of this urgency of problems prior to the discovery of their solutions ...'). On the double aspect of problems–Ideas, transcendence and immanence, see *Nouvelles recherches sur la structure dialectique des mathématiques*, Paris: Hermann, 1939, pp. 14–15.

Chapter IV Ideas and the Synthesis of Difference

1 *Immanuel Kant's Critique of Pure Reason*, transl. Norman Kemp

Smith, London: Macmillan, 1973, 'Introduction', p. 57; see Preface to the Second Edition, p. 25: 'For pure speculative reason has this peculiarity, that it can measure its powers according to the different ways in which it chooses the objects of its thinking, and can also give an exhaustive enumeration of the various ways in which it propounds its problems ...'.

2 Ibid., p. 318 (The Transcendental Ideas).

3 Ibid., p. 319.

4 Both images may be found in the 'Appendix to the Transcendental Dialectic': ibid., p. 533, and p. 542.

5 Jean Bordas-Demoulin, *Le cartésianisme ou la véritable rénovation des sciences*, Paris: Gauthier-Villars, 1843, vol. II, pp. 133 ff., 453 ff. Charles Renouvier provides a comprehensive and profound analysis, despite his hostility towards Bordas's theses: *La Critique philosophique*, 6e année, 1877.

6 Salomon Maïmon, *Versuch über die Transzendentalphilosophie*, Berlin: Vos, 1790, p. 33. See also Martial Guéroult's very important book *La philosophie transcendentale de Salomon Maïmon*, Paris: Alcan, 1929 (especially pp. 53ff., 76ff. on 'determinability' and 'reciprocal determination').

7 Jules Houël, *Essai critique sur les principes fondamentaux de la géométrie élémentaire*, Paris: Gauthier-Villars, 1867, pp. 3, 75.

8 Hoëne Wronski, *Philosophie de l'infini*, Paris: Didot, 1814; *Philosophie de la technie algorithmique*, Paris: Didot, 1817. It is in the latter book that Wronski expounds his theory and his formulae for series. Wronski's mathematical works were republished by Hermann in 1925. On his philosophy, see Francis Warrain, *L'œuvre philosophique de Hoëne Wronski*, Paris: Vega, 1933. Warrain undertakes the necessary comparisons with the philosophy of Schelling.

9 Albert Lautman has clearly indicated this difference in kind between the existence and distribution of singular points which refer to the problem-element, and the specification of these same points which refers to the solution-element: *Le problème du temps*, Paris: Hermann, 1946, p. 42. He emphasizes thereafter the role of singular points in their problematizing function which generates solutions: '1. allowing the determination of a fundamental system of solutions which can be analytically extended over every path which does not encounter any singularities; 2. ... their role is to divide up a domain so that the function which ensures the representation can be defined in this domain; 3. they allow the passage from the local integration of the differential equations to the global characterisation of the analytic functions which are the solutions of those equations': *Essai sur les notions de structure et d'existence en mathématiques*, Paris: Hermann, 1938, vol. II, p. 138.

10 C. Georges Verriest, 'Evariste Galois et la théorie des équations

algébriques', *Oeuvres mathématiques de Galois*, Paris: Gauthier-Villars, 1961, p. 41. The great manifesto with regard to the problem – solution may be found in N.H. Abel, *Œuvres complètes*, ed. B. Holmboe, Christiana, Norway: Grondhal, 1839, vol. II: *Sur la résolution algébrique des équations*. On Abel and Galois, see the two essential chapters of Jules Vuillemin, *La philosophie de l'algèbre*, Paris: Presses Universitaires de France, 1962, vol. I. Vuillemin analyses the role of a theory of problems and of a new conception of the critique of Reason in Abel, and the role of a new principle of determination in Galois, especially pp. 213–21, pp. 229–33.

11 See Louis Althusser and Etienne Balibar, *Reading Capital*, London: New Left Books, 1970, pp. 174 ff., 212 ff.

12 Jacques Brunschvig, for example, has clearly shown that the Aristotelian questions *ti to on* and *tis hē ousia* do not at all mean 'What is being?' and 'What is the essence?', but 'Which one is being (which is being)?' and 'Which one is substance (or better, as Aristotle says, which things are substances)?': 'Dialectique et ontologie chez Aristote', *Revue philosophique*, 1964.

13 Charles Péguy, *Clio*, Paris: NRF, p. 269.

14 See one of the most important books of Neo-Platonism which puts in play a serial and potential dialectic of difference, Damascius's *Dubitationes et solutiones de primis principiis, in Platonis Parmenidem*, Paris: C.A. Ruelle, 1889; reprinted Amsterdam: Hakkert, 1966.

*The term *ho synonichos* in Deleuze's text is a misspelling of *ho synochikos*, 'the one that pertains to an integrated whole, holistic', which occurs in Damascius, *Dubitationes*, p. 234. This clarification is due to Professor A.P.D. Mourelatos.

On Schelling's theory of difference and powers, see particularly his 'Conférences de Stuttgart', transl. into French by S. Jankélevitch, in *Essais*, Paris: Aubier, 1949; and *The Ages of the World*, transl. Frederick de Wolfe Bolman, New York: Columbia University Press, 1942.

15 On Plato, see *The Republic*, VI, 511b: 'by the other section of the intelligible I mean that which the reason itself lays hold of by the power of dialectic, treating its assumptions not as absolute beginnings but literally as hypotheses, underpinnings, footings and springboards so to speak, to enable it to rise to that which requires no assumption and is the starting point of all, and after attaining to that again taking hold of the first dependencies from it, so to proceed downward to the conclusion ...'. This text is profoundly commented upon by Proclus, who treats it as the expression of the method of the *Parmenides*, and uses it to denounce the formal or sceptical interpretations already current in his time: it is clear that the One in so far as it is distributed among the hypotheses of the Parmenides is not the same as the One which requires no assumption (an-hypothetical One), which is progressively attained

by the dialectician and measures the truth of each hypothesis along the way: Proclus, *Commentaire du Parménide*, transl. into French by A.E. Chaignet, Paris: Leroux, 1903.

On the transformation of hypothetical judgement into categorical judgement in the philosophies of Maïmon and Fichte, see Martial Guéroult, *L'évolution et la structure de la Doctrine de la Science chez Fichte*, Paris: Les Belles-Lettres, 1930, vol. I, pp. 127 ff.

On Hegel and the analogous transformation, see the relation between the in-itself and the for-itself in *The Phenomenology of Mind*; the relation between the *Phenomenology* itself and the *Logic*; the Hegelian idea of 'science', and the passage from the empirical proposition to the speculative proposition.

16 We refer, for example, to Philippe Sollers's novel *Drame*, Paris: Editions du Seuil, 1965. This novel takes as its motto a formula of Leibniz: 'Suppose, for example, that someone draws a number of points on the paper at random. ... I say that it is possible to find a geometric line the notion of which is constant and uniform according to a certain rule such that this line passes through all the points ...'. The entire beginning of the book is constructed on the two formulae: 'Problem ...' and 'Missed ...'. Series are traced out in relation to the singular points of the body of the narrator, an ideal body which is 'thought rather than perceived'.

On the blind spot as the original point of the work, see the interventions by Philippe Sollers and Jean-Pierre Faye in 'Débat sur le roman', *Tel Quel*, no. 17, 1964.

17. Nietzsche, *Musarion-Ausgabe*, XVI, p. 35. * See *Beyond Good and Evil*, transl. R.J. Hollingdale, Harmondsworth: Penguin, 1973, p. 231.

18 M. Heidegger, *Kant and the Problem of Metaphysics*, transl. J.S. Churchill, Bloomington: Indiana University Press, 1962, pp. 211–12.

19 No one has gone further than Gabriel Tarde in a classification of multiple oppositions, valid in every domain: *formally*, static oppositions (symmetries) as opposed to dynamic; successive dynamic oppositions (rhythms) as opposed to simultaneous; linear simultaneous oppositions (polarities) as opposed to radiating. *Materially*, qualitative serial oppositions as opposed to quantitative; quantitative oppositions of degree as opposed to force: *L'opposition universelle*, Paris: Alcan, 1897.

Tarde seems to us to be the only one to discover the consequences of such a classification: far from being autonomous, far from being a maximum of difference, opposition is a minimal repetition in relation to difference itself. Hence the positing of difference as the reality of a multiple virtual field, and the determination of micro-processes in every domain, such that oppositions are only summary results or simplified and enlarged processes. For the application of this point of view to language and the principle of a micro-linguistics, cf. *Les lois sociales*,

Paris: Alcan, 1898, pp. 150 ff. transl. Howard C. Warren. (as *Social Laws: An Outline of Sociology*, New York: Arno Press, 1899). It seems that Georges Gurvitch rediscovers an inspiration in many respects close to that of Tarde in *Dialectique et Sociologie*, Paris: Flammarion, 1962.

20 Gustave Guillaume, especially his *Conférences de l'Institut de Linguistique de l'Institut de Paris*, 1939. For an account and an interpretation of Guillaume's work, see Edmond Ortigues's fine book, *Le discours et le symbole*, Paris: Aubier, 1962. Similarly, on the expletive NE and on negation, see Ortigues, pp. 102–9; and, cited by Ortigues, *Essai de grammaire de la langue française*, by Jacques Damourette and Edouard Pichon, Paris: Editions d'Astrey, 1911–52, vol. VI, chs 4, 5. The distinction between the 'discordant' and the 'foreclusive' is due to Damourette and Pichon.

21 Louis Althusser, Jacques Rancière, Pierre Macherey, Etienne Balibar, Roger Establet, *Lire le Capital*, Paris: Maspero, 1966. (On the nature and the role of the concepts of opposition, contradiction and alienation, see Rancière, vol. I, pp. 141 f., Macherey, vol. I, pp. 233 f., Balibar, vol. II, pp. 298 f.).
*The English translation of *Reading Capital* (London: New Left Books, 1970) contains only the essays by Althusser and Balibar. For the reference to Balibar's essay, see pp. 289 ff.
On the 'problem–differenciation' schema as a historical category, see Arnold Toynbee, who, it is true, is little suspected of Marxism: 'We could say that a society confronts in the course of its existence a succession of problems that each member must solve for himself as best he can. The statement of each of these problems takes the form of a challenge which must be undertaken as a test. By means of this series of tests, the members of the society are progessively differenciated from one another': *L'Histoire, un essai d'interpretation*, transl. E. Julia, Paris: NRF, p. 10.

22 On the correlation between internal milieu and differenciation, see François Meyer, *Problématique de l'évolution*, Paris: Presses Universitaires de France, 1954, pp. 112 ff. H.F. Osborne is among those who have most profoundly insisted that life is the posing and solving of 'problems'; mechanical, dynamic or properly biological problems: *The Origin and Evolution of Life: On the Theory of Action, Reaction and Interaction of Energy*, London and New York: G. Bell, 1918. For example, the different types of eye can be studied only in relation to a general physico-biological problem and the variations of its conditions in different types of animals. The rule governing solutions is that each entails at least one advantage and one drawback.

23 Bergson is the author who pushes furthest the critique of the possible, and also most frequently invokes the notion of the virtual. From *Time and Free-Will*, duration is defined as a non-actual multiplicity (*Time

and Free-Will: An Essay on the Immediate Data of Consciousness, transl. F.L. Pogson, New York: Harper & Row, 1960, p. 84). In *Matter and Memory* (transl. Nancy Margaret Paul and W. Scott Palmer, New York: Zone Books, 1988), the cone of pure memories with its sections and its 'shining points' on each section (p. 171) is completely real but only virtual. In *Creative Evolution,* (transl. A. Mitchell, New York: Holt, 1911; reprinted by University Press of America, 1983), differenciation and the creation of divergent lines is understood as an actualisation in which each line of actualisation corresponds to a section of the cone (p. 167).

24 Leibniz, *New Essays on Human Understanding*, transl. and ed. Peter Remnant and Jonathan Bennett, Cambridge: Cambridge University Press, 1981, Book II, ch. 1.

25 Louis Vialleton, *Membres et ceintures des vertébrés tétrapods*, Paris: Doin, 1924, pp. 600 ff.

26 Etienne Geoffroy Saint-Hilaire, *Principes de philosophie zoologique*, Paris: Pichon & Didiet, 1830, p. 70. The texts of the controversy with Cuvier may be found in this book.

27 Edmond Perrier, *Les colonies animales et la formation des organismes*, Paris: Masson, 1881, pp. 701 ff.

28 Raymond Ruyer, *La genèse des formes vivantes*, Paris: Flammarion, 1958, pp. 91 ff.: 'The mystery of differenciation cannot be elucidated by making it the effect of differences in situation produced by equal divisions ...'. Ruyer, no less than Bergson, profoundly analysed the notions of the virtual and actualisation. His entire biological philosophy rests upon them along with the idea of the 'thematic'. See *Eléments de psycho-biologie*, Paris: Presses Universitaires de France, 1946, ch. 4.

29 Lucien Cuénot, *L'espèce*, Paris: Doin, 1936, p. 241.

30 The Kantian theory of schematism points beyond itself in two directions: towards the dialectical Idea, which is its own schema and which ensures the specification of the concept (*Critique of Pure Reason*, 'The Final Purpose of the Natural Dialectic of Human Reason'), and towards the aesthetic Idea, which makes schemata serve the more complex and comprehensive process of symbolism (*Critique of Judgment*, Sections 49, 59).

Chapter V Asymmetrical Synthesis of the Sensible

1 On dissymmetry as 'sufficient reason', see Louis Rougier, *En marge de Curie, de Carnot et d'Einstein*, Paris: Editions Chiron, 1922.

2 J.-H. Rosny, the elder (Boex-Borel), *Les sciences et le pluralisme*, Paris: Alcan, 1922, p. 18: 'Energetics shows that all work derives from differences of temperature, potential, or level, just as all acceleration presupposes differences of speed: it is likely that all calculable energy implies the presence of factors of the form E-E', where E and E' themselves

hide factors of the form *e-e*'. ... Since intensity already expresses a difference, it will be necessary to define more clearly what this means, and in particular to make it clear that intensity cannot be composed of two homogeneous terms but must contain at least two series of heterogeneous terms.' Rosny develops two theses in this fine book concerning intensive quantities: (1) resemblance presupposes difference; it is differences that resemble one another; (2) 'difference alone allows us to conceive of being'. Rosny was a friend of Curie. In his novels, he invents a kind of naturalism in intensity which, at the two extremes of the intensive scale, then leads into the prehistoric caverns and future spaces of science fiction.

3 *Deleuze follows Bergson in employing distinct terms for the act or process of extension (Latin *extensio*, for which Deleuze gives both *extensité* and *extension intra*: pp. 223, 228), and the result (Latin *extensum*, for which he invariably uses *étendue*). I have followed established usage in using 'extension' for the former and 'extensity' for the latter. See the note on these terms by Martin Joughin in Deleuze, *Expressionism in Philosophy: Spinoza*, New York: Zone Books, 1990, pp. 416–18.

4 See 'Valeur de la différence', *Revue philosophique de la France et de L'Etranger*, vol. CXLV, April 1955, pp. 121–39, where André Lalande sums up his principal theses. Emile Meyerson's position is closely analogous, even though Meyerson gives a quite different evaluation of the role and sense of Carnot's principle. However, he accepts the same system of definitions. So does Albert Camus who, in *The Myth of Sisyphus*, invokes Nietzsche, Kierkegaard and Shestov, but is much closer to the tradition of Meyerson and Lalande.

5 Ludwig Boltzmann, *Leçons sur la théorie des gaz*, transl. into French by Gallotti and Bénard, Paris: Gauthier-Villars, vol. II, pp. 251 ff.(*see *Lectures on Gas Theory*, transl. Stephen G. Brush, Berkeley and Los Angeles: University of California Press, 1964).

6 André Lalande, *Les illusions évolutionnistes*, Paris: Alcan, 1930, pp. 347–8, and 378: 'The *production* of difference, which is contrary to the general laws of thought, is, strictly speaking, *in*explicable.'

7 Léon Selme, *Principe de Carnot contre formule empirique de Clausius*, Paris: H. Dunod & E. Pinat, 1917.

8 (A) On the envelopment or 'implication' of depth in the perception of extensity, see the very important and little-known work of Jacques Paliard, notably *Pensée implicite et perception visuelle*, Paris: Presses Universitaires de France, 1949. Paliard analyses the forms of implication and shows the difference in nature between what he calls implicit thought and explicit thought: p. 6: 'Not only is there an enveloped implicit, but there is also an enveloping implicit'; and p. 46: 'This implicit knowledge ... seemed to us to be at once something enveloping, like

depth or the synthetic affirmation of a visible universe, and something enveloped, such as the multiple suggestions which cause details to conspire, or the multiple distancial relations within depth itself ...'.

(B) On the intensive nature of depth perception and the status of the quality which follows from this, see Maurice Pradines, *Traité de Psychologie générale*, Paris: Presses Universitaires de France, 1943, vol. I, pp. 405–31, 554–69.

(C) Finally, on intensive space and spatial operations of an intensive nature, from the point of view of activity, see Jean Piaget, *Introduction à l'épistémologie génétique*, Paris: Presses Universitaires de France, 1949, vol. I, pp.75 ff. 210 ff.

9 Hermann Cohen, *Kants Theorie der Erfahrung*, Berlin: Dümmler, 2nd edn, 1885, section 428 ff. On the role of intensive quantities in Cohen's interpretation of Kantianism, see the comments by Jules Vuillemin, *L'héritage kantien et la révolution copernicienne*, Paris: Presses Universitaires de France, 1954, pp. 183–202.

10 Plato, *Timaeus*, 35–7.

11 G.F.C. Griss founded and developed the idea of a mathematics without negation, within the framework of Brouwerian intuitionism: 'Logique des mathématiques intuitionnistes sans négation', Paris: *Comptes rendus des séances de L'Académie des Sciences*, 8 November 1948; 'Sur la négation', *Synthèse*, Amsterdam: Bussum, 1948–9. On the notions of gap, distance or positive difference according to Griss, see A. Heyting, *Les fondements mathématiques, Intuitionnisme, Théorie de la démonstration*, transl. Paulette Février, Paris: Gauthier-Villars, 1955; Paulette Février, 'Manifestations et sens de la notion de complémentarité', *Dialectica*, 1948; and especially Nicole Dequoy, *Axiomatique intuitionniste sans négation de la géométrie projective*, Paris: Gauthier-Villars, 1955, where the author gives numerous examples of proofs by Griss in contrast to proofs involving negations. The limitations of this mathematics as shown by Madame Février do not seem to us to derive from the notion of distance or difference itself, but rather from the theory of problems added to it by Griss: cf. Chapter III above.

12 On depth, stereoscopic images and the 'solution of the antinomies', see Raymond Ruyer, 'Le relief axiologique et le sentiment de la profondeur', *Revue de métaphysique et de morale*, July 1956. On the primacy of 'disparateness' in relation to opposition, see Gilbert Simondon's critique of Lewin's 'hodological space' in *L'individu et sa genèse physico-biologique*, Paris: Presses Universitaires de France, 1964, pp. 232–4.

13 Alois Meinong ('Über die Bedeutung des Weberschen Gesetzes', *Zeitschrift für Psychologie und Physiologie der Sinnesorgane*, vol. XI, 1896) and Bertrand Russell (*The Principles of Mathematics*, Cambridge: Cambridge University Press, 1903, ch. 31) clearly indicated the

distinction between lengths or extensions and differences or distances. The former are extensive quantities divisible into equal parts; the latter are relatively indivisible quantities of intensive origin – in other words, quantities which do not change without changing their nature. It was Leibniz who first founded the theory of distances, linking these to the *spatium* and opposing them to the magnitudes of *extensio* – see Martial Guéroult, 'Espace, point et vide chez Leibniz', *Revue philosophique de la France et de l'étranger*, vol. 136, 1946 (*partially translated by Roger Ariew as 'Space, Point and Void in Leibniz's Philosophy', in M. Hooker, ed., *Leibniz: Critical and Interpretative Essays*, Manchester: Manchester University Press, 1982).

14 Bergson, from the outset, defined duration as a 'multiplicity' or a divisibility which does not divide without changing its nature: *Time and Free-Will: An Essay on the Immediate Data of Consciousness*, transl. F.L. Pogson, New York: Harper & Row, 1960, pp. 84 ff.; and especially *Matter and Memory* transl. Nancy Margaret Paul and W. Scott Palmer, New York: Zone Books, 1988, pp. 206–7. There is therefore not only a difference in kind between duration and extensity, but duration is distinguished from extensity in the same manner as *differences in kind* are distinguished from *differences of degree* (two types of 'multiplicity'). Nevertheless, in another manner duration is indistinguishable from the *nature of difference* and, as such, includes all the *degrees of difference*: hence the reintroduction of intensities within duration, and the idea of a coexistence in duration of all the degrees of relaxation and contraction (the essential thesis of *Matter and Memory* and *La Pensée et le mouvant*).

15 On the reticence of the Greeks, for example, with regard to the eternal return, see Charles Mugler, *Deux thèmes de la cosmologie grecque, devenir cyclique et pluralité des mondes*, Paris: Klincksieck, 1953.

16 Pierre Klossowski has demonstrated the link between eternal return and pure intensities functioning as 'signs': 'Oubli et anamnèse dans l'expérience vécue de l'éternel retour du Même', in *Nietzsche: Cahiers de Royaumont, Philosophie No. VI*, Paris: Editions de Minuit, 1967. In his story *Le Baphomet* (Paris: Mercure, 1965) Klossowski offers a detailed description of this world of intensive 'breaths' which constitute the specific matter of the eternal return.

17 See Simondon, *L'individu et sa genèse physico-biologique*.

18 On the speed with which the type and specific form appear, see Edmond Perrier, *Les colonies animales et la formation des organismes*, Paris: Masson, 1881, pp. 701 ff. Perrier emphasizes the dependence of the notion of species with regard to sexed reproduction: 'To each new generation, the common characteristics assume a greater immutability. ... All recent research tends to show that species do not exist in those groups of the animal kingdom where reproduction is carried out with-

out prior fertilization. Thus, the appearance of species is intimately tied to that of sexual generation' (p. 707).

19 Albert Dalcq, *L'œuf et son dynamisme organisateur*, Paris: Albin Michel, 1941, pp. 194 ff.

20 Leibniz, *The Principles of Nature and of Grace, Based on Reason,* 1714, section 6, In *Philosophical Papers and Letters*, transl. and ed. Leroy E. Loemker, 2nd edn, Dordrecht, Holland: D. Reidel, 1969.

21 François Meyer, *Problématique de l'évolution*, Paris: Presses Universitaires de France, 1954, p. 193: 'The functioning of biological systems is therefore not contrary to thermodynamics but only outside its sphere of application ...'. In this sense, Meyer recalls Jordan's question: 'Is a Mammal a microscopic being?' (p. 228).

22 On the other as expression, implication and envelopment of a possible 'world'; see Michel Tournier, *Vendredi ou les limbes du Pacifique*, Paris: Gallimard, 1967; transl. Norman Denny as *Friday*, New York: Pantheon, 1985.

Conclusion

1 See Nietzsche, *On the Genealogy of Morals*, Part I, section 10.

2 The most developed attempt of this kind is that of J.-P. Faye in a book entitled, precisely, *Analogues*, Paris: Editions du Seuil, 1964. See pp. 14–15 on displacement and disguise in unspecified series, yet at the same time the consideration of repetition as an analogy for an eye which remains after all external. Also, throughout the book, the role of a death instinct interpreted in an analogical manner.

3 There is no need to enquire whether Bouvard and Pécuchet themselves are stupid or not. This is not at all the issue. Flaubert's project is encyclopaedic and 'critical' rather than psychological. The problem of stupidity is posed in a philosophical manner as a transcendental problem of the relations between thought and stupidity. In the same divided – or rather, repeated – thinking being, it is a matter of both stupidity as a *faculty* and of the *faculty* of being unable to stand stupidity. Here, Flaubert recognises Schopenhauer as his master.

4 Arthur Adamov wrote a very fine piece on this theme, *La grande et la petite manœuvre*, Paris: NRF, Theatre I, 1950.

5 See Eugen Fink, *Le jeu comme symbole du monde*, transl. Hildenbrand and Lindenberg, Paris: Editions de Minuit, 1960; and Kostas Axelos, *Vers la pensée planétaire*, Paris: Editions de Minuit, 1964, which attempt to distinguish the divine game and the human game, from a very different perspective from that adopted here, in order to arrive at a formula which they call, following Heidegger, 'ontological difference'.

6 Nietzsche, *Thus Spoke Zarathustra*, transl. R.J. Hollingdale, Harmondsworth: Penguin, 1961, Book III, 'Before Sunrise'; 'The Seven Seals'; Book IV, 'Of the Higher Men', s. 14.

7 Butler's *Erewhon* seems to us not only a disguised *no-where* but a rearranged *now-here*.

8 All sorts of examples of this kind may be found in Xavier Abély, *Les stéréotypies*, Toulouse: Dirion, 1916. One of the best clinical studies of stereotypes and iteration remains Paul Guiraud's, *Psychiatrie clinique*, Paris: Le François, 1956, pp. 106 ff.; and 'Analyse du symptome stéréotypie', *L'Encéphale*, November 1936. Guiraud distinguishes clearly between perseveration and repetition (step-by-step iterations or intermittent stereotypes). For if the phenomena of perseveration may be explained negatively by a defect or mental lack, those of repetition have the double property of presenting condensations and contractions and requiring a primary and positive principle of explanation. Note, in this regard, that Jacksonism, while it places repetition among the category of 'positive' symptoms, still maintains the principle of an entirely negative explanation; for the positivity it invokes is that of a bare and mechanical repetition, expressing a supposedly inferior or archaic level of equilibrium. In fact, the mechanical repetition which constitutes the manifest aspect of a stereotype or an iteration does not express a level of the totality but concerns essentially *fragments* or 'bricks', as Monakow and Mourgue call them – hence the importance of fragmentary contractions and condensations. In this sense, however, the true positivity is that which invests the totality of the psychic life in the fragment – in other words, invests in the mechanical repetition a repetition of a quite different kind which belongs to the sphere of the 'instincts', always displaceable and disguised [*thymie*]. It has been said that in the case of stereotypes, only the signifier, not the signified, is archaic: 'Underneath the fragmentation of the symptom, there is always a continuous signified, more or less richly endowed with sense': A. Beley and J.-J. Lefrançois, 'Aperçu séméiologique dramatique de quelques stéréotypies motrices chez l'enfant', *Annales med. ps.*, April 1962.

9 Nietzsche, *Thus Spoke Zarathustra*, Prologue 4 and 5; and Part II, 'Of the Sublime Men' for the critique of heroes.

10 Nietzsche, *Werke*, Leipzig: Kröner, vol. XII, 1, section 106.

11 See Heidegger, '... Poetically Man Dwells ...' in *Poetry Language, Thought*, transl. Albert Hofstadter, New York: Harper & Row, 1971, p. 18.

Bibliography

Index of Names and Topics
The comment following the book-title specifies the sense in which the work is cited in relation to the concerns of the this book.

Works of a particularly scientific or literary character are marked with an asterisk *.

This bibliography is obviously not exhaustive, and could not be. (For example, a theme such as that of the 'compulsion to repeat' in the unconscious involves almost the entire psychoanalytic bibliography.) Only those authors and works which have been referred to in the course of this book have been included, *even where this involved no more than a detail or a simple reference.*

Sometimes we refer in an allusive, vague and general manner to authors or works which are nevertheless essential: for example, Damascius, Schelling or Heidegger with regard to the philosophy of difference; Vico and Péguy with regard to repetition. This is because, in the case of these authors, we have not had occasion to give an account of their conceptions of difference or repetition for their own sake. In other cases, by contrast, we have been led to undertake such an account: in those of Plato, Aristotle, Leibniz, Hegel or Nietzsche, for example. Even in these cases, however, the accounts given remain completely inadequate from the point of view of the history of philosophy, since they are intended only to serve the needs of our researches.

One should therefore take into account not only the fact that there is no analysis of the theory of difference as it appears in the work of many very important authors, but also the fact that even where such an analysis is sketched, it remains partial and fragmentary.

For a certain number of authors (Plato, Aristotle, Leibniz, Hegel, Freud and Heidegger) we have put only *passim* in the column for works. This is because the themes of difference or repetition are really present throughout all their work. Undoubtedly there are some works which treat these themes more directly than others: these are the ones cited in the course of this book. In other cases, by contrast, particularly those where the work is of more literary character, we have cited only certain works considered 'exemplary', even though the whole of the author's work revolves around the themes of difference and repetition.

Abel, N.H. **Œuvres complètes*, ed. B. Holmboe, Christiana, Norway: C. Grondhal, 1839. Theory of problems, differential and determination.

Abély, X. *Les stéréotypies,* Toulouse: Dirion, 1916. Stereotypes in psychiatry.

Adamov, A. **La grande et la petite manœuvre.* Paris: NRF, Theatre I, 1950. Impersonal differences.

Alleman, B. *Hölderlin et Heidegger,* French translation, Paris: Presses Universitaires de France, 1954. Ontological difference according to Heidegger.

Alquié, F. *Le désir d'éternité,* Paris: Presses Universitaires de France, 1943. Repetition in the unconscious.

Althusser, L. *For Marx*, transl. Ben Brewster, London: New Left Review Editions, 1977; with Jacques Rancière, Pierre Macherey, Etienne Balibar and Roger Establet, *Lire le Capital* Paris: Maspero, 1966. (See Althusser and Balibar, *Reading Capital*, London: New Left Books, 1970.) Difference and contradiction: structural logic of difference.

Aristotle *Passim.* Logic and ontology of difference (generic and specific differences).

Artaud, A. **Collected Works*, transl. Victor Corti, London: John Calder, 1968. Determination, theatre and thought.

Axelos, K. *Vers la pensée planétaire*, Paris: Editions de Minuit, 1964. Ontological difference and play.

Bachelard, G. *Le rationalisme appliqué*, Paris: Presses Universitaires de France, 1949. Epistemology of problems and difference.

Beaufret, J. Introduction to *Poème de Parménide*, Paris: Presses Universitaires de France, 1955; 'Hölderlin et Sophocle' in Hölderlin, *Remarques sur Oedipe. Remarques sur Antigone*, Paris: Union Générale d'Editions 10/18, 1965. Difference, the form of time and the caesura according to Hölderlin.

Bergson, H. *Œuvres*, Paris, Presses Universitaires de France (Edition du Centenaire), 1959. Physical repetition, contraction, change; Repetition and memory, biological differenciation; intensity, quality and extension.

Blanchot, M. 'Le rire des dieux', *Nouvelle Revue Française*, July 1965; *The Space of Literature*, transl. Ann Smock, Lincoln and London: University of Nebraska Press, 1982. Difference, thought and death; simulacra.

Boltzmann, L. **Lectures on Gas Theory*, transl. Stephen G. Brush, Berkeley and Los Angeles: University of California Press, 1964. Difference and probability.

Bordas-Demoulin, J. *Le cartésianisme ou la véritable rénovation des sciences*, Paris: Gauthier-Villars, 1843. The differential Idea and the interpretation of calculus.

Borges, J.L. **Ficciones*, New York: Grove Press, 1962. Chaos, play, difference and repetition.

Bouligand, G. (with Desgranges, J.) *Le déclin des absolus mathématico-*

logiques, Paris: Editions d'Enseignement supérieur, 1949. Epistemology of problems and difference in mathematics.

Brunschvig, J. 'Dialectique et ontologie chez Aristote', *Revue philosophique*, 1964. Aristotelian difference and dialectic.

Butler, S. *Life and Habit*, London: Jonathan Cape, 1910. **Erewhon: Or Over the Range*, London: Trübner, 1872. Repetition and habit.

Butor, M. *Répertoire, I*, Paris: Editions de Minuit, 1960. Repetition and freedom according to Raymond Roussel.
**La Modification*, Paris: Editions de Minuit, 1957. Repetition and modification.

Camus, A. *Le Mythe de Sisyphe*, Paris: NRF, 1942. Difference and identity.

Canguilhem, G. *On the Normal and the Pathological*, transl. Carolyn R. Fawcett, Dordrecht, Holland: D. Reidel, 1978. Epistemology of problems and of biological difference.

Carnot, L. **Réflexions sur la métaphysique du calcul infinitésimal*, Paris, 1797 (2nd ed. transl. W.R. Browell as *Reflexions on the Metaphysical Principles of the Infinitesimal Analysis*, Oxford, 1832). Differential calculus and problems.

Carroll, L. **The Complete Works of Lewis Carroll*, New York: Random House/Nonesuch Press, 1939. Problem, sense and difference (the object = x).

Cohen, H. *Kants Theorie der Erfahrung*, Berlin: Dümmler, 2nd ed., 1885. The role of intensive quantities in the *Critique of Pure Reason*.

Cuénot, L. *L'espèce*, Paris: Doin, 1936. Difference in biology.

Dalcq, A. *L'œuf et son dynamisme organisateur*, Paris: Albin Michel, 1941. Intensity, individuation and biological differenciation.

Damascius *Dubitationes et solutiones de primis principiis, in Platonis Parmenidem,* Paris: C.A. Ruelle, 1889; reprinted Amsterdam, Hakkert, 1966. Neo-Platonic dialectic of difference.

Damourette, J. (with Pichon, E.) *Essai de grammaire de la langue française*, Paris: Editions D'Astrey, 1911–52. The differential 'Ne' in language.

Darwin, C. *On the Origin of the Species by means of Natural Selection*, London: J. Murray, 1859. The logic of difference in biology.

Dequoy, N. **Axiomatique intuitionniste sans négation de la géométrie projective*, Paris: Gauthier-Villars, 1955. Distance or positive difference in logic and mathematics according to Griss.

Derrida, J. *Writing and Difference*, transl. Alan Bass, London: Routledge & Kegan Paul, 1978. Difference and repetition in the unconscious, language and the work of art.

Duns Scotus, J. *Opus Oxoniense. (Opera Omnia*, ed. L. Wadding, 1639; reprinted Paris: Vivès, 1891–95.) Univocity, formal distinction and individuating difference.

Eco, U. *The Open Work*, transl. Anna Cancogni, with an Introduction by David Robey, Cambridge, MA: Harvard University Press, 1989. Simulacra, difference and works of art.

Eliade, M. *The Myth of the Eternal Return*, transl. William R. Trask, New York: Pantheon, 1984. Repetition, myth and faith.

Elie, H. *Le complexe significabile*, Paris: Vrin, 1936. Sense and difference in certain medieval logics.

Faye, J.-P. in 'Débat sur le roman', *Tel Quel*, no. 17, 1964; **Analogues*, Paris: Editions du Seuil, 1964. Difference and repetition in the work of art.

Ferenczi, S. (with Rank, O.) *Entwicklungziele der Psychoanalyse, Neue Arbeiten zur ärtzlichen Psychoanalyse*, Vienna: 1924. (*The Development of Psychoanalysis*, transl. Caroline Newton, New York: Nervous and Mental Disease Publishing, 1925.) Transference and repetition in the unconscious.

Feuerbach, L. *Contribution à la Critique de la Philosophie de Hegel*, transl. Louis Althusser, in *Manifestes philosophiques*, Paris: Presses Universitaires de France, 1960. Difference and beginning in philosophy.

Février, P. *'Rapports entre le calcul des problèmes et le calcul des propositions', *Comptes rendus des séances de l'Académie des Sciences*, April 1945; *'Manifestations et sens de la notion de complémentarité', *Dialectica*, 1948. Difference and negation in logic, mathematics and physics.

Fink, E. *Le jeu comme symbole du monde*, transl. Hildenbrand and Lindenberg, Paris: Editions de Minuit, 1960. Ontological difference and play.

Foucault, M. 'La Prose d'Actéon', *Nouvelle Revue Française*, March 1964; *The Order of Things*, transl. Alan Sheridan, London: Tavistock, 1977; *Death and the Labyrinth: The World of Raymond Roussel*, transl. Charles Ruas, London: Athlone, 1987. Difference, resemblance, identity. Difference and repetition in simulacra.

Freud, S. *Passim*. Repetition in the unconscious; after 1918, Repetition, Eros and the death instinct.

Geoffroy Saint-Hilaire, E. *Principes de philosophie zoologique*, Paris: Pichon & Didiet, 1830. The logic of difference in biology.

Ghyka, M. *Le Nombre d'Or*, Paris: Gallimard, 1931. Static and dynamic repetition, symmetry and dissymmetry.

Gilson, E. *Jean Duns Scot: Introduction à ses positions fondamentales*, Paris: Vrin, 1952. Difference, analogy, univocity.

Gombrowicz, W. **Cosmos*, transl. into French by Georges Sedir, Paris: Denoël, 1966 (English ed. transl. Eric Mosbacher, New York: Grove Press, 1967); **Ferdydurke*, transl. Eric Mosbacher, London: Marion Boyars, 1979. Chaos, difference and repetition.

Gredt, J. *Elementa philosophiae aristotelico-thomisticae*, I, Freibourg: 7th 1937. Analogy and the logic of difference according to Aristotle.

Griss, G.F.C. *'Logique des mathématiques intuitionnistes sans négation', Paris: *Comptes rendus des séances de L'Académie des Sciences*, 8 November 1948; *'Sur la négation', *Synthèse*, Amsterdam: Bussum, 1948–9. Distance or positive difference in logic and mathematics.

Guéroult, M. *La philosophie transcendentale de Salomon Maïmon*, Paris: Alcan, 1929; *L'évolution et la structure de la Doctrine de la Science chez Fichte*, Paris: Les Belles-Lettres, 1930; The philosophy of difference in Post-Kantianism.

'Espace, point et vide chez Leibniz', *Revue philosophique de la France et de l'étranger*, vol. 136, 1946. (Partially transl. Roger Ariew as 'Space, Point and Void in Leibniz's Philosophy', in M. Hooker, ed., *Leibniz: Critical and Interpretative Essays*, Manchester: Manchester University Press, 1982.) Distance and difference according to Leibniz.

Guillaume, G. *Passim*. The logic of difference in language.

Guiraud, P. *Psychiatrie clinique*, Paris: Le François, 1956, republished from 'Psychiatrie du médecin clinicien', 1922; 'Analyse du symptôme stéréotypie', *L'Encéphale*, November 1936. Iterations and stereotypes in psychiatry.

Gurvitch, G. *Dialectique et sociologie*, Paris: Flammarion, 1962. Difference and opposition in the dialectic.

Hegel, G.W.F. *Passim*. The logic and ontology of difference (difference, negation, opposition, contradiction).

Heidegger, M. *Passim*. Ontological difference (Being, difference and the question).

Heyting, A. *Les fondements mathématiques. Intuitionnisme. Théorie de la démonstration,* transl. P. Février, Paris: Gauthier-Villars, 1955. Distance or positive difference in logic and mathematics according to Griss.

Hölderlin, F. *Remarques sur Oedipe, Remarques sur Antigone*, 1804, French transl., Paris: Union Générale d'Editions (10/18), 1965. Difference, the form of time and the caesura.

Hume, D. *A Treatise of Human Nature*, Oxford: Oxford University Press, 1978. Physical repetition, contraction, change: the problem of habit.

Hyppolite, J. *Logique et Existence: Essai sur la Logique de Hegel*, Paris: Presses Universitaires de France, 1953. The logic and ontology of difference according to Hegel.

Joachim of Flora *L'Evangile éternel*, transl. into French by E. Aegerter, Paris: Rieder, 1928. Repetition, universal history and faith.

Joyce, J. **Finnegans Wake*, London: Faber & Faber, 1939. Chaos, difference and repetition.

Jung, C. G. *Dialectique du moi et de l'inconscient,* Paris: Gallimard, 1964 ('The Relation between the Ego and the Unconscious, in *Two Essays on*

Analytical Psychology (Collected Works Volume 7), transl. R.F.C. Hull, London/Henley: Routledge & Kegan Paul, 1966). The unconscious, problems and differenciation.

Kant, I. *Prolegomena to Any Future Metaphysics,* revision of the Carus transl. with an introduction by L.W. Beck, New York and London: Macmillan, 1950; *Critique of Pure Reason,* transl. Norman Kemp Smith, London: Macmillan, 1933. Internal and intrinsic difference. The undetermined, the determinable and determination in the 'I think' and in the Idea. The difference between the faculties.

Kierkegaard, S. *Fear and Trembling* and *Repetition,* transl. and ed. H.V. and E.H. Hong, published as two volumes in one; Princeton, NJ: Princeton University Press, 1983; *The Concept of Anxiety,* transl. R. Thomte, ed. H.V. and E.H. Hong, Princeton, NJ: Princeton University Press, 1980; *Philosophical Fragments*; or *A Fragment of Philosophy,* rev. transl. H.V. Hong, Princeton, NJ: Princeton University Press, 1962. Repetition, difference, freedom and faith.

Klossowski, P. *Un si funeste désir,* Paris: NRF, 1963; 'Oubli et anamnèse dans l'expérience vécue de l'éternel retour du Même', in *Nietzsche: Cahiers de Royaumont, Philosophie No. VI,* Paris: Editions de Minuit, 1967; *Le Baphomet,* Paris: Mercure, 1965. Simulacra and repetition; intensity, eternal return and loss of identity.

Lacan, J. *Le mythe individual du névrosé,* CDU ('The Neurotic's Individual Myth', transl. Martha Noel Evans, *The Psychoanalytic Quarterly,* 48, 1979, pp. 405–25); *Ecrits,* Paris: Seuil, 1966 *(Ecrits. A Selection,* transl. Alan Sheridan, London: Tavistock/Routledge, 1989). Difference and repetition in the unconscious: the death instinct.

Lagache, D. 'Le problème du transfert', *Revue française de psychanalyse,* January 1952. Transference, habit and repetition in the unconscious.

Lalande, A. *Les illusions évolutionnistes,* Paris: Alcan, 1930; 'Valeur de la differénce', *Revue philosophique de la France et de L'Etranger,* vol. CXLV, April 1955. Difference and identity.

Laplanche, J. and Pontalis, J.-B. 'Fantasme originaire, fantasmes des origines, origine du fantasme', *Les Temps modernes,* no. 215, April 1964. Transl. as 'Fantasy and the Origins of Sexuality', *International Journal of Psycho-Analysis,* 49, 1968; reprinted, with an afterword, in V. Burgin, J. Donald, C. Kaplan eds., *Formations of Fantasy,* London: Methuen, 1968. Difference and repetition in the phantasm.

Laroche, E. *Histoire de la racine nem – en grec ancien,* Paris: Klincksieck, 1949. 'Distribution' according to Ancient Greek.

Lautman, A. *Essai sur les notions de structure et d'existence en mathématiques,* Paris: Hermann, 1938; *Nouvelles recherches sur la structure dialectique des mathématiques,* Paris: Hermann, 1939; *Le problème du temps*, Paris: Hermann, 1946. The dialectical Idea, the differential and the theory of problems.

Leclaire, S. 'La mort dans la vie de l'obsédé', *La psychanalyse*, no. 2, 1956 ('Jerome, or Death in the Life of the Obsessional', *Returning to Freud: Clinical Psychoanalysis in the School of Lacan*, ed. and transl. Stuart Schneiderman, New Haven and London: Yale University Press, 1980, pp. 94–113); 'A la recherche des principes d'une psychothérapie des psychoses', *Evolution psychiatrique*, II, 1958; 'Les éléments en jeu dans une psychanalyse', *Cahiers pour l'analyse*, 5, 1966. Difference and repetition in the unconscious, and the role of questions (according to J. Lacan).

Leibniz, G. *Passim*. The logic and ontology of difference (continuity and indiscernibles, the differential unconscious).

Lévi-Strauss, C. *Tristes Tropiques*, transl. John and Doreen Weightman, London: Jonathan Cape, 1973. Static and dynamic repetition.
Totemism, transl. Rodney Needham, Boston, MA: Beacon Press, 1963. Difference and resemblance.

Maïmon, S. *Versuch über die Transzendentalphilosophie*, Berlin: Vos, 1790. The differential Idea and transcendental philosophy of difference.

Marx, K. *The Eighteenth Brumaire of Louis Bonaparte*, in *Surveys from Exile*, Harmondsworth: Penguin, 1973. Repetition and History.

Meinong, A. 'Über die Bedeutung des Weberschen Gesetzes', *Zeitschrift für Psychologie und Physiologie der Sinnesorgane,* vol. XI, 1896. Difference and intensity.

Meyer, F. *Problématique de l'évolution*, Paris: Presses Universitaires de France, 1954. The logic of difference in biology.

Meyerson, E. *Passim*. Difference and identity.

Miller, J. A. 'La Suture', *Cahiers pour l'analyse*, 1, 1966 (transl. 'Suture (elements of the logic of the signifier)', *Screen*, vol. xviii, no. 4, 1977/8, pp.24–34). Difference and repetition in the unconscious according to J. Lacan.

Milner, J. C. 'Le Point du Signifiant', *Cahiers pour l'Analyse*, 1, 1966. Difference and repetition in the unconscious according to J. Lacan.

Mugler, C. *Deux thèmes de la cosmologie grecque, devenir cyclique et pluralité des mondes*, Paris: Klincksieck, 1953. The role of eternal return in Greek thought.

Nietzsche, F. *Werke*, Leipzig: Kröner, 1930 (see *Werke: Kritische Gesamtausgabe*, eds G. Colli and M. Montinari, Berlin: De Gruyter, 1967–78). The ontology of difference and repetition: will to power and eternal return.

Ortigues, E. *Le discours et le symbole*, Paris: Aubier, 1962. The logic of difference in language according to G. Guillaume.

Osborne, H.F. *The Origin and Evolution of Life: On the Theory of Action, Reaction and Interaction of Energy*, London and New York: G. Bell, 1918. Life, difference and problems.

Paliard, J. *Pensée implicite et perception visuelle*, Paris: Presses Universitaires de France, 1949. Distance and depth.

Péguy, C. *Passim.* Repetition, difference, freedom and faith. Repetition, variation and style.

Perrier, E. *Les colonies animales et la formation des organismes*, Paris: Masson, 1881. Differenciation and repetition in biology.

Piaget, J. *Introduction à l'épistémologie génétique*, Paris: Presses Universitaires de France, 1949. Difference and intensity.

Plato *Plato: The Collected Dialogues*, ed. E. Hamilton and H. Cairns, Princeton, NJ: Princeton University Press, 1963. The Logic and ontology of difference (the method of division and simulacra).

Porphyry The Phoenician *Isagoge*, transl. Edward W. Warren, Toronto: The Pontifical Institute of Mediaeval Studies, 1975. The logic of difference according to Aristotle.

Pradines, M. *Traité de Psychologie générale*, Paris: Presses Universitaires de France, 1943. Depth, distance, intensity.

Proclus *A Commentary on the First Book of Euclid's Elements*, transl. Glenn R. Morrow, Princeton, NJ: Princeton University Press, 1970; Neo-Platonic dialectic of difference; Idea and problem.

Commentaire du Parménide, transl. into French by A.E. Chaignet, Paris: Leroux, 1903. Neo-Platonic dialectic of difference; Idea and problem.

Proust, M. *A la recherche du temps perdu*, Paris: NRF, 1919.
(*Remembrance of Things Past*, transl. C.K. Scott-Moncrief and Terence Kilmartin, Harmondsworth: Penguin, 1986). Difference and repetition in lived experience.

Renouvier, C. 'Les labyrinthes de la métaphysique', *La Critique philosophique*, 6e année, 1877. Critical examination of the theories of differential calculus.

Ricoeur, P. *Freud and Philosophy. An Essay on Interpretation*, transl. Denis Savage, New Haven, CT and London: Yale University Press, 1970. Difference and repetition in the unconscious according to Freud.

Robbe-Grillet, A. *Passim.* Difference and repetition, displacements and disguises.

Rosenberg, H. *The Tradition of the New*, London: Thames & Hudson, 1962. Repetition, theatre and history.

Rosny, J. H., the elder *Les sciences et le pluralisme*, Paris: Alcan, 1922. Intensity and difference.

Rougier, L. *En marge de Curie, de Carnot et d'Einstein*, Paris: Editions Chiron, 1922. Intensity, dissymmetry and difference.

Rousseau, J. J. *La nouvelle Héloïse*, 1761. The attempt at repetition in psychic life.
Roussel, R. *Passim*. Difference and repetition, variation and style.
Russell, B. *The Principles of Mathematics*, Cambridge: Cambridge University Press, 1903. Difference, distance, intensity.
Ruyer, R. *Eléments de psycho-biologie*, Paris: Presses Universitaires de France, 1946, 'Le relief axiologique et le sentiment de la profondeur', *Revue de métaphysique et de morale*, July 1956; *La genèse des formes vivantes*, Paris: Flammarion, 1958. Biological differenciation.

Saussure, F. *Cours de linguistique générale*, Paris: Payot, 1956 (*Course in General Linguistics*, New York: Fontana, 1974). The structural logic of difference in language.
Schelling, F. *Essais*, Paris: Aubier, 1949; *The Ages of the World*, transl. Frederick de Wolfe Bolman, New York: Columbia University Press, 1942. Difference, power and ground.
Schuhl, P. M. *Etudes platoniciennes*, Paris: Presses Universitaires de France, 1960. Repetition, variation and style in Plato.
Selme, L. *Principe de Carnot contre formule empirique de Clausius*, Paris: H. Dunod & E. Pinat, 1917. Intensity, difference and entropy.
Servien, P. *Principes d'Esthétique*, Paris: Boivin, 1935; Equality and repetition.
Science et Poésie, Paris: Flammarion, 1947.
Simondon, G. *L'individu et sa genèse physico-biologique*, Paris: Presses Universitaires de France, 1964. Difference, singularity and individuality.
Sollers, P. in 'Débat sur le roman', *Tel Quel*, no. 17, 1964; *Drame*, Paris: Editions du Seuil, 1965. Problems, difference and repetition in the work of art.
Spinoza, B. *Ethics*, in *The Collected Works of Spinoza*, vol. I, transl. and ed. E. Curley, Princeton, NJ: Princeton University Press, 1985. Univocity, formal distinction and individuating difference.

Tarde, G. *Passim*. Difference and repetition as categories of Nature and Mind.
Tournier, M. *Vendredi ou les limbes du Pacifique*, Paris: Gallimard, 1967; transl. Norman Denny as *Friday*, New York: Pantheon, 1985. The Other and difference.
Trubetzkoy, N.S. *Principes de phonologie*, Paris: Klincksieck, 1939. The structural logic of difference in language.

Verriest, C.G. *'Evariste Galois et la théorie des équations algébriques', *Œuvres mathématiques de Galois*, Paris: Gauthier-Villars, 1961. The theory of problems and determination according to Galois.
Vialleton, L. *Membres et ceintures des vertébrés tétrapodes*, Paris: Doin, 1924. Biological differenciation.

Vico, G. *The New Science*, transl. Thomas G. Bergin and Max H. Fische, Ithaca, NY: Cornell University Press, 1968. Repetition and universal history.

Vuillemin, J. *L'héritage kantien et la révolution copernicienne*, Paris: Presses Universitaires de France, 1954. The philosophy of difference in Post-Kantianism and the role of intensive quantities according to the interpretation of H. Cohen.

La philosophie de l'algèbre, Paris: Presses Universitaires de France, 1962. The theory of problems and determination according to Abel and Galois.

Wahl, J. *Passim*. The dialectic and difference.

Warrain, F. *L'œuvre philosophique de Hoëne Wronski*, Paris: Vega, 1933. The philosophy of difference according to Wronski.

Weismann, A. *Essais sur l'hérédité et la sélection naturelle*, Paris: Reinwald, 1892. Difference in biology.

Wronski, H. **Philosophie de l'infini*, Paris: Didot, 1814; **Philosophie de la technie algorithmique*, Paris: Didot, 1817. The differential Idea and the interpretation of calculus.

Index